Your Brain On
Childhood

Your Brain On Childhood

THE UNEXPECTED SIDE EFFECTS OF CLASSROOMS, BALLPARKS, FAMILY ROOMS, AND THE MINIVAN

Gabrielle Principe

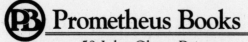 **Prometheus Books**

59 John Glenn Drive
Amherst, New York 14228-2119

Published 2011 by Prometheus Books

Cover design by Grace M. Conti-Zilsberger
Cover image © 2011 Media Bakery

Inquiries should be addressed to
Prometheus Books
59 John Glenn Drive
Amherst, New York 14228–2119
VOICE: 716–691–0133
FAX: 716–691–0137
WWW.PROMETHEUSBOOKS.COM

15 14 13 12 11   5 4 3 2 1

Library of Congress Cataloging-in-Publication Data

Principe, Gabrielle F.
    Your brain on childhood : the unexpected side effects of classrooms, ballparks, family rooms, and the minivan / by Gabrielle Principe.
        p. cm.
    Includes bibliographical references.
    ISBN 978–1–61614–425–8 (pbk.)
    ISBN 978–1–61614–426–5 (ebook)
    1. Child psychology. 2. Child development. 3. Brain stimulation. 4. Learning.
5. Cognition in children. I. Title.

BF721.P72 2011
155.4—dc23

                                                              2011020203

Printed in the United States of America

To Isabella and Dominic,

for teaching me
that the real trouble with the world
is that too many people grow up.

Contents

CHAPTER 3: THE TWENTY-YEAR   69
SCIENCE PROJECT

CHAPTER 4: NOT ENOUGH TORTOISE,   105
TOO MUCH HARE

Preface

Before you read this, find a child. Like the four-year-old scaling the stacks in the self-help section. The one wearing cowboy boots and a grape juice mustache. Strike up a conversation with him. Ask him what he does all day. He probably won't tell you that he fashions play huts out of sticks and mud, that he war-paints his body with ink extracted from urucum fruit before ambushing his little sister, that he fancies blowing darts at small game, or that his evening bath in the river helps him wind down.

Rather, he'll probably tell you the same thing that any American child would: That he spends more time tuned in to *SpongeBob SquarePants* than a typical hunter-gatherer of his age. That he is more likely than your usual nomad to be ferried in the family van to T-ball practice. That he belongs to the only hominid species whose young spend their weekdays seated in classrooms memorizing state capitals and reciting times tables. And you can see for yourself by the plastic gaming console sticking out of his overalls that he plays with toys that are very different from those of most primates.

Children today live a radically different lifestyle than they used to. The problem is, children's lifestyles have changed, but their brains have not. Modern children are born with the very same brains and accompanying tendencies, abilities, and adaptations as their nomadic hunter-gatherer ancestors dating back at least 35,000 years, but perhaps as far back as 250,000.[1] What's more, many parts of their brains originated even deeper in the evolutionary past—long before language, deliberate thought, opposable thumbs, or animals like us even existed.[2]

Why should this matter to you? Because it means that the brains inside today's children's heads were not designed with modern life in mind. They did not evolve to watch Dora the Explorer find her way to the Indies, play Frisbee® from the couch with a virtual dog, or spend their Saturdays on a newly groomed soccer field. They evolved for life in a very different world.

Consider, first, the long history of the brain. The very first brain appeared on the planet half a billion years ago and evolved for most of that time without leaving the ancient oceans, freshwater streams, and tropical forests. The *human* version of the brain emerged some two million years ago, and it didn't leave the African savannah until very recently. Civilization, in contrast, has been around for a meager ten thousand years. That's less than half of 1 percent of the human brain's entire existence. In evolutionary time, that's chump change.

Furthermore, *modern* civilization, with its highfalutin technology, formal schooling, manufactured toys, manicured playgrounds, and organized sports, has emerged only in the past hundred or so years. By the standards of evolution, that's not enough time for the brain to adjust. And this is exactly why the modern world is imposing unwanted side effects on our children's brains.

Today's children clearly have it easier in many ways than children just a generation or two ago, let alone human offspring living tens of thousands of years in the past. They no longer have to worry about catching leprosy on a play date, scrapping for meat left behind by larger predators, or fending off raiding parties of neighboring troops of toddlers. But modern life has brought about a childhood full of unnatural and often overwhelming experiences that hundreds of millions of years of evolution never saw coming.

The result of this new world on children's old brains is what you'd expect if you took any freshly minted animal brain; tacked on some general primate parts; tweaked it until it could talk, think, and walk on two legs; dressed it up in a pair of jeans and a polo shirt; and enrolled it in kindergarten. The thing is, you can dress up an old brain only so much without paying a price. Those parts of the brain that may have worked well in a young toad, a teenage monkey, or a prehistoric human do not do so well when you make them grow up in our modern world.

THE NEWEST ENDANGERED SPECIES

There is no question that children today are facing mounting problems. The evidence is pervasive. For instance, the Foundation for Child Development's 2010 Child Health and Well-Being Index says that children's health has sunk to its lowest point in the thirty-five-year history of the index.[3] Other research reveals that today's children are suffering from excessive levels of depression and anxiety.[4] Attention deficit/hyperactivity disorder (ADHD)[5] and phobias, especially school phobias, are on the rise.[6] There has also been a dramatic increase in the prevalence of developmental disorders such as autism and Asperger syndrome.[7] Because of these growing problems, modern children have become heavily medicated; rates of prescription of stimulants, antidepressants, and other mood stabilizers have tripled in the past decade.[8] Likewise, children are not faring so well in the classroom. The latest National Assessment of Educational Progress shows that only 38 percent of high school seniors are proficient in reading and only 26 percent in math.[9] Another study found that our children are slipping—that the performance of fifth graders on scientific problem-solving tests has fallen by three years' worth in the past two decades.[10] This makes today's eleven-year-old as smart as yesterday's eight-year-old.

There likely are several factors underlying children's tumbling well-being, but in this book I will try to show that some of the most common difficulties of today's children are likely by-products of the rapid and profound changes in their lifestyle. Within the space of the last two or three decades, almost everything about the environment in which children grow up has changed. Those of you who wax nostalgic about your own Red Rover childhoods, when you played without PlayStations®, kicked around balls without coaches, made friends without Facebook®, and went to school without standardized tests, know exactly what I mean. If children were any other animal, the World Wildlife Fund already would have put them on the endangered species list because biologists consider rapid environmental change to be the leading cause of species extinction. Natural changes in the environment tend to occur slowly, which gives animals time to react and readjust to new conditions. But when habitat change occurs at a fast pace, most individuals just can't keep up.

Unlike polar bears, pandas, and black rhinos, humans are an incredibly adaptable species and can grow up in an enormous range of habitats. But even though most of today's children may be capable of handling their new lifestyle, studies showing their increased distractibility, inattention, impulsiveness, hyperactivity, learning disabilities, and behavioral disorders are evidence of the pitfalls of having a brain designed for life in a different world. Young hunter-gatherers—or any animal besides us, for that matter—don't suffer ADHD. But plenty of modern elementary school children, who spend eight hours a day stuffed inside classrooms, suffer from its effects. It is exactly what you'd expect if you put any juvenile (insert your choice of species here) brain behind a desk, made it do seatwork, told it to concentrate, and didn't let it out to play.

FAIRLY ODD PARENTS AND TEACHERS

Lately, I've noticed parents and teachers behaving in strange ways with children's young brains. I've seen parents stash their infants in front of the television set and slip in a Baby Einstein™ DVD, even though research reveals that these sort of programs can delay the young brain's ability to learn language. I know of others who drop off their toddlers at early learning centers, even though such curricula can squash a young tot's creativity and drive to learn. I live across the street from a couple who indulge their children in unlimited video game play, even though the science journals sitting in my living room say that too much gaming time can overwhelm a young brain and make it have trouble paying attention. And I've watched teachers cut back on recess, even though mounds of studies have shown that free play can boost the brain's performance on academic tests and increase its ability to concentrate on schoolwork.

So if scientists know that things like early learning centers and baby DVDs can be bad for the young brain, then what's behind the odd behaviors of parents and teachers? Blame it on the fact that brain scientists rarely talk to mothers and fathers, teachers and superintendents, or pediatricians and policy makers. Scientists' knowledge mostly collects dust in journals and books, rather than getting to parents and teachers and affecting what they do. Instead, we have a self-help industry that peddles largely made-up advice to sell toys, programs, games, and gear.

The problem is, despite parents' and teachers' real desire to help young brains grow into smart and successful adult brains, most know remarkably little about how brains *really* develop. Rather, these adults are better versed in the story of brain development that marketing professionals use to sell their smart toys, video games, education programs, and parenting magazines. The problem is that the version promoted by product marketers usually is made up of claims that go wildly beyond the conclusions drawn by the scientists who actually did the research. The result is that many parents and teachers have been duped into thinking that classical music piped into the womb grows better brains, that babies require battery-powered activity gyms to achieve motor milestones, that flash cards turn toddlers into mathematical geniuses, that academic preschools are a prerequisite to a Harvard education, that handheld gaming systems boost intelligence, and that recess takes away time needed for learning.

A major goal of this book is to vaccinate readers against such widely spread brain-building mythologies and to train skeptical eyes on any such claims perpetuated in the popular press. It's time to wake up and smell the Diaper Genie®.

AND NOW FOR SOMETHING COMPLETELY DIFFERENT

The facts about brain development come from scientists working in an exceedingly diverse array of fields, such as developmental psychology, experimental neuroscience, evolutionary biology, and paleoanthropology, studying a range of species—mostly humans, of course, but also chimpanzees, rats, ducks, quail, and other animals. Remarkably, this research, despite its disparate areas of investigation and the assortment of animals under study, paints a singular picture of how human brains should be reared and educated in the modern world. The picture is this: If parents and teachers wanted to design a way of life counter to the needs of developing human brains, they'd invent something like modern childhood. They'd crowd young brains into classrooms, babysit them with widescreen televisions, design video games that flood their bodies with adrenaline, put batteries in their toys, manicure their backyards, build them artificial playgrounds, and tell them how to play at recess. But if parents and teachers wanted to create a lifestyle for which young brains were designed, they'd have to stop doing all these things and engineer a completely different way of life for today's children. That is what this book is about.

So what's the prescription? Should we revert to a more primitive and animalistic way of life to better raise today's children? While that would be fun for a while—at least until my iPad® battery wore out—it's not the solution. If our children are to grow up to be happy and successful adults, they still need to develop a portfolio of modern skills. They still need to learn how to upload onto Facebook only those vacation photos that make them look slimmer than their high school friends, prod their smartphones to find the cheapest hotel that offers turndown service with those little chocolate mints, and order with confidence at a sushi bar. The solution is merely to design children's lives to work *with* how evolution has prepared their developing brains, not *against* it. What would this look like? For starters, parents would forgo the infant bouncy seats and playpens and foreign language DVDs. They would take the batteries out of "smart" toys, limit the high technology, cut back on the organized sports, and leave plenty of time for play that's freewheeling, make-believe, and messy. Marketers would sell strollers that swivel back to face caregivers and design monkey bars with unevenly spaced rungs. Schools would stop teaching to the test and instead supply consistent opportunities for exploration, experimentation, and exposure outside of the classroom. Lessons would be individualized, recess brought back, homework minimized, and letter grades done away with.

Warning: none of these sorts of changes will make children's brains grow bigger or better or faster or stronger—as the marketers promise their products do. Rather, they will make children's brains grow *normally*.

RAISING BRAIN

Here's what I'll do in this book. I'll be your tour guide to the science behind how children's brains really develop, briefly reviewing the biology background you'll need to understand how humans' evolutionary baggage makes certain aspects of contemporary life a poor fit for the brains of today's children. I'll tell the story of brain development—unfiltered through the lens of media hype and professional marketing, so that you'll learn what scientists really know. Along the way, I will explain how evolutionary pressures have shaped the human brain, how natural selection has designed children's brains to learn, and how childhood experiences physically wire the brain. In particular, I will try to convince you that childhood is exactly what makes the human species unique. It is an adaptation designed by natural selection that makes humans develop in a radically different way than other animals, despite sharing with them most of the same brain parts. And this is why our society's collective push to speed up childhood is a bad idea.

Next, I will expose seven specific recent changes in children's lives that are having baleful effects on the development of today's children. To do so, I'll marshal compelling empirical evidence from a wide array of fields from both human and animal literatures—classical psychology, experimental neuroscience, evolutionary biology, anthropology, public health, and landscape architecture. This discussion needs to include animal research because animals can be more easily studied than humans, the conditions under which they are raised more easily manipulated, and their brains more easily altered and probed. Because human brains and behavior share deep similarities with those of animals, many of the discoveries scientists make in ducks, mice, and monkeys can be applied to humans.

In the final chapters of the book, I will work through the cultural assumptions that underlie the recent changes in children's lifestyles, and I'll show how many of these changes have been driven by quirks in human thinking and myths perpetuated by the popular media. I'll explain why well-meaning parents and educators have been making unhelpful or even harmful choices for their children. Ironically, this has a lot to do with the fact that humans have yet to evolve effective responses to contemporary forces like fear-mongering media reports, shrewd marketers, and statistics. The last chapter of the book offers practical suggestions about how parents and teachers can begin to redesign children's environments—their homes, schools, toys, and pastimes—in ways that gel with how the human brain has been designed to grow.

Rather than leaving you with a doomsday message about today's children (as do most of the books bemoaning modern childhood), readers who join me on this journey to the final pages will close the book with a sense of awe and fascination for the process of brain development and the peculiarities of the human parent and teacher, and with the knowledge to engineer a comeback for today's children. There is much to be optimistic about.

WHO DO I THINK I AM?

I am a developmental scientist who has spent nearly twenty years doing research on as well as writing and teaching about young children. I'm also a mom. I've got an eleven-year-old girl and a seven-year-old boy. So I am standing in your shoes and getting pelted with the onslaught of contemporary pressures to equip my children with the latest electronic gadgets, enroll them in every enrichment activity that comes their way, and occupy them after school with a bag of cheese curls and the Mario Bros.® while their supper of franks and beans is cooking on the stove.

Sometimes, I am tempted to cave into the pressures. To go with the status quo, even though I know better. Consider the alien battle video game that my soon-to-be eight-year-old wants for his birthday. Peoples' heads blow right off their bodies and the flying zombies give me the willies, but it's what children today like. Or what about the handheld gaming console my eleven-year-old wants to buy with her dog-walking money? These types of games seem addictive, but only the really smart children use these things, or so the evening news says. The expensive math tutor that the radio commercial told me my daughter must have if she stands any chance of getting into Harvard seems to make her allergic to word problems, but she's got to get straight As in math, or else she'll end up a forty-year-old living in my basement and greeting shoppers at Junk-Mart. There's also the baseball travel league that all the neighborhood boys are playing in this summer. Backyard pickup games seem like much more fun, but I can't let my son feel left out. But as they say in Alcoholics Anonymous, recognition is the first step. And the more parents, teachers, and policy makers recognize what the brain really needs (and doesn't need) to develop successfully, the better armed they will be to find a healthy balance between the modern world and the natural world—and to engineer a comeback for today's children.

So I invite you to join me in recovery. We have a ball at the meetings. We unbuckle the bouncy seats and hold the babies right on our laps, and no one gasps in disbelief. We take the batteries out of the talking frogs and get down on the floor with the toddlers, and no one casts a disparaging glance. We turn off the Little Einsteins and give the kindergartners old pots and pans and dress-up clothes, and no one rolls their eyes. We let the school-age children out in the backyard and strip them of their touch phones, earbuds, and gaming consoles. And if by the end of the meeting everyone's clothes are muddy, their hair is a mess, and their sneakers are soaking wet, we toast another day sober.

Chapter 1

Old Brain, New World

So, three children walk into a bar.

"Hold on," you say. "How did three children, all at the same time, manage to turn off the Cartoon Network, power down their gaming consoles, and flick off their learning laptops; have no violin lesson, tutoring session, or Scout meeting scheduled; no soccer game, karate class, or ballet recital to attend; and no science fair project, cookie drive, or word study to do?"

Good point. The setup is all but impossible in today's world. Not because the price of a Shirley Temple has inflated beyond the means of the typical four-year-old on a fixed weekly allowance, or because the usual kindergartner favors the trendy hookah lounge over the traditional bar scene. Nor is it because the hologram has made it exceedingly difficult for the ordinary middle schooler to make a good fake ID, but because childhood has changed. Really changed.

When humans first appeared on the scene about two million years ago, families lived in small, nomadic bands and made their living hunting and gathering. Children spent their days roaming in packs and playing on their own in the out-of-doors. They improvised their own fun, regulated their own games, and made up their own rules. Children's education was informal, and new skills were learned out in the world. Such was childhood for more than 99 percent of human existence.

Today, childhood is different. Infants find themselves strapped into bouncy seats and plunked in front of television sets. Toddlers are put away in play yards to listen to Baby Mozart™ and use learning laptops. Preschoolers are given talking dollhouses, robotic pet dogs, and battery-powered frogs that teach them their ABCs. Older children sit in front of computer screens with earbuds connected to their iPods®, texting their friends on their touch phones to see if they can come over and play video games. They spend their weekdays inside classrooms, seated in rows of desks, reciting times tables, drilling word banks, and memorizing state capitals. Their weekends are filled with activities that are organized, supervised, and timed by adults: sports leagues, private tutors, music lessons, math camp, dance instruction, karate classes, and Cub Scouts.

And if you think that things like high technology, formal schooling, organized sports, and manufactured toys are the major newcomers to childhood, you are being speciocentric. To come up with the list of real novelties, you'll need to stop thinking like a human and think like, say, an orangutan. Try it. Pretend you're a hairy, knuckle-dragging ape reclining in the forest canopy, lunching on a ficus fruit and dragonfly sandwich. Suddenly, new changes come to mind, like language, letters, numbers, preexisting tools, art, music, religion, market economies, morals, manners, governments, nuclear families, and stable communities.

Why should you care about how the lifestyle of the typical young orangutan differs from that of children today? Because the very parts that make up modern children's brains were originally inside the heads of nonhuman primates, like orangutans—or at least their (and your) primate ancestors. More importantly, it's because children's brains have a history not only as primates, but as mammals and reptiles and fish.[1]

"That is absurd," you say. "The human brain is inarguably the most innovative organ this planet has ever seen. It enables us to do all sorts of impressive things that no other animal can do. It gives us the ability to think about the future before it happens, understand what others have on their minds, imagine life a different way, solve abstract problems, and learn new skills just by listening. It lets us dance the rumba, play the saxophone, invent the light bulb, launch a rocket to the moon, and dream about standing behind a lectern at a 9:00 a.m. class completely naked and utterly unprepared. No other species even comes close. It's not as if chimpanzees simply speak less eloquently than we do. They can't even utter a single word. But we can say things that can get others to make us a sandwich, drive us to the mall, give us their life savings, award us a Nobel Prize, or elect us president." "So you see," you say as you tap your hairless pointer finger on a coffee table that only a human could be crafty enough to make, "our brains must have been specially made just for us with uniquely sophisticated, state-of-the-art parts."

That is a beautiful idea. It really is. And it's a deeply entrenched belief. But it is simply wrong. At every level of organization, from molecules to cells to systems, the human brain is merely a collection of old parts that have been fitted together throughout millions of years of evolutionary history. Humans, today, are born with the very same brains that resided in the heads of our Pleistocene ancestors tens of thousands of years ago, before the last Ice Age and before humans gave up their nomadic lifestyle and figured out how to domesticate plants and animals. What's more, most parts of our brains are holdovers from a more ancient evolutionary past, originating in primates, mammals, reptiles, and fish that lived long before creatures like us even existed. And the basic processing unit of the human brain—the nerve cell, or neuron—first appeared roughly six hundred million years ago inside the squishy bodies of prehistoric jellyfish.

How can I be so flippant about the human brain—the very organ that seems to make us special? Because when you look the right way at the brains of an ape, a mouse, a frog, a fish, or any other creature with a nervous system, you see that our brains are merely made up of old parts that were developed in other animals at different points in our evolutionary history. You see that the parts of the brain that enable kindergartners to design a sandcastle first appeared in nonhuman primates; that reptiles are responsible for the brain system that preschoolers activate to navigate the ball pit at Chuck E. Cheese®; that fishes premiered the cranial nerves that elementary schoolers use to coordinate their facial muscles to give their little brother a raspberry. And you see that prehistoric jellyfish developed the brain cells that middle schoolers use to roll their eyes when you tell them they can't wear their neon-yellow Chuck Taylors® and matching rhinestone-encased sunglasses for their school portrait. You see that everything seemingly unique about the human brain is merely vintage parts from brains that came before us.

What does this recognition of the deep evolutionary history of our brains mean for children today? It means that their brains were not designed with modern life in mind; rather, they evolved for life in a very different world. At different times in the brain's evolutionary history, it developed in deep seas, freshwater streams, tropical rain forests, and the grasslands of the savannahs, not in classrooms, living rooms, manufactured playgrounds, manicured ball fields, or minivans. These sorts of evolutionarily novel environments have changed the way that children behave and develop, but today's children still enter their respective worlds with a brain that never expected to find itself in any of them. It is this disconnect between children's evolutionary past and their human present that makes parts of the modern world challenging and even damaging to the development of their brains, bodies, and behaviors. But the better we understand the long history of the human brain, the better able we are to raise happy, healthy, and successful children. To see why, let's begin at our beginning.

WELL, I'LL BE A CHIMPANZEE'S UNCLE

"Well, I'll be a monkey's uncle," my grandpa Sal said when he found out that his nephew Joey was legally married in the state of Massachusetts to his longtime business partner, Bob. But if my grandpa Sal cared to characterize more precisely his primate lineage, he should have said, "I'll be a chimpanzee's uncle" or "a gorilla's brother-in-law" or even "an orangutan's nephew," because these great apes, and not monkeys, are our closest living ancestors. How close? Super close. Measured nucleotide by nucleotide, the human genome is nearly 99 percent identical to that of the chimpanzee.[2] This makes humans and chimps genetically closer than gorillas and chimps and even closer than many interbreeding animals, like horses and donkeys. This difference is so close that evolutionary biologist Jared Diamond at the University of California, Los Angeles thinks that humans really should be considered the third chimpanzee (that is, along with common chimpanzees and bonobos, or pygmy chimpanzees).[3]

If you've ever seen one of those old posters depicting the evolution of humankind as a straight progression from a hairy, knuckle-walking ape to an encyclopedia salesman, you might have the impression that the very first human was some hotshot chimpanzee who got the bright idea to stand up, shave his back, craft a business suit and an alligator-skin briefcase, and swagger right out of the African jungle. You could think of human evolution as happening that way—a straight line from chimp to man—but you'd be wrong.

Despite our genetic similarity to chimpanzees, we humans did not evolve from them. Instead, both chimpanzees and humans evolved from a common ancestor six million or so years ago.[4] The most noticeable feature that distinguished our human ancestors—early hominids, generally referred to as *australopithecines*—from early chimpanzees was their upright stance. Australopithecines' hips and legs already had been repositioned to make walking on the ground easier than moving about up in the trees, and their feet already had done away with the opposable big toe of other apes. Famed australopithecine "Lucy" stood about three feet tall and had a brain capacity of four hundred cubic centimeters—about the size of a modern chimpanzee's brain. Australopithecines made their living as nomads, gathering foods like grasses, seeds, and nuts, and about two and a half million years ago, they began to craft simple tools from stone.

The first true humans—that is, members of the *Homo* genus—appeared on the scene roughly two million years ago and went on to evolve into diverse species. Some *Homo* species looked quite similar to Lucy, and others, mainly *Homo erectus*, stood at least a foot taller and had brains more than double the size of those of the early australopithecines. *Homo erectus*'s tool manufacturing was more complex and varied than that of the australopithecines: some tools were made to cut meat and others to extract marrow from animal bones.[5] *Homo erectus* was also likely the first species to figure out how to control fire and fashion containers for food and water. Equipped with such handy skills, *Homo erectus* migrated out of Africa around one and a half million years ago and into Asia and Europe, where it remained in some areas until as recently as twenty-six thousand years ago (which would make the species contemporary with fully modern humans).

Our species, *Homo sapiens*, evolved roughly 250,000 years ago, most likely from the *Homo erectus* who stayed behind in Africa. Modern humans with large brains (about 1,300 cubic centimeters) appeared within the last 150,000 years or so, and about 100,000 years ago, they, too, began to migrate out of Africa and eventually displaced all other existing *Homo* populations (e.g., Neanderthals in Europe), either by killing or by outcompeting them for available food supplies.[6]

So it went until about forty thousand years ago, when, during the last ice age, humankind took a peculiar historical turn. Out of nowhere, we took up the fine arts. We created statues that glorified the female form, painted cave wall frescos of animal scenes and great hunts, fashioned jewelry with shells and animal teeth, and crafted musical instruments. We also carried out elaborate burials for the dead, worshiped supernatural forces, and built huts for shelter (even though we still lived as hunter-gatherers). Then, with the end of the last ice age ten thousand years ago, we settled down, built stationary communities, and domesticated plants and animals. Setting up shop in one place triggered lightning-speed growth in our technological prowess. Once it happened, we took only about seven thousand years to figure out how to build the Great Pyramids. Then only a thousand more to build the Roman Coliseum. A couple more millennia after that, we've made the space shuttle, the Magic Kingdom®, and the iPad. But the irony of our rise to the technological top is that not only are we the only species whose brains are smart enough to fashion such groovy creations, we are the only species whose brains are smart enough to meddle so much with how nature intended us to raise our children.

This look back on humankind's long evolutionary history reveals just how unnatural modern childhood is, in that most of what children do today involves experiences never encountered by our ancestors. Our history also shows just how new our contemporary lifestyle is for our species—we've been civilized for less than half of 1 percent of our existence. Fossil evidence indicates that the human brain has not changed that much over the past 250,000 years, and certainly little at all over the past 35,000 years. What this time frame means is that there simply has been far too little time for natural selection to adapt the human brain to the conditions and challenges of civilization, let alone of contemporary childhood. Children's brains were not designed for life in the modern world. They were not built to be strapped into vibrating bouncy seats, assigned to climate-controlled classrooms, or put onto padded plastic play structures. Yet this is where we've been putting them.

CLOUDY WITH A CHANCE OF BRAIN

In roughly six million years, we've gone from your run-of-the-mill ape to a uniquely clever human. The exact cause of this development has been hotly debated by scientists for a long time. But the most likely explanation has to do with a change in the weather. Paleoanthropologist Richard

Potts, the director of the Smithsonian's Human Origins Program and the curator of anthropology at the National Museum of Natural History, believes that our solution for dealing with the changing weather conditions is exactly what enabled us to cut the neurological rope from the rest of the animal kingdom and emerge as uniquely smart humans.[7]

In prehominid times, our ancestors were just another group of small apes that made their living feeding on fruits and leaves in the treetops of the tropical rain forests of northern and eastern Africa. The weather was typical jungle: uncomfortably hot and wet. But comfortably predictable. Then, beginning about ten million years ago, the weather started to change. The climate turned increasingly arid, and our reliable arboreal food courts began to dry up. As the trees disappeared, we were forced down and out of our comfortable treetop lifestyle to wander about on the forest floor to find more trees to teeter up to dine. This meant that we had to travel longer and longer distances to find a meal. It also meant that the stamina to move far across a dry savanna in a two-dimensional plane was now a much more desirable trait than the dexterity to move up and down in a three-dimensional, tree-centered environment.

The clever solution we came up with to address the demands of our new, flat environment was to stand up and use only our rear appendages for moving about. Standing up made us slower, but it freed up our hands for carrying things and using tools. And because walking on two legs expends fewer calories than walking on all fours, our new upright stance also gave us extra energy to modify ourselves to better survive in our new surroundings. But rather than taking the typical animal kingdom approach of adding more muscle to the body or sharper fangs to the jaw, we did something completely different: We added more neurons to our brains. So much so that our brains today consume 20 percent of our bodies' energy, even though they make up only 2 percent of our weight. We ended up developing a brain four to five times larger than would be expected for an animal of our size.

How did our big brains help us survive in our new flat residence? You've probably watched enough National Geographic specials to guess that the odds were stacked against us. Easily 99.9 percent of all species that ever existed are now extinct. And so are all other *Homo* species—except for us.[8] Most extinct species can blame their demises on changes to their habitats that were both too quick and too intense. This was almost the story for our kind, especially since our new horizontal digs already had tenants. Not only had our new roommates already co-opted the local food sources, but most of them were bigger and stronger and faster than us.[9] Some scientists think that our founding population of direct ancestors was weeded down to a paltry two thousand individuals. Others argue that the group was reduced to a few hundred. So how, then, did we go from a relatively wimpy and clearly endangered species to a population seven billion strong and growing?

We changed the rules of the game. Instead of trying to adapt to the changing environment, we adapted to change itself. We stopped worrying about learning how to survive in a particular habitat and instead figured out how to survive in any environment that the earth could throw at us. That's a pretty gutsy solution. It was brilliant, too, because those of us who had trouble solving new problems quickly or learning from our mistakes didn't live long enough to pass on our genes. The evolutionary result was that rather than becoming bigger or stronger or faster, we became smarter.

BRAINS FOR BRAWN

How exactly did our growing intelligence help us survive in our new, flat, occupied world? It enabled us to figure out a unique way to become the biggest around—not by taking the usual course and making our bodies stronger, but instead by making allies. By getting our friends and neighbors to cooperate with us, we were able to double and triple our strength without increasing individual muscle power. By cooperating with others, we humans—physically unimpressive members of the animal kingdom— ended up sitting at the top of the food chain. Need to fight off a saber-toothed tiger? A human alone doesn't stand a chance. But if a group of humans learns how to coordinate their behaviors and work as a team, suddenly they're a formidable opponent.

Humans are able to pull off such amazing feats of teamwork because we've developed a skill no other animal has: theory of mind.[10] Theory of mind refers to our ability to infer other people's beliefs, goals, intentions, knowledge, and motivations on the basis of their behaviors. It allows us to peer into others' mental lives and to infer why someone did something, whether they're telling the truth, whether they liked the watermelon chicken we cooked for dinner or are just saying it, or whether they know we mind that they want to work late rather than pick up the kids at the bus stop like they promised. Theory of mind enables us to coordinate impressive group behaviors because it allows us to create shared goals that take into account our allies' interests as well as our own.

Today our talent for predicting and manipulating other people is mostly automatic, so much so that most of the time we don't even realize we're doing it. But theory of mind was a development that required an exceptional level of intelligence, and consequently a tremendous amount of brain activity, one that could come only with a big brain that was much more powerful than our tree-dwelling ancestors required merely to find good fruit in a bountiful rain forest.

THE BEASTS WITHIN

If adaptability itself is humankind's slickest adaptation, then why worry about the lifestyle changes that modern life has imposed upon today's children? Since humans moved to the top of the food chain not because we were particularly well adapted to any one environment, but because we were smart enough to adapt to any environment, aren't the lifestyle changes of the twenty-first century just a new variation on an old theme, to which children's clever brains will adapt?

Even though we humans are remarkably flexible, we and our children are still very much animals. Our children are animals not because they grunt, drool, shed, and usually need a bath, but because they, like dragonflies, hammerhead sharks, elephants, and fruit bats, are card-carrying members of the animal kingdom. (Check the slot in their Velcro™ wallets behind their Lego Club™ membership cards and the Clone Wars™ sticker they got at the doctors' office. That's where my kids keep their cards.) This membership suggests two powerful reasons that the lifestyle changes facing today's children are cause for concern: all animals (1) have parents and (2) inherit from them their genes *and* an environment.

Consider, first, the statement that all animals have parents and what that might mean. (Working through this first point will take some time; we'll pick up on the second point in a few pages.) Neil Shubin, a paleontologist at the University of Chicago, refers to the fact that all animals have parents as the biological "law of everything."[11] This law means that every animal sprang from some parental genetic information and that consequently, every animal is a modified descendant of its parental genetic information. This is what Charles Darwin meant by "descent with modification." I've descended from my mother and father, but I'm not copies of them. I am a modified version of them. Likewise, my parents are modified descents of my grandparents, my grandparents are modified descents of my great-grandparents, and so on. This pattern of descent with modification defines our family tree. But just as we have a family tree that branches out with our parents, grandparents, and great-grandparents, we also have a species tree that branches out to other living beings. We can use this species tree to show that humans are modified descendants of some earlier species, which are modified descendants of an even earlier species, and so on. This family tree concept that we use to describe our family history also applies to humankind as a whole. It means that all humans are modified descendants of everything from early hominids to apes to reptiles to long-extinct prehistoric jellyfish. Our deep connections to the rest of the animal world represent a truly beautiful idea. But it's this long history that has constrained evolution's design of children's bodies and brains.

I'LL HAVE THE PRIMORDIAL SOUP

Imagine that you've been asked to design the human brain. How would you do it? You'd probably start from scratch. You'd probably use only shiny new parts engineered specifically for humankind. And you'd probably see no good reason to mix in parts already in use by other animals, like monkeys, frogs, or fish. Good thing no one asked you—with a brain designed like that, you'd never end up with a human.

The concept of descent with modification means that evolution can't just wipe the slate clean and start over with a new design. Evolution is constrained to working with what is already in place, reworking, retooling, or otherwise refashioning what's already there. This means that new forms are simply altered versions of existing ones. It also explains why we don't have three heads, six arms, or wheels instead of legs. Our heads and arms and legs are merely modifications of systems that originated in creatures existing before us and were reworked by natural selection for operation inside of us.

Because evolution is constrained to work with what is already in place, it often makes changes by piling new systems on top of old ones. John Allman, a neuroscientist at the California Institute of Technology, describes this tendency of evolution with an analogy to an old power plant he visited, where at least three layers of technology were in simultaneous use, stacked one on top of another.[12] He noticed that several generations of systems were running simultaneously. The newest computer machinery didn't operate the plant directly. Instead, it regulated a 1940s-era vacuum tube system that controlled an even older pneumatic setup. The engineers no doubt would have preferred to scrap the older systems altogether and start over with just the newest computing machinery. But the continuous need to generate power prevented the plant from ever being shut down long enough to do a complete remodel and reboot.

The same logic applies in the design of animals, humans included. Our ongoing need to survive and reproduce prevents evolution from taking its biological productions offline and redesigning them from the ground up. The consequences of this constraint, like that imposed on the power plant, are that new technologies often are built right smack on top of the old.

Consider our spines, for example. If an engineer had been called in to design the support system for the very first human—an admittedly top-heavy creature—he'd probably concoct a frame that evenly distributed the body's weight across multiple columns, each reinforced with cross braces. Instead, we support our bodies with a single column that bears tremendous weight and consequently causes a lot of people back pain. We are built this way not because it's the best means to support a biped, but because our backbone is merely a modified version of the original that first appeared in fish, a creature for which a single column worked just fine.

The same goes for our vocal system. An engineer probably would have designed some sort of amped-up stand-alone digital system. But evolution had to start with a breathing tube and tinker with it until it made sound. It did this by dividing the tube in half—half for breathing and sound, half for eating. Problem is, because everything we eat and drink has to pass over the trachea, we're at high risk for choking. Likewise, we have five fingers not because it's the best design for the human hand, but because five-pronged appendages developed in the fins of fish some three and a half million years ago.

There are countless more examples that tell the same story for every part of us, from our spines to our digits to our brains. Admittedly, it's one thing to accept that certain parts of your body, like your backbone or your fingers, originated in fish, but somehow quite another thing when it comes to your brain. But what's true of our backbones and fingers also applies to our minds.

A LOOK UNDER THE HOOD

Now that you know the constraints that our species family tree puts upon us, let's take a look under the human hood and see what we can discern about the brain's design. To take proper part in this exercise, you'll need to imagine a fresh human brain sitting on the table in front of you. What you'd see is a slightly oblong pinkish-gray mass of thickly wrinkled tissue with a deep groove running from the front to the back. If you were to slice the brain in half along this groove and then turn the cut side to face you, you might be surprised to see that really, three brains are tucked inside the human head, one piled on top of the next.[13]

At the bottom of the brain, somewhat toward the back end, is the most ancient neural structure inside the human head. This structure, called the brain stem or "lizard brain," dates back from at least half a billion years ago, and does the same thing for us that it does for a Komodo dragon. It handles most of our basic housekeeping chores: heart rate, breathing rhythm, body temperature, and sleeping and waking. It also controls some important reflexes such as coughing, sneezing, and vomiting. It's also involved in the regulation and coordination of movement, posture, and balance. And it contains primitive areas for vision and hearing that are old for us, but remain the main sensory centers of animals like frogs and lizards. As you'll see in a bit, these regions have been supplemented in us by more modern regions higher up in the brain. All the functions housed in this part of the brain operate completely outside of our awareness and are always turned on. They keep our body systems up and running 24/7—that is, regardless of whether we are wide awake, catching a wink, or three sheets to the wind. But as you'll see in later chapters, their functions can't be switched off, even when their actions cause children to behave in ways that get them into trouble at home, in school, or on the sports field.

Piled atop the brain stem is the "mammalian brain." As its name suggests, this structure appears in humans in much the same way it does in many mammals, such as rats and pigs. Most of its functions are involved in the regulation of basic behaviors that are critical for survival, or what some scientists call the "four Fs" of behavior: fighting, fleeing, feeding, and, er, reproduction. Several parts of this middle brain also are involved in making memories and regulating emotion. This is also the first place in the brain where automatic and reflexive functions begin to blend with conscious awareness. And like the reptilian regions, parts of this mammalian brain lead to behaviors that can cause problems for children in the modern world. For instance, midbrain structures regulate drives for sweet, salty, and fatty foods. These drives are adaptive for animals that never know when their next meal may come, but these same drives make today's children, who have easy access to candy, cookies, and potato chips, overweight and unhealthy.

Draped over the top is the newest addition to the brain, the "human brain" or cortex. The cortex is not uniquely human, but the human cortex, compared to the cortexes of other animals, is quite large—about the size of a baby blanket if unwrinkled and completely stretched out. It is involved in sensory and motor functions, but its most recently evolved section, known as the frontal cortex, is the region of the brain that makes possible our uniquely human talents, such as emotional regulation, delayed gratification, executive control, and long-term planning. One of its most important jobs is to compensate for the rest of the parts of the brain. In other words, it functions to inhibit the emotional and impulsive inputs from the older, deeper parts of the brain. It works by ignoring bad advice from the ancient brain, like, "Forget what your mom says and take candy from that stranger." And it gives us the ability to, say, withhold a burp during church but let loose later around the guys. The frontal cortex is also the region that gives us personality and individuality; it affects our social relationships, our outlook on life, our moral sense, and much more. Not surprisingly, other species don't have a whole lot of frontal function, which is why your pet dog will burp even when company is joining you for dinner. Nor do young children, which is why they'll burp in church without embarrassment. The human frontal cortex is pretty much the last part of the brain to fully mature. Before the age of two, we don't much distinguish ourselves in frontal function from apes.

Having finished our tour of the brain, what can we conclude about the overall principles of human brain design? First, the most sophisticated functions of the brain, those involving conscious awareness and explicit thought, are located at the very top and front, in the cortex, whereas the most primitive functions, supporting basic unconscious regulation of body functions such as breathing and heart rate, are situated in the very bottom and rear, in the brain stem. In between are centers engaged in basic drives and the crossroads where conscious and unconscious parts of the brain meet and initiate emotion and the storage of certain types of memories.

Our trip around the brain also reveals that it is built somewhat like an ice-cream cone with new scoops piled on through evolutionary time. As higher functions were added, a new scoop was placed on top, but the lower scoops were left largely unchanged. In this way, our brain stem (scoop one) is not very different from that of a frog, and our middle section (scoop two) appears in us the same way it does in many mammals. The human brain, then, was made by taking the standard mammal model and adding an extra scoop (scoop three) on the top, albeit an unusually large scoop. This ice-cream scoop design shows that when new, higher functions were added, it did not result in a wholesale redesign of the brain from the ground up—just a new scoop plopped on top. So primitive structures from our deep evolutionary past persist in the lower parts of our brains and still affect how we think and behave.

Not only have we retained evolutionarily ancient systems in our modern brains, but the old components sometimes make their presence felt in newer systems. One of my favorite examples demonstrating this is a phenomenon called blindsight, which happens because we have two visual systems.[14] We have an evolutionarily ancient one that we share with fish and lizards, but we also have a modern, more elaborate system that exists higher up in the brain (in the visual cortex). If you're a frog, the older system drives your tongue to snag insects in midair. In us, it triggers our bodies to duck when a snowball is coming for our heads. We and the frogs do these things without even thinking about them. Most of the visual input that comes into our brains via the eyes is processed in our newer system—the visual cortex. If this newer system gets damaged, most people report that they can't see anything at all. Yet if you ask them to reach for something, some of them grab it on the first try, even though they'll say they have no idea where the object is and are merely guessing. And if you ask them to judge the emotional expression on a face, they get it right more often than chance would predict, especially if that expression is anger. The explanation is that blindsighted people have lost what most of us think of as vision and are seeing with the ancient reptilian visual system. But because this vintage region is not hooked up to the more modern parts of the brain, these people have no conscious awareness of an object's location or a face's expression. To the conscious mind, the world looks pitch black, but unconsciously, the ancient system is communicating with the motor cortex (which makes the arm reach out) and the amygdala (which assesses emotion) exactly as it would in a frog.

JELLYFISH iPOD

From our grand tour of the human brain, we can conclude that it was built by piling newer technologies right on top of old components that are still operative and make their presence felt. Think about what this means for how your brain does its business. It's as if your iPod had to have a working turntable and eight-track player attached to it at all times. Not only would that make your iPod much too large to fit into your trendy exercise armband, you'd have to deal with the Neil Diamond songs simultaneously streaming out of the older systems.

If this design weren't old enough, the ancient origins of our brains become even more evident at the cellular level. Brain cells, or neurons, first appeared in prehistoric jellyfish some six hundred million years ago, and their design—that is, their overall shape and chemical composition—has not changed substantially since then. Neurons are simple devices, less complex than walkie-talkies from Sears, and they do one simple thing: namely, react to the chemicals that reach them by releasing chemicals of their own. Let's have a closer look at the biology of the neuron to understand how their ancient design has affected how humans grow up.

Neurons come in many sizes and shapes, but most have the same basic framework. Like all cells, neurons are bounded externally by an outer membrane and have a cell body that contains the cell nucleus, which is where the DNA resides. Blooming out of the cell body are branches of the neuron called dendrites, which receive chemical signals from neighboring neurons. Neurons usually have several branches of dendrites, but they also have a single, thinner appendage called an axon. The axon is the information-transmitting end of the neuron and often branches off in different directions. Axons can be remarkably long (some go all the way from the base of the spine to the tip of the toes) and usually end when they nearly touch dendrites on other neurons. At these junctions, or synapses, information passes from the axon of one neuron to the dendrite of the next. The ends of axons (called axon terminals) contain many synaptic vesicles, which are tiny membrane-covered balls loaded with molecules of a specialized chemical known as a neurotransmitter. Between the axon terminal of one neuron and the dendrite of the next is a tiny saltwater-filled gap called the synaptic cleft. The synaptic cleft is where synaptic vesicles release neurotransmitters to signal the next neuron in the chain.

Synapses are central to our story. They are the switching points between two forms of signaling that go on in the brain: chemical and electrical impulses.[15] When electrical signals traveling down the axon arrive at the axon terminal, they trigger synaptic vesicles to dump their contents, special neurotransmitter molecules, into the synaptic cleft. These neurotransmitter molecules then move across the synaptic cleft, where they contact specialized proteins called neurotransmitter receptors embedded in the membrane of a neighboring neuron's dendrite. Receptors convert the neurotransmitter's chemical signal back into an electrical signal. Electrical signals from activated receptors all over the dendrite are funneled toward the cell body. If enough electrical signals arrive together, the signal is passed farther along the chain of neurons.

MORE IS SOMETIMES OTHER

Everything you've read so far seems to point to the fact that the human brain isn't all that fancy—that it's made up of the same parts, the same chemicals, and the same physiological reactions as the brains of other animals. Our neurons are not any different from those of a jellyfish. Our neurons don't use some special-recipe neurotransmitter to communicate with one another, nor do our neurons grow bigger, jump higher, or run faster. Yet we are very different from other animals. So how does the human brain manage to create unique mental functions with its hand-me-down design and its garden-variety, vintage parts, none of which were designed specially for operation inside our modern human heads?

The answer is sheer numbers. The human brain has an enormous number of neurons, roughly one hundred billion. And with that many neurons, you can do some pretty remarkable things. To put this number into perspective, for each one neuron a fly has, we have about one hundred million neurons. We ended up with so many neurons because, rather than redesigning the original jellyfish model, we just kept tacking on more of the same over evolutionary time. To turn us into a uniquely clever animal, evolution needed an unprecedented number of neurons because frankly, neurons, as electrical devices, are poorly designed. Their exact biological story is likely to be well beyond the interest of most readers, but the quick and dirty version that will serve our purpose here concerns four features of the neuron: (1) its electrical signals travel exceedingly slowly (even the fastest conduct signals more than a million times more slowly than copper wires), (2) much of the electrical current leaks out because of the "soaker" garden hose design of the axon, (3) neurotransmitters fail to release about 70 percent of the time, and (4) neurotransmitters don't always make the trip all the way across the synaptic cleft. This slow, leaky, and unreliable design might have worked just fine for a jellyfish, but not for a creature that walks, talks, and thinks. So, to compensate for this less than optimal design, not only did the human brain grow an enormous number of neurons, it had them massively interconnected. Each neuron makes, on average, five thousand synapses (the range is zero to two hundred thousand). Do the math and you end up with an astounding network of five hundred trillion (that's 500,000,000,000,000) connections. The way that evolution created a uniquely smart human with a brain cobbled together out of old parts was to build a massively interconnected network of one hundred billion neurons with five hundred trillion synapses. The human brain enables our clever behavior not by being made out of special parts, but as the result of the sheer *number* of interconnections among neurons that, all together, can do very special things. With quantity we created quality.

If you're a little confused at the moment, help is on the way. Let's work through a phenomenon that statisticians call the law of large numbers, which explains why having more of the same (i.e., old neurons) enables us to develop capacities that are far beyond the abilities of other animals. Many people have the wrong idea about large numbers—namely, that they are like small numbers, only bigger. Consequently, many people expect large numbers to do *more* of what small numbers do, but not to do anything *different*.

We know that a couple of neurons exchanging electrochemical signals across their axons and dendrites cannot possibly produce complex behaviors like language, deliberate thought, or theory of mind. If we assume that one hundred billion of these simple devices can only do one hundred billion simple things, we would never guess that one hundred billion of them could produce a behavior that two, ten, or ten thousand could not. But complex behaviors like symbolic thought and self-consciousness arise as the result of the sheer number of interconnections among neurons in the human brain, not as a result of any one of the parts or the interconnections of just a few.

You already know this from your dog. Your dog is made up of atoms, and atoms are invisible. Therefore, your dog is invisible. The problem with this reasoning is that the whole of something doesn't always have the same qualities as its parts. Your dog, which is made up of invisible atoms, is visible because visibility emerges from the interaction of a terribly large number of terribly tiny parts that do not themselves have visibility. In short, more is not just more—it sometimes is *other*.

This more-is-sometimes-other logic can be applied to the human brain. The way that we've gotten around the constraint of descent with modification is to employ an enormous number of the same old neurons. It's the sheer number of interconnections among neurons that produces our uniquely human behaviors, even though each individual neuron is not unique.

So while the brain tucked inside the human head has enabled us humans to do all sorts of unique things, it doesn't follow that our brains are uniquely designed. Every piece of our brains has been revised, reworked, or repurposed in different ways throughout evolutionary time. This means that our brains are not uniquely designed, but historically designed. That history is our inheritance, and that inheritance can cause our children problems because they live in a different world.

HUMANS, GORILLAS, BANANAS, OH MY!

Now let's return to the second consequence of children's membership in the animal kingdom that should make us worry about today's children's lifestyle changes—namely, that all animals inherit from their ancestors both genes *and* an environment. Ever since sixth grade biology, we've known that all living things, humans included, inherit a complement of genes that is typical for their species. Common wisdom goes that it is these genes that make a sponge, a naked mole rat, and a human being the unique entities that they are. If you had sponge genes, you'd be fused to the bottom of a tide pool instead of reading this book. If a sponge had human genes, it'd be on the couch watching HGTV with a bag of Cheetos® instead of hanging from a rope in the shower. But if genes are really what make humans human, how do we resolve the fact that we share 99 percent of our genes with chimpanzees, 98 percent with gorillas, and 40 percent with bananas?

Perhaps we're more like bananas than we think we are. Or perhaps genes aren't as powerful as we think they are. The latter is the scientific conclusion that a lot of people are making lately.[16] One of the most common misperceptions about evolutionary explanations is that if a behavior is considered to have evolved, it is "in the genes" and therefore inevitable and unchangeable. But that is not how genes really work. Genes don't fire off and determine behavior. How could they, buried deep inside our cells as they are? They're obviously in no position to see the world, move our bodies, choose our words, or tell us how to think.

Genes produce proteins, not behaviors. Sure, some of these proteins have a lot to do with behavior. But genes are always expressed in an environment, and often it is this environment that regulates their expression in bodies and behavior. Put a bunch of genes in a jar, and they'll do nothing. Put them in an environment (that is, inside a cell that is inside a body that is inside a classroom) and they'll generate a behavior. Put them in another environment (that is, inside a cell that is inside the same body that is inside a backyard) and they'll generate something entirely different. This is how temperature can change camouflage patterns in butterflies, diet can change the color and shape of caterpillars, and social-group composition can change some fish from female to male. In all of these cases, genetically identical organisms develop differently based on differences in their environments.

Evolution is based on genetic inheritance, but throughout life, the environment regulates how that inheritance expresses itself. To begin to rethink the notion of genetically determined behaviors, let's visit the classic demonstration of an "instinctive" behavior that comes from the work of Nobel Prize laureate Konrad Lorenz.[17] In the 1930s, Lorenz observed that shortly after hatching, certain birds, like ducks and geese, follow the first moving and quacking thing they see. In the natural world, usually this thing is their mother, making this an adaptive behavior because it ensures that chicks stay close to their caregiver until they became sufficiently independent to survive on their own. In the laboratory, this phenomenon can be demonstrated by placing a freshly hatched chick in the center of a circular pen and playing the maternal call of the chick's species on one end of the pen and the maternal call of other species on the opposite end. Almost invariably, chicks approach the speaker playing their species' maternal call. They seem to know "instinctively" which call is their own species and which is not. Lorenz called this behavior "imprinting" and argued that it evolved to happen without any sort of prior experience. From this research came the idea that evolution preprograms behaviors in the genes and thus that behaviors can be innate. It seemed to be the perfect little proof of innate ability.

In the 1970s, the late developmental psychologist Gilbert Gottlieb of the University of North Carolina, discovered the flaw in Lorenz's assumption.[18] He decided to test Lorenz's "no experience necessary" interpretation of imprinting. In the wild, mother ducks lay several eggs and stay close until the eggs hatch, and while still in the egg, ducklings begin to vocalize. These natural conditions mean that before hatching, chicks hear not only their mother's vocalizations, but also those of themselves and their broodmates. In a series of experiments, Gottlieb systematically modified the various sources of ducklings' natural prenatal auditory experiences to see if he could find an early experience that triggered their later imprinting behavior. First, Gottlieb removed the mother, and then later, the broodmates. Under both of these conditions, he found that newly hatched chicks still reliably approached the maternal call. To examine the third source of auditory experience—the ducklings' own vocalizations—Gottlieb developed a procedure that surgically prevented the birds from making any sound while still in the egg (no worries, the effect is reversible). Under these conditions, after hatching, the birds showed no preference when given the auditory choice test. The surgically treated birds were just as likely to approach the call of another species as they were their own. This finding shows that imprinting, a behavior long thought to be "in the genes," really is dependent on a specific experience—namely, hearing one's own vocalizations prenatally. The accurate conceptualization of imprinting, then, is that ducklings clearly are prepared, or biased, by evolution to make an attachment to the call of their mother, but this is achieved not by a genetically prescribed instinct, but by a process that involves experience—a type of experience that all normal members of the species could expect to have.

Gottlieb's experiments have since been replicated many times in different contexts with different animals and different behaviors. The seminal insight from Gottlieb's work is that behaviors that seem to be "in the genes" often really are dependent on certain experiences that are typical for the species. Evolved behaviors at the human level can be viewed similarly. Strong species-wide biases may exist for certain behaviors, but the development of these behaviors is likely dependent on species-typical experiences.

Here's one example. Certain developmental psychologists, often referred to as nativists, believe that infants come into the world having evolved an innate ability to recognize the human face. Now if I didn't know about imprinting, this genetic explanation would seem reasonable because within the first few days of life, newborns—seemingly with little or no experience with human faces—can tell the difference between human faces and other designs. So it *seems* to be "in the genes."

But I hope by now you're wondering whether babies' ability to recognize the human face might require some sort of species-typical experience. And you should indeed be wondering. The problem with the nativists' interpretation is that it rests on the assumption that any behavior expressed by a young baby must be innate because either (a) young babies haven't had enough meaningful experiences in the world to matter or (b) young babies are simply too dense to learn anything substantial from the world.

The truth of the matter it that even very young babies rack up all kinds of powerful learning experiences and that even newborns can learn brilliantly from the world. A landmark finding by a rival group of developmental psychologists known as the interactionists showed that adults process human and monkey faces differently, but babies do not.[19] Babies react to human and monkey faces the same way. This striking finding tells us that babies' facility with human faces is not "in the genes." What babies' exact reaction to monkey and human faces means is that their ability to tell human faces from other designs is driven not by some inborn genetic predisposition, but by species-typical experiences—that is, simply by seeing more human faces than other types of faces. Related work using brain-imaging techniques shows that certain areas of the newborn brain are biased to process certain types of information, like human faces, more effectively than other types of information. But for these biases to take effect, babies need species-typical experience (i.e., seeing human faces). With species-typical experience, these sets of neurons become increasingly specialized, enhancing the efficiency of these brain areas for processing specific information, which decreases their ability to process or recognize other types of information (i.e., monkey faces).

The lesson that lurks in findings like these is that species-typical genes are not all that make us human (and ditto for other animals). Species-typical experiences, like early exposure to human faces for humans, are crucial for making important human behaviors happen— even those behaviors that Parenting.com told you were genetically driven. Without species-typical experience, these behaviors disappear.

WHAT TO EXPECT WHEN YOU'RE EXPECTING A HUMAN

If genes are expressed differently in different environments, how can we resolve the fact that most members of a species develop in a similar fashion? The answer, according to Robert Lickliter, a developmental psychobiologist at Florida International University, lies in the fact that humans (or chimps or ducks) inherit not only a species-typical genome, but also a species-typical environment.[20] Lickliter argues that findings like Gottlieb's require us to rethink what is inherited from generation to generation and, accordingly, what is involved in evolution. To the extent that an animal grows up under conditions similar to that in which its species evolved, development will follow a species-typical pattern, and all will be well.

So sponges evolved underwater and require wetness to thrive. Naked mole rats evolved underground and do well only underground. Both of these animals need these species-typical environments to develop properly. Likewise, young humans thrive in environments that historically have been typical for our species, such as nine months in a womb, a loving and lactating mom, and kin to share in storytelling, thumb wrestling, and fart jokes.

There is compelling evidence that species-typical experiences are exactly what make us develop in a normal fashion. Vision demonstrates this point. Contrary to what you might think, visual centers of the brain do not come prewired or rely on a genetic blueprint that automatically builds them. Even though these brain components were designed by millions of years of evolution, they (like those regulating imprinting in ducks) need species-typical experiences during their early development to grow properly. If they don't get species-typical experience as they develop, they don't put themselves together correctly. Dozens of studies have shown that if you deprive an eye in a newborn kitten of normal vision, visual centers of the brain begin to degenerate.[21] Keep that eye sutured closed for a few months, and the animal is blind in that eye when the eye is reopened. Connections between the shut eye and neurons in the brain close up shop. It's the same punch line for humans. We know this because infants who are born with dense cataracts and who consequently are deprived of species-typical visual experience develop normal vision only if their cataracts are surgically removed by the time they are about two years old.[22] Otherwise, their developing brains, deprived of expected experiences, will not wire themselves for normal vision, and these children will never be able to see—even if their cataracts are removed later in life.

So species-typical visual experience is vital for visual centers in the brain to correctly hook themselves up. Until recently, evolution all but ensured that young humans got these experiences. But the advent of the video game in the 1970s, a mere wink of an eye ago in humanity's time on the planet, plucked children from their usual outdoor regimen and stripped them of species-typical visual experience. Is this really something to worry about? Only if it bothers you that researchers have found that young children who frequently play video games are four times more likely to develop myopia than children who regularly play outdoors.[23]

These sorts of findings raise a question as well. If the deprivation of species-typical experiences can wipe out vision—a skill that seems relatively basic and that humans share with most members of the animal kingdom—then what might deprivation of species-typical experiences do to the development of much more complex and uniquely human talents?

Consider the well-known effects of exercise on children's academic performance. Why should exercise boost performance on academic tests? Because during our brain's long history as primates, we moved from active tree-living animals to active hunters and gatherers to active agriculturalists. The common theme here is the word "active." And it means that activity is a species-typical experience for us humans. Supporting this idea are dozens of studies showing that children who exercise aerobically perform better academically than their sedentary peers.[24] The bad news for today's children is that many spend a large portion of the day being anything but active. Many sit in classrooms eight hours a day, sit some more in minivans, and then come home to sit in front of television sets, behind computer screens, and at kitchen tables. So, going along with the theme of this book, upping children's activity won't boost academic performance, but it should get it back to normal. We'll get into more details and the biology of how exercise makes young brains work better in a later chapter.

You might think that evolution wouldn't favor such a high-risk strategy of relying on species-typical experience to properly build an animal. But usually such a strategy is not risky because evolution traditionally has ensured that young animals get species-typical experiences—that ducklings hear duck vocalizations from the egg and that newborn babies see human faces. So the larger meaning here is that if evolution works to provide humans (and all other animals) with species-typical experiences that make important behaviors develop, we should be wary of our attempts to dupe evolution and take away the experiences that it has designed children's brains to expect.

What's more, the disappearing species-typical experiences are being replaced by a gambit of species-*atypical* experiences—assigned seats, worksheets, word banks, video games, organized sports, and online social networks. Should we be concerned about how such *unexpected* experiences are affecting the way the brain builds itself? Remember the studies showing that children who exercised aerobically outperformed their sedentary peers on academic tests? It turns out that the cognitive gains of the physically active children plummeted if they stopped exercising. The implication, of course, is that if we take away species-typical experiences, then childhood development goes downhill.

EXPECT THE UNEXPECTED

You know what happens when three-year-olds don't get what they expect. If you promise Sally a chocolate cone and the ice-cream shop runs out of chocolate, there's screaming and banging and kicking and tears when you suggest strawberry. The brain seems to react the same way when it doesn't get what it expects.

Dozens of studies on birds, rats, and other animals reveal that providing young animals with stimulation that is outside the species norm can have negative consequences for development. Bobwhite quails, for instance, that are made to see patterned light several days before hatching (done by peeling away part of the eggshell and shining in a light) end up with better than average vision.[25] (This is an unexpected experience because quail chicks normally would not see patterned light until after hatching—and this information could be spun by marketers to argue that early experience builds better quails, or children.) But the effect of the extra light is not a straightforward case of extra stimulation leading to a better baby quail. Even though the early exposure to light boosts their post-hatching vision, they lose their preference for the maternal species call. After hatching, these quail can't tell the difference between the maternal call of their own species and that of a chicken. In fact, some even prefer the chicken call. A look at the brain in high-tech imaging equipment has revealed that what happens under these conditions is that the earlier-than-expected visual stimulation causes neurons that normally would have been dedicated to dealing with sounds to be instead used for handling sights.

Another example of how unexpected experience can disrupt normal brain development is illustrated in a study of the effects of painful stimulation in newborn rats.[26] Neural development in rats typically proceeds during prenatal times and early infancy in the absence of painful stimulation. But when newly born rats are made to experience pain, the neural circuits that respond to pain are permanently rewired, altering their response to sensory stimulation and making the animals more sensitive to pain as adults. The unexpected exposure to pain, therefore, adversely alters the course of species-typical development.

A finding like this could give panic attacks to rat mothers all over the world. Remember the time when Junior pricked his paw on that thumbtack he found in his nest box bedding? But such worries are far afield, of course, from human concerns. And that's where the next study comes in.

Neonatologist Heidelise Als and her colleagues have demonstrated a phenomenon that makes the same point for humans, seen in premature babies who end up in neonatal intensive care units in hospitals that are brightly lit and overwhelmingly loud.[27] Such sights and sounds are far in excess of what preemies expect to see and hear at that age. Because they are born early, they are expecting still to be inside of their mothers' dark and muted wombs—and consequently seeing and hearing very little. In short, they are expecting a *lack* of stimulation, at least until their due dates. As you'd expect, it turns out that, like the quails that received unexpected light in the egg, the unexpected interference from these sorts of nurseries can disrupt brain development in premature infants. This can lead to a handful of difficulties, including speech impairments, hand-eye coordination delays, impulsiveness, attention deficits, and lower IQ scores.[28]

Studies like these show how unexpected experiences early in life can make brain development go awry. It's clear from our look at the brain's evolutionary history that it's not been designed to be stuffed into classrooms, sat in front of television sets, handed battery-operated dollhouses, and told how to play ball. Yet we do all these things to the young brain, even though it doesn't expect it.

Chapter 2

Supersized Childhood

Nobody starts life with a brain. Yet everybody ends up with one. Trillions of cells arranged just the right way to enable us to breathe, think, talk, imagine, learn, fall in love, and do the Electric Slide. But how exactly does a tiny blob of squishy cells develop into the most sophisticated information-processing system on earth?

If you've seen the warning label that comes attached to brand-new brains, you already know that some assembly is required. The human brain is only partially constructed at birth. And it takes an exceedingly long time to build. It takes twenty or so years to wire together the major parts and another twenty or so to fine-tune the connections. But contrary to common wisdom, genes don't direct the building. Rather, the construction of most of the unfinished parts of the brain is brought about by children's individual experiences in the world.[1]

An extensive literature, stretching back for decades, provides unequivocal evidence that children build their brains with experience. But the gentle reader might need some convincing that experience weaves its way into the brain and makes it grow. This might seem implausible because even after a heaping day of educative experience— say, a trip to the city zoo or a visit to the science museum—your child's head looks exactly the same as it did that morning.

The problem for most is the steps that connect children's experiences with brain growth. A toddler spends the morning figuring out which gadgets in the kitchen drawers stick to his new magnet and which fall off—and that experience ends up inside his head. And somehow that experience is going to be reconstructed into brain tissue. Just think, all those afternoons of stickball and hopscotch you played as a kid are now fused into your frontal lobe.

The difficulty, I think, is that the effects of experience on the brain aren't tangible. You can't see how a finger painting gets into the head and changes the brain. But for most body parts, the effects of experience are readily visible. When children dig in the mud, their hands get dirty. When they splash in the stream, their feet get wet. When they do either of these things for several hours, their eyelids droop and their mouths yawn. And when their parents forget the sunscreen, their skin turns bright pink.

But for the brain, the skull hides the action. If we had special X-ray goggles that we could use to peer inside the heads of children as they go about their business, here is what we might see: The third grader is in the backyard pretending to be a cheetah hunting antelope for an afternoon snack. The five-year-old, scared out of his wits, crouches down behind a crab apple sapling. Instantly he is ambushed by the hungry cheetah. Click. His brain sets up a circuit linking the visual image of the tiny tree to the collection of brain cells in his head that make up his idea of failed hiding places. Later, the five-year-old goes behind the birdbath and again is snared. Click. Eighty-six the birdbath. The next day, the antelope covers himself completely in a pile of leaves, and the cheetah never finds him. Double click. Now all of these hiding efforts have been transformed into umpteen new connections among brain cells, creating an awareness that successful hiding places are those that obscure the entire body from head to toe, not those that merely block one's own view of the seeker. So, all of the sights and sounds that the five-year-old has seen and heard have been splattered all over his brain.

Still not quite sure that early experience gets inside heads and modifies developing brains? Consider an organism less sophisticated than the typical human child—namely, the *C. elegans.* The *C. elegans* is a tiny roundworm that has to generate, arrange, and wire together a neural system of exactly 302 neurons and about 7,800 synapses before it reaches adulthood.[2] For the worm, this is not a trivial process. Each and every step in the construction of its neural circuitry must be done precisely, or else the *C. elegans* will end up in a can of worms, figuratively speaking. This could mean futile squirming, a failure to find food, or the inability to stay out of danger's way. Fortunately for the *C. elegans,* it has roughly nineteen thousand genes encoded in its DNA that can help guide the development of its brain.

What's a worm brain have to do with a human brain? Making a

human brain surely is an exceedingly more complicated process than making a worm brain. A human brain has to specify correctly the locations, properties, and connections of an enormous network of one hundred billion neurons and their synapses. Considering that the typical neuron incorporates about five thousand synapses, this means roughly five hundred trillion connections need to be made. That's a big task. To put the hugeness of it in perspective, if you wanted to give away your synapses, you could give every single person in the world about seventy-one thousand of them.

We might expect that we would need many, many more genes than the *C. elegans* does. But the best estimate to date from the Human Genome Project is that we have about twenty-three thousand genes. Not many more than the *C. elegans*. And this number is nowhere near enough to genetically specify the synaptic connections of each and every neuron inside our heads.

So, there are simply not enough genes to specify the complete development of our complex human brains. There are enough to direct the overall shape, size, and large-scale brain region connections, but not enough to handle the cell-to-cell details. The only solution, then, is to leave the precise specification and wiring of the human brain to the environment.

Let's start from square one and follow the brain throughout its development, first in the womb and then during early life. By the end of this chapter, not only will you be convinced that children's experiences grow their brains, but you'll see that it couldn't be any other way. You'll also start to see how the experiences common to modern childhood are growing brains in unexpected, and unwanted, ways.

SOME ASSEMBLY REQUIRED

Here's how it happens. A few weeks after conception, one of the two layers of the one-tenth-inch-long gelatin-like embryo begins to thicken and build up along the middle. Over the next few days, the developing structure buckles, and parallel ridges rise across its surface—like the creases in a paper airplane. As the embryo grows, the ridges curl inward and fuse together to form a hollow neural tube. One end of the tube will develop into the brain, and the other end will become the spinal cord.

The empty core of the tube will form the ventricles, the fluid-filled spaces of the brain and spinal cord.

Once the tube fuses, about a month or so after conception, neurons proliferate like wildfire. The speed of production is remarkable, churning out roughly 250,000 new cells *every minute* throughout the rest of the first half of gestation. With some recently discovered exceptions,[3] nearly all the neurons the brain ever will have are created by the end of the fourth or fifth prenatal month.

Once neurons are made, they pack up and move out beyond their birthplace to their adult location in the brain. They make their way to their new homes along threads produced by a network of guiding cells. Around the time when the human fetus becomes viable—about week twenty-five—most neurons have migrated to their final destination.

After settling into their new homes, turning on their electricity, and hooking up their cable, neurons find and connect with neighboring neurons to establish their unique jobs. Neurons do this by extending their axons to meet up with partner dendrites on other neurons. The forging of these connections, or synapses, goes on at a fast and furious pace during the prenatal period and in infancy and early childhood—so much so that in the first year of life, babies mint half a million fresh brain connections every second.

THIS BRAIN AIN'T BIG ENOUGH FOR THE TWO BILLION OF US

You've just learned that most of the neurons the human brain ever will have are manufactured during the first half of pregnancy. What you haven't yet learned is the demoralizing fact that your children have truckloads more neurons than you do. The whole lot fits into their little heads because newly minted neurons take up less space than mature neurons. But children's neural abundance doesn't last long. By the time children reach adulthood, depending on the brain region, 20–80 percent of their neurons die.

What does it mean that brain cells die? Let's start with what it *doesn't* mean. It doesn't mean that you should put this book down pronto and do all sorts of special things to make sure your little Lily does not lose her congenital stockpile of neurons and fall short of her potential. But this is exactly the message that many marketers who sell battery-powered "smart" toys, electronic learning systems, and other so-called early educational gizmos are sending. They spend gazillions of dollars pitching products they say have been designed to prevent children's neurons from dying and their intellect from going to pot.

My favorite of these sorts of neuron-saving devices is the BabyPlus® Prenatal Education System. Its website says that the product's use during pregnancy prevents the dangerous die-off of brain cells that otherwise occurs during early development.[4] For only one hundred fifty dollars a pop. All Mom has to do is strap on a speaker-equipped belt pack to her belly after the eighteenth week of pregnancy, twice a day for an hour at a time, and a sixteen-lesson curriculum that remixes a human heartbeat gets piped into her fetus.

The thing is, this "Save the Neurons" pitch is not based on science, but rather on a stubborn and pervasive myth that scientists have been trying to undo for decades. Given the success of gadgets like BabyPlus, the myth has not yet been busted. So I'm taking another shot.

The BabyPlus device was invented back in the 1980s by Brent Logan. On his website, Dr. Logan writes that the idea for BabyPlus came from a radio interview with Joseph Susedik and his wife.[5] In the interview, Susedik claimed to have sired four child geniuses by playing music for them in the womb.[6]

Now, any card-carrying developmental scientist can tell you that fetuses can hear sounds outside of the womb and that newborns can recognize sounds they heard while in utero.[7] But no study has ever shown that the BabyPlus system or its growing number of impostors do any good. No matter. Since 1998, sales of BabyPlus have swelled by 15 to 25 percent each year. In 2006, BabyPlus sold an impressive eight thousand belly-pack gadgets in about sixty different countries.[8]

I am willing to get myself into trouble with the BabyPlus crowd because the burgeoning success of this device tells me that if only parents understood how brains really develop, no well-meaning pregnant woman ever would strap a speaker to her womb. Here's why: the BabyPlus promises to mitigate the dying-off of children's brain cells. But the truth of the matter is that the human brain creates many more neurons than it actually needs to function in adulthood. If children didn't lose a good deal of their prenatally produced neurons during their first few years of life, they would be, in the vernacular of the potty-training set, in deep poopy. It is a normal and healthy consequence of growing up for infants and children to lose roughly half of their prenatally produced brain cells.

Cell death might seem like a weird way to build a body part. But cell death can—at the right time and at the right place—be a brilliant design feature. The entire surface of your skin, for instance, is made up of cells that have already passed on to the Great Cellular Beyond. Your body's dead cell coating allows the rest of your organs to support your daily life without having to worry about mosquito bites, rainstorms, or spilled cheese dip at the office Christmas party.

Cell death also plays a critical role in the shaping of the body during development. Without well-timed and well-placed cell death during early embryonic development, we all still would have webbed fingers and webbed toes, making bowling alleys and toe rings passé. Cell death is the body's way of sculpting away extra tissue during early development.

So if cell death didn't happen at the right time and the right place in developing young brains, not only would children have trouble holding up their heads at the dinner table, they also would have difficulty tying their shoes, spelling their names, getting jobs, and living normal lives.

GAINING FROM LOSING

You know how three-year-olds whine about their stuff being smaller than everyone else's stuff—that their slice of cake is smaller than their big sister's slice of cake, that their underwear is smaller than their dad's underwear, and that their bed is smaller than the dog's bed? Well, the little whiners have one thing up on the rest of us: they have gobs more neuronal connections than we do. To be precise, they have a massive ten quadrillion hookups, compared to our puny five hundred trillion.

But this early synaptic abundance doesn't last long. By the time children are eight or so, their brains have ratcheted themselves back down to adult numbers. Why do brains get rid of synapses? It seems like sheer waste.

Brains lose many of their synapses because having a thousand neuronal connections to decide whether to pick your nose or suck your thumb is not an efficient way to run a child. So young brains downsize. They downsize for the very reason that organizations of people downsize. With more streamlined networks, human brains, like businesses, function more quickly and more efficiently. How do I know? Because when brain regions don't downsize normally, strange things happen. Consider synesthetes.[9] Synesthesia, in one of its most common forms, causes people to see certain colors or hear certain sounds (usually musical sounds) when they see certain numbers, letters, or symbols. Seeing the number 6 might cause an experience of bluish-purple, whereas the number 8 might be a hot pink. In other forms, synesthetes hear odors, smell textures, or even feel heat from various forms of visual stimulation. There is growing evidence that these strange perceptions come about when certain synaptic connections fail to be eliminated early in life (connections, say, from the auditory information stream to visual color areas) and their retention and elaboration in later life is what drives synesthetic experiences. And it might be that infants—before their brains shed the full complement of synaptic connections—are highly synesthetic.

Fragile X Syndrome provides another example of the potential costs associated with the failure of some children to downsize their existing supply of neurons.[10] Children born with Fragile X, a genetic disorder, have higher numbers of synapses in certain brain regions compared to typically developing children. Consequently, Fragile X children display varied symptoms that range from mild to severe mental retardation, learning disabilities, and autistic-like behaviors. Likewise, autistic toddlers tend to have large brains for their age, and there is a correlation between the degree of excess growth and the severity of autism symptoms.[11] So, like cell death, the demise of synaptic connections during childhood is a design feature, not a flaw to be fixed by flash cards, smart toys, or classical music.

USE IT OR LOSE IT

So neurons and their connections are shed with age to more efficiently run the human body. But how does the brain decide which connections to keep and which to ditch?

Experience.[12]

Each time synapses are stimulated by an experience in the outer world, they become sturdier and more resilient. Those that are activated often survive and go on to form increasingly elaborate networks that lead to even more complex jobs. Those that are not stimulated often enough tend to wither and die. But activation not only preserves and strengthens synapses, it also makes their neighbors weaker and ultimately can cause those neighbors to be eliminated. So a synapse can be "lost" or eliminated even if it is active to some degree simply if its neighbor is much more active. Experience-driven electrical activation can also cause axons to sprout brand-new branches in the formation of new dendritic spines and small dendritic branches. If you think of the brain as a block of clay, then you can visualize experience sculpting away at it not just by carving away inactive or ineffective parts, but also by sticking on extra bits in the form of newly created wiring (axons, dendrites, and synapses) in active regions. This is how experience grows the brain.

IF A LITTLE IS GOOD, MORE MUST BE BETTER

One jelly bean is good; ten jelly beans are better. One day at the beach is good; ten days are better. This mentality trickles down to thinking about how experience stimulates development of the brain. A little stimulation is good for building a brain; more stimulation is better. If you have read this far into the book, I hope you know that this is a bunch of hooey. One banana split is good; ten and you've got a horrific bellyache.

If more is not always better, then why do the media, marketers, and mom blogs send a consistent message that more stimulation—in the form of early learning centers, learning laptops, flash cards, private tutors, language DVDs, and who knows what else—is better for young brains? With apologies to Mark Twain, reports of the benefits of extra stimulation have been greatly exaggerated.

The hype that more stimulation is better can be traced back to the 1960s and Mark Rosenzweig's laboratory at the University of California, Berkeley. In a series of experiments, Rosenzweig and his colleagues found that rats raised in "enriched" environments—that is, in cages fitted with running wheels, slides, tunnels, and other fun rodent toys—ended up with brains that had more neurons with more branches and more synaptic connections than rats that grew up on their own in drab, starkly decorated cages.[13] This synaptic abundance translated into important behavioral differences. Those rats raised in the enriched cages could find their way through complicated mazes (a rodent equivalent of human intelligence tests) more quickly and efficiently than those raised in the bare cages.

These bombshell findings have since been replicated dozens of times: rodents raised in an enriched environment with lots of extra stimulation develop thicker and heavier brains than those raised alone in small, empty cages. But what exactly do these findings mean for children's brains? Should parents and teachers exercise their children on running wheels and hand out squeeze toys on their playdates? Can human children grow bigger brains, or are rat pup brains somehow special?

Let's start out with how most media outlets interpreted Rosenzweig's results. Most told the story that if rats raised in enriched environments had bigger, better brains than rats raised in barren environments, then human children raised in enriched environments would make out much better than human children raised in normal environments. This interpretation of Rosenzweig's research incited the frenzy for intensive efforts to stimulate children's brains to make them bigger and better. And this interpretation made it easy for advertisers to persuade parents that Baby Einstein, Neurosmith®, and LeapFrog® are as vital to growing children's brains as are air, water, and mac 'n' cheese.

But think about the logic behind the analogy: if rats raised in enriched environments grow bigger brains than rats raised alone *in empty cages*, then children in enriched environments should grow bigger brains than children raised *in normal environments*. Right? Wrong. The leap from barren environments to enriched environments in rats is not the same as the leap from normal environments to enriched environments in humans. The analogy doesn't work with humans because we typically don't raise children alone in empty closets. With the exception of a handful of cases of horrible deprivation, children today are raised in homes and neighborhoods and schools that automatically come with all sorts of meaty stimulation—much beefier than what one would get in an empty cage or closet.

For Rosenzweig's research to be relevant to human children, we need to see how rats raised in a normal rat environment would fare. Rosenzweig did this very study. He tested rats raised in a normal rat environment and found that these rats had the biggest and best brains of all. These natural rat experiences were superior to even the superstimulating experiences in the enriched cages. The rats that grew up in their natural environment were stimulated by all of the sights and sounds and smells that their brains had evolved to expect. In other words, these rats grew up exposed to the whole gambit of species-typical experiences. They had run-ins with spiders, snakes, and cats. They hung out with their broods, defended their burrows, dealt with fleas, and boxed with their buddies. But this third group's performance never made it into the media reports and therefore is a little-known finding. This is most probably because it is not a finding that learning toy marketers or early education professionals or anyone else could make any money on.

For the reader, Rosenzweig's findings shouldn't be a shocker. But what might be news at this point is that scientists have known since the nineteenth century—long before developmental psychology was even a gleam in the sciences' collective eye—that natural environments grow the best brains. In the 1800s, for instance, Charles Darwin examined the brains of two sets of various animals—those raised in their natural environments and those reared domestically. Foreshadowing Rosenzweig's findings, Darwin found that the brains of the naturally reared animals were 15 to 30 percent larger than those of their tame, domestic counterparts.[14] The natural world wired the animals' brains best.

These findings might seem far afield from human concerns, but they speak to a point that I hammered at last chapter: that modern children are living an unnatural lifestyle. Like Rosenzweig's super-stimulated rats, today's children are dealing with all sorts of extra and artificial stimulation. But does this mean that today's children's brains, like Rosenzweig's rats' brains, would do better if they moved out of their hyper-stimulating contemporary environment and spent more time in a natural environment, one that they evolved to face? If you think of children as the animals they are, the answer is a resounding "You betcha." The rest of the chapter will tell you why.

TOO MUCH OF A GOOD THING

Ever seen a baby's eyes glaze over while watching a Lady Gaga video? Know why? It's called neurological crowding, which is what happens when too much information comes into the brain at one time and jams up the synaptic network. Imagine this: You and your grocery cart, full of

Starbucks® beans and Ding Dongs®, are waiting in one of the only two open lines at the supermarket. It's quitting time, and your cashier shuts down her lane. A few exchanged glances, a couple of curse words, and everyone rushes and pushes and squashes themselves into a single, crowded line, and it takes forever and a day to pay for your groceries. The same goes for neurological crowding. Too much stimulation too early in life leaves little space left for growth later on in later childhood and adolescence. It takes a couple decades for the brain to finish its wiring, and as such, it seems wise to keep some lines open for growth during the later brain-building years.

The notion of crowding may be one of the best arguments for why today's super-stimulating artificial environments can interfere with normal neural development. Let's start with rats to tell this part of the story.[15] There are dozens of studies showing that when rats are made to learn common rodent intelligence tasks (like mazes) early in puphood, they do less well than those rats that begin their training at a later age. One study found, for instance, that pups that trained on a task beginning when they were ten days old did much worse on the task at days fourteen and fifteen compared to rat pups that started their training at either twelve or fourteen days of age.[16] Not only were there no benefits associated with an early start, the pups that started learning early performed more poorly than those who began later.

These sorts of "too much, too early" findings show up in other animals, too. Primatologist Harry Harlow showed that monkeys that began training to learn how to discriminate between various objects, like objects of different colors, at 155 days of age or younger learned less quickly than monkeys that held off training until 190 days of age or later.[17] So the monkeys that started at 190 days outperformed those that started on day 155 even though the 155-day starters had more experience on the task.

In another case of trying to train young primates too soon with artificial stimulation, consider the gobs of human parents who are plopping their infants in front of television sets to watch early learning DVDs like Baby Einstein in the belief that they are expanding their babies' brains. They think this, of course, because the Baby Einstein box told them so.[18] But a 2007 study carried out by Frederick Zimmerman, chair of the Department of Health Services in the School of Public Health at the University of California, Los Angeles, and his colleagues revealed that each hour per day eight- to sixteen-month-olds spent watching these videos translated into a 17 percent decrease in vocabulary acquisition.[19] More specifically, these children learned six to eight fewer new words for every hour of screen time a day than did babies who had no screen time. Yes, you read that correctly. The more educational "brain science" videos the children watched, the fewer words they knew. In fact, there is growing evidence from Zimmerman's laboratory and others that the more screen time children have early in life, the shorter their attention span is later on. Infants just are not ready for much television. This is why the American Academy of Pediatrics recommends zero screen time for children two years of age and younger.[20] But given marketing forces, you're less likely to know this than to know that Baby Einstein has won an *American Baby* Best of the Year (AMBY) Award for the past six years in a row.[21]

The same is true for early learning centers. These centers, which are becoming increasingly pervasive in the modern world, train infants with letter and number flash cards and later give preschoolers a full curriculum of reading, math, science, art, gym, and more. But Temple University psychologist Kathy Hirsh-Pasek and her colleagues have found that rather than producing super-smart kids, as these programs' literature says, program graduates often have later difficulties with test anxiety, show less creativity than their peers in socially oriented programs, and display a less positive attitude toward school in general.[22] And any academic gains, like knowing more letters or numbers, fade away by first grade. Contrary to the story pitched by learning toys' marketers and academic early learning schools, dozens of studies have told the same story over and over again: rushing young children with these sorts of artificial stimulation can hinder rather than benefit their development.

Findings like these perhaps can explain why famous genius Albert Einstein was an average student rather than an early superstar. Perhaps the slow start allowed Einstein's brain to avoid crowding. Supporting this possibility is a recent study revealing that the brightest children tended to have a burst of brain development three to four years later than children of more average intelligence.[23] So the take-home message is that rushing with extra artificial stimulation might get your two-year-old to recite the ABCs in three different languages, which might make it seem as if your child is ahead of the curve for good, but too much too early and you've just shot the neural works. It seems best to cool the artificial attempts to pump up the brain until it has had some time on its own in its natural environment to get the basic wiring in place.

If you've taken Psychology 101, you've probably heard at least one professor compare the human mind to a computer. Both human minds and computers process information, both deal with symbols of things, and so on. But I trust that by now you can see why the computer analogy doesn't exactly fit if you're dealing with brain development. Stuff a computer to the gills with information, and you can buy more space to get it to process even more information. Stuff a kid's brain with information, and your options for getting it to do more are severely limited.

WHEN THE BRAIN STILL HAS THAT NEW-CAR SMELL

By now, I hope to have convinced you that you are unlikely to build a better brain by stimulating children to the hilt. But surely you've heard that the first few years of life are critical for brain development. The most widely cited such claim comes from the 1997 White House Conference on Early Brain Development, when then First Lady Hillary Clinton stated that "young children—particularly infants and toddlers—are biologically primed for learning, and . . . these early years provide a unique window of opportunity or prime time for learning."[24] You don't want children to miss out on the window of opportunity that is wide open in the first three or so years of life, do you?

The "critical period" argument is perhaps the most frequent argument that the marketplace of artificial kid stimulation waves in front of our faces. Take the Your Baby Can Read® system. You've seen the infomercial if you've watched any of the preschool television networks. The Your Baby Can Read box promises that its contents can teach babies to recognize words. The problem, it says, is that children usually are not taught to read until after they start kindergarten, and therefore, most sadly miss the "natural window of opportunity."[25]

But there is no reason to suspect that the brain pays any attention to what the Your Baby Can Read box says. You didn't learn how to read when you were a baby, yet you are a proficient reader. And Finnish children, who don't begin formal reading instruction until age seven, consistently come out on top in international assessments.[26] The same goes for Austrian children. That's the same Austria with a per capita Nobel laureate rate many times higher than that of Japan, the country responsible for Junior Kumon®—a widely used tutoring program for preschoolers whose website says that "it's never too early to get started with your children's education."[27]

There is, admittedly, some reason for the critical-period hype. There are critical periods in fetal physical development. For instance, if a fetus is exposed to the drug thalidomide between four and six weeks after conception, then its arms and legs won't grow normally.[28] But the role that critical windows play in childhood brain development is less clear cut.

There is evidence that in certain regions of the brain, there are critical periods in early life where experience must be present or the fine-scale wiring will degenerate and never regrow in later life. One of the best examples comes from vision. Much like the experiments with kittens in chapter 1, if an infant develops a cataract in one eye that is dense enough to block out most visual experiences, then the infant can permanently lose sight in that eye if the cataract is not removed early in life. The same cataract on the eye of an adult for the same amount of time will not cause any lasting damage. The reason for the blindness is not that the eye has stopped working, but rather that the cataract deprived the eye of expected visual experiences that are needed to keep the eye connected to the brain (the visual cortex) during the critical period for vision.[29]

The story is the same for some higher, uniquely human cognitive processes. Consider the well-known story of thirteen-year-old Genie, who was raised in near isolation beginning at about twenty months of age.[30] She had almost no human contact, other than when her parents left her food. Years after her rescue, she spoke with the vocabulary of a typical five-year-old, but she never got the hang of grammar. It seemed as if Genie's brain had missed a critical window for language input.

There are also widely cited stories of infants who were raised in horribly inadequate Romanian orphanages and later adopted into American upper-middle-class homes.[31] During infancy, these institutionalized children were confined to isolated, empty cribs. They had only fleeting contact with caregivers—who showed up only to prop up bottles and change diapers—and virtually no stimulation. If adopted by their second birthday or earlier, most of the children eventually regained normal intellectual functioning and reached a normal early childhood IQ of around 100. But those children who remained institutionalized were severely mentally retarded and only able to communicate with simple gestures by age four or five. Even if adopted in later life, these children never reached the normal intelligence of their counterparts who were adopted before two years of age.

Findings like these are powerful evidence of a critical period for normal brain development. But the Your Baby Can Read interpretation of these findings is that if children don't get mounds of store-bought stimulation during an early window of opportunity, brain development is stunted for good—like those of the Romanian orphans. Yet, how many children in the modern Western world grow up in such deprived conditions? The environments in these orphanages were horrifically barren and unimaginably isolated—not unlike those of Rosenzweig's empty-cage rats and completely unlike those of most modern children. What the studies on infant cataracts and Romanian orphans really and sadly show is that severe environmental deprivation leads to major developmental problems. They cannot, however, be used to justify the contention that children need extra stimulation during infancy and early childhood to develop into successful adults in the modern world. However, these studies can be used to support the idea that there are critical periods for *normal* stimulation for different brain systems, and unless your children live in a closet, they can't help but get it.

But what if you really wanted your child to develop some sort of specialty, to stand out from the crowd? You've heard the predictions about how, in today's downsized and outsourced economy, our children may be the first generation to be worse off than their parents. You want to do all you can to help your children get ahead. Doesn't this justify piano lessons at one, golf camp at two, and a math tutor at three? Plainly, no. There is plenty of empirical evidence to support the fact that most skills that are uniquely human, like violin playing, rocket building, and poetry writing, have always-open windows of opportunity. Most of these sorts of skills can be picked up by the brain throughout childhood and, in fact, throughout our lives, so you need not worry about the window slamming shut on skills if you don't enroll your child in the right class by the ripe old age of three. This is because even though the major brain construction is complete by around age twenty, our brains continuously rewire themselves throughout life. The truth of the matter is that during your entire life, there is constant redesign inside your head. Even as you read this sentence, some of your neurons are breaking old connections, sliding around to fresh locations, and hooking up with new neighbors. Some are going to decide to stay put and strengthen budding relationships, while others soon are going to pack up and leave. Even though you can't feel it, right now your brain is bustling with change, all so you can learn a few things about rats, orphans, and Hillary Clinton.

YOU KNOW WHAT THEY SAY ABOUT BIG HEADS . . . BIG BRAINS

In the first chapter, you learned that humans are well endowed when it comes to gray matter. Our brains, relative to body size, are bigger than any other mammal's. They're an impressive four to five times larger than would be expected for a mammal our size. Because the brain is made up of inefficient jellyfish neurons, we needed a big fat brain to build the clever species we are today. What you haven't yet learned is that it's the *development* of these old parts that allows us to do new tricks.

Human brains generally are constructed like those of our primate relatives. But one thing that we do differently is to uniquely prolong the fabrication of neurons during prenatal development. Instead of throwing in the towel after four or five rounds of cell division, human neurons extend the number of cell duplications by one or two or more rounds. Each cell division is a big deal because it essentially results in a doubling of the number of neurons. Many of these neurons die, of course. But this is exactly what happened repeatedly over the course of primate evolution in the brains of our *Homo* ancestors.

Generating new neurons is only part of what it takes to build the special human brain. Neurons also must relocate to their proper location in the brain, and once they've moved in, they must establish synaptic connections with their new neighbors. Such processes take place in all mammals' brains and are especially rapid during prenatal development for all primates, including humans. But while brain growth pulls back after birth for chimpanzees, macaques, and other primates, it does not for humans. The pace of human brain development that started prenatally carries on throughout the first few years of life. So humans' whopper brains are achieved mostly by keeping up the rapid rate of pre-natal growth into postnatal life and letting the brain finish up its development outside the womb. And this is how we've cut the neurological rope from the rest of the animal kingdom.

IS THIS ANY WAY TO BUILD A BRAIN?

The human baby is *the* most helpless creature on earth. By five months of age, most animals are fending for themselves. We humans can't even sit up on our own. Compared to the rest of the animal kingdom, human beings come into the world neurologically immature and are very slow to develop.

Why not do more of the neural construction job in the womb? Wouldn't it make better sense to keep human infants inside the womb until the brain is fully developed, rather than evicting them before they have the wherewithal to turn over on their bellies or wipe their own noses?

The answer is a simple one: if a species has a big brain, it also must have a big skull. And a big skull has to find some way out of the womb. If the human brain followed the same prenatal growth rate as the rest of the body, and if humans were born with the same degree of neurological maturity as their ape relatives, pregnancy would last twenty-one months. Not only would twenty-one months be an excruciatingly long time to carry around a fetus, a twenty-one-month-old skull—no matter how well you positioned it—simply could not fit through the human birth canal. So, instead, what we humans have is a pregnancy that lasts nine months and a creature who is born neurologically immature.

Back to the evolutionary drawing board. Perhaps natural selection could tinker with the female form and widen the hips a smidgen to allow a larger skull to squeeze through. This wouldn't work because hips any larger would make upright walking nearly impossible (recall from chapter 1 that bipeds evolved before big brains). An upright-walking pelvis—and birth canal—can only be so wide. A lot of mothers and infants died on the way to reaching an anatomical compromise as our kind was giving birth to children with larger and larger heads.

The only tenable solution to big-brained humans is premature birth. Human mothers give birth while the baby's head is still small enough to fit through the birth canal and allow it to finish its development outside the womb.

But this solution creates a new problem—namely, supersized childhoods.[32] It means giving birth to a creature that is vulnerable to predators for years and not reproductively fit for more than a decade. That's an eternity if you are an uncivilized hunter-gatherer living outdoors, which was the case for us for greater than 99 percent of our existence. With all the malaria, leprosy, and wild beast maulings, it is quite astonishing that any of us made it to maturity to mate.[33]

Compared to the rest of the animal kingdom, we humans ease into adulthood. We take longer to reach maturity than any other animal on the planet. Even chimpanzees, which share nearly 99 percent of our genetic makeup, grow up faster than we do. Even our hominid ancestors grew up faster than present-day humans. How do I know? One way is to look at dental development. The eruption of the first permanent molar in chimps occurs at 3.1 years in chimpanzees and is estimated to have been about the same in *Australopithecus*, at 5.0 years in late *Homo erectus*, and at 6.2 years in modern humans. A look at skull size tells the same story. For example, based on dental development, a well-preserved skeleton of a Neanderthal child who was believed to have been about two years old when it died had a skull size equal to that of a modern six-year-old child.

Given that reproduction is evolution's bottom line, putting off maturity seems like a risky way to build an animal.[34] But evolution is too smart to favor a high-cost/low-profit strategy. Childhood is exactly what makes us human. During this time of extreme vulnerability, we are creatures fully capable of learning just about anything. The problem is, for at least the first few years, we are not good for doing much else.

UNFINISHED ON PURPOSE

If you have young children, then you might not remember the last time you've read an entire novel, seen an R-rated movie, been out on a dinner date, or even taken a shower. If this is you, then you might need some convincing of the benefits of humankind's supersized childhood. Growing up super-fast makes sense if you're an antelope living in the open plains of South Africa. The faster you learn how to run, the less likely you are to find yourself featured on the early-bird menu at the Café du Lion. But we humans have a very good reason for growing up slowly. Our slow-cooking brain is exactly what enables us to do all of our special human tricks. Humans are a unique animal because of the number and sorts of things we need to learn to be successful adults. No other animal on Earth has so much to learn, and for us it takes an extra-long childhood to learn it all.[35]

You might be thinking that if evolution really was smart, wouldn't it have hardwired human brain development with genetic programs that simply activate during childhood to bypass the risk of having a bad environment screw things up? That is, if the problem is that big brains don't fit through limited-sized birth canals, why not just design a brain that doesn't need experience to wire it, but just happens, the way our hands develop five fingers and our heads grow hair? Why rely so much on experience?

Because of the variability of environments in which humans live and the fact that new brains never know where they'll find themselves, the human world is too diverse; building everything in would mean a lot of waste. In addition, we don't know where we'll end up until after we're born. Birds automatically develop wings because they know they'll be in the trees. Fish automatically develop gills because they know they'll be in the water. But humans grow up in all sorts of idiosyncratic environments—in the Arctic, in the tropics, and everywhere in between. So a brain driven by inborn genetic programs would never work in the human head because there is no one size that fits all when it comes to human society. New human brains need the flexibility to adapt themselves to wherever they're born.

As discussed in the last chapter, it is human intelligence, particularly our ability to adapt to the varying demands of the environment, that stands out as our hallmark. In addition to helping us survive and thrive in the disappearing rain forest millions of years ago, this flexibility and plasticity in the nervous system allows children today to set up their own brains to exactly match their culture—the spoken language, the written characters, the regional customs, the local faux pas, the community trades, and the neighborhood party tricks. This is a much more flexible and powerful solution than relying solely on genes. But it means that more than any other species, human brain development is dependent on appropriate cultural stimulation. It also means that we need to be more careful than other species in making sure that our children get the right sorts of experiences as their brains are developing.

RABBLE ROUSERS, ROADRUNNERS, AND RUMPUS ROOMS

When I was a kid, my father, a World War II Army Air Force veteran, would bribe me with cookies and milk to sit with him and watch old war movies. I never paid much attention to the goings-on, lost in my chocolate-chip stupor, except to scribble down the secret passwords the Pacific Theater soldiers muttered to one another—"rabble rouser," "roadrunner," "rumpus room"—and then later impress my backyard clubhouse mates with these new watchwords to keep out the kids from Mr. Sherman's class. We all thought the alliteration was brilliant, even though we had no idea why the passwords invariably were overrun with the letter *r*.

But now I know. Native Japanese speakers can't pronounce the letter *r*. Instead, they say "ell." Nor can they hear the distinction between *r* and *l*.

But six-month-old Japanese infants with no exposure to the English language have no trouble telling the difference.[36] Because the sounds of *r* and *l* don't exist in the Japanese language, the loss of Japanese infants' ability to make the distinction between them happens simply because Japanese people don't hear these sounds regularly. We know this because if we take a native-born Japanese child and raise him in an English-speaking country, his brain will wire itself to tell the difference between *r* and *l*.

This example illustrates one of the many extraordinary feats of the human baby. But the slick adaptation comes at a cost. When infants are born, they can distinguish between the sounds of every language on the planet. Between six and nine months of age, infants lose this ability. By their first birthdays, babies can distinguish only the sounds of their native language. What changes in us between six and nine months of age? Experience. Specifically, experience hearing a particular language (or languages). This trains or tunes the brain with respect to how to place language sounds into a template for comparison. Not hearing *r*'s on a day-to-day basis, Japanese infants lose the ability to hear them or later say them.

Experience tunes our brains to a great many things besides just language sounds. My favorite example of neurological tuning explains the familiar saying, "You seen one monkey, you seen 'em all." You can demonstrate this by taking three sets of folks: six-month-olds, nine-month-olds, and adults. Show them pairs of photos of human and monkey faces—some of which they've seen before and some new. Everyone in all three groups will be able to tell you (or demonstrate behaviorally, for the babies) if they've already seen a human face. But *only* the six-month-olds will be able to distinguish an old from a new monkey face. The ability to tell a new from an old monkey is gone by nine months because experience tells the human brain that it really doesn't need that ability to get by. So, in humans, a general knack for recognizing sounds or faces is jettisoned in favor of a more specific and intense ability—understanding and speaking English or telling apart your entire first grade class.

These sorts of examples demonstrate what a brilliant design concept the human brain is. Grow a big glob of cells, make them compete for their survival, and then keep only the ones that are stimulated by the organism's experiences in its environment. Tinker with the wiring to make the thing perfectly fit its surroundings, and there you have it—the most finely tuned piece of machinery on Earth.

A VERY FINE WHINE

This brings us to a not-so-frequently made insight about childhood. As explained by Florida Atlantic University evolutionary developmental psychologist David Bjorklund, childhood is an adaptation. It is an adaptation designed by evolution to make sure that the human brain gets hooked up properly and to enable the array of behaviors that makes humans different from any other species.[37]

Many people today think of childhood as a necessary evil, that it's something we must get through on our way to adulthood, the time in our lives when the real action of humanity takes place. We often see children's brains and bodies as inefficient versions of the smoother-running adult model. Consequently, we try to rush children through childhood: praising them when they act mature, learn a new skill before their classmates, or choose to do their homework rather than play in the backyard. Thinking that the sooner they are like us, the better off they will be.

But given that childhood is really an adaptation that evolved to make us human, it is not something to be rushed or speeded up. Humans need long childhoods to learn the complexities of life. The slow course of neural development is adaptive and has been shaped through evolution to give us a brain that tunes itself by experience to operate smoothly in whatever environment it finds itself.

IT'S ALL IN THE TIMING

Now we know how human brains create modern human mental function with a hand-me-down design and a mess of garden-variety, vintage parts—none of which, mind you, have been designed specifically for operation inside our modern heads. The answer, in a word, is childhood —and an extremely long one at that. The human brain comes into the world astonishingly unfinished and spends much more time than does any other animal on the planet in finishing its development outside the womb. This extended period of neurological immaturity gives humans an unusually long time in which our brains are especially responsive to experience, and thereby transform us from your ordinary primates into prolific learners. The way that we've become clever humans is not by developing new brain parts, but by slowing down and extending the growth of the old parts. This way we can continue to wire our brains with experience to do all sorts of unique things long after this opportunity is gone in other, faster-developing species. Rather than thinking about how we can speed up childhood and make children's brains bigger, better, stronger, and faster, we should ask: why are we so hell-bent on doing so?

Chapter 3

The Twenty-Year
Science Project

There's a Super Ball® in my chandelier. If you'd walk through my front door and look straight up, you'd see it dangling about ten feet above your head. It's wedged between the clear glass shade and one of the three type A bulbs. It's a bright neon-green one, about the size of a small plum. It doesn't go well with the bright yellow wall in the foyer or the bamboo blinds on the bay window, yet I like it right where it is.

My son, Dominic, is responsible for this decorative eccentricity. It happened on a rainy Saturday afternoon when Dom was only two. He was sporting his usual pretend play gear—namely, a pair of lensless 1980s metallic sunglasses and a hooded baby towel hooked on the top of his head. He was tall enough now that the blue and yellow polka-dot towel flowed behind him as if he were some washed-up superhero too down on his luck to afford a proper cape.

Dom was busy saving the good people of Duploville from the wrath of the evil Dr. Diaperpants. His arch-nemesis, also known as big sister Izzy, had affixed a smiley-face-sticker-covered Pamper to her head. True to her role, she was tormenting the population of Duploville by popping off their oddly square heads and their three-fingered hands. "You mean!" Dom said more and more loudly as his round belly led him around the house to reattach the discarded body parts. As soon as I saw that Dom couldn't keep up with his sister's dismemberment, I stooped down, gathered the two enemies, and asked them if they'd like to finger paint. They cheered at the suggestion, stripped off their war gear, and stood straight up, awaiting Dad's old T-shirts, er, art smocks. As I popped Izzy's head

69

through her smock, I saw Dom sweep a Super Ball up off the floor and begin to whip his arm around like a windmill. "No throwing balls in the house, young man," I reminded Dom. "OK, Mommy," he agreed and put the ball down on the counter. I slipped the art smock over his head and smooched him on the cheek, and he pivoted to make his way to the kitchen table but then turned back and asked if he could have a drink. "Lemonade all around," I said and opened the fridge.

As I pulled the pitcher off the shelf, I thought I saw Dom's fist whirl around and then release something with surprising velocity for a toddler. I turned around, and all three of us watched the ball ricochet off the kitchen floor, speed up to the ceiling, smack one of the moving blades of the fan, rebound off the ceiling, and then drop into the chandelier's glass shade.

"Oh no, Mommy!" said Dom.

"Oh no, Dom," I said and realized that I had been outwitted by a two-year-old. The boy wasn't thirsty at all; he just needed a diversion.

This was the official opening of a new attraction of my son's childhood known as the "terrible twos." It was a bumpy opening day for Dom and me. Neither of us expected it to kick off with a Rube Goldberg sequence and a permanent toy in one of my lighting fixtures. Yet once we talked about the day's events and all agreed to keep the ball throwing outside, I smiled. The cognitive abilities that two-year-olds muster to distract their mothers so they can test the physics of bouncy balls are the same ones they'll use in a couple of decades to discover better medical treatments, alternate forms of energy, new information technologies, and a way to make tofu taste like bacon. We humans are natural-born scientists from the very start, even if the habit sometimes gets us into trouble with our mothers.[1]

Humans' scientific research program kicks off at birth. During the first year of life, infants center their studies on the physical properties of things. They use their entire set of senses to actively test and systematically analyze their world. And, much like scientists, they are very serious about collecting as much data as they can before the next nap time or meal. They make observations by squeezing things, pushing things over, tearing things apart, banging things into each other, dipping things into the dog's water bowl, dumping containers full of things onto the floor, sticking things in their mouths, and giving things to you so that you can stick them in your mouth. Often this means that their laboratory is messy. Occasionally things get broken.

Once they've collected sufficient pilot data, babies begin to design specific experiments to learn about things: "What happens if I let go of Mom's coffee mug?" "If I hide Mom's car keys underneath the pile of dirty laundry, will they cease to exist?" As their program of research progresses, children's experiments become increasingly sophisticated. "If I drop Mom's sunglasses on the floor, will they bounce?" "If I throw them up in the air, how high will they go?" "If I throw them with more force, will they go higher?" "Will they go faster?" "Can I get them to go through the ceiling?"

From their observations, children soon form hypotheses about the world, design and carry out experiments to test these hypotheses, and draw conclusions from their data: "Yesterday when I threw Mom's sunglasses down the stairs, both lenses cracked. I hypothesize that that same thing will happen today if I throw Dad's sunglasses down the stairs." When the data don't pan out as expected, children self-correct, revise old hypotheses, and go back into the lab for additional experimentation: "Mom's coffee cup did not bounce when I dropped it on the hardwood floor. Perhaps it will bounce if I stand up on the kitchen counter and drop it." Their laboratory manner is aggressive, inspired, and maddeningly persistent.

As children move into their second year, they extend their studies to the social world—that is, to people: "If I put blue finger paint on the dog, will Mom get mad?" Like good scientists, they often tweak their methods to examine their research topic programmatically: "Will red paint on the dog make Mom mad too?" "What about on the guinea pig?" "Or my baby brother?" They broaden their work to different populations to see if their results generalize: "Will finger painting the pets make Dad mad too?" And they replicate their experiments to be sure that their findings are stable: "I'm going to finger paint the dog one more time just to make sure that Mom still gets mad."

Through their studies, they begin to learn how other people are different from one another and different from them. That Dad doesn't want a new My Pretty Pony® set for his birthday and that Mom doesn't enjoy the feeling of Jell-O® smashed between her fingers. Through experimentation, they also figure out that just because they know something, the whole world doesn't too: that just because they know the television remote is hidden in the dog food bag, Mom isn't aware of it, unless someone tells her or she finds it herself in the morning when she scoops out Fido's breakfast kibble. The lesson here is that what often look like deliberate attempts to defy, annoy, or subjugate Mom and Dad are merely natural extensions of the research program that your child started at birth.

This experimental style of learning is the way our brains have been designed to learn. We developed it in the Serengeti plains of Africa and literally have depended on it for millions of years. When we came down and out of the trees to make our living on the savanna, no one said, "Find me a textbook, or better yet, an online course, so that I can learn how to survive and reproduce in this new environment." Our success was not dependent on a standard, planned curriculum. Instead, it was dependent on how quickly we could learn from our own information-gathering experiences. "That plant with bunches of small white flowers that I found near the water hole . . . I ate it yesterday and I got a terrible bellyache and my head felt funny" would have been an important observation for our Pleistocene ancestors. Better yet are the further steps we made: "I hypothesize that if I eat more of that same plant I'll get sick again." Those who weren't so quick to learn from their mistakes didn't survive long enough to pass their genes to the next generation. This Serengeti mind-set, and the self-correcting, scientific style of learning it favors, is not something that we have outgrown in the modern world. Sure, there aren't a whole lot of bookless folks still living like nomads in the grasslands. But millions of years later in the contemporary high-tech world of formal education we've fostered, our children still have brains that are built to do most of their early learning through the children's own active observations and experimentation.

LIKE LEARNING FOR CHOCOLATE

What drives children to discover and explore their world? You were a Sunday regular *Wild Kingdom* viewer back in the day, so you think you've got this one. You recall the usual segue into the commercial break: "Just as the mother lion protects her cubs, you can protect your children with an insurance policy from Mutual of Omaha." So you say, "It's for the good of the species. Children's drive to explore developed because this behavior increases the likelihood of the species surviving and multi-plying, right?" Nope. That style of thinking went out with Marlin Perkins. Evolution is not about traits and behaviors that are for the good of the species, but rather traits and behaviors that optimize the number of copies of one's own genes that get passed on to the next generation. It's for the good of the individual. Does this mean, then, that children experiment on their world to maximize the number of copies of their genes in the next generation and thereby enhance their reproductive success in the general population pool? Not quite. Two-year-olds typically don't leaf through evolutionary biology textbooks before they head out to play in the sandbox. Children behave as they do because they are born with a deep desire to understand the world and an incessant curiosity that compels them to aggressively explore it. Children are driven to learn like you're driven to chocolate. The desire is insatiable, and once you get it, nothing is better.

You can see this unquenchable thirst for knowledge most clearly in the youngest of our species. They are constantly experimenting, asking extraordinary questions about ordinary things. Their natural learning style has not yet been contaminated by our modern ways of teaching. And so much is still new, so they are constantly seeking to understand and master everything in their world. It's why they dip their hands into the birthday cake you just finished icing, skip through rather than around the muddy puddle on their way to the family portrait sitting, and take fif-teen minutes to walk from the front porch to the minivan. The twenty feet between your house and the van door is their field laboratory, and it is full of all sorts of natural phenomena that demand immediate study. There's the dandelion seed head that compels the young scientist to his knees to regard, pluck, and then blow it. When one of the seeds lands near an army of ants carrying half a Goldfish® cracker, he must lie flat on his belly and carefully observe the collaborative operation. He tries to thwart the group with a twig as a breeze blows a crumbly brown leaf into his sights. He snags the leaf, crushes it in his fists, and erupts with the cackle of a new discovery. A field cricket springs by, and he stands up to follow the insect when he hears his sneaker push something on the pave-ment. He crouches down and picks up a flat black rock. He lets the sun shine off it for a moment before he decides to bang it on the driveway. Then there is a butterfly, a puddle of rainwater, a rusty penny, and a stray tennis ball. All of this demands study, and the professor has only made it a quarter of the way to the minivan. What a shame that his mother interrupts his field work to buckle him into his car seat and drive him to preschool. There he spends the rest of his morning sequencing story cards, coloring animal drawings inside the lines, hearing tales of a faraway forest, and matching pictures of trees and flowers to their printed names. He very much likes the school curriculum's theme of the week: The Great Outdoors. But he would much rather be in his lab, digging worms out of the vegetable garden to study their lifestyle and piling up the wet sand in his sandbox to learn something about the physics of gravity.

Children are driven to explore their world because new discoveries bring them joy.[2] This "learner's high" then compels them back out into the world so they can make more discoveries and experience more joy. It's a straight-up reward cycle that, if allowed to thrive, will persist for a lifetime. As children's learning becomes more sophisticated with age, it brings them not only joy but also mastery. Mastery then gives them the capacity to take intellectual risks in their domain of expertise: to make the next smart car, wonder drug, or iThing. But as I'll discuss in a bit, it is possible to break this natural cycle, to squelch children's drive to explore, and to seep the joy out of learning.

The childhood drive for exploration is so strong that many scientists consider it a universal human drive like hunger, thirst, and sex. "Wha?" you're thinking. "If children are driven to learn like they are driven to eat and drink, then why is it nearly impossible to get Junior to do his word study homework, but I've never had to force-feed him a bag of cheese curls and a juice box?" It's because much of the learning you're asking him to do doesn't satisfy his drive to actively explore and experiment on the world. Memorizing the life cycle of a grasshopper, reading about the physical properties of a paper clip, and mapping the major battles of the Revolutionary War so that he can pass the fourth grade doesn't satisfy the drive to explore any more than an evening of cardboard hamburgers, imaginary milkshakes, and dry humping would satisfy your other three drives.

No matter how much we make children watch educational television programs, sort new vocabulary words, and fill out math worksheets, their experimental style of learning is something that they will not outgrow during their school years. Their brains were built for a very different kind of learning. They're compelled to take on the world as their laboratory so that they can master new things, not spend their days with multiplication flash cards and word sorts, preparing for the next standardized exam. This disconnect between children's brains and the ways in which we ask them to learn is why many children rarely find joy in learning and why it is tough to motivate many children to do well in school.

FANTASTIC SCIENTISTS

You probably think that I'm pushing this analogy of children as scientists a little far, right? You've seen both scientists and two-year-olds, and you've noticed glaring differences. One wears a lab coat; the other, a diaper. One publishes his findings in prestigious journals; the other merely makes mental notes. One has a rich fantasy life, and the other doesn't. Two-year-olds can get away with acting as if two-headed monsters live under their beds, a jolly old man delivers them presents from a reindeer-propelled flying sleigh, and the empty chair next to them at the dinner table is occupied by a talking pink rabbit that is invisible to everyone but them. Scientists can't. It seems as if the experimental life of the typical two-year-old generally is less bound to reality than that of the Harvard astrophysicist. But it's not. The very best scientists—those who change the world with their ideas—dabble in the nonexistent and dream up imaginary worlds. Then they try to make their fantasies come true: a world where Alzheimer's disease is nonexistent, cities are fully powered by renewable energy, and Play-Doh® never dries out. University of California, Berkeley, developmental psychologist Alison Gopnik says, "It's not that children are little scientists but that scientists are big children."[3] It's the two-year-olds' facility with fantasy that makes them not your ordinary scientists, but Super Scientists.

To see where I'm coming from, let's work through why most preschoolers would prefer to prepare a dinner of mud pies and grass-clipping sun tea than bake a real pie and brew a real drink. Initially, psychologists thought it was so children could work out their problems—that children pretend to have fussy babies and stressful day jobs in order to work through the frustrations of being the neglected middle child. But this explanation is not supported by research. In fact, it's just the opposite: the more pressure and problems children have, the less likely they are to play. Other psychologists have proposed that children's frequent slips into fantasy occur because they can't distinguish the real from the make-believe. But there is no evidence for this either. Have you ever seen a preschooler actually try to eat the plastic meal they've prepared in their play kitchen or try to make a real phone call to their grandmother on a banana? They know better than that. If you don't believe me, the next time you visit the ice-cream shop with your two-year-old, get yourself a double scoop of cookies and cream, hand her a plastic cone, and see what happens.

Children indulge in fantasy not because they can't appreciate the truth, but precisely for the opposite reason. Gopnik believes that children's frequent forays into the imaginary have everything to do with their quest to understand their world. To understand why Gopnik likely has it right, take a moment and imagine being inside the head of a baby. The best way to do this is to pretend that you've appeared suddenly on a strange alien planet. You know nothing about this new world. You have no knowledge of its laws of physics, biology, psychology, or anything else. You wonder, "Is that space rock alive? Does it get scared when it's alone in the dark? What does it taste like? Does it fit in my ear? Does it cease to exist when I cover it with my blankie?" The sounds you hear coming out of the mouths of other, bigger organisms don't help you make sense of anything. But the one who smells familiar and just changed your diaper hands you a pair of stuffed animals. You smash the yellow doggie against the pink bunny just to see what happens, and the familiar-smelling person says, "Thedogkissedthebunny. Makethemdoitagain." You have no idea what this means, but the attention feels good, so you crash the two together again. You plan on spending indefinitely long figuring out this new world because—let's face it—you have no plans, no goals, and no responsibilities. Your calendar is wide open for at least a decade. And your mom and dad are there to protect you from harm, prepare your meals, kiss you good night, and make sure you don't crawl out into the middle of traffic.

In the previous chapter, we learned that humans have a longer period of neural immaturity than any other species. But as this strange-planet example illustrates, children's lives also are less regulated, more protected, and perhaps even more interesting than our lives. Combine this open schedule and protected life with twenty years of neural immaturity, and parents have on their hands a being who can think and learn and experiment on the world without the practical constraints of adulthood. This gives children the wherewithal to imagine the nonexistent, explore alternate worlds, and generally make things up as they work toward understanding their real world with minimal, if any, consequences. If you had this freedom, you might very well also pretend that you were a race car driver just so that you could learn a little bit more about the physics of centrifugal force and inertia from a bag of marbles and a plastic Hot Wheels® track. But you can't do this because you're too busy answering e-mails, returning phone calls, and writing presentations, and because the rest of your family would worry that you'd gone off the deep end. What makes children Super Scientists is that they don't have to play by the adult rules of probability and practicality. Their experiments can be out-of-this-world fantastic, and they can let their imaginations rip. They're as free to make up an improbable world where stuffed animals rule humans as they are to consider the more probable world of an afternoon T-ball game. They're as free to act as if American settlers lived in tempera-painted appliance boxes in carpeted living rooms as they are to consider Gettysburg.

Of course, no real scientist would propose that Candy Land® or Toontown® actually exists. But real scientists often propose things that seem utterly fantastic at the time. Pretend for a second that you're a seventeenth-century Greek commoner. For you and your village mates, it's common knowledge that the earth is the motionless center of the universe. Not only does the Bible say so, but everything about your everyday experiences suggests it is so.[4] You think that the earth must be the center of the universe because things, like the rain, autumn leaves, and spilled mead, fall toward it. And the earth is clearly stationary because you don't feel it moving beneath your feet. Furthermore, if the earth were spinning, things not firmly attached to the ground, like pack horses, plague-bearing rats, and your three children, would be hurled off into space. Ever try standing on a spinning merry-go-round without holding on? You'd also encounter 788 mile-per-hour head winds if you went outside.[5] Things in the sky, like clouds, dragonflies, and geese, would be left behind by the spinning earth. Geese would have to fly 788 miles per hour just to keep up. And since you'd be constantly moving relative to fixed stars, they'd seem to be shifting their place in the sky relative to one another. The constellation Hercules would look like a heroic warrior one moment, egg salad the next, then Flat Stanley, and then back to heroic warrior. So when Galileo wrote in his 1632 *Dialogue Concerning the Two Chief World Systems* that the earth moved and the sun was the stationary center of the universe, it's no surprise that these fantastic ideas got him sentenced to house arrest for the rest of his life.[6]

Scientific genius is proposing the fantastic. No one would accuse me of scientific brilliance for presenting the theory of general relativity or being able to write at great length about microorganisms. But they would if I were the first person ever to do it. Imagine what your great-great-great-great-great-great-grandparents would think of the technologic discoveries of the past few generations. A round bulb of glass that produces light? A heavier-than-air flying machine? Swallowed capsules that cure a festering infection? A handheld device that enables you to throw your three-year-old twins a kiss good night from a hotel room three hundred miles away in Shreveport, map the quickest route to a Starbucks even though you have no idea where you are, set the DVR in your family room to record an entire season of *Glee*, and broadcast a homemade video of your pugs dressed up on Halloween as Yoda® and Princess Leia®? All of these things surely seemed utterly fantastic before they were conceived and built. Their eventual invention depended on a healthy dose of the fantastic. Unimaginative scientists don't produce radically new ideas. And children invent new ideas when they're given the room to create, consider, and immerse themselves in worlds that don't exist.

Fantasy benefits us regular adults, too. Mainly, it helps us avoid making terrible mistakes—like a crawfish jambalaya ice-cream sundae. You know that you wouldn't want to eat this, right? But it's not because you've whipped it up, downed a few gooey bites, and then decided that it tastes terrible. It's because you can *imagine* that a mixture of cool and creamy crawfish, drippy hot fudge, and marshmallow cream would taste awful. Imagination gives us the ability to try out experiences in our heads before we give them a go in real life. Just as pilots use flight simulators so they can minimize mistakes out in the real world, our imaginations are a built-in experience simulator that does essentially the same thing. It's a handy adaptation that we can imagine that things like camouflage golf balls, crepe-paper umbrellas, and rubber tissues would be lousy inventions without having to leave the comfort of our armchairs.

But somehow fantasy has gotten a bad name. We think that learning takes place in the reality of classrooms and textbooks and not in the imaginary world conjured up while playing in a pile of dirt. If you took twenty minutes to walk from your front door to the minivan, to stoop down and explore the new anthill forming between your sidewalk cracks, or to see how high a mound you could form with the gravel in the driveway, your neighbors wouldn't think you were learning. They'd think you were goofing off. But the reality of the matter is that fantasy is a normal, and sometimes superior, means of learning. People who get paid to learn new things about our world (i.e., scientists) have a pervasive and active fantasy life. Some of them sit in their offices and imagine the past. What did Neanderthals eat? How was the universe created? Why did dinosaurs become extinct? Others imagine worlds that don't yet exist. A world without lower back pain, traffic jams, human-made CO_2 emissions, and dryers that lose socks. And they act to make these imaginary worlds real. Think about it. Everything in the room you're sitting in right now—from your sticky notes to your contact lenses to your smartphone—certainly would have seemed as imaginary or fantastic from the perspective of our hunter-gatherer ancestors as Middle Earth does to us.

Granted, a scientist's imagination is more disciplined and systematic than the more lawless child version. Children can imagine a rocket to Mars powered by spaghetti and meatballs, but this sort of irrational invention wouldn't fly for scientists. Scientists combine logic with imagination to articulate possible worlds and then make them real. And this is exactly what children do as they get older. Their imaginations develop in ways more informed by their knowledge of how things really work. This knowledge gives imagination power. Consider this: you drive by a beautiful old farmhouse and you notice the inviting rocking chairs on the front porch, the mature fruit trees in a grove off to the side, the well-stocked fish pond with a skiff tied to the deck, and the "For Sale" sign in the front yard. You wistfully imagine your family sharing stories and hot cocoa by the hand-laid stone fireplace in the family room while you prepare the horses for a late-afternoon ride. Perfect. Then you imagine all you'd need to do to keep up the property. That you'd need to care for the horses, mow the four-acre lawn, maintain the algae-bloomed pond, and deal with the asbestos in the attic, the raccoon family between the floors, the lead pipes in the bathrooms, and the radon in the basement. Not perfect. This second round of imaginings needs to be directed by reality and is the layer of imagination that makes adults' fantasy lives adaptive. Of course, you could imagine hiring a pack of farm gnomes to keep up your property in exchange for a home in the barn or planting a money tree in your backyard to sprout the cost of the needed renovations, but it's better not to rely on such fantasies. You're better off if you construct your fantasies in ways informed by your knowledge of how things really happen.

Constraining fantasy by knowledge doesn't make fantasy redundant as we get older because we rarely have an exact formula that we can dial up to get us through complex situations. We more often have to work out our course of action by thinking through the possibilities in ways that are both imaginative and realistic. Growing older and gaining knowledge doesn't crush imagination; rather, it gives this adaptation the power to change the world and, with apologies to Monty Python, to provide something completely different. If you're a seventeenth-century Englishman and read Isaac Newton's manuscripts on centrifugal force and gravity, then with the right mix of speed, weight, and steel, you can build one heck of an amusement ride. Of course, in Newton's time, no one had any idea how to build a roller coaster with an inclined, diving loop and a wraparound corkscrew, but his ideas told you what would happen if you did. The uniquely human evolutionary gift is to combine imagination and logic to articulate possible worlds and then make them real.

But even though fantasy and imagination give children the room to make important insights and discoveries that are not amenable to classroom learning, formal instruction nonetheless is necessary to teach children how to become twenty-first-century adults. No matter how many science experiments they carry out in their backyards or how often they fantasize about imaginary worlds, they won't learn necessary modern skills. They won't learn how to write a sentence, how to make change at the supermarket, or how to drive a car. Children need some degree of intentional tutelage—this much is clear. Drop a newborn on a deserted island, and she might pick up for herself some skills for dealing with the physical world, but her skill set would not be particularly impressive. With no one to teach her and no one to imitate, she'd likely not invent the English language or Arabic numerals. Nor would she figure out for herself how to read the newspaper, balance her checkbook, tell time, file her federal income tax, or make a grilled cheese sandwich. These sorts of abilities are the product of direct instruction.

MIND-READING TEACHERS

We humans like to think we're different from the rest of the animal kingdom. It's why most of us feel a proprietary twinge when we read news reports of other species doing things we thought only our special species could pull off. It makes our uniqueness among earth's creatures seem frankly shaky. There are bonobos that use language, chimpanzees that practice charity, hyenas that cooperate, crows that craft tools, whales that teach, bees that communicate, and elephants that show empathy. Is there anything left?

You might think that we at least enjoy the advantage of being more intelligent. No other animal can solve monic polynomials, engineer Silly String®, invent penicillin, or design the Golden Gate Bridge. It seems as if our smarts are so impressive that the gap between us and whoever comes in second place is unbridgeable. We all thought this was the case until Michael Tomasello, the codirector of the Max Planck Institute for Evolutionary Anthropology, and his colleagues gave a comprehensive battery of cognitive tests—the equivalent of a nonverbal IQ test—to a large number of chimpanzees, orangutans, and human two-and-a-half-year-olds.[7] Think the toddlers made us proud? Think again. The human children were not more intelligent overall. They performed at an equivalent level to the chimpanzees on tasks that measured their understanding of the physical world of space, quantities, and causality. This is a truly striking finding. Even more so if you consider the great apes' added disadvantage: they had to deal with a test battery that was not only designed but administered by a different species.

Even more demoralizing to our presumed lofty status in the animal kingdom is a study by Andrew Whiten, head of the Scottish Primate Research Group at the University of St Andrews, and his colleagues.[8] Whiten pitted two- to six-year-old chimps from a Ugandan nature reserve against three- to five-year-old humans. Both groups were given boxes with a pair of compartments. In each box, the top compartment was empty and the bottom contained a species-appropriate goodie—food for the chimps and stickers for the children. Before getting a go at the boxes, the chimps and children watched a researcher lift the lid on the top of each box and then poke a stick around in the empty compartment as if trying to skewer the prize. Thing is, this demonstration was purposely misleading. The snack and stickers could be accessed only by opening a flap at the *front* of the box. When the boxes were handed over, the chimps immediately realized that the poking motion they had just seen demonstrated was useless. Instead, they flipped up the front flap and grasped the snack. What was more remarkable, and frankly disappointing, was that the children continued to stab futilely at the empty top compartment. They did this even when they were left alone and secretly filmed so as to eliminate the chance that they were carrying out the unsuccessful motion merely to please the researchers. Even though a few children figured out how to get the sticker after much fruitless poking, clearly the chimpanzees solved the task using a more intelligent approach. The chimps quickly worked out that the poking motion was ineffective, whereas the children mindlessly copied what they saw.

I have nothing against nonhuman primates, but these findings make me worry that *Planet of the Apes* might have been on the right track. And once science starts backing up old Charlton Heston science fiction movies—well, if you've seen *Soylent Green*, you know we're in trouble.

However, things might not be that bad after all. If we go back to the Tomasello study with the two-year-old humans and adult great apes, it turns out that there were a number of tasks on which the children outscored the apes: those measuring social-cognitive skills such as social learning, communicating, and understanding the intentions of others. On these measures, the children far outscored the great apes.

Tomasello thinks that it is this suite of social-cognitive skills that makes all the difference between us and the rest of the biological world.[9] They don't give us more individual brainpower. They give us the ability to learn from other people and their artifacts and to collaborate with others in collective teaching and learning activities. "Wait a minute," you're thinking, "on the network Animal Planet, there are great apes that learn new behaviors from others." There are young chimpanzees that learn how to coordinate a stone hammer and tree-root anvil to crack open nuts by watching others practice the technique. This sort of learning, however, is really individualistic social learning. Chimpanzees learn the technique merely by gathering information unilaterally from unsuspecting others. The elder chimpanzees have no idea they're teaching the watching youngsters anything. They're just trying to open up nuts for their own lunch. And the juveniles have no idea that they're actually learning something when they try to imitate.

Young humans, in contrast, imitate the actions of others readily and sometimes with the apparent motivation of not just solving a problem but of demonstrating to the adult that they are "in tune" with the current situation.[10] Great apes simply don't do this. Likewise, human adults often teach children by demonstrating what they should do—and the children respond by imitating what is learned. Adult great apes don't typically demonstrate things for youngsters. Even human infants seem to understand the collaborative nature of teaching and learning. When imitating back, one-year-olds often direct the actions back to the imitator, making it clear by looking to the demonstrator's face that they see this as a collaborative activity. Chimpanzees don't look at their partner's face in this manner.

These comparative investigations support Tomasello's view that humans are super-smart because we have a package of social-cognitive skills that make us hyper-educable. They permit the transition of knowledge from one generation to the next to an extent that far exceeds that seen in any other species. And they create the possibility of intentional teaching, or pedagogy—in which adults impart information by telling and showing, and children trust and use this information with confidence. Not even our nearest primate relatives teach and learn in this manner. Certainly our primate kin can pick up certain behaviors like nut cracking, termite fishing, and grooming from watching others carry out these actions, but I've never seen a mother chimpanzee call over her brood and deliberately teach the oldest how to make a sandwich. She'd never do this because she is not equipped with the social-cognitive gear to know that he doesn't know how to make a sandwich. Nor would the oldest know that his mother is making those hand motions with bread and bologna to show him how to make a sandwich. But we humans would, and it's these abilities that permit pedagogy.

A common thread in this bundle of skills that permits our hyper-educability is the capacity to consciously think about what's going on in our own and other people's heads.[11] This ability falls under the umbrella of skills known as theory of mind, and it is something humans have to the exclusion of all other animals. We know what's happening in someone else's head without ever opening it up. We are so good at this skill that we don't even need to be in the vicinity of people's heads to figure out what's happening inside them. Consider the first sentence of Cormac McCarthy's *The Road*: "When he woke in the woods in the dark and the cold of the night he'd reach out to touch the child sleeping beside him."[12] This opening line works so well because you have a theory of mind. From this one sentence, you know what this nameless "he" is feeling, and you know that it's not looking good.

This intuitive mind-reading ability gives us the capacity to engage in pedagogy—to deliberately learn when we're children and to deliberately teach when we're adults. Theory of mind is essential for this to happen because if the instructor wasn't aware that the pupil didn't know what was being taught, parents and teachers never would have been motivated to pass on information to children. If you didn't realize that Junior didn't know how to tie his shoes, you'd never teach him. If adults could not infer what children do not know, intentional teaching would never have emerged, and formal schooling would never have come about. The same goes for the pupil: "Why is my teacher scribbling lines on my paper with her pencil? She's trying to teach me how to write my name." If children didn't know what their teachers were up to, they'd never put up with school.

Yet formal instruction is a foreign element in the brain's natural ecology. During the brain's history, it never needed a classroom to learn how to find buried food, recognize relatives on the first encounter, or fly thousands of miles to the exact same spot every spring. It didn't need a textbook to learn how to detect the electrical fields in the muscle twitches of hiding prey, sense impending earthquakes, intuit human epilepsy seizures, or predict the outcomes of World Cup matches. Yet now we ask it to come into classrooms and think big, think out loud, and think out of the box. We ask children to rack their brains, collect their thoughts, put on their thinking caps, and get bright ideas. It all sounds so neurologically dangerous. I worry that too much brainstorming about how to design a leafcutter ant diorama for the elementary school science competition might generate a power surge that completely shorts out a fourth grader's frontal lobe.

GOLD STARS, CHOCOLATE CHIP COOKIES, AND As

If you've ever tried to get a fourth grader to do a diorama for science class, her word study homework on a school night, or a summer vacation book report, you know that children are not always ready and willing to learn. No matter. You took Psychology 101 in college, and you know about B. F. Skinner, the late, esteemed Harvard psychology professor who discovered that you can trick all sorts of animals into behaving however you want merely by reinforcing, or rewarding, the behavior of choice. There are all sorts of demonstrations of this. Rewards can get rats to press levers; bears to ride bicycles; squirrels to water-ski; and monkeys to fetch bologna sandwiches, open cabinet doors, and turn magazine pages for quadriplegics. So rewarding children for doing their schoolwork seems, from this perspective, a reasonable way to motivate children to learn new things. If dead fish can motivate a killer whale to balance a human on its beak, then surely a Mickey Mouse sticker can motivate Sam to do his best on his finger painting, a chocolate bar can motivate Ramona to read about Jonestown for her social studies class, and an A grade can motivate Alexander to do his best on his science fair project.

Many school districts have taken Skinner's philosophy and put it into practice. Some schools have thrown money at the problem—literally.[13] New York City fourth graders can earn a maximum of twenty-five dollars in cash per standardized test, and seventh graders can earn up to fifty bucks a pop. In Chicago, children are paid fifty dollars for each A grade, thirty-five for each B, and twenty for Cs, up to two thousand dollars a year. Dallas schools target the youngest children: every time second graders read a book and complete a computerized quiz about it, they earn two bucks. Other districts, uncomfortable with such a pay-to-learn philosophy, dole out goodies like small toys, extra recess time, smiley-face stickers, "Good Job" certificates, and class pizza parties. These practices are incredibly common in our schools. For instance, in a recent survey of young adults, 70 percent said that their elementary school teachers had used candy in the classroom as a reward.[14] I don't know if I'm more upset that my children are being stoked with chocolate bars in school or that my boss has never offered me even a single M&M® for all the hard work I do.[15]

Being a developmental psychologist, I've met a lot of children, and I've never met one who doesn't enjoy pocketing rewards for schoolwork. But does rewarding children for schoolwork actually succeed? It's one thing to use Snausages® to get your dog to shake hands, but quite another thing to use Cheese Nips® to get your child to do long division. Is there any evidence that rewards work in humans the way they do in animals? That they can trick children into doing things? You bet there is. Rewards make it as easy as pie to, for instance, get children to eat their vegetables. Forget about secretly tucking lettuce into turkey sandwiches, grating carrots into muffins, and hiding spinach in lasagna. If you want to get children to eat their vegetables, just give them prizes for doing it. In a recent study, vegetable consumption among elementary school children in their lunchroom was substantially boosted when the youngsters were rewarded with plastic tokens that they could trade for swag like colored pencils and stickers.[16]

But this rewarding business can be tricky. Say you mistakenly reward the wrong behavior. Then you end up with something you didn't expect. When I was in second grade, my school decided to give out a prize to the student who read the most books by the end of the year. The prize was a coveted color-changing fiber-optic disco light—the kind with the thin plastic spaghetti fibers that spray out like a mushroom top. Everyone wanted the light, but the more industrious of us downgraded our typical reading to simpler, less challenging picture books. I went from reading J. R. R. Tolkien to Dr. Seuss. I doubt that was the school's intent. There's also the issue of what happens when the rewards stop. If your third grader is working math problems because you're rewarding her with chocolate chip cookies, what happens when the cookies stop? If you guess that she'll stop doing her math work, you're right. That's exactly what happened in the vegetables study described above. The children stopped eating vegetables at lunch as soon as the reward program stopped.

The tendency of rewarded behaviors to stop once the reward stops seems obvious. It's why we tell big sisters to ignore their pesky little brothers. If you ignore them (i.e., stop rewarding them with attention), they'll stop making silly monkey faces when you're trying to talk with your friend about the new boy in Mrs. Lee's class. It's why you've stopped making that special lemon chicken recipe for your family. And it's why "You must be a parking ticket because you've got 'Fine' written all over you" never lasted long in any normal person's repertoire of pickup lines.

For a while, psychologists thought they had come up with a clever solution to the vanishing-rewards problem by using a reinforcement system known as a token economy.[17] In a token economy, whenever a certain behavior occurs (e.g., doing homework), a token (e.g., a ticket) is handed out. Once a certain amount of tokens are accumulated, they then can be traded in for rewards (e.g., a small toy). The idea was that once the desired behavior occurs regularly, the rewards could be phased out and the behavior would persist. So once Max is practicing his violin routinely, his Pokémon™ card reward could be dropped down to 75 percent of the time, then 50, then 25, and so on, eventually down to zero. It seems that this progressive process would gradually motivate the desired behavior without the reward. There's certainly lots of evidence that intermittent rewards create greater motivation to carry out a behavior than when a reward is handed out every time. It's why activities like gambling and fishing can be so addicting. If you can't predict when the reward is coming, you're compelled to keep trying. But once it's clear that the rewards have completely stopped (e.g., because the slot machine is fixed or the lake is dry of fish), you return to behaving as you did before the rewards began. This news is not good—especially if you can't get your son to do his social studies review sheet or your daughter to do her book report without promising a reward. So is your best option to stock up on Twinkies® and resolve that at least your rewarded children are doing more learning than they would if you didn't dole out the rewards? Absolutely not. In 1959, Harvard psychology professor Richard White published a paper that turned the business of rewarding children for learning on its head.[18] White made the seemingly simple argument that learning is driven not by external rewards but by internal motivation. That mastering new things simply feels good. That exercising and extending knowledge is inherently satisfying. Most people ignored White's paper because it seemed well established that learning was a behavior that needed external prodding. Indeed, this idea lingers today in American child rearing and education ideology. But today it's clear that the idea that learning is motivated by rewards was formulated by psychologists who were too busy rewarding pigeons to play Ping-Pong® and pigs to push grocery carts to spend any time watching real children interact with their world.[19]

White's proposal that learning is internally motivated is something to be taken seriously if it turns out to be true. This chapter so far has made it sound like rewards will motivate any behavior so long as the reinforcement keeps coming, but the behavior will return to where it started once the reinforcement ends. This is usually true, but not always. If we're dealing with a behavior that does not come naturally and needs some *external* motivation, then the pattern holds. But if we are talking about behavior that is enjoyable—in psychologist-speak, *internally* motivated—when the rewards stop, the behavior will occur even less than it did before the rewards started.

There are volumes of studies showing that internally motivated behaviors can be seriously squashed by rewards. A classic demonstration was carried out by Stanford University psychologist Mark Lepper and his colleagues.[20] Lepper gave three groups of preschoolers magic markers and construction paper. One group was offered a "good player award"—a certificate with a gold star and a red ribbon—for drawing a picture. The second group got the reward but didn't know it was coming. The final group just drew. A few weeks later, the markers and paper reappeared in the classrooms, and not all of the children were equally willing to draw. Those children who'd received the expected reward spent half as much time drawing during this second round compared to those who'd never seen the groovy certificate or those who were awarded it as a surprise. The promise of a reward seemed to have snuffed out the first group's enjoyment in drawing. The reward had turned play into work.

This pattern has been replicated using all sorts of rewards and in all sorts of learning situations.[21] It even persists in adults. For instance, University of Rochester psychologist Edward Deci gave two groups of college students a series of block-building puzzles.[22] One group received one dollar for each puzzle solved, and the other got nothing. Later, when the students were told that the experiment was over (though it really wasn't) and that they had a few minutes to relax, work more puzzles, or read, those who were paid for their solutions were likely to put the puzzles down. In another study, Kenneth McGraw and John McCullers at the University of Mississippi paid undergraduates to solve a series of nine problems that required pouring a specific amount of water into a jar from bottles of varying sizes.[23] When presented with a tenth problem that demanded inventing a new type of solution, the rewarded students took much longer to solve the problem than those who hadn't been paid. These studies suggest that rewards not only sap the fun out of play, but that they also lead to less skilled play.

What's going on here? How can getting a reward drain your motivation for doing something that's already rewarding? The answer lies in the overjustification effect, which can be summarized in five words: extrinsic rewards decrease intrinsic motivation.[24] The thinking goes that when an intrinsically rewarding behavior is reinforced with external incentives, like prizes or money, we begin paying more attention to the incentives and less attention to the pleasure that comes from doing the behavior. This shift in attention brings about a shift in motivation to extrinsic incentives and ostensibly disables the existing intrinsic motivation. When children are rewarded for doing something they already enjoy, the reward alters their locus of motivation from internal to external. In Lepper's study, children who initially drew because it was fun shifted to drawing in order to get the certificate. Later, when no certificate was promised for drawing, the children's thinking went, "I drew last time because I wanted the certificate, so why should I draw for nothing now?" And that's how you take a behavior that children do because they like doing it and change it into a behavior that children expect a reward for doing.

Many of us promise our children rewards for reading, writing, and studying because they'll do more of those things if we promise them pizza parties, extra recess time, and prizes. But in the process of rewarding them for good behavior, children go from learning because it's fun to learning in order to get a gold star, special privilege, or a high letter grade.[25] The goodies, rather than an internal drive, motivate learning. Grades are a particular sore spot among developmental psychologists. For a long time, many of us have been arguing that grades are the reason so many students dislike school or lack interest in schoolwork. Almost everything that children do in school is graded, and students quickly come to expect a grade in exchange for any piece of schoolwork. As a college professor, whenever I assign a writing assignment or class project just for fun, I'm immediately told by my students that if they're going to invest their time and effort into something for class, they darn well better receive a grade. And whenever I give them something like a series of questions to consider as they read through a difficult but provocative text, they're disappointed if I don't collect and grade their work, no matter how much working through their answers before class prepared them to react to the queries I posed in class. Most of them just can't seem to wrap their heads around the idea of doing some learning without receiving a grade.

The problem with grades is that once they're introduced as something children get in exchange for their performance at school, the grades themselves rather than any internal factors come to motivate schoolwork. So even things that were initially fun are turned into grubwork that children will do only for external incentives.

Since at least the early 1900s, a number of prominent thinkers whose voices have not been sufficiently heard have been making the argument that a critical problem with our educational system is its failure to sustain and make use of children's internal motivation for learning and exploration.[26] Sure, motivation is a product of many factors and is not solely driven by incentives doled out by teachers and parents. Putting one smiley sticker on a spelling test won't completely squelch all internal desire to learn. But why risk it? Why put a gold star on the leaf rubbing that the kindergarten class did just for fun? Why not just make school intrinsically interesting from the very beginning? This is a tall order for sure. But if teachers and parents could figure out how to keep learning fun, they'd never have to promise a reward or offer a bribe—which is how the whole problem with motivation starts in the first place. Once children realize that acquiring new knowledge not only feels good but gets them something, the fat lady has sung.

In my day job, I've lost track of the number of times students drop by during my office hours, open up their textbooks on my desk, and ask flatly, "Just tell me what I need to know to get an A." The times I'm in class bursting over a brilliant new experiment, and a student raises her hand and asks, "Excuse me, Professor, but will this be on the test?" And the times I'm helping a student make up his spring course schedule who is struggling to figure out the meaning of life and I suggest that he take Philosophy 340 (a.k.a. "The Meaning of Life"), but he only wants those courses that are guaranteed "easy As." These experiences with college students are typical business rather than the exception. But I'm sure that when all of them were younger and experimenting in the world of leaf piles, they didn't care if the lessons learned in their backyard would be tested on a later exam or get them into a good college. I bet they never said, "Mom, building this block bridge is a waste of time because I don't plan on becoming a civil engineer" or "Dad, I don't want to play catch because I'll never play ball professionally." Something happens between the leaf piles and college. Learning goes from fun to drudgery. It likely starts when we bring children into the classroom and ask them to learn things in a manner that isn't fun, so we offer up rewards to egg them on.

It's time we worked toward making learning fun throughout the life span. We need to figure out ways to maintain children's internal motivation for learning so that it isn't completely undermined by rewards once they reach the first grade.

WHY YOU DON'T NEED SMART CHILDREN

Did you hear that? That was your psychobabble alarm going off. It went off because you're thinking, "Reeeeally, the best way to raise a successful child is to maintain her internal motivation for learning? That never got anyone into Harvard. A high IQ does."

Dear Ivy League Admissions Officer:

I understand that I am competing against many other impressive high school seniors for limited spots at your esteemed institution. I understand, too, that most of the other young applicants have IQs of 145 or higher. I have an utterly average IQ of exactly 100, but I am the *only* student in the tristate area who has preserved an internal motivation for learning throughout my entire public school career. Given this unparalleled and paramount achievement, I look forward to receiving an acceptance letter and official notice of my full scholarship (plus room, board, and textbooks).

There is no doubt that IQ does a reasonably neat job of predicting all sorts of things most of us would consider measures of success. Generally, people with healthy IQs are more likely than those with lesser IQs to do well in school and in the real world, to land good-paying jobs with short commutes and have happy and lasting marriages, to stay out of jail and off drugs, and so on. But a high IQ guarantees none of this. It can't even guarantee an A on a spelling test. But you already know this. Remember that brainiac in high school who aced every chemistry exam, presided over the debate club, and was voted Most Likely to Win a Nobel Prize? Today he's cleaning toilets in the mall. And you hear stories in the news about children with exceedingly high IQs who fell into mediocrity as adults. There's William Sidis, who was reading the *New York Times* at eighteen months, taught himself to speak eight different languages by age eight, and enrolled at Harvard at eleven.[27] These were very impressive early achievements, but other than a seemingly neurotic collection of streetcar transfer tickets, Sidis's adult life was unexceptional.

Though IQ is a reasonable predictor of success, it can't predict greatness. It can't forecast who will become a Nobel Prize–winning scientist, a Hall of Fame athlete, *Time* magazine's "Person of the Year," an honorary knight for humanitarian work, or a classical violinist who brings audiences to tears. IQ can't even anticipate who will show inklings of genius. The trouble is that IQ is merely a measure of verbal and analytic skills. These skills surely are associated with success in everyday life, but they are a far leap from assuring the exceptional creativity, unprecedented originality, and extraordinary dedication you need to develop genius. Which is why even people with ho-hum run-of-the-mill IQs can be geniuses. William Shockley, who won the 1956 Nobel Prize in physics for inventing the transistor, was excluded as a child from Louis Terman's famed study of genius because his IQ score wasn't high enough. It was the same story for 1968 Nobel Prize winner Luis Alvarez. Alvarez, too, was left out of Terman's study.[28] In fact, none of Terman's high-IQ children (fondly referred to as "Termites") has ever won a Nobel Prize.[29] My favorite ordinary IQ Nobel Prize winner is Richard Feynman. Feynman, who was declared by *Omni* magazine to be "The Smartest Man in the World," often boasted that his winning a Nobel with a regular IQ was a more impressive feat than winning one with a lofty IQ.[30]

Acknowledging that IQ doesn't predict genius has real implications for how we raise and educate our children. It means that we don't need to build exceptionally high-IQ children to end up with adults who do extraordinary things in their chosen field. A high IQ is a good ingredient but not necessary for success. It also means that parents shouldn't become discouraged if their child doesn't score in the 97th percentile on an IQ test. She likely has other amazing talents in her pocket that simply are not tapped by a standard IQ assessment. So, rather than pining for a child who is one of the chosen few with a gifted-grade IQ, instead muster whatever resources you can to keep your child's desire to learn and achieve ignited. This exuberant learning, rather than IQ, is what makes all the difference.

STOP SAYING THEY'RE SMART

If you're one of those parents who think your child must have skipped their naturally ambitious stage and went straight to underachiever, you're wrong. Spend a few moments with an infant fiercely trying to grasp a toy, a baby restlessly trying to figure out a zipper, or a toddler thirstily trying to speak her mind. These skills are not the ordinary sort, like the times table your second grader is cultivating in math. Rather, they are the most difficult tasks of a lifetime, like learning how to walk, talk, and think. No matter how tough the going gets, babies would never throw in the towel or complain it's too hard or not worth the effort. They don't worry about making mistakes, humiliating themselves, or getting a failing grade. No matter how many times they stumble, they get up and barge ahead, headstrong on mastering the day's missions.

Several years later, for many children, the fire seems to go out. Somewhere around the beginning of middle school, many children seem to lose their natural drive to succeed and downgrade themselves to underachievers. For parents, this switch from exuberant learner to slacker can be a bewildering and frustrating experience. The problem is that ambition can't be taught like other subjects at school. It's not that simple.

There is a way to make ambition bloom, however. Children have to know that intelligence is malleable. That it's a process that can be developed through dedication and effort, not a thing that you either have or you don't. Thirty-some years of research by Stanford University developmental psychologist Carol Dweck provides compelling evidence that this "growth mindset" is the key to lifetime motivation and success.[31] Study after study shows that a growth mind-set leads to a love of learning and a resilience that is essential for intellectual growth. These are the children who go at life vigorously, delight in persevering when the going gets tough, and rebound in the face of failure. How do you raise children to develop these characteristics? First, stop rewarding them for learning. Then stop telling them they're smart.

You know about the downside of rewards from the discussion earlier in this chapter, but stop telling children they're smart? That's ridiculous. Our children are smart, and we tell them so because we don't want them to sell their intellectual talents short. Plus, if our children believe they're smart (having been told so regularly), they won't be intimidated by new challenges, and their feelings won't be hurt by academic failures. Most of us praise our children liberally for their smarts; a recent survey found that 85 percent of parents do so. But I think that even this might be an underestimation.[32] Every parent I know does it constantly. "You are so smart, kiddo" just seems to roll off the tongue. It's in our official job description as parents to cheer on our children and tell them they are brainy, even when they do less than perfect work. We tell them they're smart with handwritten notes in their lunchboxes and magnetic star charts on our refrigerators, the way we brag on the phone to their grandparents, and the "I'm with Genius" T-shirts we wear to their parent-teacher conferences. We saturate our children with messages that they are doing terrific and were born with what it takes. The thing is, thirty-some years of evidence accumulated by Dweck and her colleagues suggests that we have it wrong. Telling children they're smart does not inoculate them against underperforming. It might actually cause it.[33]

For a long time, parents and teachers carried on under the assumption that praise boosts children's self-esteem and consequently their success. Self-esteem gurus, like Nathaniel Branden, told us to praise our children liberally and lavishly because self-esteem was the number-one most important feature affecting well-being and life success. Brandon's 1969 book, *The Psychology of Self-Esteem*, launched a movement that propelled everyone to take whatever lengths were necessary to achieve high self-esteem.[34] California even signed into law a self-esteem task force to study how self-esteem is "nurtured, harmed, and rehabilitated." Assemblyman John Vasconcellos, who created the task force, argued that raising Californians' collective self-esteem would do everything from lowering dependence on public welfare to decreasing teen pregnancy.[35] Efforts to nurture children's seemingly fragile self-esteem became an unstoppable train. Anything at risk of bruising children's self-esteem was given the boot. Academic contests and talent competitions were bad-mouthed. Sports leagues stopped counting goals, runs, and touchdowns and instead handed out trophies, medals, and ribbons to everyone. Teachers threw out their red pencils and instead invested in gold stars and smiley-face stickers. In the air was the idea that any criticism was to be replaced with praise, even if the praise wasn't entirely deserved; undeserved praise was considered healthier for children's self-esteem than any deserved feedback because criticism might pop children's self-esteem bubble. No kidding, in the 1980s there was even a school district in Massachusetts that had children "jumping rope" without a rope to remove the risk that one of the students might suffer the self-esteem-squashing shame of tripping.[36]

FOR THE DOGS

After decades of rampant and impartial praise, Carol Dweck began to wonder whether we might be overdoing it. She wondered whether too much praise might actually cause children harm. And in the 1970s, she began a body of research that has produced a series of results that can take your breath away. Sure, praising children boosts their feelings of self-worth and confidence, but only so long as they never fail, face difficulty, or make mistakes. Study after study by Dweck and her colleagues demonstrates that the consequences of praise backfire the first moment children are stumped.

The intellectual seeds that planted the idea that praise might promote unintended behaviors came from a series of 1960s experiments by University of Pennsylvania psychologist Martin Seligman, carried out in his animal laboratory. Seligman placed dogs in situations in which they received inescapable and uncontrollable electric shocks. Eventually, most of the dogs stopped trying to escape the shocks and merely accepted their condition. Thing is, once this "learned helplessness" developed, when given a way to escape or terminate the shocks, the dogs failed to learn to do so. These dogs could not cope. They'd learned that they were powerless. These experiments had a huge impact on psychology, mostly in our understanding of disorders like depression and post-traumatic stress disorder because they suggested that experiences with uncontrollable stressors can produce the learned helplessness that is common to these pathologies.[37] Dweck took Seligman's laboratory findings in an entirely different direction. She wondered whether a tendency to attribute aversive events as uncontrollable would lead to feelings of learned helplessness that would in turn affect children's academic performance.

To test this idea, Dweck gave fifth graders a series of puzzles that were easy enough for all of the children to solve.[38] After the test, the children were told their score and then heard a single line of praise. Some were praised for their *intelligence* and told, "You must be smart at this." Others were praised for their *effort*: "You must have worked really hard."[39]

Then, in a second round, the children were given a similar test, but this time it was rigged so that none of them would succeed. When questioned about why they thought they had failed, the two groups reasoned differently. Those children who had been praised for their effort earlier reasoned that they simply hadn't tried hard enough on the second round. These children generally were very engaged in the second test, willing to test different sorts of solutions, and some even remarked spontaneously that they were enjoying the challenge of the difficult tasks. But those children who had been praised earlier for being intelligent reasoned that their failure was evidence that they weren't really smart at all. As you can probably guess, these children generally had a miserable time with the test.

Even more remarkable is what happened next. After artificially inducing failure on the second round, Dweck gave the children a final series of puzzles engineered to be as easy as the first set. Those children who were initially praised for their effort did better than the first time around. These children raised their score by about 30 percent. But those who had been told they were smart performed worse than they did on the first test by about 20 percent. Some of these children took much longer than the first time around to solve the very same sorts of puzzles, and others suddenly couldn't work them out at all. So after a failure, those children who were praised for their smarts developed trouble with tasks they had solved just moments earlier.

What happened? Telling children they are smart sends the message that they are naturally endowed. The problem is, this "fixed mind-set" praise takes the control out of children's hands and leaves them with no formula for responding to failure. Like Seligman's learned-helpless dogs, when faced with failure, the "smart" children didn't seem to realize or were unable to respond to the fact that their environment had become controllable. Emphasizing effort, however, gave children a variable they could control. These children felt as if their success was in their control and therefore they weren't thwarted by failure. In follow-up interviews, Dweck discovered that children who believe that innate intelligence is the key to success discount the importance of effort. These children reason, "I am smart, so I don't need to put out the effort." For these children, effort is stigmatized as public proof that you can't cut it on your natural endowments.

A subsequent round suggests that once children latch onto the idea that their innate smarts are responsible for their successes, they become reluctant to take on tasks that don't come with a guarantee of success. After being praised for their intelligence or their effort on a first set of easy puzzles, children were given a choice of a second set of puzzles. They could pick either an easy set similar to the first round or more difficult puzzles that they were told they would be learning something by just trying. Ninety percent of the children who were praised for their effort on the first test choose the *harder* set of puzzles. The majority of children praised for their intelligence, however, picked the *easy* set. The "smart" children took the easy way out. Dweck argues that praising children for their intelligence sends the message that what's most important is to appear smart and to avoid the risk of making mistakes. When you say to your children, "You got a perfect paper! You're so smart!" they also hear, "If you don't get a perfect paper, you're not smart." When children come to believe that intelligence is a fixed trait, they don't take any risks because failure would mean they lack competence or potential. In this study, the "smart" children took the easy option, thereby ensuring they'd look smart and skirt any chance of failing.

Other studies show that "smart" children will go as far as to lie about their performance to protect their intellectual reputation.[40] In a similar study, children who were praised for either their intelligence or their effort were asked to write letters to students at another school, describing their experience in the study. Remarkable differences emerged: 40 percent of those children praised for their intelligence lied about how they did on the puzzle tasks and inflated their scores upward. Of those praised for their effort, very few lied. The children who were praised for their intelligence likely weren't routinely deceptive children—they simply did what almost everyone does when they're immersed in an environment that celebrates them solely for their innate talent. This belief creates an urgency to prove you've got a healthy dose of talent. So when times get tough and there's a risk of appearing deficient, these children would sooner lie than try harder or admit they had trouble.

"I don't care what Carol Dweck says," you say. "My children have no idea who she is, and they are doing just fine." Your spouse chimes in, "This Dweck study is a one-shot deal, and we want our children to have a long-term belief in their innate abilities." A study done by one of

Dweck's colleagues, Lisa Blackwell, might make you think otherwise. Blackwell traveled to the Life Sciences Secondary School in East Harlem.[41] Life Sciences is a health-science magnet school with high aspirations and whose seven hundred students are predominantly minority and low achieving. In an effort to improve the children's math skills, the school offered a semester-long series of classes that taught basic study skills. Half of the children also were taught that intelligence is not innate and that the brain grows when it works hard. What happened? The teachers—who were not aware of which students were assigned to which group—could pick out who had been taught that intelligence was malleable. These children also developed better study habits and increased their grades. In a single semester, Blackwell reversed the students' longtime trend of decreasing math grades. Most importantly, this was done not by teaching math, but by teaching a single idea: that the brain can change. Giving it a harder workout makes you smarter. That alone improved their math scores.

A fixed mind-set often becomes especially troubling when those who had sailed through elementary school run into subjects in middle school that require effort. Because these children believe intelligence is fixed and nothing can change that, when they start to make mistakes, they conclude they've been dumb all along. They don't try harder or study more diligently because they believe that talent alone creates success, without effort. Their grades merely are proof that they can't cut it—that they're no longer smart. In interviews, many children with fixed mind-sets confess that they have "seriously considered cheating."[42] They turn to cheating because they have no good recipe for overcoming failure. It takes only a few hits of this brick wall before they're discouraged and then depressed. Quite simply, many children at this point quit trying.

It turns out that even Roy Baumeister, the self-proclaimed self-esteem guru, is on Dweck's side of the argument. In 2003, the Association for Psychological Science asked Baumeister and others to review the more than fifteen thousand scholarly articles on self-esteem.[43] The group concluded that having high-self esteem doesn't increase children's academic performance, make people more likable, improve personal relationships, or elevate career success. It doesn't even protect children from drinking or engaging in early sex (if anything, high self-esteem may increase these behaviors). And it especially does not decrease violence of any sort. In fact, highly aggressive, violent people happen to think very well of themselves, debunking the theory that people turn to aggression to make up for low self-esteem. At the time, Baumeister was quoted as saying that his findings were "the biggest disappointment of my career."[44]

Now Baumeister is working in a similar direction as Dweck. He recently published an article showing that for college students on the verge of failing in class, esteem-building praise causes their grades to sink further. The lesson here is that all praise is not equal and, as Dweck demonstrated, the effects of praise can vary significantly, depending on the praise given. Rather than praising children for being smart, youngsters should be praised for their effort, for working hard. Rather than saying, "Look at that report card. You're so smart," you should say, "Look at that report card. You must have studied really hard." This sends the message that their smarts are under their control rather than due to unchangeable talent.

TRY AND TRY AGAIN

"It's not that I'm so smart," Albert Einstein once said, "it's just that I stay with problems longer." Einstein's statement captures well the growth mind-set that Dweck wants children to have—a solid belief that they can achieve great things through hard work and dedication. Sure, this try-and-try-again philosophy sounds awfully cliché, but there is growing evidence that it is persistence, not IQ, that's the difference between mediocrity and enormous success.

To demonstrate that persistence and effort is the key to success, psychologist Anders Ericsson wondered if he could train a regular person to carry out extraordinary feats of memory.[45] So he took an ordinary person who had an ordinary short-term memory, able to recall seven digits at a time, and got him to be able to regularly recall an astonishing eighty-plus digits. Ericsson concluded that with enough persistence, "there is seemingly no limit to memory performance."[46]

Interestingly, persistence is more than conscious perseverance; it also is driven by an unconscious response circuit in the brain. Robert Cloninger at Washington University in St. Louis and his colleagues found this circuit in a part of the brain called the orbital and medial prefrontal cortex.[47] This switch monitors the reward center of the brain and intervenes when there is a dearth of immediate reward. When it turns on, it sends the neural message, "Keep on trying—dopamine (the brain's feel-good chemical reward for success) is on the way." While looking at people's brains by way of a magnetic resonance imaging (MRI) scanner, Cloninger saw that this switch turned on regularly for some but barely at all for others.

What makes some people wired to have an active circuit? Cloninger answered this question by training rats and mice to develop persistence. He trained rats and mice in mazes to develop persistence by not rewarding them when they made it to the finish. He argued that intermittent reinforcement is the key to persistence because the brain has to work through frustrating spells and reward itself for slow and steady progress rather than the more thrilling instant gratification.

If we can marry this neurobiology with Carol Dweck's psychology in motivating students to work harder, we may actually get closer to a real recipe for greatness that could be useful to any parent, teacher, or coach. People who grow up getting too much praise—particularly fixed mind-set praise—will not have persistence because they'll quit when the rewards disappear. Collectively, this research sold me. I'd thought "praise junkie" was just an expression, but suddenly, it seemed as if I could be setting up my kids' brains for an actual chemical need for constant reward. Could I really give up praising my children so often? Me telling them that they are smart feels good to them and to me. It feels right. But leaving it up to my son and daughter to reach their own conclusions about their own intelligence is the right thing to do. Jumping in with "You're so smart, kiddo" is like jumping in too soon with the answer to a homework problem—it robs kids of the chance to figure it out for themselves.

WHAT DOES "SMART" MEAN?

But what if intelligence really isn't innate? For a long time, we've been under the impression that intelligence, or IQ, was something you were endowed with—whatever you got, you got. So it's worth looking at how this belief came about.[48] In late nineteenth-century France, psychologist Alfred Binet developed the very first IQ test as a way to measure academic skills and identify those children who were not learning as fast as they could or should. It was not designed to separate innately smart people from less innately smart people. He saw intelligence not as a thing, but as a process of acquiring certain thinking skills, and he never, ever, wrote that it was innate.

Then along came Lewis Terman, a Stanford psychologist in the early twentieth century, who proclaimed that intelligence was a certain innate quality with which each person came preloaded. Terman repackaged the IQ test and sold it to American intellectuals and policy makers as a way to separate the intellectual wheat from the idiotic chaff.

In 1979, University of Minnesota psychologist Thomas Bouchard added to the popular confusion by adopting what he thought was a method to statistically distinguish genetic influences from environmental influences. His method was to compare the level of similarity between separately raised identical twins and separately raised fraternal twins. Identical twins share 100 percent of their genetic material, whereas fraternal twins share 50 percent, so comparing these two sets of children gives you a tidy statistic. This convenient statistic, however, led to a mess when Bouchard and his colleagues published a paper that seemed to say that intelligence was 60 to 70 percent inherited and therefore mostly set in stone by our genes.[49]

But now we know better.

DOGGING THE CENTRAL DOGMA

We know better than Bouchard because since 1979, we've learned a lot more about what genes do and don't do. As we discussed in chapter 1, genes don't produce behaviors. Genes make proteins. Sometimes these proteins influence behavior, but only in the sense that they generate *tendencies* to respond to the environment in certain ways.[50]

But what about news reports that researchers have discovered a "smart" gene, or a gene for obesity, aggression, depression, or impulsivity? This is nothing more than the media overstating findings. It's true that variants of certain genes are associated with higher intelligence scores, more aggressive tendencies, or weight, but only in certain environments. Having an obesity gene does not cause obesity—eating too much and not moving around enough does.

To begin to undo the notion of genes producing behaviors, consider depression. Not everyone with a genetic disposition for depression gets it, and not everyone with depression has a genetic disposition for it. Genetic status is really not very predictive of depression, in and of itself. Even when one identical twin has depression, it is not inevitable that his or her genetic clone also suffers depression.

The fact that identical twins, who share 100 percent of their DNA, don't behave identically should tip you off to the fact that genetic influence is not about inevitability. One of the biggest clichés in psychology is to talk about how genes do different things in different environments. In fact, they don't teach you the secret handshake in graduate school until you mutter something at least twice a day about genes and environment interacting. Yet this fact rarely makes it into the popular press. *Newsweek* and *Time* have told us that scientists have discovered genes for sexual orientation, religiosity, happiness, and intelligence. But the truth of the matter is that scientists have never, nor will they ever.

If you're still not convinced, consider a study by Avshalom Caspi and his colleagues at King's College in London.[51] The group discovered that a certain gene, called 5-HTT, is linked to depression. The gene comes in two variants, and what Caspi found needs to be stated carefully. He didn't find that one variant of the gene caused depression. He didn't even find that one variant increased the risk of depression. Well, not exactly. He found that one variant of the gene greatly increased the risk of depression *only in a certain environment*. People born with the bad 5-HTT version had a higher risk of depression than those with the good version *only* if they had experienced stressful events early in life. Those who had the bad gene but a generally stress-free childhood had no higher risk of depression than those with the good 5-HTT version—which means that whether you have the good or bad 5-HTT gene isn't even a valid worry. What matters is what your version of the gene had to do with your risk of depression in a certain environment.

The moral in Caspi's work is that for human behaviors that have a genetic component, like depression, happiness, and intelligence, the environment regulates their expression. Genes clearly play a central role in human behavior—to an overwhelming extent in some cases. But if you take Caspi's findings seriously, they mean that it's important to think about how the environment you create for your children might affect even those behaviors that *Newsweek* told you were genetic.

This idea is kind of a mind-blower, and it takes some getting used to, but the bottom line is that children's behaviors are the result of a dynamic process—and we influence that process with our parenting, our teaching, our communities, and our culture. We also know from Dweck's research that intelligence is malleable, and getting children to understand that malleability is vitally important. Having an "I can improve" mind-set rather than a "some kids are just smart and others aren't" mind-set is critical to children's learning. So we need to talk about abilities like intelligence as a matter of development rather than innate ability.

GENIUS RECIPE

So, the broadly accepted view that people are born with a given intelligence or musical ear or athletic ability is flat-out wrong. Geniuses are made, not born—they are people who refine skills through extraordinary dedication and persistence. But what skills do they have? Parents want to know. One way to examine this is to look at the minds of people who have achieved enormous success for their groundbreaking ideas, like Apple's Steve Jobs, Amazon's Jeff Bezos, and eBay's Pierre Omidyar and Meg Whitman. If only we could look at the inner workings of their minds, perhaps we could discover how innovation really happens. This is exactly what Jeffrey Dyer and his colleagues did. They undertook a six-year study to cast light on the origins of creative business strategies in especially innovative companies, putting entrepreneurs under the spotlight to examine how and when they came up with their key ideas.[52] Studying the habits of twenty-five innovative entrepreneurs and surveying more than three thousand executives and five hundred people who had started innovative companies or invented new products, they discovered some patterns.

First, such people delight in asking questions that challenge the status quo—that shake things up. They spend a tremendous amount of time thinking about how to change the world, asking "What if?" "Why?" and "Why not?" and opening themselves up to new possibilities. Second, they have the ability to closely observe details; they keep their eyes and ears open, and from these observations, they can work out new ways of doing things. Third, they have an unquenchable desire to experiment and tinker with things and new ideas. Finally, they excel at associational thinking—making connections across seemingly unrelated ideas, questions, and problems or fields. They see both the forest and the trees.

How can we sum this up? One of the authors of this study, Hal Gregersen, told the *Harvard Business Review*, "You can summarize all of the skills we've noted in one word: 'inquisitiveness.' . . . It's the same kind of inquisitiveness you see in small children." Of children, he said:

> If you look at four-year-olds, they are constantly asking questions and wondering how things work. But by the time they are six-and-a-half years old they stop asking questions because they quickly learn that teachers value the right answers more than provocative questions. High school students rarely show inquisitiveness. And by the time they're grown up and are in corporate settings, they have already had the curiosity drummed out of them. Eighty percent of executives spend less than 20 percent of their time on discovering new ideas. Unless, of course, they work for a company like Apple or Google. We also believe that the most innovative entrepreneurs were very lucky to have been raised in an atmosphere where inquisitiveness was encouraged. We were stuck by the stories they told about being sustained by people who cared about experimentation and exploration. Sometimes these people were relatives, but sometimes they were neighbors, teachers or other influential adults. A number of the innovative entrepreneurs also went to Montessori schools, where they learned to follow their curiosity. To paraphrase the famous Apple ad campaign, innovators not only learned early on to think different, they act different (and even talk different).[53]

That's a heartbreaker. Why we've designed our schools to value getting the right answers rather than cultivating inquisitiveness just doesn't make sense. But there are things you can do as a parent to encourage and not squash your children's natural desire to explore—starting with understanding how inquisitiveness contributes to your child's intellectual success.

Chapter 4

Not Enough Tortoise, Too Much Hare

You've heard that forty is the new twenty, right? At least, that's what the women's magazine in my doctor's office said. But did you know that three is the new six? I didn't know either until a recent neighborhood picnic. I was sitting in my lawn chair with a plateful of melon when I spied three-year-old Tad waddling around in the sort of straddled way you do if you're either keeping balance on the high seas or have a load in your pants. I tipped off Tad's parents, and his mom took him by the hand to find a private spot for a fresh diaper. Tad's dad stuck behind to explain, with unapologetic conviction, that his son just was not developmentally ready to be potty trained. I nodded with understanding and shared that my daughter was almost four before we got her off the Pull-Ups®. But then the dad leaned in and dropped the bomb. He said that even though Tad was not potty-ready, he could read. And add. And name all of the basic two- and three-dimensional shapes. Tad could carry out these impressive feats and more because his parents drill him daily with first grade vocabulary flash cards and set him up on his learning laptop every night before bed to review Euclidian geometry.

So three is the new six. At least for children like Tad who are rushed along. But how did this happen? I thought that middle-aged moms going through divorces and dads going through midlife crises were the only ones who got away with not acting their age. Not anymore. The age shift for the younger set is captured by the term Kids Getting Older Younger (KGOY). Youth market analysts coined this initialism to describe the reality that many of today's preschoolers play with toys, electronics, and other products initially intended for preteens. Now, if you see nothing wrong with your three-year-old playing handheld Texas hold 'em, going steady with the popular guy in Mystery Date®, and spending the afternoon at the mall getting a Hannah Montana® makeover, you're not ready for this chapter just yet. But if forty is the new twenty, and three is the new six, doesn't this mean that our children soon will be older than us? Perhaps Tad can help us with the math.

So why do we treat three-year-olds like they're six? It's not our fault, but rather a side effect of a nasty disease known to laypeople as Super Baby Syndrome (SBS). Even though I don't know you, I bet you think you're immune to SBS—that only *other* people get it, and that you have none of the risk factors. After all, you exercise and eat right. But the two major risk factors are being a parent and wanting to do what's best for your children. Without these two risks, almost no one develops SBS. But if you've got both, watch out.

Symptoms of SBS include a persistent feeling that child development is a race, and thus the faster your children finish, the better. SBSers believe that the sooner children have the basics under their belts, the quicker they'll advance to more complicated material and the more successful they'll be in life.

The scary thing about SBS is that it compels its sufferers to do all sorts of odd things. To buy their babies talking frogs, quiz their toddlers with letter flash cards, enroll their preschoolers in academic learning centers, buy their kindergartners learning laptops, and sign up their elementary schoolers for summer science camps. Most get those What to Expect books to make sure their children are reaching their "developmental milestones" on time—or, better yet, early. "Aw, look, little Betsy is using her Toddlers' Guide to Feng Shui to draw up plans for her Lincoln Logs® cabin. Can you believe she's only three years old? The book says that's really early to show such obsessive-compulsive behavior."

If you have SBS, you're not alone. It is more widespread than you think. See that mom over there in the smart toy aisle, dropping the dozen AA batteries she needs to power her toddler's learning laptop as her nine-month-old gets his head caught in the arch of rattles, mirrors, and propellers that's been clipped over his stroller? She's got SBS. So does that dad rushing by in the family minivan to bring his daughter to ballet class without her new leotards, which he couldn't find in time, but will show up in a few days, stuffed into his daughter's viola case. I bet he's out of the house ferrying around his children so much that he doesn't even see the irony in being called a stay-at-home dad. And look at that poor grandmother trying to stuff a Learn 'n Jump Playaroo into her Cadillac so that little Maisy has somewhere to practice her standing while she watches her Your Baby Can Speak French DVDs.

Here's my point: once you've come down with SBS, it's a chronic, lifelong condition. It follows a predictable course, with its symptoms most pronounced while your children are still living in your house. Once they go off to college, SBS usually goes into remission. It can, however, flare up again if you have grandchildren.

I got hit with SBS when I was pregnant with my first child. With the help of my family, I was able to keep my SBS in check for quite some time. That is, until I had a particularly nasty relapse when my daughter was a little less than a year old. A neighbor had asked if we'd like to join a mommy-and-me playgroup that met weekly in her house. I agreed, even though I was well aware that babies really don't play; they just suck on their pacifiers and drool. Nonetheless, when we arrived at our first get-together, I plunked my daughter, Isabella, down on the carpet in the middle of a bunch of other babies, handed her a board book, and popped open a plastic container of Goldfish crackers. She gurgled and grabbed a fistful of crackers. Suddenly, ten-month-old Ben waddled over to his mother and wailed, "*My* book!" "Yes, Ben," said his mom, "That is your book. But let Isabella see it, OK?" Meanwhile, Isabella, oblivious to Ben's apparent grandstanding, was babbling some gibberish and pointing to the soppy Goldfish leaking out of the side of her mouth. Ben said, "Yes, Mama," and in snuck a nagging worry that my daughter had fallen behind the crowd. That I had to do something before it was too late. And that Baby Einstein might not be so bad after all. At this point I was sure a blinking neon SBS sign had appeared above my head, so I stopped trying to fight the flare-up and just went with it. That is, until I saw the flash of boredom that bloomed across my daughter's face the third time I flipped through the pack of nature discovery cards—the ones with pictures of things like clouds, grass, and leaves. So I took her hand and walked her outside. I plunked her down in the middle of some real grass under some real clouds, she crinkled some real leaves, and I really tried not to be too angry at myself for wasting my money on a product clearly designed to flimflam cash from hapless SBS sufferers.

I relapsed with my second child, Dominic. Right around the time of his third birthday, I couldn't stop signing him up for just one more summer enrichment activity, and I started lying about the numbers of educational video games I had purchased online. I hit rock bottom when my husband found my stash of math flash cards in the minivan glove box.

If there's a positive side to being a recovering SBSer, it's the sympathy I've developed for other sufferers. I try to quiet my inner judge when I encounter someone making a parenting choice that is different from what I would do. I try not to feel smug about my parenting style—that I'm a better mother somehow than the harried ones I see rushing to sign up their kids for after-school math tutoring as they're on their way to their Saturday morning karate classes and jazz dance lessons. Rather, I assume positive intent in everyone's teaching and everyone's parenting. At the core of it, we all want the best for our children.

Just as it should, SBS is gaining recognition as a serious illness. I'm sure it's just a matter of time before we get our own ribbon or minivan magnet to raise awareness. When we do, it'll simply say, "Childhood is not a race." And our celebrity spokesperson will spread the scientifically sound message that children who reach their developmental milestones quickly are no better off than those who ease into them. She'll tell families what developmental psychologists have known for decades: that trying to rush children into adults is about as good an idea as trying to rush unripe tomatoes into mature fruit. Neither will do anyone any good.

BUILDING BLOCKS AND BUILDING RÉSUMÉS

All of us have fallen prey to this mentality to some degree. We compare our children endlessly to others. I do it all the time. There's the eighth grader down the street who is spending the summer in Guatemala building houses for Habitat for Humanity. And the homeschooler who makes backpacks for the homeless out of recycled soda cans. And the ten-year-old chemist who developed an adhesive in her garage that the science fair judges say will revolutionize the waterproof bandage. How do my kids stand any chance? My seven-year-old still needs help tying his shoes, and my eleven-year-old still can't cut her own fingernails.

My generation of parents has been swept up in a flurry of assumptions about how to raise and educate our children. The media tell us that faster is better and that we should push learning along at a rapid pace. These assumptions about children and how they learn have propelled my generation of parents into the grip of marketers—marketers who have sensed these pressures on parents and have been happy to develop products designed to help. Products that they say boost brain development and are going to give our children a head start. And we're suckers for the message they're selling because we all want to do everything we can for our children and set them up with every opportunity to get ahead.

All concerned parents have the best of good intentions. That goes without saying. Life *is* competitive. There *are* more children than spots in Harvard. And we've all heard the warnings that in our downsizing and outsourcing economy, our children might very well be the very first generation of Americans that is worse off financially than its parents.[1] But the thing to keep in mind is that the goal of marketers is to get our attention and make us buy more of what they're selling, not to accurately inform us about child development.

Parents' focus on boosting their children's brains to the exclusion of other organs is understandable. A superior colon will get you only so far in life. Good skin might get you on the cheerleading squad, but it probably won't get you into Princeton. But a better brain—now that's the golden ticket to all things in life. And frankly, that's why the brain is the only organ to get its own decade.

The U.S. Congress officially designated the 1990s the Decade of the Brain. President George H. W. Bush proclaimed, "A new era of discovery is dawning in brain research."[2] Media coverage of brain development boomed, boosting the public's interest in the effects of early experience on this already interesting organ.[3] There was a Pulitzer Prize–winning series of articles on brain research by *Chicago Tribune* writer Ronald Kotulak, a Carnegie Corporation report titled "Starting Points: Meeting the Needs of Our Youngest Children," and a massive public information campaign coordinated by Rob Reiner's I Am Your Child Foundation. The campaign included a White House conference on early child development, a special issue of *Newsweek* (with an essay by Hillary Clinton on "Doing the Best for Our Kids"), a weeklong series of segments on *Today* and *Good Morning America*, and the distribution of more than eight million copies of a parenting video.

This media attention effectively moved many science findings concerning early brain growth out of the laboratory and into the living room. Families and teachers were told that the first three years of life are a special time of both neural opportunity and vulnerability, that brain growth doesn't follow an automatic genetic blueprint, and that parents and teachers matter. These sound bites were solid, but the media generally ignored less splashy but not necessarily less important findings. No one heard much about the significant brain growth that happens after age three, that the brain continues to reshape parts of itself across the life span, and that even old people can learn certain new tricks.

More worrisome than the exclusion of certain pieces of the story of brain development are media accounts that exaggerate and overstate what is known. Let's face it: "Let your kids play with blocks and they'll turn out swell" lacks the punch and glamour of "Scientific ways to make your child smarter." Some media accounts have overpromised applications of new scientific knowledge; others have generalized from existing knowledge to issues that had not yet been or could not be studied; and some have been flat-out wrong, like when Rob Reiner, speaking to the National Governor's Association in 1997, said, "We now know through science that the first three years of life is the most critical time period . . . but by age ten your brain is cooked and there's nothing much you can do."[4] Not only has the public ended up with a set of myths about the developing brain, but researchers worry that parents, teachers, and policy makers may lose interest in applications of brain science if the currently advertised products and practices do not result in the super brains that the media promises. Parents like guarantees. But if they do all the things the evening news and *Parents.com* tell them to do and their children still don't get into Yale (or a child from the most awful parents turns out fine), confidence in the brain sciences may erode.

Marketers also have exploited exciting findings of early brain development to sell billions of dollars' worth of educational toys and programs.[5] We'll get to some of these products later in this chapter and throughout the book. The problem is that the repackaging of data often leads to promises that go way beyond the conclusions made by the scientists who conducted the research. There are countless products on the shelf that say they are scientifically proven to build better brains when in fact they have absolutely no basis in science. This marketing is appalling to us in the research community because we are well aware that no brand of baby toy or program has ever been demonstrated to make superior brains. Yet the marketing is so persuasive that well-intentioned parents (through no fault of their own) buy all sorts of goods and services in the hope that the promises on the packaging hold some grain of truth. The fact is, children not only don't need most of these goods and services, but some of them may be harmful to developing brains. Once you understand what types of stimulation brains really need to develop, you will see why so many of these products are nothing but smoke and mirrors.

No doubt there still are some readers out there who believe marketers can't make misleading promises. They are correct in thinking that the Marlboro Man cannot say that smoking is good for your health, and the Hamburglar® cannot tell parents that Happy Meals® reduce the risk of childhood obesity. It's the law that advertisers must tell the truth and not mislead consumers. But if you're a company that makes baby products, it's pretty hard to make money if you tell parents that your products really are unnecessary and sometimes even harmful.

Let me give you one heartbreaking example that'll shake your faith in product packaging. The risk of Sudden Infant Death Syndrome (SIDS)—the leading cause of death in infants between one month and one year of age—is reduced by placing babies to sleep on their backs on a firm surface. In 1994, the National Institute of Child Health and Human Development and others launched a public information campaign known as "Back to Sleep" that recommended that caregivers place infants to sleep on their backs on a firm surface and avoid using soft objects like pillows, blankets, stuffed toys, and crib bumpers. The campaign has been wonderfully effective. The number of infants placed on their backs to sleep has increased dramatically, and overall SIDS rates have declined by more than 50 percent.[6]

Now here's where slimy marketing comes in. Capitalizing on the "Back to Sleep" recommendation, several companies developed what are known as infant sleep positioners. These "safety devices" are essentially soft-taco forms with foamy sides that you fill with a back-lying baby. The sides are meant to prevent infants from rolling over and are marketed as an invention that increases sleeping safety. First Years™' Airflow Infant

Sleep Positioner says it keeps "baby safe and comfortable throughout the night." The DexBaby™ Sleep Positioner says it's "designed to cradle a baby on its back as recommended by the American Academy of Pediatrics and the Surgeon General." And the Safe Lift™ Deluxe Crib Wedge says it is "doctor approved for providing your baby with a safe and comfortable night's sleep. The gentle angle elevates your baby's head for easier breathing and better digestion. Now baby can breathe easier! Promote the proper sleeping position recommended by most pediatricians with the Safe Lift Deluxe." The Basic Comfort™ Supreme Infant Sleep Positioner is so great that it received the iParenting Media Award.[7]

These medical-sounding claims are enough to make one believe that these devices can keep babies safe while they sleep. But the reality is that the Food and Drug Administration has never cleared any positioner for safer sleeping. And they never will—there is no scientific evidence that positioners benefit sleep, but there is evidence that they can be very dangerous. So much so that in 2010, the Consumer Product Safety Commission and the Food and Drug Administration distributed a press release that warned parents to stop using infant sleep positioners.[8] What could be so bad about a spongy truss that holds babies firmly in the recommended sleeping position? Everything. Positioners increase the risk of death while sleeping because infants can suffocate if they roll onto their stomachs or become trapped between the positioner and the side of their crib or bassinet. Since 1987, thirteen infants between the ages of one and four months have died from suffocation associated with sleep positioners. The lesson here is that you shouldn't trust anyone who says their gadget has been proven scientifically to be good for your children. Do your research. Watch your wallet. And read on. I'll tell you the facts you need to know about brain development, and I'll save you a bunch of money along the way.

BRAIN SHAMS

As I shared in chapter 2, my favorite brain improvement sham product is the BabyPlus Prenatal Education System. I have a special affinity for it because it is the near-perfect example of a product that uses fake science to sell smoke and mirrors to well-meaning but ill-informed parents. No study has ever been published in a peer-reviewed journal that demonstrates that this product—or any other commercial product—does anything to improve brain development during the fetal period. Nor would we expect this. The very best feature of the womb, from the fetus's point of view, is its *lack* of stimulation. The womb has been designed by millions of years of evolution to be dark, warm, and muted. If there were some advantage to a noisy womb, women would have evolved some sort of abdominal stereo jack to plug in sounds from the outside world. But women haven't because it's best to leave the fetus alone. It is busy churning out thousands of new brain cells every second, and the last thing it wants is to be bothered by Mom and Dad. Besides, the brain isn't even hooked up to the ears until midway through pregnancy.

If what I have pointed out is true, then why is the BabyPlus such a success? It is a commercial success because most pregnant women don't consult developmental neuroscience journals before registering for baby shower gifts. Instead, they are more likely to know that famous mothers like Gwen Stefani, Nicole Richie, and Trista (the Bachelorette) Sutter used the BabyPlus.[9] Or to have heard about it on *The Rachael Ray Show* or *The View*, or to have read about it in *Pregnancy* magazine or on the website Hot Moms Club. Or to have seen its blue-and-white box adorned with an "Award of Excellence" sticker from the Toy Man®. It's all very persuasive. If you want to see for yourself, click on to BabyPlus.com.[10] Go ahead. I'll wait. I just logged on and saw pregnant Olympic gold medalist Shannon Miller sporting a BabyPlus and promising that its prenatal curriculum gives children "an intellectual, developmental, creative, and emotional advantage from the time they are born." How could she possibly know that? Well, she "knows" it because there are a slew of testimonials saying just that from professionals who seem like they know what they're doing. Like Rene Van de Carr, medical doctor and author of *While You Are Expecting*, who says, "For their child's lifetime development, every parent should hear about this discovery, an innovation representing the single most significant step science has taken toward increasing infant potential."[11] That's major. And if you're expecting when you read this, you're missing "the single most significant step science has taken toward increasing infant potential" if you don't immediately run out and buy one.

The feeling you get in your gut from Van de Carr's appraisal of the BabyPlus is exactly why this device shows up on pregnant bellies everywhere despite the complete absence of science supporting it. It's because anecdotes are persuasive. Let me demonstrate this point by a study of condom choice. Social psychologist Timothy Wilson gave University of Virginia college students two sources of information about two brands of condom: Brand A and Brand B.[12] The students read the results of a large scientific study that demonstrated that Brand A was far more effective than Brand B. Then they heard a single anecdote from a fellow student who recommended Brand B because his Brand A condom had burst in the middle of Saturday night's hanky-panky, which, of course, caused some stress about a possible pregnancy. Most students agreed that, generally, a scientific study is a more reliable source of information than a single person's anecdote. But when asked which condom they'd choose for themselves, nearly a third of them were persuaded by the anecdote and went with Brand B. This is even though the scientific evidence showed that Brand A was far more effective. These are the sorts of findings that make researchers throw up their hands, shake their heads, and mutter a collective "Why do we bother?" because they demonstrate that people are more likely to listen to Shannon Miller than a bunch of scientists.

But it's not just one doctor spouting the success of BabyPlus; there are countless moms and dads who say, hands down, it works.[13] How can the experiences of so many people be at odds with science? Let's break this down. First, there's Kathy Corsi, a teacher who began using BabyPlus at the recommended eighteen weeks gestation, who says, "I just love your BabyPlus! I would recommend it to anyone! My son . . . is now sixteen months old and has more than fifty words in vocabulary, listens intently, [and] watches lips. . . . I credit half of this development to BabyPlus!!" This sounds impressive until I tell you that the *average* sixteen-month-old knows more than sixty words (so ten-ish more than Baby Corsi).[14] And listening intently and watching lips are typical first-year baby behavior. There is nothing special happening here. What we have is a mom unknowingly gushing about how her BabyPlus baby is, er, normal.

What about testimonials of faster-than-typical development? Like the one that says, "Our daughter . . . has reached all of her developmental and motor milestones on an average of 3 months earlier than expected and always a lot sooner than her peers," or the one that says, "We were delighted (but not surprised), to find that both babies had already hit their one month developmental milestones by their first week pediatrician appointment."[15] These babies are ahead of the curve. But *why*? Their advancement might be due to the BabyPlus, but it also might be due to something else that has nothing to do with the sounds that their mothers piped in during pregnancy. The most likely explanation is that parents who invest in things like prenatal learning systems also do other things after birth that really do boost early development. If this is the case, then why give BabyPlus the credit? Because as soon as you shell out one hundred fifty dollars for a belly pack that you cinch on twice a day, there's a certain incentive for you to think that your efforts somehow turned your child into a genius. What we have here is one big fat placebo effect. A mother uses the BabyPlus, and her baby turns out swell—and so it's easy for her to attribute her baby's swellness to the expensive prenatal learning device.

The only way to know if BabyPlus really improves babies is to randomly assign some mothers to use the system and others to refrain. Then compare the two groups at various times after birth. You wouldn't want to give your children a medication that wasn't tested in this typical fashion—even if there were scores of web testimonials touting its effectiveness: "My husband and I were thrilled that our twins were much more alert and energetic than the rest of the babies in the hospital nursery. The other babies mostly lay in their basinets and slept. But ours constantly giggled and smiled. We highly recommend all parents give their newborns crystal meth from the get-go."

If, however, you are one of those parents who have felt all along that BabyPlus was a sham, you might be thinking, "What is Kathy Corsi thinking? Her brain and the rest of those snowed by BabyPlus advertisements must work differently from logical minds like mine." Well, you might be right. There is increasing evidence that your brain functions differently once you've decided that something works. Consider a study carried out by Uffe Schjoedt at Aarhus University in Denmark. Schjoedt had strongly religious Christians (mostly from Pentecostal congregations) and nonreligious people listen to speeches made by three groups of people: non-Christians, "ordinary" Christians, or Christians who believed they had healing powers.[16] Importantly, the Christian listeners believed in the existence of particular individuals on whom God had bestowed special healing powers, but the non-Christian participants did not. While the two groups listened to the speeches, they stretched out in functional magnetic resonance imaging (MRI) scanners equipped with big magnets that measure neural activity. Among the nonreligious people, Schjoedt found no differences in brain activity no matter what they listened to. Among the Christians, Schjoedt found that when they were listening to the words of Christians who claimed to have healing powers, they had a massive deactivation in certain brain areas. The biggest decreases were in parts of the brain known as the frontal executive network and the social cognitive network. The former is a complex set of neural structures known to be involved in high-level organization, assessment, and analysis of information. The latter is essential for perceiving and understanding others' affects and intentions. In other words, when religious subjects listened to Christians, they turned down the logical parts of their brains and effectively handed them over to someone else. Most fascinating of all, Schjoedt points out that similar alterations in brain activity have previously been observed in people undergoing hypnosis. The point here is not that atheists think more clearheadedly, but that one's preexisting beliefs in something can interfere with the brain's ability to process and judge information about that something. So if you believe in the power of BabyPlus, and you go to the website and read the barrage of testimonials from celebrities and caring moms who say this product works, then you've put the logical parts of your brain at risk for malfunctioning like those of Schjoedt's believers. This is my fair warning that visiting the BabyPlus website may cause you to buy a prenatal education system, only to later ask yourself, "What was I thinking?"

THE MYTH OF THE MOZART EFFECT

Now that you know that the BabyPlus is a sham, perhaps you're thinking, "Not the Blaby too?[17] The Blaby is different. Better, in fact. You can record yourself reading *Goodnight Moon* or transfer songs from your iTunes® playlist. Surely some Bob Marley is better for the brain than those BabyPlus remixes of a human heartbeat." As you upload your Margaret Wise Brown soliloquy onto your Blaby, you know better than to heed the concern you read on BabyPlus.com that "the spoken word is too difficult for the developing child to understand and music is too complex."[18] But as you talk about the "great green room," you wonder if you really need this belt to pipe your story into your belly because there's plenty of evidence that fetuses can hear their mothers' voices just fine.[19]

Geof Ramsay, designer of the Blaby Music Belt, explains his motivation for developing this product: "We wanted to let the mothers record their own lullaby, so you can record anything you want on the belt, or simply play pre-recorded music."[20] Ramsay wants to market the Blaby to mothers who think playing music—particularly classical music—can crank up children's intelligence. His idea is based on a phenomenon known as the Mozart effect. The popular version of this effect is that "Mozart makes children smarter"—but this has never ever been demonstrated by anyone. The Mozart effect got its start in a 1993 paper in noted science magazine *Nature* by Frances Rauscher and her colleagues at the University of Wisconsin's Oshkosh campus.[21] They found that college students who listened for eight minutes and twenty-four seconds to the first movement, "Allegro con spirito," of Mozart's Sonata KV 448 for Two Pianos in D major scored eight to nine points higher on a small portion of the Stanford-Binet intelligence test—one that measured spatial-reasoning ability by way of a paper-folding task—than those who were instructed to relax or those who just sat there in silence. Mind you, Rauscher did not administer a full-blown IQ test to achieve a proper measure of general intelligence—but merely a paper folding task. So there you have it—Rauscher and colleagues found that Mozart temporarily improved the spatial intelligence scores of college-aged students. This is not even close to the same as showing that listening to Mozart increases intelligence in children.

How, then, did we get from Rauscher's modest finding to the idea that "Mozart makes children smarter?" The media and marketers. A 2004 Stanford study tracked the media's coverage of Rauscher's study relative to other studies published in *Nature* around the same time period. In America's top fifty newspapers, Rauscher's paper was cited 8.3 times more often than the second-most popular paper.[22] For the past fifteen years, this idea has been turned into hundreds of products such as CDs, DVDs, and toys, and promoted in books like Don Campbell's book *The Mozart Effect: Tapping the Power of Music to Heal the Body, Strengthen the Mind, and Unlock the Creative Spirit* and CDs for sale at www.mozarteffect.com. On his website, Campbell claims that "playing music early in life helps build the neural pathways that allow language, memory, and spatial development to take place," and that his eleven-dollar CD *The Mozart Effect Music for Children, Vol. 1, Tune Up Your Mind* "increases verbal, emotional, and spatial intelligence; improves memory and the ability to concentrate; enhances 'right-brain' creative processes; and strengthens intuitive thinking skills."[23] There's also the best-selling Baroque-A-Bye Baby® CD, whose makers claim that "slow Baroque music—60 beats per min.—same as mother's heartbeat, has a calming effect on babies, while its mathematical perfection and symmetry will stimulate your child's brain."[24] In 1998, Georgia's governor mandated that the parents of each newborn in the state be given classical music CDs.[25] In Florida, state-run child-care centers were required to pipe symphonies through their sound systems.[26]

Had anyone been paying attention to the scientific literature, they would have known that in 1999, Rauscher's findings were officially refuted. The authors of reports in two top scientific journals—*Nature* and *Psychological Science*—could not reproduce Rauscher's findings.[27] And in a recent summary of follow-up studies, researchers at the University of Vienna performed a meta-analysis of nearly forty studies and found no evidence that listening to Mozart's music "enhanced" cognitive abilities or IQ in any way.[28] Raucher herself said, "I would simply say that there is no compelling evidence that children who listen to classical music are going to have any improvement in cognitive abilities. It's really a myth, in my humble opinion."[29]

This doesn't mean you should throw out your classical music CDs and DVDs. It just means you shouldn't expect that Mozart (or any other music) will make your children's brains grow in ways that make them smarter. But what you might want to know is that there is evidence that listening to music, especially music that makes us feel good, does have beneficial effects, at least temporarily. There is even research showing that listening to music that makes us happy can also make everyone *around us* look happy.[30] These results suggest that the basis of Rauscher's original effect was the good mood induced by music, rather than the music itself. For a long time now, developmental psychologists have been pulling their hair out trying to convince parents that listening to Mozart does not guarantee genius or even increase the chances of genius.

YOUR BABY CAN MEMORIZE

In July1993, the cover of *Life* magazine announced, "Babies are smarter than you think. They can add." Inside, the article claimed that infants as young as five months not only could add, they also could subtract.[31] Very cool findings—unless you have a twelve-month-old who can't even count to three. Because if five-month-olds can add and your twelve-month-old can't even count, your child must be way behind, right? So what do you do? Many a parent would run out to the mall to buy a box of those dot-patterned flash cards that say they can teach babies to do math. In the eyes of some, flash cards are a must-have, if you want to boost your baby's brain.

No doubt that with some daily practice with a deck of Baby Pythagoras, your little Einstein would learn her numbers. But what the cards don't tell you is that identifying numbers on them is not really counting, nor is calling out "four" in response to the "2 + 2" card you've seen for the eightieth time. This is what cognitive psychologists call paired-associate learning—which might sound more impressive than "counting" and "adding" until I tell you that even a pigeon can be taught to do it.[32]

How could your child give the right answer to two plus two and not know how to add? There's a famous turn-of-the-century story about a horse named Clever Hans that was considered clever because he seem-ingly could add and subtract.[33] When Hans's owner would give him a math problem—say, six minus two—he would tap out the correct answer with his hoof. Hans answered without error to all sorts of questions— that is, until psychologist Oskar Pfungst blindfolded him. It turns out that when the horse couldn't see its owner, it couldn't figure out the answer. Why not? Pfungst discovered that rather than doing math, Hans was responding to unwitting nonverbal signals from its owner. When-ever Hans got to the right answer, the trainer would stand straight up, and Hans learned to interpret this behavior as "stop tapping." Hans's real skill was in reading the nonverbal cues of its owner, but the horse knew nothing of math.

Like Clever Hans, children can learn to give correct answers without really understanding. They might know, for example, that a certain symbol on the flash card you're showing them is a three, but that doesn't mean that they know that three is more than two and less than five. They might mem-orize that "six" is the right answer for "three plus three" the same way they memorize that "yellow" is the name for a certain color and that "foot" is the name for a certain body part. So even when they can tell you that the "three plus three" flash card equals "six," it's not at all necessary for them to under-stand what any of these numbers really mean.

Another popular product that disguises paired-associate learning as something else is Your Baby Can Read. *Creative Child* magazine awarded this product the 2010 "Media of the Year Award," and the Tillywig Toy Awards Program gave it a 2010 "Brain Child Award."[34] Tillywig wouldn't give a product an award if it was a scam, would it? What we really have here is a product that should be named "Your Baby Can Memorize." Most of the early readers taught by this program aren't reading at all. Rather, they're demonstrating that they've memorized lots of words by sight. Here's what you'd see if you slipped in one of these videos. First, you see a picture of something—say, a dog—over and over and over. Then you see the word printed out under the picture so that you learn to associate that letter sequence (d-o-g) with that picture. Then the picture goes away and the word is repeated a few more times. This is repeated for every word you are "taught." What ends up happening is that instead of understanding that each letter in each word has both its own name and its own sound or group of sounds, you—like our early ancestors—see each word as a whole symbol for each object or action you're taught. So if you take a child who has learned to "read" with the program and change "dog" to "dot," she's likely to think it still means man's best friend until she memorizes that "dot" means something completely different from "dog."

If you really want your youngster to "read" in the Your Baby Can Read style so that you can show her off at dinner parties and save yourself some money, just read the age-appropriate books you already have on hand over and over and over to your baby, and your baby will "read." She'll be able to "read" these books because she'll have memorized the letter sequences, and she'll be able to pick out these same sequences in advertisements and signs and other books. Your guests will be so mesmerized that they'll never realize she isn't really reading.

But even if Your Baby Can Read doesn't teach reading, what are we to make of Dr. Robert Titzer's claims at the Your Baby Can Read website that "the current practice of starting to teach reading skills in school is too late and children benefit greatly from getting a much earlier start since a child basically has only one natural window for learning language—from birth to age four."[35] Maybe Titzer is right because his website says that his research has been published in scientific journals, including "the prestigious *Psychological Review*." That sounds impressive until you look up Titzer's publications (he has two) and see that neither has anything even remotely to do with reading.[36] Or until you learn that the consumer watchdog group Campaign for a Commercial-Free Childhood recently filed a complaint with the Federal Trade Commission alleging that Your Baby Can Read uses deceptive marketing to get parents to buy its videos, flash cards, and other materials.[37]

"So what?" you say. "What harm could encouraging your children to read at a young age do?" I say: what harm is there in starting later? In Denmark, where formal teaching of reading and writing in kindergarten is prohibited by law, literacy rates are higher than in the United States. So starting later doesn't seem to reduce overall literacy.[38] Why would it? You're able to read this book, and your parents didn't use Your Baby Can Read on you. As it happens, a handful of studies have shown that not only do the initial advances evidenced by early readers wash out a few years down the line, but early readers often face reading difficulties as their reading skills progress. Illinois educator Carleton Washburne compared the reading development of children who started reading at several different ages, up to age seven, and found that children do best when they begin to learn to read around age six and not before.[39] Even though children who learned how to read at young ages had an early edge in reading level, by middle school, the differences between children who started early and those who started later disappeared. However—and this is a very important point—those children who started young were less motivated and less excited about reading than those who began later. More recent research also raises doubts about the push for early readers. A cross-cultural study of European children shows that boys and girls taught to read at age five had more difficulties than those who were taught at age seven.[40]

But how can learning later be better if we want to give our children a head start? Later is better when it comes to reading because reading is a difficult task. As Maryanne Wolf, the director of Tufts University's Center for Reading and Language Research, puts it, learning to read is nothing short of a miracle because it is a complex process that involves building an extraordinary number of new connections among various spatially segregated regions of the brain.[41] This includes areas that control attention; memory; and visual, auditory, linguistic, and conceptual activity. Building these pathways simply takes a lot of time. For fluent reading, neural impulses must flow smoothly and quickly throughout the brain. For this to happen, brain cells first must wrap themselves in a sheath of what's known as myelin, or a sausage-shaped layer of dense fat tissue that wraps around the axon. Myelin works to speed up information transmission in much the same way that rubber insulation works on a wire—it keeps the signal strong by preventing electrical impulses from leaking out.

Myelin is the secret sauce for developing complex skills like turning the small black squiggly lines on this piece of paper into a meaningful story without even being conscious you're doing it. Basically, your little sausages of myelin get thicker when the associated brain cells are repeatedly stimulated. The thicker the myelin gets, the better it insulates the neuron, and the faster and more accurately signals travel across the brain.[42]

Brain imaging data show that most areas of the brain needed for reading are not myelinated at mature levels until somewhere between the ages of five and seven, with boys usually coming in a bit behind girls. This is why it takes so long to learn complex skills like reading, and it is why, in most places across the world, training in reading is not begun until five to seven years of age. Teaching children to read before this time is potentially counterproductive. Some researchers argue that these findings demonstrate why pushing literacy too soon can be harmful. Lilian Katz, a professor emerita of education at the University of Illinois at Urbana-Champaign, says, "It can be seriously damaging for children who see themselves as inept at reading too early,"[43] Many in education hold the opinion that forcing children to read too early may actually cause a learning disability. The brain is not ready, and forcing may do damage. When we try to teach younger children to read, we are asking them to do something for which their brains simply are not ready.

NATURALLY SPEAKING

Some of you who are reading this are still not convinced. You've got a nagging feeling that Your Baby Can Read's Titzer might be right when he says that "the best and easiest time to learn a language is during the infant and toddler years, when the brain is creating thousands of synapses every second—allowing a child to learn both the written word and spoken word simultaneously, and with great ease."[44] Here, the good doctor has confused language learning with reading learning. Learning how to speak and learning how to read are two different skills. Lots of people can speak and understand others just fine, but they have no idea how to read. Language is something that comes naturally, just by way of vicarious exposure to other people who speak it. This is not the case with reading. Reading is not exactly natural—we invented it only a few thousand years ago.

Language is natural? It doesn't need to be directly taught? Without structured language lessons, many parents are convinced that their children will be left behind. They may believe that their kids are already behind that two-year-old down the street who drops the words "quiescent" and "melancholic" when she's pretending in the sandbox, and the three-year-old in their playgroup who orders takeout for his parents in Chinese.

You want your children to be accelerated, too. What can you do? A quick trip to KidSmart® tells you there are scores of language-learning computer programs, DVDs, and drills. Yet even though these products are marketed as educational programs that boost language acquisition, they really don't. If anything, they slow it down. There's increasing evidence that interventions like computer programs and DVDs hinder rather than help language development.

Babies and young children don't benefit from artificial means of learning language. They've been designed to learn language through social interaction.[45] They need to hear fleshy people engaged in meaty conversations to learn language. Real people in real social contexts, not DVDs, motivate young language learners to express their needs, thoughts, and feelings. A talking television set isn't motivation enough to jump into a conversation on the screen and ask for something—a book to read or a hand to hold. And even though computer programs are built to interact with users, these programs cannot mirror the finely tuned way real humans interact. They don't pause long enough or they pause too long before giving a response or asking a new question. Nor do they adapt when children try to drive the conversation. No matter how hard Mollie tries to get her computer to talk about the yellow finch that just landed on the bird feeder in her backyard, her computer is going to persist in continuing the conversation about the pineapple. Real people, however, can steer the conversation in whatever direction children want to go. They can work to keep the youngest of conversational partners, those who don't even talk yet, to hang in there and take their turn.

Here's how we know. The University of Delaware's Roberta Golinkoff filmed families at mealtime and found that babies as young as eleven months will hang in there for an average of eleven conversational turns to get across that they'd like some applesauce and not some carrots. Or that they're pointing and babbling at the Barcalounger® not because they want to sit in it, but because they want you to get the Super Ball that's squeezed underneath it. Such back-and-forths are where word learning occurs, as parents struggle to figure out the exact word that their baby wants to hear.[46] As parents cycle through the alternatives to zero in on what the baby wants, infants hear many words over and over again. "That's the chair. That's Daddy's chair. Your daddy's brown chair. You want to sit on Daddy's chair? You want Rover to get off the chair? Take a hike, Rover. Look at that, Rover was laying on the remote. You want the remote? No remote with those applesaucey hands. Daddy left his slippers under the chair. You want to wear Daddy's slippers? Let's get Daddy's slippers. Oh, look at that—there's a ball under the chair. You want the ball? It's your brother's yellow ball." If babies weren't rewarded with the actual ball they've been gesturing at, they wouldn't be motivated to try eleven times to learn the word "ball." Real-world motivation and rewards is exactly why no DVD, computer program, or educational toy could ever be superior to the everyday verbal interactions that go on between babies and other people.

One of my favorite demonstrations of just how motivated children are to learn to communicate with others comes from Susan Goldin-Meadow and her colleagues at the University of Chicago.[47] Goldin-Meadow had a sample of hearing parents who wanted their deaf children to learn lipreading and speech. These parents didn't want their children to pick up the crutch of sign language (from their perspective), so they refused sign language training and didn't sign themselves. What Goldin-Meadow observed was remarkable. The children, on their own and without any outside help, had spontaneously invented a gestural language to communicate with one another. Surely it was not as rich as a conventional sign language system, but it's clear evidence that if you put children in a natural social context, language emerges naturally.

There's also overwhelming evidence that efforts to formally teach language are superfluous. Language emerges naturally so long as the developing brain is exposed to the everyday conversational interaction it expects. Language simply occurs as a natural byproduct of hearing language or, as in the case of the deaf children above, being exposed to communication situations. A fantastic example of this comes from a study in which researchers dropped American nine-month-olds into the same room as Chinese speakers.[48] Can you guess what happened? The infants immediately were able to distinguish sounds in Chinese. The implication of these sorts of studies is that all we need to do to foster language acquisition is simply talk with our children and keep the conversation going. We don't need to do anything artificial or extreme.

KINDERCRAMMING

Did your parents send you to preschool? Mine did. I went for a couple of hours twice a week in a dingy church basement. Just long enough for my mom to pick up some groceries and for me to share some blocks and bacteria with my people my own size. At least, I think that's what happened. I don't exactly remember going to preschool. But I'm sure I did because I've seen the pictures of four-year-old me in my matching orange orangutan Garanimals® T-shirt and skort set, playing four square with my classmates out in the parking lot.

In all the old, faded photos, I look like I'm having a lot of fun. Though I can't help but notice that my preschool looks bleak compared to the jam-packed classrooms I see today. Did my parents send me to a low-budget program because they didn't expect much out of me? I don't think so; no one in my grade school group went to one of those souped-up preschools. Yet we all still managed to grow up and become successful adults.

But perhaps all of us could have achieved much more had we gone to better preschools. I almost think this when I look at advertisements for preschools in my area. "Watch your child develop into a happy, confident learner—ready for lifelong success." But doesn't that seem like a lot to expect from a bin of blocks and some crayons? "Our well-rounded schools are designed to reveal your child's full learning potential." Don't most parents just want their preschoolers to learn how to make friends and take turns? "Your child has ample access to computers, becoming familiar with the necessary skills to move to the next technological level." Technological skills? How about they learn how to use scissors first? "Children are placed into three classrooms according to ability." What abilities are they talking about? Who's best at swiping toys from their classmates? "Music appreciation, art history, foreign language, and world cultures are incorporated into your child's lesson plans." All I wanted for my daughter when I enrolled her in preschool was for her to learn that "elemeno" was not the letter of the alphabet between "k" and "p." When I see these signs, I wonder if the people who run preschools have gone completely mad. We're talking about three- to five-year-olds here, right? When we were preschoolers, we were happy as pie to spend our couple of hours finger painting, stacking blocks, doing puzzles, and playing tag. Imagine how you might have felt back then if someone took away your crayons, glitter, and glue stick and asked if you'd like to sit quietly at your table and do your language arts worksheet.

Of course, preschools advertise this way because no parent would sign up for a program that tells it like it is. "We'll keep your kid busy for two hours with some homemade Play-Doh so you can go home and shower in peace for a change." "Your kids will have a ball playing with our bins of donated toys, but we can't guarantee that they won't someday be flipping burgers at Dairy Queen." "Not one of our alumni has won a Rhodes Scholarship or a Nobel Prize." Surveys show that parents are increasingly demanding "academic" preschool content. In a recent paper in the *American School Board Journal*, one preschool director said about parents, "They agree in theory that play is important, but they say, 'Could you just throw in the worksheets so I can see what they are learning?'"[49] The focus on academics is so intense in some classrooms that teachers have taken away some of the usual staples of preschool, like dress-up areas and blocks.

There is also evidence that children are playing less in preschool. One compelling example comes from three studies that examined the prevalence of social pretend play in low-income community-based child-care centers from 1982 to 2002.[50] During this period, social pretend play for four-and-a-half-year-olds dropped from 41 percent to only 9 percent of the observed time. The irony of this drop is that play is a central means of learning.

Play is a means of learning? "Play is certainly fun," you say, "but children learn from direct lessons, books, and worksheets, not from pretending that they are housewives or cowboys." Not true. Young children show more advanced language skills when playing than in any other context. New words embedded in playful contexts are learned better and faster than words picked up outside of play.[51] This happens because when young children are given the freedom to play, they naturally incorporate rich literacy materials, like storybooks and writing materials, into their pretending. They also engage in high levels of storytelling and emergent reading and writing ("reading" stories by reenacting the pictures, "writing" stories with letter-ish forms or random strings of letters, and "reading" their own printed messages). These early literacy activities develop the exact skills they need to learn how to read and write in the conventional sense. For instance, in their attempts to write out a shopping list while playing house, young children will experiment with squiggles, letter-like forms, and perhaps even imitate cursive by forming wavy scribbles. Later, they use their knowledge of letter sounds to invent their own spellings. They'll even "read" back their own messages to keep the play going. Children's early written forms will develop into standard letters, and their early invented spellings will develop into conventional words. Likewise, young children will "read" books by weaving a story from picture to picture, often imitating the words and intonation patterns they remember hearing from adult readings. Eventually children attend to the print and begin to decode words using meaning, grammar, and letter cues.

Several studies have compared the effects of early high-academic preschool programs that emphasize direct formal instruction versus programs that are child-centered or "developmentally appropriate," in which play is a central means of learning. If you walked into a developmentally appropriate preschool classroom, you'd see children taking care of plants; experimenting with sand, water, and pebbles; building with blocks; dressing up and playing pretend; drawing, painting, and cutting; singing and dancing; predicting the weather; and climbing, running, and jumping outside.

The notion that play can lead to intellectual growth better than formal instruction might seem odd, but there are a growing number of studies showing that more playful learning environments are better for younger children.[52] Likewise, there is increasing evidence that academic classrooms for young children are associated with higher levels of stress, anxiety, and problem behaviors and lower levels of creativity and enthusiasm for school. There's also no scientific support for the idea that direct instruction classrooms boost academic achievement—not a single study has found that academic preschools increase intellectual performance in school. In fact, in one study carried out by Deborah Stipek, the dean of the School of Education at Stanford University, and her colleagues, preschoolers and kindergartners in classrooms that emphasized basic skills scored lower on math and reading achievement tests than did children in developmentally appropriate programs.[53] Stipek found that the same negative effects were also evident one year later, at the end of kindergarten and first grade, respectively.

Academically oriented preschool programs also can reduce children's motivation for learning, lower their own expectations for success on academic tasks, and decrease the pride they feel in their own accomplishments. Further, academic preschools can make children more dependent on adults for permission and approval and increase worries about school.[54] The significance of these findings should not be underestimated.

Even more striking is growing evidence that the effects of an academic focus in preschool can persist into the teenage years. In one study that examined the long-term effects of preschool programs for lower-income children, fifteen-year-olds who had attended academic preschools felt more alienated from school, home, and society compared to those who had gone to more play-centered preschools.[55] Although there were no differences in grades or IQ scores at age fifteen, those teens who had attended academic programs as preschoolers engaged in twice the number of delinquent acts and had lower educational aspirations than those who had attended developmentally appropriate programs.

What does all this mean? Let's start with what it doesn't mean. It doesn't mean that all attempts to directly teach infants and young children are bad. Instead, it suggests that when parents push too hard and too soon, they're attempting to artificially accelerate a delicate developmental system designed by evolution and set firmly in place for millions of years. And that can't be good.

THE TUTOR DYNASTY

It's a shame that humans use only 10 percent of our brains. If only we could tap into the other 90 percent, we'd be an even more impressive species. We'd probably be able to figure out exactly how wormholes work, how to cure cancer with a single pill, and how to halt global climate change. We'd probably even have telekinetic powers.

This is an alluring idea. But it's totally wrong. We use virtually every part of our brain, and most parts of the brain are doing something most of the time. Frankly, the brain is probably the busiest and most involved organ in the human body. It makes up only 3 percent of our total body weight, but it uses up 20 percent of the body's energy. The simple act of grasping a block, balancing it on the top of a wobbly tower, and then planning your next architectural move engages everything from your occipital and parietal lobes to your motor and sensory cortices, basal ganglia, cerebellum, and frontal lobes. Lightening storms of neuronal activity crackle across the entire skull in just the few seconds it takes to transfer a block from your hand to the top of a tower.

Nonetheless, the idea that the brain holds untapped intellectual potential is a hope that tutoring centers like Kumon, Kaplan, and Princeton Review have capitalized on to boost their business. This type of company originated as a means to provide after-school supplemental education to underachieving students and students with learning disabilities. Responding to growing pressures from parents who want to keep their children competitive in the academic world, most tutoring companies have widened their targets to the intellectual mainstream, and consequently, tutoring has grown into a booming multibillion-dollar industry.[56]

In recent years, the tutoring industry also has ratcheted down the minimum age it serves. One of the quickest-growing markets for tutoring is preschoolers and kindergartners. There's Sylvan Learning Centers, which now offer pre-K reading programs that "focus on the building blocks of reading including phonics, phonemic awareness, oral comprehension, and vocabulary."[57] Kumon, a Japanese company that refers to itself as "the world's largest after-school math and reading enrichment program," has developed a Junior Kumon program that teaches basic math and reading skills to children as young as three and aims to "instill a desire to learn for life."[58] Preschool tutoring doesn't come cheap. Kumon charges the pre-K set about $125 a month for thirty-minute sessions twice a week to memorize flash cards and letter and number charts. If Kumon is too steep, there's KnowledgePoints®, which promises to have your preschooler "prepped for reading after only 40 hours of instruction."[59]

To some degree, this preschool-tutoring phenomenon is driven by parents who hope that if their children learn how to read and do basic math before they start kindergarten, they will excel in school, get into a good college, and eventually land a good job. That's a lot to expect from knowing how to sound out *cat* and *dog* when you're five. But with years of Baby Einstein marketing ringing in our heads, it's hard not to think that the more reading and math preschoolers master, the better.

Plus, there seems to be some empirical evidence supporting the tutoring industry's marketing. Consider, for example, an examination of nearly thirty-six thousand preschoolers carried out by Greg Duncan, a professor of education at the University of California, Irvine, and the president of the Society for Research in Child Development, and his colleagues.[60] Duncan found that the strongest predictor of achievement in later school years was children's kindergarten-entry math and reading skills. Those children who understood the order of numbers and the sounds of letters at the start of school were more successful than those who hadn't yet had these basics under their belts. For sure, these results underscore the importance of preschool mastery of early math and reading skills. But as Duncan himself warns, his findings should not be spun as an endorsement of direct academic instruction for preschoolers because "the kind of skills that matter in affecting later learning are things parents can pretty easily convey to their children in the home."[61] Young children can learn their letters and numbers at home from Mom and Dad and do just fine. Yet this straightforward advice from the president of the world's leading professional society for child development researchers doesn't seem to be enough to counteract the preschool-tutoring industry's bells and whistles, like Sylvan's trained and certified tutors and Kaplan's customized learning plans, computer-adaptive testing, and real-time online progress reports.

THE AMERICAN QUESTION

When did the race to grow better, faster, smarter children begin? It is a relatively recent phenomenon; we humans have not always viewed childhood in the idyllic way we do now. Historically, children haven't been treated very well at all.[62] In ancient Greece and Rome, many parents offered up their children as religious sacrifices or to be buried in walls of buildings so as to "strengthen" their structure. During the Middle Ages in Europe, parents routinely (and legally) killed newborns who weren't born perfectly healthy, were female, or were illegitimate. Less murderous parents merely abandoned unwanted infants outside the city gates, sold them into slavery, or used them as collateral for loans.

During the Industrial Revolution of the eighteenth and nineteenth centuries, our conceptions of childhood started to shift. We began to see childhood as special time, a separate and different period from adulthood. Nonetheless, we still put children, at quite young ages, to work on farms and in factories, mills, and mines. I like to tell my children these stories when they grumble about having it so hard. Sure, picking up the toys in your bedroom might not be the most thrilling thing to do on a Saturday morning, but isn't it better than a twelve-hour shift two miles underground?

Once we developed a conception of childhood, common wisdom for a long time was to take it slow. In the eighteenth century, social philosopher Jean-Jacques Rousseau wrote in his classic *Emile* that damage is done to the bodies and minds of children by "the desire to make men of them before their time."[63] A century later, writer Henry David Thoreau expressed a similar idea when he said, "the more slowly trees grow at first, the sounder they are at the core, and I think the same is true of human beings."[64] Likewise, Friedrich Froebel, inventor of the kindergarten, wrote, "The child, the boy, the man should know no other endeavor, but to be at every stage of development, what that stage calls for."[65] In fact, the prevailing view of academically gifted children was that because of their precociousness, they were only tenuously holding on to their sanity.[66]

But then the 1957 launching of Sputnik happened, and concerns about rushing childhood evaporated almost overnight in America. The fears sparked by the Soviet Union's startling success in space, says David Elkind, author of the 1981 best seller *The Hurried Child*, spurred Americans to ratchet up their educational demands and put heavy academic pressures on children.[67] Much of the blame goes to Admiral Hiram Rickover, who famously attributed Sputnik to the Soviet Union's superior educational system. He lamented that Soviet children were "learning math at an early age while our children were finger painting."[68]

Capitalizing on this desire to produce children who could pull off

Sputnik-like successes, the 1960s saw a slew of books like *Give Your Child a Superior Mind* that promised ways to produce children who could do something as impressive as Sputnik. The 1960s also saw Head Start, a federal program aimed at closing the achievement gap by better preparing poor children before they entered school.[69] At Head Start's inception, only thirty-two states had kindergarten programs. Preschool programs for four-year-olds were almost unheard of. The most immediate effect of Head Start was not a boost in the achievement of low-income children, but rather tantrums from middle- and upper-class families because of the unfortunate name given to the program. These parents also wanted for their children the secret sauce that Head Start was handing out.

Brain science had nothing to do with this increased emphasis on early enhancement. There was no new brain-boosting knowledge coming out of the scientific community during these years. Attempts to jump-start the preschool mind were nothing more than an overreaction to a pissing match we lost with the Soviet Union. When Swiss psychologist Jean Piaget traveled to the United States to give his famous lectures on child development, he often referred to the "American question."[70] His American audiences wanted to know: how could a child's development be accelerated?

THE AMERICAN QUESTION ON STEROIDS

Not that long ago, everyone thought that babies were born blind at birth. But then came a collection of scientific papers that turned this assumption on its head. In 1973, Joseph Stone, Henrietta Smith, and Lois Murphy published *The Competent Infant*. This volume provided evidence that not only do infants have all their senses up and running at birth, they are socially and intellectually competent creatures.[71] This was a brand-new world for researchers. And it was in this atmosphere that some began to argue that infants should exercise these newly discovered capabilities. For example, Glenn Doman, director of the Institutes for Achievement of Human Potential and author of *How to Teach Your Baby to Read*, *How to Teach Your Baby Math*, and *How to Give Your Baby Encyclopedic Knowledge*, argued (and still does) that it is easier to teach an infant anything than it is to teach an older child.[72] Not many child development scientists would agree with Doman, but he is not alone in advocating formal instruction in the early years of life.

In recent years, this popular hysteria to rush children through childhood has gotten particularly intense. The rush is fed by growing research findings about infant capabilities. With the development of new methodologies for studying infants that were made available in the 1980s, we began to discover that the infant's world was not a blooming, buzzing confusion. We learned that newborns analyze speech, are calmed by music, and can distinguish between two visual patterns, and that young infants can identify their mothers on the basis of smell and remember previously seen visual images. This barrage of findings about the amazing capabilities of infants led to an even more fervent belief that if babies can have all of these basic understandings of how the world works, shouldn't we build on this core knowledge with deliberate teaching? The thought was that if infants understand gravity at eight months, then maybe we should produce educational toys that encourage the learning of physics. If infants know that three is different from two, then possibly we should build toys that teach math. If infants are sensitive to sounds in all of the world's languages, we should expose them to DVDs so that they can become bilingual.

To all of these suggestions, the answer is a resounding no. This far into the book, it should be obvious that children learn best while engaged in everyday, natural activities, not artificial ones. Babies learn physics not from blinking and beeping stationary saucers, but from watching what naturally goes on around them, from manipulating objects already in your home, and later, by moving themselves around the house. They learn about gravity by dropping their teddy bear out of their playpen, inertia by pushing a toy car across the kitchen floor, and friction by riding their bicycles through the backyard. They learn language not by watching a video or listening to an electronic storybook, but by having back-and-forth conversations with real people. They learn math not by being drilled with number flash cards, but by asking for more applesauce and by setting their tea party picnic for three and not four.

HIDDEN MICKEYS

The study responsible for the widespread belief that infants can add and subtract was conducted in the 1990s by Yale University developmental psychologist Karen Wynn.[73] In a famous experiment, Wynn showed five-month-old babies a Mickey Mouse doll sitting on a stage. When the baby's interest in the doll began to wane, a screen would be raised that entirely hid the doll. Next, the baby would see an outstretched arm that placed a second Mickey Mouse behind the screen, which logically would make two dolls sitting on the stage. Wynn was interested in whether or not her babies would realize this. Did they understand that one plus one equals two?

To test this knowledge, Wynn lowered the screen. Sometimes it revealed the expected two dolls, but other times there was only one. Wynn studied babies' reactions to these two different results and discovered that they looked longer and more surprised during the impossible (one doll) than the possible (two doll) revelation. She concluded from this that babies could "add," and by doing the study in reverse that babies could subtract—with two dolls shown to begin with and then one taken away. Again, babies looked longer at the impossible result.

Do these findings really mean that babies can add and subtract? They clearly mean that babies know something about numbers, or at least something about amounts of "stuff." They also mean that babies understand something about how these amounts could change. This is truly an extraordinary finding. But before you get too excited, you should know that rhesus monkeys do the same thing when they are shown similar impossible conditions with lemons (something monkeys find much more interesting than Mickey Mouse dolls).[74] Same goes for newly hatched chicks, according to Rosa Rugani of the University of Trento in Italy, who used plastic containers (that look like large jellybeans) on which the newborns had imprinted (so the chicks considered them their parents). And no one is suggesting that we create Baby Einstein math flash cards for chicks.[75]

So the question is whether Wynn's findings demonstrate actual addition and subtraction as we understand those concepts, or whether something else is going on here. The answer is more complicated when we consider research by Janellen Huttenlocher of the University of Chicago, who explored the basic math skills of your average two- to four-year-old.[76] In a typical experiment, a two-and-a-half-year-old is seated across from an experimenter, who shows her three red blocks. Then the researcher covers up the blocks with a large box. To make sure the youngster understands the game, she is asked to show the researcher, using another set of blocks, how many the researcher has hidden under the box. Most children this age can oblige and will line up three blocks on their side of the table. Then, with the original blocks still hidden, the researcher adds another block underneath the box and asks, "Can you make yours look like mine?" All the child has to do is pick up one more block and place it in the pile to make a total of four blocks. But most children at this age can't perform the task. It'll be another year before the child will be able to work with small numbers like $1 + 1 = 2$ or $3 - 1 = 2$. And not until she's almost four will she be able to do tasks with larger numbers like $2 + 2 = 4$.

If you're a little confused, you should be. Why should five-month-olds pass the Mickey Mouse test in Wynn's lab, only to later fail a similar task in Huttenlocher's lab at age two and a half? The answer is that babies have only rudimentary number skills—a sensitivity to quantity—but not an awareness of the kind of math we think of when we talk about addition and subtraction. What most scientists think babies are doing in Wynn's studies is recognizing amounts like more or less, not specific quantities like two of something or four of something.

Consider a study conducted by Melissa Clearfield of Whitman College and Kelly Mix of Indiana University in Bloomington.[77] Seven-month-olds were tested using what's called the habituation method, in which children are shown something over and over again until they get bored. A hidden researcher, who is watching the kid, presses a button connected to a computer to record each child's looking time. When a child's looking time falls below a certain level, the child is shown something new. If she can distinguish the new from the old, she will start looking again. If she can't distinguish the new from the old, she will just continue to be bored.

Using this method, Clearfield and Mix showed their seven-month-olds two medium-sized squares placed on a board over and over again until the children got bored and stopped looking. Next, the infants were shown two different scenes: one with two larger squares (the same number but a *different amount*) or one with three little squares (a different number but the *same total amount*). If the infants understood number, they have should looked longer at the three-square scene because the number had changed. If amount was what infants attended to initially, they should have looked longer at the two-square scene because here the amount had increased. In the end, emphasis on amount prevailed. The babies looked longer at the scene where the two larger squares appeared and seemed uninterested when the three smaller squares, with the same original amount, were seen. This pattern suggests that babies focus on amount, not number. What should we make of this finding? One conclusion is that infants are capable of noticing only amounts of stuff and are not really tuned in to number at all. Another is that Wynn has it wrong. These findings definitely fall short of claiming that infants can add and subtract, instead suggesting that what young infants really have is elementary conceptions of "more" and "less." Some argue that these conceptions are what animals use when foraging for food. It is clear, nonetheless, that infants are not performing addition and subtraction calculations in any way that resembles what older children or adults do, or even what preschoolers do. Products marketed to boost babies' abilities to add and subtract are misguided because it's not until much later that children are capable of elementary math.

LESS IS MORE

I certainly am not the first to bemoan the race to adulthood. Every few years, a new book or magazine article warns that kids are being rushed through childhood. The most famous is David Elkind's *The Hurried Child*, but there is also Marie Winn's 1981 work titled *Children without Childhood* and Neil Postman's 1982 book, *The Disappearance of Childhood*. More recently, works titled *The Over-Scheduled Child: Avoiding the Hyper-Parenting Trap* by Alvin Rosenfeld and Nicole Wise, *Putting Family First: Successful Strategies for Reclaiming Family Life in a Hurry-Up World* by William Doherty and Barbara Carlson, and Ralph Schoenstein's *My Kid's an Honors Student, Your Kid's a Loser: The Pushy Parent's Guide to Raising a Perfect Child* have appeared in bookstores. Warnings to slow down have trickled down to children as well. There's *The Berenstain Bears and Too Much Pressure* and self-help books like *Stress Can Really Get on Your Nerves* and *Getting Out of a Stress Mess! A Guide for Kids*. Girl Scouts can earn "From Stress to Success" and "Stress Less" patches by making a stress kit, journaling about ways to quell stress, or doing deep breathing exercises.[78] The preschool set is even getting the message to slow down in picture books like Eric Carle's *Slowly, Slowly, Slowly, Said the Sloth*.

So if the word is out that today's children are feeling stressed from the rush, then why do parents keep emphasizing the acquiring of skills earlier and earlier in life? My best guess is that it has something to do with the fact that the experts who are touting that we slow down childhood are not heeding their own advice. Even Rousseau shelved his five children in foundling homes because they got in the way of his work. Many authors who have written about the stresses of modern childhood have embarked on their own frenetic public advocacy campaigns for more downtime. For instance, psychiatrist Alvin Rosenfeld, who coauthored *The Over-Scheduled Child*, has created two websites to try to get children to slow down and plan at least one evening a month with their families (check out Rosenfeld's website at: www.hyper-parenting.com/nationalfamilynight/). Rosenfeld wants to involve "politicians, civic, educational, business, and entertainment leaders" in this effort.[79] This sounds like a great idea, but doesn't *planning* what Rosenfeld himself refers to as "unscheduled activities" miss the point? It would seem that Rosenfeld is advocating that parents *schedule* unscheduled together time with their children!

Other child development experts have even less laid-back means than Rosenfeld's of getting us to slow down childhood. The University of Minnesota's William Doherty, author of *Putting Family First*, has a website by the same domain name that intends to spread the word about clearing children's after-school calendars. The site also offers handy suggestions for activities that families can do together. This seemed like a good idea until I scrolled down the home page, found a user-submitted list of "21 things to do before summer ends," and then got completely stressed because it's already June and my children and I haven't done a single thing on the list.[80] My husband and I saw the final item, "Complete a triathlon," and dubbed ourselves losers because there was no way we could get ourselves in shape enough in time to do even one leg of the three. Frankly, though, we felt better when we read about Doherty's challenge to families to spend "21 minutes each day around the family table and get the kids to bed on time."[81] So we followed Doherty's link to a printable version of a calendar that we could use to track our time, send in, and be eligible to win unlimited rides at the park at the Mall of America for an entire year. Here's a contest Doherty might want to hold: How many more times can families hear about planning less planned time before they sock a child development expert right in the nose?

The irony of these campaigns is obvious: the movement to slow childhood down is frankly stressful. Sure, parents and teachers need to stop pushing so fast, but it doesn't take a labor-intensive community organization to carve out a round of backyard kickball or some free space in your family room for a Lincoln Log fort. Nor do we need Joe Biden, Donald Trump, and Beyoncé as national spokespeople to muster a backyard pickup game. This campaign based on the regret that "parenting has become the most competitive sport in America"—a favorite refrain of Rosenfeld's—is anything but mellow. Slowing down with the Joneses is the get-ahead thing to do. It totally stressed me out when I realized I missed Stress Awareness Week. "This is how to raise children who will succeed in life!"[82] The message? Slowing down is not for slouchers.

My main message here is that we don't need a national campaign to slow down childhood. Parents don't need a nonprofit agency to schedule downtime for their children. And we don't need to schedule time to relax with our kids. We merely need to open up the calendar, wipe clean the whiteboard, and just be. Any time an extra class/activity/club/competition for your children comes your way, just ask yourself if it is really worth reducing their free, unstructured playtime further. Do you really need to shell out more cash and spend more time in the minivan? Are you considering it because the media told you it was a good idea or because the marketing is persuasive? Science tells us that the rushing of childhood is not a positive choice, so resist. Let childhood simmer.

THE TORTOISE AND THE HARE

All of this brings us back to that surprising study discussed in chapter 2 that gives late bloomers a cause for celebration. Philip Shaw and his colleagues at the National Institutes of Mental Health carried out a series of MRI brain scans on children and teens ranging in age from five to nineteen and found that those who had "superior intelligence"–level IQ scores had brain cortexes that matured much later than those of average intelligence. The cortexes of the smartest children peaked by around age eleven or twelve, whereas the average children peaked by around age eight.[83] This is a striking study. It suggests that the brain wants us to slow down.

I am not proposing that parents throw a party if their child makes it to age six without reading a single word. But those children whose parents resisted the Your Baby Can Read pressure may not only catch up to their early-reading peers, but actually outdo them. These MRI data tell the same story as those showing that early brain-boosting experiences like academic preschools not only don't boost brains, but actually may hinder children's potential for success.

On the flip side, there's also growing evidence that rapid early brain growth is associated with developmental abnormalities, like autism. Autistic toddlers tend to have larger brains for their age. But they do not start out with larger than average brains; their brain volume appears quite normal at birth. However, University of California neurobiologist Eric Courchesne and his colleagues discovered that by two to four years of age, 90 percent of autistic children have larger than normal brains. There's also a link between the degree of early growth and the severity of autistic behaviors. Although why excessive brain growth is related to autism is unclear, the findings suggest that abnormal neural growth patterns early in development lead to a number of consequences in brain structure and function.[84]

We must be careful what we do with findings like these. Preschools should not try to profit from these findings and change their names to "Slowly Growing Brain Day School." Nor should they hold Brain Imaging Days where the students slip into MRI scanners for a quick session to measure their progress. Parents should not hang their children's slowly growing brain scans on their refrigerators or post them on Facebook. Nor should toy companies develop electronic games that slow down brain growth or market puzzles with labels that warn, "Your brain must be this small to play." These are all totally wrong ways to take these brain growth findings. The right way is to be patient. It'll pay off.

THE BUTTERFLY EFFECT

One of the reasons that we parents fill our children's schedules with "enriching" activities and "early learning" products is our hope that these efforts will have some later payoff in adulthood. We buy our children learning laptops, sign them up for T-ball skills camps, or enroll them in Scouts because we think we are doing something that will help prepare them for a competitive future.

But what parenting books, mom blogs, and your MOPs (Mothers of

Preschoolers) groups never tell you is that much of what happens during childhood will have absolutely no *long-term* consequences of any significant degree. So, yes, that girls' weekend beach trip you passed up to take your daughter to the Mommy and Me Clappy-Hands Feel-Good Sing-Along Jamboree won't make an ounce of difference in the long term. But it will make a huge difference *now*, as your daughter is clapping her hands and singing out loud and having a grand old time.

What I'm not doing here is suggesting that you suspend everything "enriching" because it might or might not have some later effect. Instead, I'm telling you that the things that we do for our children because it will be good for them in their future may not always be justifiable on those grounds. I'm asking you to rethink the possible consequences of the life you make for your children and realize that much of what you do will have no bearing on whether they get accepted at Harvard, but it will certainly enrich their lives now.

One of my colleagues at work refuses to take his children to Walt Disney World® until they're old enough to remember it: "Why waste thousands of dollars on a trip they won't even remember?" I suggested that if a memory is what he wanted, the easiest thing to do would be to create Photoshop pictures of his children at the Magic Kingdom and then "reminisce" about the trip.[85] This hesitancy to take children too young to remember on a special vacation illustrates that, as parents, we often focus our energies on the adults our children will become, rather than on the children they are now. It doesn't only matter whether or not your children will remember a childhood trip to Disney. What also matters is the here and now. Children need to feel good now and enjoy themselves now, not merely rack up experiences that may or may not matter later. Parents with the happiest children are those who are most in tune with their children's emotional cues in the here and now.[86]

One of the reasons we focus so much of our energy on our children's future rather than their present is that most of us see human development as a progression.[87] We see our children as starting out as immature and inefficient beings who develop into mature and efficient ones. Most of us see infants and children as unfinished and incomplete versions of adults.

From this viewpoint, the immaturity of children—all the mayhem and mess of it—seems merely a necessity that our species has to endure on our way to adulthood, the period of life that really "counts." And if adulthood is what counts, then of course you'd want Suzie to learn as quickly as possible how to ask for more grape juice, tie her own sneakers, make her own bologna sandwich, balance her checkbook, read the *New York Times*, and eat a meal without forming her mashed potatoes into Mount Vesuvius and pretending it's erupting gravy lava on a village of unsuspecting peas.

There is, however, another way to view development that doesn't have this idea of a linear progression from the immature to the mature. Florida Atlantic University developmental psychologist David Bjorklund points out that many insects and amphibians metamorphose: they change their form from caterpillar to butterfly, or from tadpole to frog.[88] Based on its appearance, you'd never guess a green-and-yellow-striped worm-like insect would turn into a beautiful flying creature with black-and-white-striped wings. You'd never guess that the two were the same species. Likewise, you know the story of Leo Lionni's *Fish Is Fish*. Even the fish is flabbergasted when the tadpole sprouts legs and hops out of the pond.[89]

There is an extreme remodel that takes place between stages of development, and the animal at each stage—as a caterpillar and then as a butterfly—has its own set of abilities, characteristics, and adaptations. At each stage, the animal has "its own integrity."[90] The life of a caterpillar is just as sophisticated and dynamic as that of a butterfly. The caterpillar is not merely an immature butterfly, but rather an animal with its own body, brain, and behaviors that are adapted to its present life as a cater-pillar and not its future life as a butterfly.

Children, of course, don't spin cocoons and later emerge as completely different animals. But Bjorklund argues that just as the caterpillar has its own integrity, so does the child. Just as caterpillars have their own set of abilities and characteristics that are adapted to the environment they inhabit, children, too, have their own set that is fitted to their environment. When you look at childhood with this lens, all the mayhem and mess of children's immaturity is not a necessary evil but rather may play an adaptive role right now in their current lives. In other words, not all the characteristics of infancy and childhood are unfinished versions of the adult form. Some function to adapt children to their immediate environment, and they disappear when they're no longer needed. Characteristics that have such an adaptive value only during a specific time in development are known as *ontogenetic adaptations* (sometimes *transient ontogenetic adaptations*, to emphasize their temporary nature).

Ontogenetic adaptations are such an important concept in developmental psychobiology that you're not given your membership card until you use the term in conversations at least once a day. And like any concept that is ubiquitous and foundational to one branch of science, everyone else pretty much ignores it. Developmental psychologists, who you'd think would be familiar with the idea, generally pay it no mind because they are focused on finding infant and child behaviors that red-flag potential later troubles or predict later success.

The most obvious examples of human ontogenetic adaptations happen early in life. A human fetus, for instance, gets its food and oxygen through the placenta. At birth, an extreme transformation occurs. The old ways of getting food and oxygen disappear, and the newborn eats and breathes in an entirely different way. In infancy, there are a whole set of reflexes, like the sucking reflex, that promote well-being for newborns but would be just plain embarrassing if they were retained in adulthood. Similarly, newborns imitate others' facial expressions for the first few weeks of life, but this behavior disappears by about two months. Imitation reappears around the first birthday, but it seems as if this later version serves a different function than it does in the newborn. Bjorklund thinks the newborn version fosters mother-infant bonding during a time when babies cannot direct their gaze or control their head movements. His interpretation is supported by a link between research findings showing that the higher the amount of newborn imitation, the better the quality of the mother-infant bond at three months.[91]

Developmental biopsychologists Gerald Turkewitz and Patricia Kenny have proposed that the early immaturity of newborns' sensory and motor systems should be viewed as adaptive.[92] They argue, for instance, that the limited motor capacity of baby animals prevents them from wandering far from their mothers, thus enhancing their chances for survival. The sensory limitations of many young animals are seen as adaptive because they serve to reduce the amount of information infants have to deal with, which facilitates their ability to construct a simplified and comprehensible world. The various sensory systems develop in an uneven order for all vertebrates—for instance, hearing emerges before vision. That means that early-developing systems don't have to compete for real estate in the brain with the other developing senses. The idea is that limited sensory functioning (fuzzy eyesight, for instance) reduces sensory input and serves to decrease competition between developing senses. From this perspective, immature sensory systems are not handicaps that must be overcome, but are adaptive and necessary for proper sensory development and sensory learning.

Is there evidence to support this proposal? Robert Lickliter's bobwhite quails from chapter 1 provide evidence that earlier than expected visual stimulation results in auditory deficits. Other research shows that earlier than expected auditory stimulation can interfere with the subsequent development of other sensory systems—visual development in quails and olfaction in rats.[93]

It's a bit more difficult to come up with examples beyond the neonatal period, but if you know where to look, they can be found. For instance, Elissa Newport in the Department of Brain and Cognitive Sciences at the University of Rochester has proposed that infants' and young children's immature cognitive skills facilitate early language learning.[94] The idea is that cognitive limitations reduce competition, thus simplifying the breadth of language the infant and young child must process, thereby making it easier to learn language. Supporting this idea are findings that young children in the early stages of language learning start out slowly—actually more slowly than adults learning a second language. They perceive and store only component parts of complex stimuli. In other words, they start with single morphemes (usually a single syllable) and gradually increase complexity and the number of units they can control. They are able to extract only limited pieces of the speech they hear. But this results in a simplified set of data that actually makes the job of analyzing language easier. Adults, in contrast, start out learning a second language more quickly than children; they are more competent initially, producing more complex words and sentences. They more readily perceive and remember the whole of the speech they hear. But this advantage is short lived. Adults extract more of the input but are then are faced with the more difficult problem of analyzing everything at once.

Egocentricity is a classic example of children's immaturity. Ask a three-year-old what gift her mommy would rather have for her birthday: a diamond tennis bracelet or a pony. You're likely to hear "pony" because a child of this age generally sees the world only from her perspective. Of course Mommy would rather have a pony than a silly bracelet—wouldn't everyone? As it turns out, this self-centered perspective serves an important function in childhood. It's well known that people tend to remember things best when they reference the information to themselves. Young children overdo this self-referencing. They, for example, tend to misattribute the actions of others as something they themselves did (but they don't make the opposite error of attributing their own actions as having been done by someone else). This bias, it seems, gives young children a boost in learning and remembering because misattributing the actions of others to themselves results in children linking the actions to a common source (themselves), which produces better-integrated and more easily retrievable memories. Support for this idea comes from studies that show that children who collaborate with adults on spatial memory tasks (such as placing miniature furniture in a dollhouse) tend to make egocentric attribution errors when tested for their memory (saying, for example, "I placed the table in the kitchen" when, in fact, the adult had) but remember more overall items in their correct locations than children who carry out the task independently.[95]

Another classic example of childhood immaturity is young children's poor metacognitive, or self-knowledge, skills. Younger children typically believe they are stronger, smarter, and generally more skilled than they really are. I have fond memories of teaching my son how to hit a baseball. Every time he'd miss, his response was not, "Mom, I screwed up," but that I had made a bad throw. Supporting the adaptive nature of children's tendency to overestimate their abilities are findings by Bjorklund and colleagues that three- and four-year-olds who overestimate their imitative abilities have more advanced verbal skills than the more accurate children.[96] However, this relation disappeared by age five. How could such overestimation be adaptive? Children who overestimate their own abilities may attempt a wider range of activities and not perceive their less than perfect performance as failure. If you have ever seen a preschooler dancing to the band at a wedding reception, you know exactly what I'm talking about. Children who believe they are skilled in a domain are likely to attempt more challenging tasks and persist at them longer than less optimistic children, and this, in turn, will influence how much they learn.

Private speech is also an example of the benefits of immaturity. Whereas adults tend to think in our heads when we work out difficult problems, young children often talk about their struggles out loud. Sometimes adults talk out loud—but when we do, it's usually with new and difficult problems. Preschool children, for whom so much is new and difficult, benefit from the extra support.[97] They talk out loud not merely to describe what they're doing, but to direct their own behavior and guide their own problem solving. Young children who talk to themselves while working on challenging problems tend to be the brighter children.

The primary message here is that many of the seeming limitations of childhood really are adaptations that give children advantages in their here and now. Behaviors like egocentricity, poor self-knowledge, and rampant private speech are not limitations of childhood, but rather adaptations to childhood. So there's no reason to try to overcome these as quickly as possible. Plus, it's irrational to worry about your fetus getting into Harvard. There's no basis for a belief that speeding up children's development, then or later, will do any good.

Essentially, in terms of development, the evidence suggests that childhood experiences are like the body's need for vitamins. You need a minimum dose, but beyond that, taking extra won't help. That is, exposure to spoken language, narrative, and music, and the ability to explore, play, and socially interact are important for youngsters. But beyond these basic experiences that are already present in most middle-class homes, there is no reason to believe that further "enrichment" confers any benefit to the structure or function of children's developing brains.

Chapter 5

The Worst Seat in the House

Your average five-month-old gopher can run, wrestle, find water, forage for dinner, groom its siblings, defend its territory, and navigate through dense grasslands without getting lost. At five months, humans can't even sit up without help. Let's face it: by comparison to most other species, we humans have wimpy babies. But this doesn't mean that we should store them away in bouncy seats, bungee jumpers, and high chairs until they can manage on their own. If we do, how are they supposed to learn about the world? Young babies need to touch, taste, look at, listen to, and explore everything—people included. Older babies need to push, pull, and manipulate objects, crawl, climb, and pull themselves up to a stand. They need to reach for and grasp things to learn the difference between hot and cold, wet and dry, bumpy and smooth, and heavy and light. They need to stack blocks, roll balls, and drop toys to learn basic physics. They need to ask for more milk and give each friend two and not three cookies to learn elementary math. They need to have exchanges with living, breathing people to learn language and be happy. But all of this is hard to do if you're strapped into a bouncy seat or shackled into a stroller and pointed at the television set.

Many babies today go an entire day without a single opportunity to explore their world—they go from the crib to the bouncy seat, from the swing to the saucer, from the bungee jumper to the high chair. When they begin to move around on their own, many are confined in a playpen or behind a baby gate. These constraints certainly make life easier on Mom and Dad. But they deprive young infants of needed opportunities to explore their world, to learn how to regulate states of wakefulness and sleepiness on their own, and to make eye contact with their caregivers. For older babies, such confines deny them needed chances for experimenting on their environment and hinder the attainment of joint attention, a skill critical for language, social, and cognitive development. Joint attention is attention shared with another person on an object or event. This skill permits infants to communicate with caregivers by way of eye contact and gestures and it enables them to learn new information by following the gaze of others. Infants who have trouble engaging in and reacting to joint attention often develop a diminished capacity for relatedness and relationships. In fact, clinical research indicates that autism is characterized by chronic, pronounced impairments in initiating joint attention.

BLOOMING, BUZZING CONFUSION

For a long time, infants weren't given very much credit. In 1762, Jean-Jacques Rousseau called the baby "a perfect idiot," and in 1890, psychologist William James famously described an infant's mental life as "one great blooming, buzzing confusion."[1] For nearly a century, we viewed infants as simple-minded creatures who grasped barely the basics of the world and merely mimicked the emotions of happiness, anger, and sadness. We thought they took years to have any clue about the world—to learn even the most elementary physical facts (like that objects continue to exist when they are out of sight) or even the simplest things about people (for example, that they have thoughts going on inside their heads). The thinking went that if babies have the mental life of a pet rock, then there's no harm in keeping them busy in bouncy seats, stationary saucers, bungee jumpers, and play yards—at least until they develop the lower body strength to break out.

This pet-rock view has persisted for so long because scientists didn't know how to go about studying the minds of babies. It's certainly a challenge to study what's going on inside the head of any animal that can't speak for itself, but human babies are especially difficult because, unlike other animals, they are physically inept: they can't run mazes or peck at levers. As discussed in chapter 4, in the 1980s, developmental psychologists began exploiting one of the few behaviors that young babies have under their control: their eye movements. The eyes, it turns out, are a window to the baby's mind. Like adults, when infants see things that capture their interest or surprise them, they usually look longer than at uninteresting or expected things. Also like adults, when looking at two different things, infants typically look more at the more pleasing thing. Once psychologists realized these tendencies, they began using "looking time" to measure what babies know about their physical world. More recently, psychologists have begun making use of electroencephalographs (EEGs), MRI scans, and eye-tracking technologies to get a deeper view of what's going on inside babies' heads.

As researchers began to make use of looking-time methodologies, they began to uncover unexpected things about what infants know.[2] These discoveries led to the realization that Rousseau and James were sorely mistaken. In the past thirty or so years, developmental psychologists have revealed that infants and toddlers have stunning capabilities. They might act like pet rocks, but they are dynamic explorers of their world who perform complicated statistical analyses of the input to figure it all out. Newborns remember things they heard in utero, they analyze the sounds of speech, they have complex emotions (like empathy and frustration), and they can distinguish between two different visual scenes. They can identify their mothers on the basis of smell alone, and they can remember things they have recently seen. By four months, they have advanced powers of deduction, an ability to decipher intricate patterns, and long-term memories. By six months, they are learning by reaching and grasping and are starting to communicate by cooing and babbling. Soon they are crawling, and by one year, they are standing, using some first words, and engaging in an impressive range of social behaviors that, without much language, can command any adult within eyeshot.

WHY THERE'S A HOLE IN YOUR REFRIGERATOR

This past summer, my family spent our summer vacation in the Outer Banks in North Carolina. We spent our days swimming in the warm ocean, playing games in the sand, and riding our bikes around town. At night, we ate fresh seafood, watched the sunset from the pier, and took long walks by the bay. Almost every evening was topped off with a scoop or two of homemade ice cream. It was a spectacular experience, except we really didn't experience any of it.

All that reaches us from the outside world as we experience it is a barrage of colors and shapes and light and sound.[3] Your children aren't really sitting in the backyard swinging. They're really sacks of skin, topped with hair and wrapped in a polyester-cotton blend, balancing themselves on suspended pieces of plastic. On each skin bag, there's a pair of little black dots just under the hair that move in unison. There's also an opening underneath the dots that morphs in shape and makes a stream of sounds.

Whenever you move about, the objects around you continuously change shape. You walk toward the table to pick up your coffee mug, and it gets bigger and bigger as you move closer and closer. The refrigerator changes shape from a flat rectangle to a three-dimensional box as you walk around it. You also notice the holes in the front of it, where you've hung your children's artwork. As you sip your coffee, the entire contents of the mug change shape. Then you lose sight of your drink altogether, but you feel something warm and yummy coming into your body.

Such is life. It's one big stew of sensations. It's not really children and coffee and refrigerators. It's photons hitting the retinas in the back of your eyes, molecules of air vibrating your eardrums, and brushes of pressure on your fingertips. Your brain predicts that children and coffee and your refrigerator are the most likely causes of your sensations because it has some prior ideas of what these things are like. This prior knowledge has created a model, or representation, of these things in your mind, and it uses these representations to make further predictions: for example, that you'll find fresh fruit for snacking if you open the fridge, or that your children will whine if you tell them to stop swinging because it's time for bed.

Our sensory systems are limited in what they pick up. They don't detect the whole of everything that's out there in the world for sensing. For instance, we see things only within certain wavelengths of light (we don't see the ultraviolet urine trails of field mice as hawks can), we hear things only within a certain frequency range (we don't hear the higher tones that bats and whales do), and we smell only some of the world's odors (a dog's sense of smell is about twenty-five times better than ours). So really we're only peering into a keyhole of what's really out there.[4]

This all sounds nightmarish, but it's what we really see, hear, and feel. Luckily, it's not what we experience. Our brain turns the chaotic onslaught of ongoing sensations into a seamless story of experience that makes sense. Images are turned into people who have intentions, beliefs, and desires.

The series of air disturbances is turned into words we understand, ideas we remember, and songs we sing. The pressure on our hands becomes a mug or our pet dog. Because our brain learns how to turn sensory information into meaning, our world is not a blooming, buzzing confusion.

How do babies figure out what this flow of raw sensations means? How do their brains discover how to turn the external world into something they can understand? The task seems incomprehensibly difficult—yet they learn how to do it without teachers and classrooms and formal curricula. Developmental psychologist Alison Gopnik explains that babies are essentially one big fleshy computer.[5] We don't exactly understand the programs inside, but we know children come equipped with powerful learning mechanisms that allow them to spontaneously revise, reshape, and restructure the world as sensory input arrives. Also, children have A-plus tech support: us.

DEEP BLUE BABIES

We really didn't figure out that the world as we know it is not what's really there until we tried to build machines clever enough to perceive the world just like we do. Because our perception of the world seems immediate and easy, we figured it would be a breeze to make a machine that could have the same one. Almost every animal recognizes familiar others, so it seemed as if it should be easy to build a machine that could do this. Building a machine that could do uniquely human and high-order skills like playing chess and answering trivia questions—that should be hard.

As it turns out, we had it completely backward. It proved fairly easy to build a machine that could play chess, and play the game well. In 1997, IBM's famous Deep Blue® computer beat grand master Garry Kasparov.[6] Fifteen years later, in three rounds of *Jeopardy!*, IBM computer Watson easily dusted Ken Jennings, famous for winning a record seventy-four games in a row on the television quiz show.[7] But building a computer to perceive like us or to recognize faces—that's proved impossible so far.

What's so hard about perception? Take a look out your front window. It's a mess of objects. Some of them overlap each other, and some of them are moving about. How has your one-year-old learned how to separate one object from another? How does she know that the black tires on your car are part of your car and not part of the blacktop driveway? How does she know which patches of green go with the tulips and which go with the bushes? She knows because as she moves around the car, the tires move with the car and not with the driveway. Her brain links the common motion of the car and the tires. She knows the tulip leaves are closer to her than the bush leaves because as she moves toward them, the bits of the tulips move past her eyes faster than the bits of the bush. Importantly, she knows all this because it's not the car and tulips that are moving, but it's she who is moving. In our brains, perception and action are linked. We use our bodies to learn about the world. Hearkening back to earlier in the book, we do things to the world with our bodies to see what happens, and our brain crunches the numbers and draws conclusions.

This is what computers lack. It's why they'll never be expert per-ceivers like us. They don't have a body. They just look out at the world. They can't do things and see what happens.

The lesson here is that movements help our perception. Movements plus goals help even more. It's one thing to move about, but it's another to do so with goals. As you're reading this book, you're aware that your spouse has just placed a plate of freshly baked chocolate chip cookies on the side table next to you. What you're not aware of is that your brain has already worked out how to shape your hand to grasp a cookie.[8] This preparation and anticipation happens even when you have no intention of picking up the cookie.

Part of your brain represents the world around you in terms of actions: the actions you need to pick up your pen, the actions you need to make a peanut butter and jelly sandwich, the actions you need to tie your shoes. Your brain is continuously and automatically predicting the best move-ments for the action you might need to perform. Whenever you carry out an action, your predictions about the world are tested. If things don't work out as smoothly as predicted, you refine your representation of the world. As you handle your pen, you develop a better idea of its shape, and the better you'll be able to "see" its shape next time you need it.

For children to learn about the world in this manner and build up representations of the things and people around them, they need to expe-rience the world by acting on it. Shackle them up in a stationary carrier or bouncy seat, and you've essentially turned them into Watson—a clever computer without a body.

SEEING EYE TO EYE

Babies come into the world nearsighted. The fuzziness is only temporary, but they arrive with their vision preset at about one foot. So things closer or farther than about one foot are too out of focus to capture their interest. This fixed field seems like a limitation of the newborn's visual system, but it more likely is an adaptation (ontogenetic, that is) that works in the newborn's favor. When babies are held—football style or when nursing—the distance between the caregiver's face and the baby's face is, you guessed it, about one foot. This preset one-foot distance puts the caregiver's face in focus and guarantees that a newborn will attend squarely on that face. If you've ever locked eyes with a newborn, you know that such attention makes you feel an immediate connection, and it compels you to interact, to smile, and to tell her all about her new world. This tendency of newborns to fix their gaze on their caregivers' faces is adaptive because so many of their early lessons depend on attention to things happening on and coming out of those faces.[9] But this tendency becomes useless if the newborn spends the majority of its time in bouncy seats, baby carriers, and infant swings.

STROLL PATROL

There comes a time in all parents' lives when their style of living is determined by one thing: their stroller. The stroller calls the shots. It puts limits on mobility. It can cramp one's lifestyle. It can keep you off of subways and buses and even taxis if you haven't yet worked out its moody folding mechanism. It bans you from riding the escalator at the mall. The narrow aisles of your local superstore become maddening. Your favorite sandwich shop won't let you past the front door. And you can forget your favorite Saturday morning farmer's market—the one with freshly baked chocolate chip muffins that taste like heaven if heaven were a muffin—because it sets up its vendors on a gravel path.

In the movie *Away We Go*, there's a scene where an unmarried thirty-something couple proudly gives a friend, a mother of young children, a stroller. This friend doesn't have a stroller, so you'd think she'd react graciously. But she doesn't. The gift makes her fly into a mad rage and fling the stroller out of her house. She barks, "I love my babies. Why would I want to push them away from me?" Her over-the-top reaction is a hoot. But her question, I think, might be exactly what some babies are asking their parents.

Certainly, the mere act of pushing your baby around the block in a stroller doesn't mean you don't love her. It's a convenient way to take a walk on a nice day. But consider the ride from your baby's point of view: as she's wheeled around in her stroller, her line of vision is about two feet off the ground. Things look very different and really less interesting from down there than they do from on your lap or in your arms. Get on your hands and knees and crawl around the block to get an idea of what she sees. From stroller height, all she sees are dog faces, license plates, and mailboxes. If you stop and talk with a neighbor, she sees kneecaps rather than eyes and facial expressions. Doesn't your baby deserve a better view than Mr. McGrady's knees?

If you consider, too, that you are the center of your baby's social and emotional life, you might think she'd also like to be able to look at you while you motored her around. You could do this if you raised the stroller up and flipped it around to face you. Sure, a stroller like this would require some explaining, but there is growing evidence that forward-facing strollers might be having a negative effect on children's early language development, perhaps even their well-being.

Look at it this way: if your baby is facing ahead as you wheel her around town, she is going to have trouble interacting with you. Imagine trying to have a meaningful conversation with your spouse if he were crawling on the ground about two feet in front of you. If you're on a loud city street or in a suburban mall, he probably couldn't even hear you talking. The potential problem with being wheeled around in a forward-facing stroller is that it cuts short infants' opportunities to learn about the world and words through social interaction. As we learned in chapter 4, babies' language skills are driven by their everyday conversations with caregivers. But if these caregivers who push forward-facing strollers can't see what babies are looking at and reacting to, then valuable language lessons are missed.

Interestingly enough, strollers haven't always faced forward. When they were designed originally in the nineteenth century, they were made so that infants faced the person pushing them. It wasn't until the late 1960s that collapsible strollers emerged, and engineering constraints caused them to face forward. To explore the effects of this switch in position, Dundee University's Suzanne Zeedyk and her colleagues watched 2,722 families pushing infants and young children in cities and villages throughout Britain. As you'd expect, they found that forward-facing strollers were the most common and that these infants also were the least likely to be interacting socially with others. When traveling with their babies in forward-facing strollers, caregivers were observed speaking to infants only 11 percent of the time, whereas the figure rose to 25 percent when caregivers used rear-facing strollers. The figure was even higher for those caregivers who carried their infants.[10]

These data suggest that stroller positioning influences the frequency of social interaction, but it's also possible that parents who purchase toward-facing strollers simply talk more than those who buy away-facing ones. To test this possibility, Zeedyk gave mothers a chance to try out both stroller types and recorded their conversations. It turns out that the mothers talked twice as much to their children during rear-facing trips than during forward-facing ones. So simply by flipping the stroller around, mothers' rates of talking to their infants doubled. The infants in the rear-facing strollers laughed more, too. In fact, only one baby in the entire study laughed when facing away, whereas half laughed during the face-to-face stroll. There was also a suggestion in Zeedyk's data that rear-facing strollers might be more comforting to infants than those that face away. When babies were placed in the toward-facing strollers, their average heart rates fell slightly, relative to trips in away-facing units.

Zeedyk's work is just one study, and clearly more research is needed to fully understand the impact of stroller positioning.[11] But it nonetheless raises a red flag and should prompt parents to think about how their babies experience stroller rides and other forms of getting about, like car seats, baby carriers, backpacks, and shopping carts. It also raises the point that parents should talk to their babies whenever they get the chance. What are we to make of the heart rate finding? While it's clear that stressed babies grow into anxious adults, there's no evidence here that forward-facing strollers will create a generation of distressed adults. These findings do, however, raise the possibility that a walk in an away-facing stroller might not only be socially impoverished but also a bit stressful. And if you want to arrange experiences in infancy that are all good, then consider minimizing the time infants spend in forward-facing strollers.

BABYWEARING

As we've just seen, there are hints in the research community that stroller positioning might matter, but what about those trendy bag-style baby slings? These minimalist baby wraps are hardly new and are traditional in many parts of the world. They're convenient for sure—your hands are free to text, make lunch, or steer around your other children. There's also the common wisdom that babywearing helps to bond the caregiver and the baby.

"Wearing" one's baby has taken on a certain cachet in Western nations. Magazines and websites often picture celebrities with their babies strapped onto their sides. Just a few years ago, it was tough to find any sort of baby sling, but today they are everywhere. Between 2006 and 2008, sales of such carriers rose 43 percent to $21.5 million.[12] They're so widely available and produced in such a variety of patterns and fabrics that some moms even collect them like handbags.

But are baby slings a good idea for babies? Their safety has been questioned, as they have contributed to the suffocation deaths of several infants. The Consumer Product Safety Commission warns that slings can be especially dangerous for very small babies.[13] Babies too immature or fragile to control their head movements can suffocate should their nose and mouth become pressed up against the fabric or their body become curled in a dangerous chin-down position. In response to such warnings, many specialty stores no longer sell bag-style slings, and if they do, they instruct buyers to position their babies upright and tight against the caregiver.

Dr. William Sears, a pediatrician and author of more than thirty parenting books, is responsible for the term "babywearing."[14] He and his wife coined the term in 1985 when they fashioned a sling from an old bedsheet to carry around their infant son. Sears is a hearty advocate of the practice, and he tells parents that "sling babies" are more intelligent, more attentive, cry less, and develop more regular sleep/wake routines than nonsling babies.

Is there any empirical evidence to support Sears's claims? Not much. There are no studies demonstrating a link between babywearing and things like higher intelligence levels later in life. Nor would we expect there to be; complex behaviors like intelligence are regulated by so many different biological, familial, social, and cultural factors that we wouldn't expect something as simple as whether or not a baby was "worn" to have any discernible effect.

There is a single 1986 study that supports the idea that babywearing reduces infants' crying and fussiness.[15] But the bulk of the literature shows no discernible relationship between infants' crying and fussiness and the manner in which they are carried.[16] And fussiness might not be a bad thing at all. Over the past four decades, Jerome Kagan, professor emeritus of psychology at Harvard University, and his colleagues have shown that fussy, highly reactive babies end up with some positive characteristics in childhood.[17] They're more likely than less reactive babies to comply with their parents' wishes, make more friends, and get better grades in school later on in life. Fussy babies develop these competencies because they seem to be the most sensitive to their environments, even if they fuss a lot along the way. On the other hand, calm, low-reactive babies are more likely to grow into children who engage in delinquent behaviors because things like parental threats (that would throw a high-reactive child into a fit) don't seem to faze the Zen composition of low-reactive types at all.

Besides, isn't crying a core experience of new parenthood? You don't get to wear the "I Survived New Parenthood" T-shirt without the seemingly unending bouts of unsoothable fussiness. Crying can be a terribly stressful experience, especially when it comes in extended and intense doses. So we'd like for something as simple as a baby sling to abate crying.

There's also the common wisdom that babies cry to alert caregivers to their needs and that once their needs are met, they'll stop crying. But this belief is not common everywhere. Most North American parents view persistent crying in a negative manner. But impoverished Brazilian mothers see it in a positive light. They conceptualize it as a signal of a strong and healthy infant who is willing to fight for her own well-being.[18]

Evidence suggests that the Brazilian mothers might be on to something. Crying, at least during the first three months, is merely a standard feature of babyhood. It comes with all models. Careful research shows that crying is a fairly poor signal of need. In more than 95 percent of observed crying bouts, researchers found nothing discernibly wrong and no discernible need. Crying doesn't even seem to be related to the baby's level of physiological arousal. Even crying in colicky infants doesn't signal a need or sickness. In the absence of other risk factors, prolonged crying in the first three months has no negative effects on children's later growth, development, or behavior.[19]

Most experts think that all of this crying happens in the first few months merely as a by-product of the humongous degree of reorganization of brain systems that happens during this period. It's simply the mental version of growing pains. If this is the case, it means that lots of early crying is simply unavoidable—sling or no sling. And it provides a reason why it's tough to soothe a small baby. Simply knowing that most crying is not a signal of something wrong should make new parents feel less helpless if they can't come up with a way to console their newborn.

So if crying doesn't do anything, why did evolution design such a noxious feature into new babies? If you're asking yourself this question, then you're thinking only about what crying does in a house like yours. If you put your baby in a more historical environment—say, in a nomadic hunter-gatherer tribe of the sort humans have lived in for more than 99 percent of our history—crying might make more sense. It's only within the last hundred years or so, and only in certain parts of the globe, that babies are kept safe and out of harm's way. But in ancient times, the baby who cried the loudest and longest might have been more likely than the other, quieter babies to have been helped if its small band of relatives ran into a pack of hungry predators, an irate neighboring tribe, or a scarcity of food. This pattern, then, would have boosted the survival of the noisiest and more persistent criers and consequently increased the likelihood they'd pass on their genes to the next generation. As University of California, Davis, anthropologist Sarah Blaffer Hrdy puts it, loud crying might send a message that this is "an infant worth rearing."[20]

TUMMY TO PLAY

You've already learned about the Back to Sleep campaign that advocates placing infants to sleep on their backs and has served to reduce the incidence of SIDS. What you haven't learned yet is one of the unintended consequences of this campaign: it has also reduced the number of infants who are placed on their bellies to play. It's been estimated that more than a quarter of parents never have placed their babies on their bellies to play.[21] Why? Because they fear the prospect of SIDS. While it is true that belly sleeping (also known as the prone position) does put infants at an increased risk of SIDS, wakeful time in the prone position is not a risk factor for SIDS.

This might not seem like a big deal until you learn the normalcy and importance of "tummy time" for infants. It's well known that infants who sleep in the dangerous prone position reach motor milestones sooner than those who sleep on their backs. This isn't an argument for putting infants to sleep on their bellies; other studies have found that some time on the belly during the day can normalize motor development. Some time spent belly-down is needed to develop a youngster's motor head control and stability in weight-bearing positions like pushing up with arms, getting on all fours, and sitting. Lack of belly-down experience during play slows down motor achievements.[22]

Some marketers and media reports claim that infant-positioning equipment, like swings, carriers, and bouncy seats, can provide needed nonback time, but there's no evidence to support these claims. Time strapped into such confines can prevent babies from exploring their environment and exercising their motor skills. Also, the increased use of baby gear like car seats, baby swings, and bouncy seats has been linked to a concurrent rise in the incidence of positional plagiocephaly—which is the head flattening or misshaping that can happen from leaving infants placed in the same position for long periods of time.

How serious is the problem? At four months of age, between 20 and 48 percent of infants have noticeable head flattening and asymmetry of the skull base and face. Most can be treated by more frequently varying their position. But some require more aggressive treatment, like an orthotic helmet, custom cranial bands, or even surgery.[23] As a result of this increase in plagiocephaly, the name of the original baby-positioning campaign has been tweaked. It's now Back to Sleep, Tummy to Play. The American Academy of Pediatrics recommends preventive measures to parents, such as "avoiding too much time in car seats, carriers, and bouncers while the infant is awake," holding the baby, and generally varying her position when awake.[24]

PLAYTIME PRISONS

Baby gear companies don't actually make prisons for children's play. I'm just having a good time alliterating to describe those folding mesh containers that busy parents use to store their babies so they can fold the laundry, pay the bills, and update their status on Facebook. Sure, playpens are convenient, but they quash your baby's planned living-room expedition for the day. If learning were all in the head, then morning after morning of diddling with an assortment of battery-powered baby toys in the playpen might be sufficient. But learning is not *only* in the head. It's also in the hands and feet and arms and legs. The entire body from head to toe is one big instrument of learning. If you constrain that instrument, then learning is constrained as well.

How much play yard time is too much? Studies carried out by New York University psychologist Karen Adolph using diaries and step counters show that the typical toddler travels a daily distance of more than thirty-nine football fields and falls (usually inconsequentially) about fifteen times per hour.[25] That's a whole lot of time spent motoring. Adolph also has demonstrated that movement experience drives the development of motor skills. The duration of experience is a better predictor of motor development than either body maturation or chronological age. Rote repetition of specific actions won't do. To progress, children need varied experiences and a wide variety of activities.

Motor learning takes the very same trial-and-error path as cognitive learning. Motor skills don't unfold according to a biological timetable, but rather develop in a flexible manner as children solve problems. It has to be this way because children's bodies and their environments are constantly changing. Imagine if you just figured out how to crawl on all fours, and suddenly you grow a couple of inches and develop new muscle mass in your quadriceps, and your center of gravity shifts up a bit. To make matters worse, someone has just stuck a diaper on your bum, mopped the kitchen floor, and offered to dog-sit the Debkowskis' boxerdoodle. Adapting to such everyday and unexpected changes in one's body and environment must involve a continual process of online problem solving—which is something you can't do if you're stuck in your playpen. Imagine the motor difficulties you'd have if you suddenly became eight months pregnant, slipped on a pair of high-heeled shoes, and were confronted with a brand-new gravel floor in your kitchen. If children don't get out there and practice as the changes are happening to their bodies and in their world, they are in for a rude, high-heeled awakening.

THE EYES HAVE IT

As we learned in chapter 4, a hallmark of humans is our social-cognitive abilities. This suite of skills gives us the capacity to do all sorts of uniquely human things. However, before infants have developed fully their social-cognitive and language skills, they communicate with others and engage in social learning by following the gaze of others and by making use of eye contact and gestures to show and direct the attention of other people. Psychologists refer to this skill as "joint attention." It is important in infancy and remains a critical skill throughout our life span.

At the 1775 Battle of Bunker Hill, Colonel William Prescott is said to have given the order, "Don't fire until you see the whites of their eyes." As Michael Tomasello, the codirector of the Max Planck Institute for Evolutionary Anthropology, points out, had the opposing army been a troop of chimpanzees rather than British men, the American colonists would have been overrun immediately. Why? Because humans are the only primate that has whites of the eyes, or at least whites that are easy to see.[26]

The whites of our eyes are several times larger than those of any other primate. This nifty adaptation lets others know where we're looking, even if our head is turned in a different direction. Not so for a nonhuman primate. If a chimpanzee looks in one direction but points its head in another, we can be easily fooled about where it's looking.

When Tomasello had an adult human look up at the ceiling with her eyes only and kept her head straight forward, most infants observing her also looked to the ceiling. However, when the adult shut her eyes and pointed her head to the ceiling, the infants tended not to follow. When this experiment was repeated with our nearest primate relatives—chimpanzees, bonobos, and gorillas—as observers, exactly the opposite pattern of gaze following emerged. When the human looked up at the ceiling but kept her head straight ahead, the great apes followed the human's gaze only rarely. But when she closed her eyes and pointed her head up, they usually followed. The conclusion: humans are sensitive specifically to the direction of the eyes in a way that our nearest primate relatives are not. Tomasello has discovered an actual behavioral function for humans' unique whites of the eyes.

This human adaptation is important because it allows us to take the first step into someone else's mental world. If we know where others are looking, we can discover what's interesting to them, what they're thinking and feeling, and what they're planning to do next. At around their first birthdays, before language acquisition has begun, infants follow the direction of another person's eyes, not their heads.

Tomasello argues that infants go beyond merely following gaze, but use this whites-of-the-eyes adaptation to share attention with others in close-range cooperative activities. This sort of joint attention is not merely two people doing the same thing at the same time, but two people doing the same thing at the same time and *knowing that they are doing it*. This common psychological ground is critical for our species because it's what enables all sorts of uniquely human cooperative things that require shared intentions, such as language, governments, schools, maps, credit cards, and rock bands.

WHY APES DON'T HAVE FACEBOOK PAGES

Except for humans, no other animal attempts to share attention with its own kind or with us. Here's a demonstration: If you're playing hide-the-beanbag with a one-year-old human and you point to a bucket, she's likely to infer that you're pointing to clue her in on the location of the hidden object, rather than to direct her attention to the color of the bucket or the design on its front. But if you're playing hide-the-beanbag with a chimpanzee and do the same thing, he'll have no idea why you're pointing. It's not that he doesn't pick up on the directionality cue. You already know that he can follow head direction. Nor is it that pointing is completely unfamiliar to his kind. Chimpanzees raised near humans will gesture to communicate to us—to tell us objects they want (even objects that are hidden), tools they need, and places they'd like to go.

The problem is that great apes simply don't understand the meaning of the pointing cue.[27] They don't share with us the joint attentional frame of the hiding-finding game. They'll follow your point to the bucket but say, in effect, "A bucket. Who cares? Gimme food!" They don't understand that the pointing is part of the searching game that you two are sharing.

This pointing example demonstrates a major difference in the motives that underlie human versus great ape communication. Chimpanzees and other apes gesture only in order to manipulate others. But humans, even from a very early age, communicate to share information, to tell others helpful things, and to relate their experiences. We humans are motivated to share interest and attention with others in a way that our nearest primate relatives are not. This is why a chimpanzee never will have his own Facebook page. As early as nine months of age, humans gesture to initiate joint attentional interactions. By their first birthday, infants point at things simply to share interest and attention about them. They'll point to something they see, like an airplane in the sky, and then look toward you. They also begin to point to inform others of things they don't know. If it's clear you've misplaced your reading glasses and your one-year-old spies them, she'll gesture to share their location. Apes don't point for any of these reasons.

JOINT ATTENTION–GETTING DEVICE

Joint attention in humans is an especially critical skill early on, before language has emerged. It provides a means of communication—a means of learning—for infants before they develop language and mature social cognition. Infants can communicate with caregivers by way of eye contact and gestures, which enables them to learn new information about the world by following the gaze of others.

Joint attention contributes greatly to early language development. Infants and toddlers who experience it sustain attention longer, comprehend more language, produce meaningful gestures and words earlier, and show faster vocabulary development.[28] How does joint attention promote language learning? For instance, when a mother names a new object during a natural interaction ("Oh, what a beautiful *butterfly*!"), the infant can infer to which object his mother is referring by following her gaze and thus incidentally learn the new word. Joint attention serves as a means for infants and young children to map overheard speech to objects and actions during the course of everyday social interactions with family members and friends.

Infants, however, who have trouble engaging in and reacting to joint attention often develop a diminished capacity for relatedness and relationships.[29] In fact, clinical research indicates that children with autism show chronic, pronounced impairments in initiating joint attention with others and responding to others' attempts to establish joint attention.[30] It appears that an impairment in joint attention prevents children with autism from fully participating in cooperative tasks with others and thus hinders the development of skills that emerge during the course of cooperative interactions. There is also evidence that individual differences in joint attention are related to the degree of social competence, responsiveness to therapies, and the long-term social functioning of children with autism. Often when children with autism begin to communicate, they are strong when it comes to communicating their needs and requesting what they want. However, they are less likely to communicate for joint attention. In fact, this may be one of the first indicators that communication is not developing as it should.

A LITTLE MORE CONVERSATION, A LITTLE MORE ACTION

Ten-month-old Sam gets propped up in his "stationary entertainer" at least once a day for an hour in front of the television set. No big deal; that's the national average for his age. His mom says his favorite program to watch is Baby Einstein and that he's learned all sorts of things from it—colors, numbers, shapes, and new words. Sounds like a win-win situation. Sam is learning while his mom pays the bills, washes the dishes, mops the floor, and makes lunch.

Baby Einstein is common baby gear. One-third of all American babies between six months and two years of age have at least one Baby Einstein DVD.[31] But are these DVDs really educational? Can they really turn your toddler into a genius while you do the laundry? Simply, no. There is no scientific evidence that DVDs can increase infant intellect. More important, there are studies that show that watching television during infancy can hinder language acquisition and lead to later attention problems.[32] So, as a lot of us in the research community had feared all along, all those happy puppets, bright colors, and silly songs are simply a mind-numbing way to occupy infants while parents do something else.

In 2006, the Campaign for a Commercial-Free Childhood went to the Federal Trade Commission to complain about the educational claims made by Baby Einstein and Brainy Baby®. As a result, the companies dropped the word "educational" from their marketing.[33] When later threatened with a class action lawsuit for deceptive practices, the Walt Disney Company (which acquired Baby Einstein in 1991) announced refunds, or "enhanced consumer satisfaction guarantees," for up to four DVDs per household.[34]

Now the word "educational" is gone from Baby Einstein's marketing, but the hint of educational benefits still lingers. The Baby Einstein home page says that the company's products offer "a whole new way for your baby to discover the world." This sounds promising until you learn that this "new way" is "three types of media—DVD, CD, and book or cards—all working together to provide different ways of experiencing a baby's world."[35] But the world isn't on DVDs, CDs, books, and cards. It's there in the living room, in caregivers, in the toy box, in the fish tank, and outside the door in the backyard, on the playground, and in the neighborhood.

Granted, the baleful effects of television on language and attention are at least in part due to children being stashed in front of the television by themselves. Baby Einstein acknowledges this by promoting their products as encouraging interaction between caregivers and children. For instance, the Baby Einstein Baby's Favorite Places DVD "presents a fun way for parents and little ones to 'go exploring' . . . with a playful introduction to 20 words for the names of familiar locations."[36] But any parent who thinks that the best way to "go exploring" with their infant is on a television set is missing the whole idea of how babies learn. What young children need is to explore with their entire bodies, not watch two-dimensional "familiar locations" on a screen.

They also need to interact with real people and not television sets to learn words. Patricia Kuhl at the University of Washington and her colleagues had a native Mandarin speaker play with a group of babies while speaking Chinese for twelve sessions of twenty-five minutes each over a four-week period.[37] When the babies were tested later, they recognized Mandarin sounds. But when Kuhl repeated the experiment with three control groups—one set of babies that watched the Chinese speaker play with babies on television, another that listened to an audio recording of the Chinese speaker playing, and a third that had no exposure to the Chinese speaker—none could distinguish the Mandarin sounds. Apparently, the presence of a living, breathing human was essential for language learning to take place.

There's also evidence that viewing DVDs with parents—as Baby Einstein now promotes—doesn't help either. University of Virginia developmental psychologist Judy DeLoache and her colleagues found that babies who viewed infant-learning DVDs regularly for one month, either with or without their parents, showed no greater understanding of words from the program than babies who never saw it.[38] The only infants with a word-learning advantage were those in a no-DVD condition whose parents tried to teach them the same target words from the DVD during everyday activities without ever showing the program. DeLoache won't reveal what DVD she used, although she says it is "one of the best available," but it's clear from logs parents kept during the study that infants were enraptured by the DVDs. One parent noted, "She loves the blasted thing," and another wrote, "It's like crack for babies." DeLoache's findings are in line with the idea that children learn best by interacting in the real world. The takeaway message here is that what matters for language learning is face time, not DVD time. Words need to be delivered through social interaction, not the television set or the computer screen. When the brain picks up this social interaction, its neurons begin churning away. The brain has been designed to develop from the kind of information-rich, give-and-take stimulation that only another human being can provide. As such, it seems that even the most sophisticated electronic toy, computer program, or DVD can't mimic human social interaction. Likewise, these artificial experiences can't engage the entire gamut of senses—sights, sounds, smells, tastes, and tactile sensations. Young children need rich sensory experiences to learn.

MOVING CONDITION

The brain comes into the world expecting the body to move. The whole reason a nervous system was invented in the first place was to coordinate movement so that the body could go find food instead of waiting for it to come to the body. Jellyfish and sea anemones, the first animals to develop neurons, had a major advantage over the brainless sponges that just sat there on the ocean floor. Through our evolutionary history, we've been active beings; in fact, there's growing evidence that movement, or exercise, boosts brain power. Children who exercise outperform their couch-potato age-mates on tests of attention and memory.[39] Brain regions involved in maintaining attention and executive control and memory also are heftier in exercisers.[40] Movement can improve thinking: working memory performance is better in children when they're walking than when they're sitting down.[41]

So, slide your babies out of their bouncy seats, hold them on your laps, and let them play on their tummies. Turn off the television sets, and make sure your kids get plenty of face time and opportunities to be active and explore. It won't turn your children into little Einsteins, but it will make them normal.

Chapter 6

Toying with Children

I love words. I love the way they feel in my mouth. I love the way they look in print. As a teacher and a writer, I love the way they can make others see the world differently, think extraordinary new thoughts, and even improve how they live their lives. I love how a carefully crafted set of words can make people break out in a cold and clammy sweat, suddenly feel their heart beating inside their chest, end up on the floor in a silly ball of laughter, or stand up and cheer. But as a parent, I have no idea what I'm doing with words. I terribly mistreat them. Frankly, I'm ashamed.

I've heard myself say, "Please use both hands," when I really meant, "Spill that grape juice on your shirt one more time, and you're eating breakfast shirtless from here on out." I've said, "Put your Star Wars® toys away in their bin where they belong," when I know damn well that C-3PO® doesn't care if he spends the night in the middle of the kitchen floor or tucked in snugly next to Princess Leia. And I've said, "I'll make three dozen cupcakes decorated in school colors for the kindergarten bake sale," when I really meant, "I have zero kitchen skills and even less free time. OK if I donate twenty bucks instead?" But despite my own shameful mistreatment of the English language, I can no longer ignore the rampant misuse of one of my favorite words. That word is "play." I know exactly what it means. The true definition is clear. But someone has seized it, capitalized it, and commercialized it. And everybody's playing along.

Play is a fun and freewheeling activity that children do naturally. They don't need special equipment, advanced preparation, or much help from us to do it. But lately the Internet, my television set, and the magazines in my dentist's office have been telling me that I need to get certain things in order for my children to do this natural activity. They've switched the word's meaning from a focus on *activity* to a focus on *things*.

The first time I noticed the shifting of this word's meaning was when my daughter took her favorite lime-green magic marker and printed out the word PLAYSTATION in the number one position on her "Things I Want for My Birthday" list. I reacted coolly by asking why she thought she needed a *station* (a thing) in order to *play* (an activity). Wasn't her takeover of the family room enough? Couldn't we just call the space piled high with blocks and plastic animals under the kitchen table her "play-station"? I volunteered to make a poster-board sign saying so and even offered to tape it onto the backs of the chairs.

I backed down from my interrogation when she crouched down and slid my soapbox out from under the couch. I agreed that video games were indeed fun, that I was no stranger to Mr. and Ms. Pac-Man™, and that Dad and I sometimes fought a virtual grappling match after she went to bed to work out who was going to do the dinner dishes.

But then I stooped down, looked her straight in the eye, and told her that a round of Super Mario Bros. was not, by any definition of the word, play. Attaching painted toilet-paper-tube horns to your headband, getting down on all fours, and roaring like a parent-eating two-headed rabid monster is play. Pushing joystick buttons to make an Italian plumber bounce off mushrooms while you recline on the Barcalounger is not.

We are constantly being told that we need to buy our children all sorts of *things* in order for them to play, when in fact these things almost always lead to something other than play—something other than a rowdy, raucous undertaking done for the sheer joy of it. We're told we need to buy play mats, play trays, playpens, play tables, play yards, play zones, play centers, play huts, play sets, Pack 'n Plays®, Play n' Learns, play lands, Playhouse Disney®, Wii Play®, and backyard play systems. But most of these things have nothing to do with real play. In fact, they often hamper it. Imagine if this linguistic strategy were applied to adult activities. Instead of golf balls, golf shoes, and golf carts, sporting goods stores would sell golf bricks, golf stilettos, and golf unicycles.

So for our children, play usually comes in a box. No matter that the box is often more beneficial for brain development than what's inside it; they and we think that the more the thing in the box costs, the better it is for play. I can buy a bag of two hundred mixed Lego® blocks on eBay for about ten bucks. But if these very same pieces are predesigned to form themselves into a medieval castle and fire-breathing dragon and come in a box that shows these finished works, the price increases ten-fold. Want to guess which option my seven-year-old wants for his birthday? How did this happen?

The shift in the meaning of the word "play" started on October 3, 1955. That's the day the Mickey Mouse Club® made its debut on television. But that's not the event that triggered the change in play. The culprit was a commercial that aired during this first episode for a toy gun by the Mattel Toy Company called the Thunder Burp.[1] The advertisement promised an extraordinary toy: "It's broken the sound barrier. It's the Mattel Thunder Burp with the real vibrosonic sound chamber that's loaded forever and ever. No batteries, no caps. That Thunder Burp looks like real, sounds like real."

The commercial was so significant because it was the first commercial ever for a toy outside of the Christmas season. Until that afternoon, no company had tried to sell toys on television year-round. According to Howard Chudacoff, a cultural historian at Brown University, after this commercial, almost overnight, children's play became singularly focused on toys rather than the activity itself.[2]

In his book *Children at Play*, Chudacoff documents the radical changes to play that have occurred in the past few generations. He combines squishy evidence from diaries and autobiographies with more solid numbers from surveys to demonstrate that as parents began to equip children with more and more specific toys with predetermined scripts, play largely lost its fluid and improvised qualities. Fifty years ago, it was common for a tree branch to change from a rattlesnake to a samurai sword to a fishing pole, all within the same play session. Today's electronic lightsabers, talking kitchen sets, and motorized pet dogs leave no room for such fluidity and inventiveness.

But today's toys are pretty fun, right? What seven-year-old wouldn't rather play-fight with a glowing, buzzing Darth Vader® lightsaber than a dried-up stick that snaps in half on contact? The problem is that highly structured toys impose a ready-made story on children's play and leave little or no room for imagination. Like it or not, if your daughter is playing with a doll that talks, a convertible that revs up, and a playhouse that tells her what's for dinner, who's at the front door, and when the baby needs a nap, there's little room left for her to start her own conversation, make fun car sounds, or script her own story with the other dolls in her toy box.

Scripted toys also squash the flexibility of simple objects. A sock puppet can be a beauty queen in the morning, a secret agent by lunch, the tooth fairy for nap time, and a crotchety old man before bed. But it's hard to make a deep-breathing, armored Darth Vader action figure into anything but what it is. And no toy company in its right mind is going to sell old socks. There's absolutely no economic reason to put Grandpa's old socks in a box and try to sell them. In fact, there's no economic reason for toy companies to sell *any* simple toy. They'll make much more profit off a ninety-dollar life-size palomino that neighs and bucks and chews fake carrots than a five-dollar miniature one that does absolutely nothing.

OK, I know what you're thinking. If I'd get down off of the soapbox that my daughter handed me from under the couch, I could clearly see that your preschooler would be sorely disappointed if she got a sock puppet rather than a Barbie® brand doll, car, and house for her birthday. But hear me out.

We've known for decades that play with objects follows a distinct and universal developmental pattern. Those what-to-expect sorts of books lay out these milestones. Generally, children move from merely reacting to the features of objects, to exploring objects, to using them symbolically as one object begins to stand for another. What the what-to-expect books don't tell you is that the characteristics of objects determine the sorts of play children do with them. For instance, less structured toys, like blocks, produce much higher levels of interactive pretend play than more structured toys, like tea sets.[3] Pretend play with less structured objects also coerces children into stretching their linguistic and cognitive legs more than play with highly structured objects. For instance, if your preschooler is playing pastry shop with a variety of fake cookies, it's easy for her to ask her playmate if he'd prefer peanut butter or chocolate chip. However, if she is in the backyard fashioning mud pies, simply asking, "Peanut butter or chocolate chip?" won't cut it when she offers her friend two handfuls of soppy dirt. She has to figure out how to communicate about something that's not really there and exists only in her mind. She has to provide the right contextual cues to get her playmate to buy into the game. But this isn't the case with scripted or structured toys, like the Little People® Dance 'n Twirl Palace™, Thomas & Friends™ Rock Quarry Run, and Playmobil®'s Jewel Thieves,[4] because the context and even the story line is already there.

TOY STORIES

The other day, in the checkout line at the grocery store, I was waiting behind a young girl who was sitting in the front of her mother's shopping cart. She was very busy reprimanding her stuffed blue elephant for his misbehavior during Mrs. Kitty's tea party earlier that morning. "Peanut," she scolded, pointing her finger at his trunk, "you were rude to eat Fluffy's cake. You are big, but that doesn't mean you can eat other people's portions." Good point, I thought. Perhaps I'd try to use that one on my husband next time we ordered a pizza.

The mother then complimented her daughter: "That's very good pretending, Emma." I agreed. "But I think you can do better than that," she added and handed Emma a pink cat in a polka-dot sundress. "Try again with Fluffy." I saw Emma's face drop as she reached out for Fluffy. Was Emma pretending at a subpar level? I hadn't noticed. Did Emma need remedial help? Are there parents out there who chastise their children for run-of-the-mill sidewalk chalk drawings, unexceptional rounds of hide-and-seek, or mediocre armpit farts?

Commercialization isn't the only reason that play has changed. There also seems to be a growing number of parents who think that camping under the kitchen table or making a marching band out of pots and pans is an inferior version of play compared to play with "educational" toys that are "designed to maximize brain growth." These parents seem to be on a mission to siphon all the fun out of play and replace it with education.

Toy companies are responding to and prospering off of this change in parents' definition of play. Barry Levenson, chief marketing officer at Knowledge Adventure, a major producer of educational software designed for children four and under, says, "Everything we do is academic, even for toddlers and babies. There's nothing in there that's just purely for fun."[5] Parents who want to do what's best for their children eat up this marketing, and for many, "educational" toys have become status symbols. Having a $2,599.99 (plus $95 shipping) Little Tikes™ Young

Explorer™ in the family room now carries more cachet than a Hummer® in the driveway.[6] The truth is, this giant plastic cubicle, whose marketing promises an "enriched learning" environment, is more likely to tell children that they'll never be a Nobel Prize winner, but just a part of the office grind.

Educational toys are nothing new. They've been around for decades. We had them when we were kids. Remember Boggle™? I had Boggle, but it was so boring that it rarely, if ever, made it out of the game closet. Heedful of the Boggle effect, today's so-called educational toys have kicked it up a notch. They are a different breed of educational toy and would be completely unrecognizable to Boggle. Twenty-first-century educational toys are loud and fun and brightly colored—and frankly, quite mesmerizing. There are frogs that talk, books that play games, magnets that recite the ABCs, handheld computers that let kids play online, and bicycles that control the television set. There are even toys that e-mail parents periodic reports of their children's play and learning progress. Today's educational toys seem so much more advanced, entertaining, and neurologically effective than, well, Boggle. Surely a talking frog promotes neural growth much more effectively than a cardboard box filled with lettered dice and a plastic hourglass timer.

But the talking-frog breed of toys are mostly smoke and mirrors. If they're really superior, then shouldn't our children be way smarter than us? There is not a single study that shows that any of today's educational toys, video games, or electronic learning systems give children an intellectual edge over playmates who stick to building blocks and baby dolls. Nor will there likely ever be.

The problem is that most of today's high-tech "educational" toys turn children into passive learners. Sure, they market themselves as "interactive," but no toy could ever be programmed to respond in the nuanced, fine-tuned, fleshy way that caregivers do. Nor could any toy teach children about the real world as well as interacting with the real world can. It's almost silly to think that children can learn about the real world by burying their faces in a handheld electronic learning system or a plastic miniature table with buttons and lights. By now you know that it's critical for children to engage in the real world—to observe it, touch it, and manipulate it. It's how children have been learning for millions of years—how children's brains have been designed to learn. But if your toddler is sitting in the middle of her living room with an electronic toy that does everything for her—if it sings and beeps and talks and shows pictures—then what does she have left to do? These brain-training gadgets miss the point of what toys really are about.

THESE TOYS ARE MADE FOR PLAYING

The current "educational" toy market started when developmental psychologists began trumpeting the benefits of play. In the 1990s and 2000s, a healthy literature developed that demonstrated that play has all sorts of social, emotional, and cognitive benefits.[7] Then, in 2007, the gold seal of approval came from a paper in the journal *Pediatrics*, published by the American Academy of Pediatrics. The paper argues that ample opportunity for unstructured play is a required ingredient in a healthy childhood.[8]

Marketers took this literature and discreetly substituted the word "toys" for "play." "Toys—that children *play* with—are essential for brain growth," is the message parents received. But this is a mistranslation of the research. Toy companies and marketers have become very clever at taking empirical work and crafting stories about how their particular brand of toy enhances the sort of play that child development scientists are talking about. Today, the educational toy market is a multibillion-dollar industry. But if you go back and look at the 2007 *Pediatrics* article, the word "toy" is mentioned only three times: once to say that toys like blocks and dolls are "true toys" and twice to say that play with heavily marketed, specialized toys is inferior to unstructured play.

Now that our family rooms and toy stores are filled with beeping, buzzing, battery-powered "educational" toys, how do we remedy children's play? At home, take the batteries out of toys. Your children will interact more actively rather than passively with them. If your daughter's Barbie Dream House no longer tells her that the microwave popcorn is ready for movie night and that the baby is ready for a nap, she'll create story lines herself. If your son's spaceship no longer tells him to prepare for landing, he'll keep the craft in the air a little longer and decide for himself when it's time to touch down. If your toddler's stationary entertainment center no longer lights up and sings nursery rhymes, you'll take a break from your housework, get down on the floor, and sing her a song.

When you're shopping for toys, remind yourself of the real definition of the word "play." Play is an activity that doesn't require too many special things. It's the activity of play, not the things of play, that promotes brain growth. Kathy Hirsh-Pasek, a developmental psychologist at Temple University, offers the following helpful suggestion for parents: buy toys that are 90 percent child and 10 percent toy, as opposed to the other way around.[9] So buy toys that demand children's active interaction, persuade them to problem-solve, and encourage them to think creatively. Resist those electronic toys that turn children into passive observers, merely feeding them sights, sounds, and information. Keep in mind that those toys that market themselves as "interactive" aren't really if children are just pushing a button or tapping a screen. If you feel yourself slipping, repeat this mantra: Real interactions don't happen with machines. Real interactions happen only with real people in the real world.

Remember, too, that toys that market themselves as "educational" are merely preying on your fears and the public's tendency to lean on exaggerated science. Remember: there's never been a single study showing that any toy marketed as "educational" is better for children's brains than simple toys like blocks, dolls, and balls. Sure, math flash cards can get your two-year-old to parrot numbers, and a learning laptop can help your child memorize addition equations. But if you want to make math interactive and quantity meaningful, sit down at the kitchen table with your three-year-old and play around with M&Ms. Ask her to sort them by color, dole out equal portions, or give you 2 + 3 to eat. All the educational toys your child needs are probably already in your house and backyard and at the neighborhood park. Science lessons happen while exploring anthills, physics is taught while tossing heavier and lighter objects down the stairs, imaginary worlds are created in piles of dirt, observational abilities are fostered in hunts for crawdads, social skills are built by pretending with friends to be astronauts, problem-solving skills are fostered in backyard pickup games, story lines are developed as cardboard boxes become faraway castles, inventions are made with glue and paint, and creative thinking is sparked by building forts with sticks and branches.

To help parents reacquaint the word "play" with its original meaning, I've developed an electronic learning laptop that you can use to identify real instances of play. My beeping, blinking, brightly colored laptop has all the flash of real learning, but its programs rely only on rote drilling, so that parents memorize the right answers without any true understanding. Parents who complete all six learning levels will be rewarded with their choice of prize for their children: a Veg-and-Learn walker, a Slack-and-Learn laptop, or a Slouch-and-Learn handheld console. You'll love my new learning laptop, but in case you don't, I've glued a sticker onto the box. It says, "Promotes Brain Growth." That should do it.

RISKY, AND COSTLY, BUSINESS

If you've ever seen children playing, it looks like a purposeless activity. Stuffing one's pants with dried leaves, collecting flower petals and small stones to mix a magic potion, and chasing each other around the backyard appears to accomplish nothing. It certainly doesn't look like learning. Children learning in the classroom look very different from children playing in the backyard. Children playing in the backyard simply look silly. The thing is, this silliness is play's special sauce. Its frivolity is essential to its definition. Biologists often use phrases like "apparently purposeless activity" when they describe play. To see how such silliness could have been selected for by something as smart as evolution over millions of years, you'll need the right pair of lenses. Read on, and I'll adjust your eyeglass prescription.

Humans, of course, are not alone when it comes to play. Certainly, you've seen puppies romping or bear cubs tumbling with one another. Our shared playfulness suggests that playing is an ancient behavior, that it's been around for a long time. But this long history doesn't tell us if play is still useful to our children, or if it's merely a useless remnant of our animal past, like the appendix.

One way of getting at this question is to compare play in children and animals. When we do, it's clear that in both groups, play is the first thing to go when basic needs are unmet. In times of famine, danger, or sickness, play is almost always affected. In most animals, play will entirely disappear when times are hard. This suggests that play is sort of a biological luxury item. It's certainly not essential. Even human children can survive without play. But as illustrated in George Eisen's *Children and Play in the Holocaust*, children's drive to play remains, even under terribly devastating conditions such as widespread war, famine, displacement, or physical abuse.[10]

If children can do without play, then why has it persisted? There are several reasons why you'd think evolution would have weed it out. First, play is biologically expensive. Juveniles spend between 2 and 15 percent of their daily calorie budget on play—calories that could be used instead for growing.[11] Evolution usually doesn't keep around such high-cost adaptations.

Play is also dangerous. It can pull youngsters away from the protection of their families; it can distract them and make them vulnerable to predators; and all that running, jumping, and tumbling can cause injury and even death.

But the young brain seems to have not gotten this memo. Children continue to play, even though each year in the United States, two hundred thousand of them end up in the emergency room from injuries that happened on the playground.[12] One of the most impressive examples of the brain's disregard for the danger of play comes from observations made by zoologist Robert Harcourt at the University of Macquarie in Australia. Over a period of nine months studying South American fur seals in Peru, Harcourt witnessed twenty-six seal pups die at the hands (well, fins) of sea lions.[13] Of these twenty-six, twenty-two were killed while playing out of the protective range of their parents. So nearly 85 percent of the pups that had been killed were playing.

ALL PLAY AND NO WORK

Play is biologically costly and can be very dangerous. Both factors seem like good reasons to get rid of it. But since play is still around, it must have some humongous advantage; otherwise, evolution would have winnowed it out a long time ago.

Neuroscientists are increasingly making the argument that play is needed for typical brain development to occur. Play seems to be a central means through which juveniles build complex, skilled, responsive, socially adept, and cognitively flexible brains. Granted, there may be other means to these neurological ends, which is why play isn't absolutely necessary. But increasing evidence suggests that play is the most efficient—and likely the most fun and fulfilling—way of developing a skilled and flexible brain.

Neuroscientist Sergio Pellis at the University of Lethbridge in Alberta, Canada, for instance, uses a rat model to understand how playing affects brain development. In one series of experiments, Pellis raised rat pups, didn't let them out to play, and then compared their brains with those that had plenty of opportunity to play.[14] Is it fair to compare rat play to children's play? Rats don't use building blocks, finger paint, or play house, true, but we can't ethically deprive human children of play and then flip open their skulls to check out their brains. Plus, rats do play—just in ratty, rough-and-tumble ways.

To manipulate rats' play, Pellis raised rat pups either with other juveniles or with adults only. Adult rats rarely play with juveniles, even their own offspring. So Pellis knew that this arrangement would pretty much eliminate play. Importantly, it didn't affect all the other typical pup social experiences—grooming, nuzzling, sniffing. When Pellis looked at the brains of both groups as they reached puberty, he found astounding differences. The play-deprived animals had a much more immature pattern of neuronal connections in their brains' medial prefrontal cortex. Like humans, rats and other mammals are born with an overabundance of cortical brain cells and connections, which are pruned and selectively eliminated as the result of feedback from experiences during the juvenile period. Play had been thought to be one of the juvenile experiences that helps in this pruning, and Pellis's findings provide the first direct evidence that play deprivation interferes with it.

Do Pellis's findings mean that if your children don't get enough playtime, their pruning will be behind that of their age mates, and they'll have more trouble in the social world of childhood? We don't exactly know that yet. Pellis and his colleagues interpret their observation of a more tangled, immature medial prefrontal cortex in play-deprived rats to mean that such rats will be less able to deal with their social world. But we don't know yet if this pruning could happen later in life or be achieved by taking some other route not related to play. However, other work in Pellis's lab showing abnormal play in rat pups whose medial prefrontal cortices have been damaged first seems to confirm the direct role of play in brain development.[15] This supports the idea that play is not a purposeless activity, but an adaptation that plays an important role.

FLAVORED PLAY

Play comes in all sorts of flavors. There's tag, which is not the same as wall ball, dressing up, pretending to be Martians, playing four square, or battling with army men. The almost unending variety of play makes Marc Bekoff, an evolutionary biologist at the University of Denver, think that its kaleidoscopic quality must be an adaptation.[16] Specifically, he thinks that play's many flavors are an adaptive way for juveniles to develop a diverse array of behaviors. Think of it this way: if the only sort of play the human child did was hide-and-seek, all the time, then the behaviors fostered by play would be limited. But since play comes in so many types, it teaches a wide array of skills and essentially trains children for just about anything life might throw their way. Those in the business of play refer to this idea as the flexibility hypothesis and describe it as the notion that a big menu of play supports the growth of more supple and flexible brains.

As we discussed in chapter 2, behavioral flexibility and variability is adaptive. It's important to be able to change your behavior in response to a changing environment. It's beneficial to have a broad set of behaviors in your arsenal, given that you never quite know what to expect. Flexibility is a hallmark of humans—it's what helps us survive and thrive in many different environments across the globe. For humans, play is essentially training for what the brain can't predict.

The flavorfulness of play is also likely why researchers have found that it has so many benefits to humans during our early development.[17] There's an enormous literature, for instance, showing that play builds attention and self-regulatory skills. Also, children who indulge themselves regularly in play tend to have advanced language abilities, display more creative thinking, exhibit better memory, and show better problem-solving skills. They also tend to be less stressed and have strong social skills. Chicken-and-egg questions arose from these data for some years, but today it's clear that play causes these advantages and not the other way around.[18]

CHANGE IN PLAY, CHANGE IN CHILDREN

The changes to play brought about by commercialized toys are recent-ish. If you stand back and look at human history in its entirety, the more dramatic change is the move away from play as something that's been largely independent, improvised, and imaginative for most of our existence. This general loss of autonomous, creative play is what's most worrisome.

It's worrisome because when children use their imaginations—by improvising with props, creating their own games, and developing new story lines—they stimulate the growth of brain cells in the executive portion of the frontal cortex, an area that lays the foundation for the circuitry of what's known as executive function. Executive function refers to a set of skills important for several cognitive functions, such as attention and memory. It's also involved in self-regulation—a critical skill for controlling emotions, resisting impulses, and exerting self-control and discipline.[19]

Children who are highly self-regulated can wait their turn on the playground, resist the temptation to snatch a desired Imperial Stormtrooper® action figure out of their brother's hands, clean up after a playdate with little or no nagging, automatically help another child who's struggling to stack a straight block tower, and persist at a challenging puzzle. Well-regulated children also actively try to control negative emotion. They usually do so by talking out loud to themselves (e.g., "I'll get another chance to play with Avery's new puppy") or changing their goals (e.g., when someone else is using the swing, they turn to play on the slide instead).

Free play develops self-regulatory skills because it puts the action in children's hands. If Ava makes up a pretend story line where she's the teacher and her playmates are the students, Ava's friends have to follow her rules if they want to play along. Or they may push and pull and argue with one another to agree on a set of rules and negotiate how they'll be reinforced. Either way, this is the development of self-control in action.

Children's private speech also builds the self-regulatory skills.[20] During play, children often talk aloud to lay out ground rules for themselves or to direct their next set of moves. If you listen closely to children talking to themselves while they're playing, you'll hear them working through what they're going to do and how they're going to do it. If you listen to them often enough, you'll learn that this sort of self-regulating language is highest during periods of pretend play. Adults use private speech, too, but not when we're pretending. We tend to break it out when we need to surmount some obstacle during a cognitively challenging task or when we need to manage an overwhelming emotion.

I bring up self-regulation because it's not only a key ingredient for a successful childhood, it also predicts effective development in just about every domain. In fact, self-regulation is a better predictor of school success than IQ.[21] The importance of this pattern cannot be emphasized enough because it challenges the common wisdom that an atmosphere of rote drilling is the best way to boost intellectual performance.

Also, an interesting relationship exists between the recent falling-off of children's free play and changes in children's self-regulatory skills. If you'd put up a graph charting recent changes in children's free playtime next to a graph charting changes in children's self-regulatory skills, you'd see that both have been plummeting along the same curve. Today's five-year-olds seem to have the self-regulatory skills of three-year-olds in the 1940s. In the late 1940s, researchers asked three-, five-, and seven-year-olds to stand perfectly still without moving. The three-year-olds, as you might guess, couldn't do it at all. The five-year-olds stood still for an average of about three minutes. The seven-year-olds could stand pretty much as long as the researchers asked. When this experiment was replicated in 2001, the five-year-olds behaved as the three-year-olds did sixty years before, and the seven-year-olds behaved like the 1940s five-year-olds.[22]

Because we know that unstructured play builds self-regulation and that both have decreased in recent decades, you have to wonder whether the drop in free play has caused the drop in self-regulation. To be sure, more research is needed. Nonetheless, this pattern should serve as a red flag to parents because poor self-regulatory skills are associated with an increased risk of all sorts of problem behaviors, like attention deficit/hyperactivity disorder (ADHD), school dropout, drug use, and crime.

The more we structure children's play by making up the rules, scripting their toys, and generally butting in, the less likely children are to engage in private speech. The more children's play is focused on soccer clinics, karate classes, video games, and battery-powered toys, the fewer opportunities they have to practice self-regulation and to police themselves. There's also growing evidence that children's reduced self-regulatory skills might be showing up in the increased numbers of ADHD diagnoses. That is, some children might get diagnosed with ADHD (and be prescribed stimulants like Ritalin) simply because they never learned early in their lives how to exercise self-control, self-regulation, or the executive functions.

PLAY IT FORWARD

This focus on the advantages that play confers suggests that play has only long-term benefits, which is exactly what a lot of people think. For instance, in his book *The Genesis of Play*, Gordon Burghardt, an evolutionary psychologist at the University of Tennessee, refers to play as an activity that has a "limited immediate function."[23] So, notwithstanding the idea that play is preparation for the future, Burghardt thinks that play has little, if any, immediate benefit.

Perhaps Burghardt has never seen a three-year-old splashing in puddles with joyous abandon. If he had, he would clearly see an immediate benefit of play. Play is great fun. The more a three-year-old plays, the richer her life—the more fun she has, the more social relationships she builds, the more physical activity her body gets, and the more stimulation her brain experiences. Without play, childhood simply would be unfulfilling and unhealthy.

Developmental research has demonstrated other, less obvious, immediate benefits of play. For example, children tend to persist longer at challenging tasks during play than they would otherwise. The fun of it all motivates them to keep noodling away. My seven-year-old son will push himself to make sure that he gives his friends exact play-money change at his makeshift Martian convenience store and motel. But ask him to figure out five different ways to make change for a dollar for his math homework, and suddenly the task seems too big for him.

Likewise, play is often a context where problems are solved more creatively. The lack of real-world consequences during play can lead children to arrive at something better than the first, good enough solution. One of my favorite studies demonstrating a novel solution discovered by juveniles comes from a troop of Japanese macaque monkeys that lived near the ocean and were provisioned with food by scientists.[24] During a bout of play, one of the juveniles washed a handful of sweet potatoes in the sea before snacking on them. Not only did the washing remove the sand from the potatoes, it also gave them a salty taste. Other juveniles picked up the trick, but few adults were observed to clean the potatoes before eating. Nonetheless, when the juveniles grew up and had their own families, some of them passed on the behavior to their infants.

Human play certainly is much more complicated than typical

monkey play, and not many innovations that adults can use in the real world emerge from children's play. Yet play gives children important insights and discoveries that cannot be as easily acquired through formal instruction. There's also a certain satisfaction that comes from discovering your own answers and a certain motivation to push yourself beyond what you thought were your limits. Success feels good, and play is a context that gives such benefits to children in the here and now.

The main point of this discussion is that you really don't have to stay up till the wee hours on Christmas Eve putting together dollhouses and racetracks that would perplex Albert Einstein. Children's play contributes to a suppler brain and a more varied behavioral repertoire, but children don't need special equipment to do this. Play might look silly and purposeless, but it warrants a place in children's daily lives because it's more essential to healthful neurological development than flash cards, alphabet drills, battery-powered toys, or electronic learning consoles.

Chapter 7

Wii Little Children

When the Martians finally come to Earth and try to understand human behavior, the first thing they'll have to sort out is our obsession with screens—movie screens, television screens, computer screens, tiny handheld screens. They'll wonder why we spend so much time staring at them while the real world goes by. They'll wonder why we'd rather build and furnish an entire simulated house than paint our own peeling bathroom wall. Why would we rather watch strangers play football than play a pickup game with our friends in the backyard? And why do we prefer to text the latest gossip to our neighbor, rather than walk down the street and enjoy a couple of laughs over coffee?

I'm not a total technology grinch. Sometimes I read the *Times* on my iPhone® while checking my e-mail on my laptop and listening to my iPod. Other times I troll the Internet for Hollywood gossip, post summer vacation photos on Facebook, Skype® my out-of-state family, and e-shop for gifts. I might also judge people I see penciling their appointments in their leather-bound daily planners. But high technology also has its glitches. We have fewer conversations with real people, we make more errors because we're multitasking, our attention spans have gone to pot, and we . . . ooooh, look at the bird . . .

OOH, BABY, BABY, IT'S A WIRED WORLD

When it comes to children, we really have no idea what their constant exposure to screen-based technology is doing to their brains. Other than some work concerning television I'll discuss in a bit, the research literature on technology's effects on children's brains and behavior is an absolute mess. There are sloppy study designs, small sample sizes, biased agendas, overstated conclusions, and loud opinions. Getting at the real story requires slipping on the garden gloves and doing some deep weeding. But it's yard work worth doing because, like it or not, screen time is a standard feature of modern childhood.

Children between the ages of eight and eighteen expose their brains to seven and a half hours a day of high technology—and that's not counting texting.[1] If you do the math, that's fifty-three hours a week—more than your full-time job. This seven-and-a-half hour estimate doesn't include children's simultaneous use of different media, or media multitasking. If you figure that in, then the total is ten hours and forty-five minutes of media content every day. And if you add in texting, this number mushrooms. Half of all twelve- to seventeen-year-olds send fifty or more text messages a day, and one-third send more than one hundred daily.[2]

These numbers have ballooned in recent decades. Just within the past five years, children's time with high technology has shot up more than an hour a day (even though time spent watching television has dropped). If you figure in media multitasking, total media content has increased by more than two hours a day in the past five years. This boost in time is driven mostly by portable media like smartphones and iPods.

BRAIN CHANGE

Near the end of Stanley Kubrick's film *2001: A Space Odyssey*, as astronaut Dave Bowman is disconnecting the malfunctioning supercomputer HAL, it pleads, "I'm afraid, Dave. Dave, my mind is going. I can feel it. I can feel it. My mind is going. There is no question about it. I can feel it." I wonder if this is exactly what our children are feeling as they spend more and more time using screen-based technologies and less and less time engaging in direct social contact and real hands-on play.

Gary Small, a neuroscientist and professor of psychiatry at the University of California, Los Angeles, thinks our daily exposure to high technology is changing our brains.[3] In one study, Small asked frequent Internet users and Internet novices to read pages from a book while he scanned their brains. He found no differences in brain activity between the two groups. But when he asked them to do a simulated Google search, compared to the novices, the frequent users showed twice as much signaling in a specific brain network that's responsible for decision making and complex reasoning. Isn't that something? This is solid evidence that technology can make our brains more active.

Then Small did something *really* interesting. He wanted to know how quickly the brain could build up new pathways. After finding the initial differences in brain activity among the Internet novices and experts when googling, Small gave both groups homework. For the next five days, both groups were asked to search the Internet for one hour a day for the next five days. After these five days, everyone returned to Small's lab and repeated the original study. He found that the exact same neural circuitry in the front part of the brain became active in the Internet novices. Small had changed their brains. Think about how weird that is. Five hours on the Internet, and people's brains had already rewired themselves.

These findings made a big splash with the media. The evening news exhausted every possible pun about teaching old brains new tricks, and science bloggers wrote essays about whether we should make grandpa google to boost his forgetful brain. But what do these findings mean for children who are exposed to extreme amounts of technology from very early ages? If five hours of Internet searching can change an adult's brain, then what could an entire childhood heavy with technology do to a developing neural system? Just picture redoing Small's experiment with children, except replace the one hour a day for five days with seven and a half hours a day for ten years. You'd expect a whopper of an effect.

But Small's findings really should come as no surprise. They fit well with the adult literature showing that heavy technology users quickly develop some physical and cognitive advantages.[4] For example, your average video gamer has better short-term memory skills, faster reaction time, sharper peripheral vision, and superior hand-eye coordination than those with only minimal technology experience. There's even evidence that laparoscopic surgeons who are regular gamers make fewer operating room errors than their nongaming peers. Thank you, improved hand-eye coordination and depth perception. Small's findings also complement other work showing how high doses of specific types of experiences can strengthen supporting brain regions. For instance, professional musicians have more gray matter in areas of the brain involved in finger movements. Likewise, athletes' brains are meatier in regions responsible for hand-eye coordination.

Other work suggests that you might not actually need to do anything at all to change your brain—merely thinking about doing things can change it. Harvard Medical School neuroscientist Alvaro Pascual-Leone asked volunteers to learn and practice a little five-finger piano exercise.[5] They visited his lab two hours a day for five days to play. At the end of the five days of practice, Pascual-Leone took a look at the volunteers' brains. He found that after just these five days, the parts of the motor cortex devoted to the needed finger movements had overtaken surrounding areas. Extraordinary stuff. But even more extraordinary is what happened when Pascual-Leone asked another group merely to think about practicing the piano exercise. These volunteers imagined moving their fingers to play the music piece, but they held their hands entirely still. When Pascual-Leone imaged their brains, he found that the very same portions of the motor cortex that had expanded in the group who actually played the piano also had grown in those who had merely imagined playing.

This means that the "power of imagination" isn't an eye-rolling metaphor. Imagination has the ability to change the physical structure of the brain. But what worries me is that if something as innocuous as imagining a piano lesson can bring about a visible physical change in brain structure, and therefore some presumably minor change in the way a player performs, what changes might something like long stints of imaginary warfare during violent video game play bring about? We don't know. Given children's more frequent exposure at an early age to technology, we'd assume that children's neural networks differ in substantial ways from those of adults whose basic wiring was done when technology was less pervasive. We have some idea of how adults' heavy use of technology can affect their brains, but we shouldn't automatically apply these findings to children. This research still needs to be done. Technology clearly has changed children's lives. How it's changing children's brains is anyone's guess.

ANTISOCIAL NETWORKING

One thing we know for sure is that as children spend more and more time with technology, they spend less and less time socializing with real people. Social interaction is a species-expectant experience for us humans, and without heavy doses of it during childhood, we might be developing circuitry for Internet social networking rather than playground social interacting. Children's perpetual technology use is changing the very nature of their friendships.

Certain types of technology, such as texting and social networking, seem to be making teens less interested in face-to-face communication with their friends.[6] Elementary schoolers play sports on television sets, and even kindergartners play side by side on handheld gaming consoles during playdates. Preschoolers play over Skype with peers across the globe. The worry is that as children center their friendships on screens, they are missing out on the fleshy face-to-face experiences that help them develop empathy.

There isn't much research yet to confirm these suspicions, but there's plenty of evidence that as adults, heavy technology users often lack social skills. Add to that the fact that children who have trouble reading the feelings of others and the intentions of playmates, and who lack a sense of timing and smoothness in social interactions, are the least popular in any group. Not only can social awkwardness make childhood rough sailing, such children are more prone to academic failure, dropping out of school, and having trouble with the law. On the flip side, high levels of social intelligence benefit children not only during childhood, but also throughout life. Children who are socially intelligent will pretty much stay that way throughout life and, consequently, tend to be very successful adults.[7]

Whether technology will make for socially unaware children is conjecture at this point and will remain so until scientists do the right long-term studies. But after my children are in the digital world for a few hours, their glazed eyes and garbled speech make it seem as if someone has tinkered with their brains—like someone went in there when I wasn't looking, rewired their neural circuitry, and reprogrammed how they regard the world. Small's research suggests that parents and teachers should be able to direct some of this technological wiring by giving children a range of experiences that involve high technology. And if so, then there seems to be a way to reap the cognitive benefits of modern technology while preserving traditional social skills: make sure your child makes time for both. Balance is likely the key.

THE GREAT ELECTRONIC BABYSITTER

In his 1953 short story "The Murderer," Ray Bradbury said that television, like the mythical figure Medusa, "freezes a billion people to stone every night."[8] He was exaggerating, of course. But the fact that even a millisecond of *SpongeBob* makes both my children freeze in their tracks and stare deeply at the television set makes me wonder if Bradbury was on to something.

We listen to the American Academy of Pediatrics when they tell us to put our babies to sleep on their backs, buckle them into car safety seats, slide them into bicycle helmets, and slather sunscreen on their skin. Yet when they tell us that children under two years should have no exposure to television, we completely ignore their advice.[9] Forty-three percent of children under the age of two watch television every day, and 20 percent have a television set in their bedrooms. A third live in homes where the television set is on most or all of the time, whether or not anyone is watching.[10]

But how can television be bad for infants and toddlers if there are so many "educational" programs and DVDs designed with them in mind? One reason is that time spent in front of the television set takes away opportunities to explore their environment and interact with real people to develop cognitive, social, and emotional skills.[11] The bottom line is that all these advances in media technologies are making it even easier for young people to spend more and more time with media and less time with people. For instance, increases in children's time spent watching television—with or without parents or siblings—are linked to decreases in time spent with parents or siblings in other activities, time doing homework, and time engaged in creative play.

For decades, we've known that there's a relationship between the amount of time children spend watching television and their subsequent hostile interactions with others. For a while, the relationship between television viewing and hostility was a chicken-and-egg thing: does television make children more hostile, or do hostile children simply watch more television? But now we know that this relationship starts with the television and that television leads to hostility because it messes with children's ability to regulate their emotions.[12] In one study that looked at bullying, researchers found that the more television watched daily by children at age four, the higher their levels of bullying behavior toward others at ages six through eleven.[13]

Television can also be toxic to attention. Attention development is something you don't want to mess with because when it comes to intellectual abilities, attention is the holy grail. It's the gateway to the brain. Everything that you're conscious of, everything you let in, and everything you remember and forget depends on whether you were paying attention to it in the first place. If you're not paying attention, it might as well not have happened.

Now, if you've ever seen a baby watching television, her trancelike stare might give you the impression that it fosters the development of attention. Set a one-year-old in front of an episode of *Umizoomi*, and her eyes and ears will lock on the screen. She'll appear mesmerized, and when I tell you it's not good for her, you'll tell me, "Mia loves this show! She can't stop looking at it!" Of course she can't stop looking at it. She can't because of what Ivan Pavlov (the Russian scientist most famous for describing a learning process that involves what he termed "conditioned reflexes") called the orienting reflex. When a baby is confronted with a novel sight or sound, he or she can't help focusing on it. By rapidly changing colors, sounds, and motions, television effectively forces a baby's brain to stay at attention. If his or her gaze wanders, the action quickly rivets it back to the screen.

The University of Washington's Dimitri Christakis and his colleagues found that for each additional hour of television watched by a child under the age of three, the likelihood of an attention problem by age seven increased by about 10 percent.[14] So a three-year-old who watches three hours of television per day is 30 percent more likely to have attention problems than a child who doesn't watch television. This is true at older ages, too. The more television teenagers watch, the more likely they are to develop attention problems and have difficulties with school, such as not doing homework, having a negative attitude toward school, earning poor grades, dropping out of school, and not going on to college.[15] Importantly, this relationship is not the other way around. It's not that teenagers who don't do so well in school watch more television. But, reducing television viewing can have positive effects.

Given the findings connecting television viewing and attention, some people have tried to make links between television and attention deficit/

hyperactivity disorder (ADHD). But this hasn't been established. Television is linked with attention difficulties; there is no evidence that it causes ADHD.

Others are making the argument that television causes autism. In recent years, there's been an alarming rise in autism in the United States. In 1970, its incidence was thought to be just one in every 2,500 children; today about one in 110 children in the United States falls somewhere on the autism spectrum.[16] Some of the spike can be reasonably attributed to a new, broader definition of the disorder; better screening procedures; mandatory reporting by schools; and greater awareness of autism among pediatricians, parents, and educators. Still, there's a nagging sense that something we're doing to children's environment tips genetically susceptible children to autism.

Cornell University's Michael Waldman and his colleagues have data they say suggest that that trigger might be television.[17] They found that as cable subscription rates grew in certain counties in California and Pennsylvania, so did autism rates, and that autism rose most quickly in those counties with the fastest-growing cable. They also found the same relationship between autism and rainfall patterns in California, Pennsylvania, and Washington State. In counties or years when levels of precipitation were unusually high (and children presumably watched more television because of the weather), autism rates shot up, whereas in places or times with low levels of precipitation, autism rates were low.

This paper caused quite a stir when it was published, but what does it mean? How can Waldman and his colleagues say that television viewing causes autism if they never even measured television viewing? They can't. More important, correlational data like these are hard to tease apart. How do you know, for instance, that it's not the mold or mildew in rainy counties that is causing the autism? Or how do you know that as counties get more cable access, they don't also get more parents who are likely to pack unhealthy lunches, pay less attention to their children, or pressure their pediatricians for a diagnosis? You don't. It would take a lot more research to confirm whether these correlations have any true significance. In my neighborhood this past December, a rise in purchases of Silly Bandz® co-occurred with an increase in cases of the flu among children. Yet without further research, I'm not willing to say that the Silly Bandz, or children's heightened exposure to silicone rubber, caused the boost in flu cases. Plus, on a biological level, there's a body of evidence that suggests that autism begins to develop long before children are born.[18] So it's likely the trouble started long before television watching, or Silly Bandz wearing, began.

BEYOND THE BOOB TUBE

As I mentioned above, the literature on screens and children is muddled. The one thing that does seem to pervade, regardless of the type of technology, is content. If the electronic content that children are consuming is some behavior you'd prefer they not do, then you might want to unplug your children.

The reason is that children are really good at imitation, especially deferred imitation—that is, repeating behavior they've seen at some earlier time. Like the time when you accidentally blurted out that your mother-in-law is a witch and then your children repeated the sentiment in front of your husband. Infants as young as thirteen months can imitate an event they saw a week before.[19] By the time children are about a year and a half old, they can act out something they saw only one time four months prior.[20] So beware. Imitation is a skill that never leaves children. If a toddler can embed into his memory a complex series of events after only one exposure, imagine what months of television or gaming can do.

GAME BOYS AND GIRLS

Video games are bad for play but good for fun. The reason has something to do with the fact that it's easier to ride a virtual skateboard than a real one; that it's easier to tackle an avatar than a real fifth grader in a youth football league; and that in the game, it's possible to blast aliens with plasma pistols. It also has something to do with the fact that video games fulfill basic psychological needs. The University of Rochester's Richard Ryan and his colleagues argue that the psychological pull of games is largely due to their capacity to engender feelings of autonomy, competence, and relatedness.[21]

The variable reinforcement nature of video games is part of the pull, too. Games are teeming with rewards (extra lives, bonus points, new levels, special powers), but you never know exactly when they'll happen.

You know that if you play long enough—hours, days, weeks—you'll eventually get rewarded, so you keep on playing. This reinforcement pattern is very hard to walk away from. Noted behavioral psychologist B. F. Skinner found that when he shifted to reinforcing a pigeon on a variable and infrequent schedule, the pigeon continued to peck at a disk 10,000 times without reinforcement, as if still expecting reinforcement![22]

On a biological level, playing video games triggers the release of the chemical dopamine in the brain. Neuroscientist Jaak Panksepp calls the dopamine system the brain's "seeking" circuitry. Dopamine is not the reward itself; rather, it's what motivates us to seek new avenues for reward and then go for them.[23] If you design a video game that's loaded with rewards that players know are there, and you make these rewards achievable through fulfilling basic needs, such as competence and relatedness, human brains will be drawn in—you've got video game nirvana. This is exactly why The Sims™ is the best-selling PC franchise of all time.[24]

Game platforms like Nintendo's Wii™ and Microsoft's Kinect™ give players even more immersion. Both platforms translate your body's movements directly onto the screen. So when you swing your arm, you hit a tennis ball; when you turn to the left, Mario turns to the left; and when you jump, so does your Mii®. Using your entire body like this does something powerful—it makes video games more emotional.[25]

To some degree, your brain determines what emotion you're feeling by reading your body. Sweaty palms, racing heart, dilated pupils, and skipping legs tell your brain that you must be in love. So, unlike other gaming consoles that leave you on the couch, pressing buttons with your thumbs, when you're playing The Clone Wars® on the Wii, you're jumping, stabbing, slicing, and spinning. You're actually involved in hand-to-hand combat, and so your pulse quickens, your blood pressure rises, and blood is redirected to your arm muscles. Your bloodstream is flooded with adrenaline. Your brain picks up these changes in your body, and bingo—you're scared. You're suddenly terrified by a cartoon Jedi®.

You might have heard about Steven Johnson's book *Everything Bad Is Good for You*. In it, he talks about the benefits of video game play (and other media) for children.[26] He describes video games as a rich, positive basis for learning and reasoning. And so they can be. A person can acquire a magnificent body of knowledge and can considerably refine perceptual, cognitive, and motor skills by gaming.

But like many other newcomers to the human experience, video game play brings with its benefits some unwanted side effects.[27] Long stints of video game play can suppress the development of attention, the ability to communicate face to face, and the emergence of abstract thinking skills. Plus, if we take the mantra of content, there is plenty of evidence that violent video games are especially detrimental.[28] One study showed that after only half an hour of a violent wartime game, teenagers exhibited increased activity in a part of the brain that governs emotional arousal. The same teens showed decreased activity in areas of the brain involved in focus, inhibition, and concentration.[29] A review of thirty-five studies with a total of 4,262 children showed that the correlation between video game violence and increased aggressive acts, such as hitting and kicking, among children is as strong as the effect of condom use on the risk of HIV infection.[30]

I don't mean to sound like a curmudgeon about this subject. Playing games delivered by the computer or game system can be darn captivating and happily entertaining, and it can have very useful learning dimensions. But I do strongly believe that a parent should understand that, as with any serious, rewarded activity, a child spending hours each day playing video games pays a price for it. This focus can change his interests and personality and socialization and brain in ways that are not in every way positive for his intellectual and social development.

DIGITAL OVERLOAD

Scientists have long thought about how new forms of media affect our mental systems. In Plato's dialogue *Phaedrus*, Socrates complained that writing would be a problem. He feared that as people started to rely on the written word as a substitute for knowledge they carried inside their heads, they would "cease to exercise their memory and become forgetful." Because they could receive information without proper instruction, they could feel very knowledgeable when "they are for the most part quite ignorant."[31] I'm sure that Renaissance mothers worried about the effects the printing press was going to have on their children's ability to pay attention. Common wisdom is that too much digital stimulation can affect adults. Too much can take people who would otherwise be OK and put them in a range where they're not psychologically healthy.

Steven Yantis at Johns Hopkins University is particularly worried about the effects of media multitasking.[32] Given the data I shared above about how often children multitask their media, this is some science that warrants our careful attention. It seems that high levels of multitasking can lead to shallower thinking, weakened concentration, reduced creativity, and heightened stress. The constant switching also reduces the ability to think deeply about complex topics.

When people engage in frequent multitasking, they often escalate to partial continuous attention—that is, constantly scanning the environment for the next exciting bit of news: the next text, tweet®, e-mail, ping®, or post. When this happens to us, it interrupts our focus and revs up the dopamine reward system as we constantly anticipate something new and more exciting than whatever we're already doing. Partial continuous attention also seems to put the brain in a bit of a heightened state of stress, giving it no time to unwind, reflect, contemplate, or make thoughtful decisions. Instead, this partial continuous attention puts the brain in a constant state of tension—on alert for new news at any moment. Once people get used to this pattern, many thrive on the perpetual connectivity, which can be irresistible.

This work has yet to be done on children, but we should at least be wary when children are constantly checking their smartphones, their iPods, the Internet, and their handheld gaming consoles. It seems that if you give children's brains a chance to chill, the cognitive and emotional costs of multitasking will decline.

TECHNOLOGY IN THE CLASSROOM

Is media technology a boon for children? Can accessibility to computers make today's children better educated, more globally connected, and better informed than children of any other generation before them? The US government seems to think so, as federal subsidies provide billions of dollars for computer access in schools and libraries.

Research by Heather Kirkorian and Daniel Anderson, both at the University of Massachusetts at Amherst, and Ellen Wartella of the University of California, Riverside, reviews studies showing that infants and young children don't learn easily from electronic media because they need direct experience and interaction with real people to develop cognitively.[33] Other research confirms that direct interaction is better even than learning via touch-screen technology.[34]

Media technology is often being used in schools as a teaching tool for older children. Marie Evans Schmidt of Children's Hospital Boston and Elizabeth Vandewater of the University of Texas at Austin show that well-designed content can help learning and that some video games can boost children's developing visual and spatial skills, such as visual tracking and mental rotation.[35] But a Kaiser Family Foundation study found that heavy media users report getting lower grades. This doesn't mean that heavy media use causes lower grades, but there are differences between heavy and light media users in this regard. About half of heavy media users say they usually get fair or poor grades (mostly Cs or lower), compared to about a quarter of light users.[36] Further, although video games, websites, and computer software can benefit children's learning in a variety of ways, there is no evidence that media technologies used in schools are any more effective than traditional teaching techniques. Until there are empirical demonstrations of the superiority of electronic media, it seems best to do most of the teaching with real people rather than computers.

There's also the story of the One Laptop per Child program—a program that provides laptops to children in developing nations. Economists Ofer Malamud and Cristian Pop-Eleches found that for many children, the computer can become more of a distraction than a learning opportunity.[37] They found that children in households who received computers spent a lot less time watching television. But that's where the good news ends. "Computered" children also spent less time doing homework, got lower grades, and reported lower educational aspirations than those who didn't get computers. Computer use also crowded out homework—children with computers spent, on average, two hours a week less on their schoolwork. The lesson here is not that computers are bad, but that parents need to work to ensure that computers don't become a tempting distraction from school. Supporting this conclusion is the fact that when the researchers looked at families with stay-at-home moms who were around to do more policing of computer use, the negative effects of the computers on children were greatly reduced.

BRINGING UP BLACKBERRY®

A general theme of our discussion here is that one of the major side effects of high technology is that it has persuaded children to spend less time engaging in species-typical childhood experiences. Video games likely satisfy basic human needs, such as mastery of skills and developing camaraderie, but they do so without the benefits of real hands-on play with real people in real settings. Pressing keys, clicking a mouse, and using a controller are not like building real things, playing real games, and making real friends.

Granted, there are likely benefits of technology. In his book, Steven Johnson makes video games sound almost like discovery learning.[38] He says the rules of most video games are only sketched out lightly at the beginning and that children need to discover for themselves how to outsmart villains, earn bonus equipment, find shortcuts, and get extra lives. He also says video games require hard work, a lot of motivation, and the ability to tolerate frustration and persevere in the face of failure. All of this sounds good, but aren't these the qualities of real play, too?

There's still a lot of work to be done before we understand the effects of new technologies on children's brains, but it seems that exposing the brain to some forms of technology too early in life can impair the development of certain abilities, while other forms of technology later on in childhood can boost the brain's capacity.

It's also important to ask ourselves what it is we expect our children to get out of watching television or playing video games. If we expect an uninterrupted shower, then a bit of age-appropriate video games or television is just fine. But if we expect the computer or television set to transform our children into geniuses, then we should rethink.

Many parents with older children know that glassy-eyed look that can happen if we let our children play an intense video game for too long. But would you ever think that video game playing could become an addiction? A council of the American Medical Association does.[39] The group is lobbying to have video game addiction classified as a psychiatric disorder and have it added to the American Psychiatric Association's diagnostic manual. They want to make the public more aware of this alleged disorder and make treatment for it covered by insurance.

According to them, it's a widespread epidemic possibly affecting up to five million children.

You might think that comparing addiction to video games with addiction to something like alcohol is a stretch. But even so, these children wouldn't have become "addicts" in the first place without a little enabling from their parents. An alcoholic wouldn't become one without having access to a bunch of booze. A kindergartner wouldn't become a sugary-cereal addict without being constantly served it for breakfast. And a sixth grader wouldn't become addicted to video games if strict limits were enforced as soon as a Wii or Xbox® entered the house. If you've already got a child who you think might be addicted, try my cure: it involves a swift kick out the door and into the backyard.

Chapter 8

Organized Crime

I sat in my backyard one summer morning, enjoying a handful of freshly picked blueberries and the warm breeze that wafted across my hammock. The chickadees were merrily chirping, the cicadas were humming in the trees, and my children were screaming bloody murder.

Apparently, one board on ropes screwed to a tree branch isn't sufficient when you have two children who want to swing. Izzy, the child who was swinging, was taunting the heck out of Dom, the child who was not swinging. She pretended to be done with her turn, only to pump her legs even harder. Dom, crouched on the ground in a predatory pose, was ready to pounce on the swing if his sister left it for even a nanosecond. When Izzy made the mistake of leaping from the swing and flying through the air, Dom swept in and snagged it. Both kids erupted. "Mom, it's my turn!" "Mom, he stole my swing!" Really? I hadn't noticed.

So I did what any mom in this situation would do: I piled both kids into the minivan and we headed to the home improvement store to buy a swing set. After that, my husband, Nick, and I toiled for two days with ungodly heavy wooden posts and eight hundred thousand screws. When we finished, we ceremoniously hung the two new blue plastic swings from the top of the set. Click. Click. Breaded with sweat and sawdust, my husband and I wrapped our arms around one another and stood back to admire our handiwork. We were heroes. We were the parents we wanted to be. We rocked.

Now we needed our kids. We flipped around to find them staring at us with their faces pressed against the sliding glass door. We called them out. Enough swings for everyone's rears. Let the backyard fun begin. Dom and Izzy burst out of the house. Two little bodies streaking wildly toward their new pair of swings.

Nick and I headed for the house to grab a tall glass of lemonade and some air conditioning. But wait—what was that? Did you hear something? Is that a wild coyote attacking someone in our backyard? Call an ambulance! Call animal control! Help! Oh, never mind. It's just Izzy and Dom fighting over who gets to ride the *one* teeter-totter that came with the new swing set.

So how did I handle this? Did I go out and buy them another teeter-totter? Or did I take the high road and lecture them about the decency of taking turns? Of course not. I did what any mom in this situation would do: I laid a guilt trip on my kids. I whined about the wonderful thing their dad and I had just done for them. I carried on about our slaving away in tropical jungle conditions for the sake of their childhood happiness. Both pairs of eyes looked up at me, swelled with understanding. I had gotten to them. They understood that their parents would do anything for their happiness. And they had learned to treat each other in the same selfless manner. At least, I thought so until Izzy said, "You're right, Mom. It is as hot as a tropical jungle out here. Too hot to swing. Let's go inside and have some lemonade."

So we went inside and had some lemonade. As I poured the drinks, I peeked out the kitchen window and saw the two empty swings swaying in the breeze, mocking me. They weren't the eight-hundred-dollar ticket to the backyard silence I thought I had bought.

The real ticket was free and merely involved having the patience to allow Dom and Izzy to figure it out on their own. If I don't let my children figure out how to negotiate swing–turn taking on their own, then how can I expect them to deal with the more complicated problems that will come their way beyond the backyard? If I jump in and help resolve every conflict now, then how will they learn when to back down, how to stick up for themselves, and what it feels like to share?

This example not only illustrates that swing sets are ridiculously expensive, but also gets at a larger problem with childhood today. We parents constantly butt into our children's lives and try to organize everything neatly for them. We schedule their soccer games, pick their teams, tell them our rules, and decide whether the ball was in or out. But how are they supposed to learn how to manage their time and make up their own rules if we always do it for them? We assign them desks in the classroom, seats in the cafeteria, benches on the bus, teams in the baseball league, and packs in Cub Scouts. But how are they supposed to figure out who their friends are if they never get to pick them for themselves? Imagine if your boss made you eat lunch every day with that creepy guy from tech support.

There's growing evidence we'll discuss in this chapter that suggests that the rapid rise in organized sports and scheduled activity is doing children more harm than good. When left to their own devices, children are likely to invent their own games, develop their own rules, pick their own teams, and make their own choices. These experiences encourage cooperation, build social problem-solving skills, and develop conversational abilities. For such competencies to take off, however, the play must be initiated by children themselves, not shaped by the soccer coach or directed by the gym teacher. Such capabilities, referred to together as "emotional intelligence," are essential for a successful adult social life. And the development of these skills is not so easily achieved when children's most frequent social play is done in organized T-ball lessons or peewee football camp.

DOING NOTHING IS DOING SOMETHING

A lot of people think that doing nothing is a waste of time. When you see children doing nothing, it certainly can look that way. But it's not. Doing nothing is essential if you're a child. It only looks like a waste of time to someone who doesn't know what it does for their development.

Let me give you one very clear example of what doing nothing can do. Picture two preschoolers left to their own devices in the family room. They invent what they're going to do. "OK, let's play house. I'll be the mommy. You be the baby. Here you go—eat your cereal. Now it's time for a nap. Lay down right here. Pull up your blanket. I'm going to read you a story. Stop barking, you're not the pet dog." See what's going on? They're creating their own rules, negotiating their own roles, and agreeing to subordinate any internal impulses that don't conform to the story line. That's an extremely sophisticated set of behaviors—a chimpanzee couldn't pull it off. It is also a powerful context for developing emotion-regulating and social skills. But that doesn't hit you in the face when you see two children playing house. It looks like they'd be better off using that time doing worksheets or studying flash cards.

This misperception we have about doing nothing causes us to do all sorts of weird things to our children. Beginning in babyhood, we take them to Mommy and Me Jamboree (where your baby gets to sit on a tiny carpet square and rattle a bell in time with banjo music, when she'd rather be exploring the music room and its instruments on her own and at her own pace). In toddlerhood, we progress to hip-hop dance classes (please leave your Air Yeezys at home because they smudge up the gym floor). Soon there's fine art lessons (which result in an overwhelming number of art pieces involving glitter and uncooked pasta that fall apart the moment they pass through the front door). We sign up our preschoolers for bowling leagues (with gutter guards so that children don't experience or learn how to deal with failure). By kindergarten, they join the local soccer club (where no one keeps score and all players, even the losers, are winners). In between, we arrange playdates (so our children don't have to pick their own friends) and we closely monitor their backyard play (so they don't experience or learn how to handle minor conflicts). In the summer, once they're older, we ship them off for at least a week to Camp Sleep-Away (mainly so they do something other than sit in their rooms and play video games).

This kind of parental behavior seems odd when you consider our evolutionary backstory. During 99 percent of human history, we parents pretty much left our children to their own devices. We were fine with them spending their days doing nothing. Today, there aren't many children who still live the hunter-gatherer way. But millennia later, their brains are still expecting a heavy dose of nothing.

The issue is not that every ounce of our organizing childhood is bad. Children—especially in the early years—need some degree of adult scaffolding. The problem is that as children spend more and more time doing things organized, supervised, and officiated by adults, they spend less and less time left to their own devices. Today's children spend more of their free time engaged in organized activities than any earlier generation did. Consequently, the amount of unstructured time children have has dropped dramatically in the past few decades.[1]

Do we fill children's schedules because we don't trust them to be constructive on their own? The media tell us that what goes on in the early years is critical for success in later life. And so maybe we've been tricked into thinking that our children can't handle life on their own. I heard an example of this mind-set recently that illustrates our mistrust of children. It comes from an acclaimed guidebook for elementary schools developed by Curt Hinson and PlayFit Education. The guide tells school officials that "recess should be a productive learning time where everyone has a purpose and works to fulfill that purpose. In essence it's still free time, but time that must be used to accomplish specific outcomes."[2] What did he say? If children's recess time is used to meet some specific outcome—one that's established by the school and not the children themselves—then it seems to me that it is *not* free time. The very definition of free time is that it's free. The guide goes on to say, "Children on the playground who perceive that recess is their free time often push the limits of irresponsible behavior, acting as though recess is a time for them to do what they want. Unfortunately, this type of 'ego-centric' attitude causes problems for teachers."[3]

Unfortunately, this view of recess leaves no room for what's good about recess. Recess is supposed to give children the freedom to do what they want; that's the point. It gives them access to something their brain is expecting: the freedom to direct their own play, to develop talents of their own choice, and to discover the world at their own speed. And it gives them a delightful sense of power.[4] For people who are being told all school day what to do—to sit still, be quiet, do their desk work, keep their hands to themselves—having a sense of power not only helps them develop self-control, it feels good.

UNORGANIZED SPORTS

Baseball Hall of Famer and former Cleveland Indian Bob Lemon said, "Baseball was made for kids, and grown-ups only screw it up." Lemon wasn't talking about organized youth leagues, but he might say the same thing about them if he were around to see what they've done to pickup games. Today, 27 percent of nine- to thirteen-year-olds play in an organized league, but only 6 percent play baseball on their own. Participation in Little League has dropped 14 percent from its peak in 1997, but spontaneous baseball play—pickup games, pickle, and catch—has declined twice as rapidly in the same time frame.[5]

This changing relationship between children and baseball says a lot. It illustrates that a good deal of children's play—especially their physical play—is organized, supervised, and timed by us. We form the teams, schedule the games, make the rules, coach from the sidelines, and call the fouls. This is surely good fun, and there's much to be gained. Such organized games boost children's rule-governed behavior and cooperative interactions with peers. But you get a very different flavor of play when you remove the adults and leave children to their own devices. Their free play doesn't have built-in rules like organized sports. Or if it does, the rules are developed, negotiated, and enforced by children themselves. So free play affords more creative behavior. Free play also challenges children's brains more than merely following predetermined rules. When children are playing on their own, they can try out their imaginations, experiment with making and breaking their own rules, and test out new roles.

Unlike humans, animals don't play organized sports. I've never seen a band of chimpanzees challenge a neighboring troop to a round of flag football. Free play, however, appears in many members of the animal kingdom—suggesting that it has a deep evolutionary history and serves an important function for youngsters.

But how can afternoons of free play—games of four square, backyard mock battles, and rounds of sardines—benefit children? Not only does it look entirely pointless, it never got anyone into an Ivy League school. It's one thing to write on your college application that you're the captain of the high school basketball team, but it's another to say you play a mean game of playground three-on-three.

Free play is critical because it helps children develop strong social skills that are important for success in childhood and throughout life. Children who are interpersonally skilled—who have a high social intelligence—do well in just about everything, even on things in the cognitive and academic realm. This is true both now and later. Those who are socially awkward not only risk being unpopular in childhood, but their lack of social skills increases their tendency toward later academic failure, criminality, drug abuse, and emotional disorders.[6]

SECRET SAUCE

Children can't learn how to become socially competent from coaches and parents telling them how to behave. Rather, they need to interact freely with peers to develop sophisticated social skills. Why? What do peers have that we don't?

Unstructured play with peers is a demanding and motivating context like no other, both socially and cognitively.[7] This double whammy of high demands and high motivation is free play's secret sauce. Consider the social-cognitive demands associated with sustained peer interaction. Children have to figure out what's acceptable social behavior and what's not. If they lose control of their emotions, refuse to take turns, or otherwise break the rules, they'll lose playmates. But because children enjoy playing so much, it means that they are motivated to do the prerequisite social-cognitive work to accomplish high-level tasks. They learn to cooperate, pay close attention, filter out distractions, follow negotiated rules, and regulate their emotions. When there's no adult authority to mediate disagreements, children learn how to do it themselves and negotiate among themselves as equals. To keep the play going, they'll also learn to consider others' feelings and desires and learn how to see situations from others' points of view. As they do, they'll develop social skills like persistence and negotiating abilities. Keeping play with peers friendly also demands effective communication—arguably the most valuable social skill of all. Importantly, these are all social-cognitive skills that help not only on the playground, but also in the classroom. Free play with peers helps children learn how to control their emotions, organize their behavior, and listen to the teacher.

We know these things not only from observational studies, but also from what happens when there's a lack of free play. Because you can't ethically deprive a young human of play, we look again to the rats. Young rats denied opportunities for rough-and-tumble play develop numerous social problems. They fail to recognize social cues and the nuances of rat hierarchy; they aren't able to mate. Vigorous social play also releases brain-derived neurotrophic factor (BDNF), a protein that stimulates the growth of new neurons, in brain regions involved in emotional reaction and social learning.[8]

EVERYONE'S A WINNER

I haven't downed my entire glass of organized-sports Haterade. I don't think organized sports itself are a bad thing. I think they're bad if they're the *only* game play that children do. There's also the business of not keeping score.

At my son's soccer games, we don't keep score. Well, not officially. My husband and I keep score, of course. My son, his teammates, and his coaches do, too. And so do all the other families, or else they wouldn't yell like crazy at their kids from the sidelines whenever they miss a goal.

We don't keep official score because we've been told that losing could damage children's self-esteem. But as discussed in chapter 3, we now know that self-esteem isn't the ticket to success that Nathaniel Branden told us it was in *The Psychology of Self-Esteem*.[9] Rather, it turns out that teaching our children they're all winners was a bad idea. We should go back to keeping score and giving trophies only to the ones who win.

I played softball in a summer city league when I was in elementary school, and we lost almost every game. But we didn't mind. Know why? Because we tried our best, accepted that we weren't all that good, and focused on the fun. And it didn't hurt that we had the coolest terry wrist sweatbands in the league.

We were unfazed by our failures because our coach taught us that self-respect was more important than self-esteem. Our parents felt the same way; they never yelled at us angrily from the stands when we struck out, dropped a fly ball, or threw a line drive over the first baseman's head. Instead, they cheered our efforts. Several decades of research by Ellen Langer and her colleagues at Harvard University show the benefits of focusing on self-respect rather than self-esteem.[10] But Nathaniel Branden—I'm guessing he was one of those kids who needed to show off his Little League "participation trophy" in a fancy display case above his dresser.

Self-esteem and self-respect sound similar, but the differences are crucial. For instance, I absolutely love to dance to bubblegum pop music. I do it all the time—when I'm packing the kids' lunches, clearing the dinner table, folding the laundry, and dusting the furniture. I dance so much that you might think I'm good at it. I'm not. I'm a terrible dancer. I look absolutely ridiculous bobbing around to Bruno Mars. But I'm not saddened if my family or friends poke fun at my moves. Nor is my self-esteem deflated by my lack of talent. I accept the way I dance. And because I accept it, I can groove to the *Glee* soundtrack without being hard on myself or concerned about what others think.

This idea of acceptance might sound familiar. We've been encouraged by both our spiritual leaders and our psychotherapists to "accept the things we can't change, change the things we can, and have the wisdom to know the difference between the two." But this isn't the version of acceptance Langer is talking about. I'm certain I could change the way I dance. If I took dance lessons, I'm sure I could improve. So my acceptance has nothing to do with a knowledge that I can't change. Nor is my acceptance based on resignation; I'm not resigned to the belief that I'm a terrible dancer, and I'm not committed to any particular belief about my future dancing.

I simply like myself. That sounds terribly corny, but it means that my self-respect is not contingent on success because there are always failures to contend with. Nor is my self-respect the result of comparing myself with others—there are lots of people who are better. These are the sorts of things you focus on if you want to boost self-esteem. But self-respect is something you either have or you don't. With self-respect, you like yourself because of who you are, not because of what you can do—how well you dance or how many runs you score while playing softball.

How can you tell if you've got a child with self-respect? Here's a simple test. Suppose you tell your middle schooler that she excels at spelling her first name correctly and does a superb job feeding herself her morning cereal. Chances are these compliments won't boost her self-esteem. She knows she does the first well and doesn't care about the second. This illustrates that when children aren't evaluating themselves, praise, rewards, and trophies don't matter. Try to give your third grader a gold ribbon for using the toilet all by himself and see what happens. For all those instances where your child doesn't "take the compliment," it is because she is not evaluating herself. The reward is unimportant, and that's good. The fewer instances in which your child evaluates herself, the less vulnerable she'll be to insult and failure. That's why instilling high self-respect is much more advantageous than protecting high self-esteem by not exposing your children to failure. Langer's research shows that compared to those people with high self-esteem for whom evaluation is sought, those with self-respect are less prone to blame, guilt, regret, lies, secrets, and stress.[11] As a parent, then, encouraging your children to like themselves and to have self-respect is better than focusing on raising their self-esteem. So go ahead and keep score at those soccer games; don't focus on protecting and preserving children's high self-esteem. It's better to develop self-respect and to acknowledge that failure can provide harmless but valuable life lessons. Sure, a loss might sting no matter what, especially if you're only five years old and winning seems terribly important, but it's a golden opportunity for parents and coaches to teach children to feel good about who they are.

CAN'T TEACH THAT

One takeaway lesson that I alluded to above is that you can't directly teach children social skills. There's no workbook, textbook, or set of flash cards that'll help. Some people have tried to steer children toward social competence by rewarding good behavior. The Scouts have several pro-social badges and belt loops. But there's evidence that this can backfire.

Consider a study carried out by Michael Tomasello and colleagues that explored the influence of rewards on the helping behavior of toddlers.[12] He gave twenty-two-month-old children several opportunities to help an unfamiliar adult by doing things like fetching an out-of-reach object or opening a cabinet door when the adult's hands were full. Some of the children were given a reward—a small toy—every time they helped. Others got nothing, not even a smile or thank-you from the needy adult. Most children helped every time the adult seemed to need help. But later, when the children were given an opportunity to help again, those who had been rewarded on the first round helped much less than those who had not been rewarded. How could this be? Don't rewards boost behavior? Usually they do, but this is again a case of the overjustification effect we discussed in chapter 3. When you reward an internally motivated behavior—like helping—you undermine it.

LIGHTLY SCAFFOLDED

The idea that play is essential for developing brains is not new. A 2005 article in the *Archives of Pediatric and Adolescent Medicine*, published by the American Medical Association, focuses on "resurrecting free play in young children" by arguing that beyond its benefits for physical health, play enhances well-being, including attention, affiliation, and affect.[13] Play has lots of advocates: experts have written theses on it, created organizations about it, and have made artificial places for kids to do it. In short, because play is so important to the brain's development, it cannot be left in the hands of children. So now we have play associates. Yep, you heard that right.

In New York City's South Street Seaport, there's a "next-generation playground." Imagination Playground™ was designed by architect David Rockwell, who's known for creating fun indoor spaces such as Nobu and Emril's.[14] The playground is filled with firm foam loose parts that can be moved, canals of water that can be dammed, and a set of lifts and pulleys that can transport sacks. It's very neat. But play is proctored and interaction fostered by a staff of city workers trained as "play associates." These folks are trained to facilitate children's play and to demonstrate new ways to interact with the playground objects and environment. Of course it's great to get kids outdoors to play, but why not leave them to explore and investigate on their own?

Sure, play sometimes needs a boost, especially if you're new at it. When a child is a year old, most pretend play is initiated by others. By the end of the second year, toddlers and caregivers equally initiate play. In the preschool years, caregivers work mainly as preparators—as play with them precedes play with peers and prepares children for it. But there's a fine line that parents and other caregivers need to be careful not to cross too often between encouraging children's play and directing it.[15] When adults are in the driver's seat, young children's pretend play often reverts to simple and immature manipulation of toys, or it stops entirely. Among older preschoolers, adults tend to dampen complex forms of free play, but age mates facilitate it.

Certainly, some parental play scaffolding is needed some of the time. But generally, older children do better on their own. We also know that merely watching children's play can reduce its occurrence later on. In one classic study, preschoolers were given novel puzzles to play with however they pleased.[16] Some were told that their play would be monitored via a television camera, and others simply played without being watched. Two weeks later, when the children were given the puzzles to play with again, those who were monitored on the first round spent less time with and showed less interest in the puzzles than those who played initially without being watched. So merely knowledge that one's performance at play is being observed and evaluated by someone else appears sufficient to decrease later interest in further play. The implications are huge: parents' mere watching of children playing organized games like soccer undermines the extent to which such play might occur spontaneously later on. I'm not suggesting that you use this as an excuse to stay home from your kids' soccer games, just that you be mindful of how your presence can affect their play.

We've also talked about how children's playful interactions with peers generally are cognitively and socially more demanding than their interactions with adults. As you might guess, children's exhibition of skills is often more sophisticated when they play with their peers than when they play with us. For example, in a university preschool, University of Minnesota educational psychologist Anthony Pellegrini and his colleagues found that when adults participated in children's immediate groups, children's play and oral language production were less sophisticated than when the groups were made up of children only.[17] Children's use of oral language with their peers, relative to language used with adults, was more explicit (e.g., saying that "Sally" spilled the crayons rather than "she" spilled the crayons) and more narrative-like (e.g., use of temporal and causal phrases that include words like "if," "then," "later," and "because"). Importantly, this more sophisticated language is predictive of children's early literacy and early school achievement. Also, Pellegrini found that children's pretend play was richer, more varied, and more often included language directing their playmates (e.g., "You be the student. I'm the teacher.") when they were playing alone than when playing with an adult. These findings fit well with the idea that to pull off successful episodes of sustained play with peers, children are required to exercise high-level social skills (like cooperation and perspective taking) and cognitive skills (like the ability to communicate clearly and concisely) when adults aren't there to jump in and take over the difficult work.

Engaging in games with rules (and without adults)—tag, wall ball, four square, dodgeball—is also an important developmental task for young children.[18] Preschool children who have had a good deal of playground experience with these sorts of games do very well transitioning into elementary school. Since both playground games and the elementary school classroom demand rule-governed behavior and cooperative interactions with peers, the link between the two makes sense.

There's also evidence that children's outdoor play behavior changes depending on whether or not they're supervised. Roger Mackett at the Centre for Transport Studies at University College London gave eight- to eleven-year-old children GPS monitors to wear and diaries to track their activities.[19] Mackett found that when outdoors, children tend to walk faster and straighter when they're with an adult than when they're unsupervised. These findings suggest that when children are without adults, they meander more, take more time to explore their environment, and more often go off the beaten path. Mackett also found that lightly supervised children were more likely to go out of the house on their own more often and spent more time playing with peers.

Collectively, the evidence presented in this chapter makes a strong case for parents to tame their inner helicopter—to spend less time hovering over their children structuring, organizing, and supervising their young lives. What do you remember most fondly from your own childhood—the tap dance lessons, T-ball games, or Scouts? Or maybe it's the winter weekends spent building snow forts with your brother, the summer afternoons exploring the neighborhood on your bike, or the Saturday mornings playing at the local park with your best friend? Give your kids plenty of time to do nothing—to indulge in pretense, create their own fantasy worlds, and foster their own happiness. It helps their brains build the circuitry to impose self-control, negotiate social rules, act in socially acceptable ways, cooperate willingly with others, make friends, and see the perspectives of others.

Chapter 9

An Inside Job

As recently as fifty years ago, some sixty million roamed the wilderness across much of North America. But for the first time in their two-million-year history, they have nearly vanished from the outdoors. Today, most children worldwide are bred in captivity and raised indoors.

To raise awareness, the World Wildlife Fund has put children on the top of its endangered species list. The main culprits of this species' disappearance from its natural habitat are electronics, homework, and extracurricular activities. But children can thrive if their parents unplug them, clear their schedules, and release them out the back door.

A large segment of North America's backyards and neighborhood streets, areas where children formerly thrived, is now designated as critical habitat for this endangered species. As the result of this designation, and in line with Section 7 of the Endangered Species Act, federal agencies now are required to ensure that the activities they authorize, fund, or carry out are not likely to destroy or adversely modify children's critical habitat.

Later this week, leaders from thirteen countries are gathering for a historic event: a Heads of Government Child Summit. They are meeting to develop a "Global Child Recovery Program" to serve as a blueprint for introducing the species back into its natural habitat. The heads of government, recognizing that the limited resources devoted to child conservation have not slowed video game console sales or deterred the syndicates that traffic homework, will seek to double the number of children in the wild by 2022.

The summit's efforts will not succeed without financial support. You can help by purchasing "Save the Children" T-shirts and bags at your local Bullseye store. A percentage of the profit will be given to the Global

Fund for Saving Children. The US Postal Service also offers a premium-priced postage stamp and dedicates the additional revenue to child conservation projects. Next week, the World Wildlife Fund is launching a Texting for Tots promotion. You can text "TOTS" to 20222 from a cell phone to make a ten-dollar donation to support WWF's efforts to protect children. Messaging and data rates may apply. The WWF also is encouraging people on Facebook and Twitter® to spread awareness about the current plight of children. Supporters can use WWF's new Facebook application to add sunshine, grass, and trees to their profile pictures and tag their tweets with #savechildrennow.

THE CHANGING HABITAT OF CHILDHOOD

If you're thirty-something or older, your childhood probably went something like this: You and your friends were pretty much on your own when school let out. The minute you came home, you dropped your books, slipped outside, and played and played and played until it was time for dinner. In the summer, you and your friends went back out after dinner and played and played and played until it got dark out, you dropped from exhaustion, or someone took the ball home.

You don't remember doing much homework, though you must have done some. What you do remember is blowing dandelion tufts, playing hide-and-seek, skipping stones, diving in leaf piles, hurling snowballs, catching fireflies, building makeshift forts, and creating imaginary worlds.

You had the freedom to do all this because you didn't have much else going on. You weren't signed up for ballet classes, lacrosse league, painting studio, clarinet lessons, drama club, Girl Scouts, and a math tutor all in the same week. Adults didn't schedule, drive you to, and coach your pickup games. You and your friends just kicked a ball around. If you wanted to play with someone, your mom didn't make a playdate; you just walked over to your friend's house, knocked on the front door, and asked, "Can (*insert name here*) come out to play?"

You got skinned knees, muddy hands, tangled hair, and sand in your eyes. You used your outside voice and explored the neighborhood on your bicycle, and not a single grown-up ever butted in. You invented your own games, made your own rules, and formed your own teams.

In retrospect, childhood was damn fun.

But within the space of two or three decades, the fun has stopped—or moved inside.[1] Unstructured outdoor play has nearly disappeared from the lives of most modern children. This change is worrisome because when outdoors, play is different and different standards apply. Outdoors, children are more likely to tackle something new, take a risk, or create their own worlds. And they can get away with a whole slew of things that would get them in deep trouble indoors. They have the freedom to run, roughhouse, get messy, and use their outside voices. But the days of "Be home for dinner!" are gone.

Today, children ride skateboards on the television set, hold mock battles on the Internet, play ball games on their laptops, text their friends the latest gossip, and share the day's events on Facebook. Their imaginary worlds have already been created for them by adults and loaded onto their handheld gaming consoles. They're cocooned inside and constantly supervised. When they make it outside, it's to a manufactured playground that's been designed by adults. Or to an organized sports game on a manicured field that's scheduled, officiated, and coached by adults. Even sidewalk chalk drawing has been made criminal in some jurisdictions.[2]

Today, children can grow up, get a job, and get married without undergoing the ancient rites of dodgeball, tag, or sardines. It seems almost Orwellian.

Am I overreacting?

Nope.

Children today spend an average of less than thirty minutes a week in free outdoor play, an amount that shrinks yearly. In this brave new world of Twitter, Google, YouTube®, and Wii, children are spending increasing time with technology. A kindergartner starts school with five thousand hours of television under her belt, enough time to have earned a college degree. The typical elementary schooler spends more than forty hours a week with technology—a full-time, virtual job.[3]

Today's children can name hundreds of brand logos and Hollywood celebrities on sight. McDonald's for dinner. "I love Katy Perry." "I need an Aeropostale® hoodie." Children can identify more Pokémon characters than local wildlife species.[4] Even preschoolers are more likely to know the words to "California Gurls" than what a house finch sounds like.

Children's move indoors can also be seen in their bodies. In the 1960s, less than 5 percent of children were obese. Childhood obesity has more than quadrupled since then. Nearly 20 percent of children today are obese.[5] According to the Foundation for Child Development's 2010 Child and Youth Well-Being Index, children's health has sunk to its lowest point in the thirty-five-year history of the index.[6] The World Health Organization is concerned enough to have issued a global alert regarding the deterioration of children's physical health, largely due to a decline in physical activity (and diet, too).[7] As a result of the health issues associated with a sedentary lifestyle and extra weight, the *New England Journal of Medicine* has raised the alarming possibility that for the first time in modern history, children might live shorter lives than their parents.[8]

Children who spend more time outdoors are more active than children who spend less time outdoors.[9] There's indeed a connection: researchers have found that the greenness of children's neighborhoods is directly linked to their body mass index (BMI).[10] The more vegetation in the area, the lower the BMI—even after controlling for a number of factors, such as residential density.

Growing numbers of children are vitamin D deficient.[11] Nine percent of American children, or 7.6 million, are vitamin D deficient, and 61 percent, or 50.8 million, are vitamin D insufficient. Vitamin D is produced primarily in the skin after exposure to sunlight, and its deficiency is associated with cardiovascular risk factors. The body can't absorb calcium and harden bones without vitamin D; low levels of vitamin D, combined with children's lack of exercise, are contributing to a decrease in children's bone mass and an increase in their risk for fractures and later osteoporosis. Consider this: The dominant arm of a tennis player has 35 percent more bone than the nondominant arm. But today, US children break their arms more often than they did four decades ago—girls do so 56 percent more often, while boys break their arms 32 percent more.[12] The increased time indoors also seems to be contributing to the rise in myopia, or nearsightedness, in children. Youngsters who spend a lot of time indoors doing close-up work are two to three times more likely to develop myopia than those with high levels of outdoor activity.[13] The protective mechanism of the outdoors is likely to be high intensity light—something that doesn't happen in the family room.

The effects of the move indoors can also be seen in children's brains. Today, nearly 10 percent of children, or 5.4 million, have been diagnosed with attention deficit/hyperactivity disorder (ADHD).[14] The percentage of ADHD diagnoses has increased an average of 3 percent per year from 1997 to 2006, and an average of 5.5 percent per year between 2003 and 2007.[15] Two-thirds of all children with ADHD are taking medication to control it; these 2.7 million children represent 5 percent of children nationwide. The thing is, playing in natural settings has been found to lengthen children's attention span.[16] Even increases in children's proximity to natural outdoor spaces that occur because of a family move can boost children's ability to focus.[17] Other research shows that symptoms of ADHD dissipate when children take a walk outside.[18] Exposure to natural settings improves brain performance, it seems, because it provides a mental break from a world stuffed with artificial stimuli.

We parents and teachers have had a hand in our children's retreat indoors. Our No Child Left Behind Act has effectively glued children to their seats, attached No. 2 pencils to their hands, and piled endless worksheets on their desks. If our children are playing outside, it's because we drove them to the ballpark and are waiting for them on the sidelines, sitting in our folding camp chairs.

We've also collapsed their geographic world. Today, the radius that children are allowed to freely roam outside of their homes has shrunk to one-ninth of that of children growing up in the 1970s.[19] I remember daylong excursions in the nearby woods with friends and biking miles on the city streets to go to the library—all without a cell phone, a Family Locator app, or even a dime. But then again, every other child was outside, too. It wasn't just brave me on my bike; I had plenty of company.

Perhaps that's why letting kids go into the woods alone today is unthinkable. It's because they'd essentially be alone. Remember Lenore Skenazy, the New York City mother who let her ten-year-old son ride the subway alone? We wanted to turn her in for child abuse. The news networks called her America's Worst Mom.[20] Now, I'll let my children walk down the block to a friend's house by themselves, but they've never been allowed to go into the woods at the end of our neighborhood alone. The outdoors is just too dangerous today—at least, that's what the evening news tells me. There's so much to be afraid of: pesticides, power lines, ultraviolet rays, bad ozone, distracted drivers, Lyme disease ticks, West Nile mosquitoes, strangers, and kidnappers. So even if my child doesn't get nabbed by the boogeyman, she'll certainly get sick or worse from all the other hazards outdoors.

The fact is that children are safer now than at any time since 1975. Since then, violent crimes against children have dropped by more than 30 percent.[21] This means that the world was actually more dangerous for children when I was growing up than now. The rate of child abductions has not changed for decades. It's around one hundred per year—about the same risk as being struck by lightning. More than fifteen times as many children are killed each year in auto accidents.[22] Our children are in more danger driving around in the family minivan than playing alone in the neighborhood park.

If the outdoors isn't as dangerous as we think it is, then why are we so hesitant to let our children play alone outside? Because of the media. Whenever a terrible crime is committed against a child, CNN™ and Fox News® run loops covering the story over and over again, sometimes for days. These horrible stories seep into the emotional parts of our brains and jam up our rational thought. They make us think that the boogeyman is right outside the front door, waiting for our children. And they change the way we parent. We can easily picture six-year-old Christopher Barrios, who allegedly was snatched from a neighborhood swing set, sexually abused, and suffocated to death by a convicted sex offender.[23] This unthinkable story then turns our natural desire to protect our children into crippling paranoia. And the unthinkable makes us worry more about the dangers lurking outside—no matter how unlikely. We are far more concerned about these dangers than those posed by a sedentary childhood spent indoors: obesity, hypertension, behavioral and learning problems, and other chronic health conditions—all of which, by the way, have doubled between 1996 and 2004, according to data from the National Longitudinal Study of Youth.[24]

NATURE-DEFICIT DISORDER

The most dangerous consequence of children's migration indoors is perhaps what's termed nature-deficit disorder. This condition was coined by journalist Richard Louv in his book *Last Child in the Woods: Saving Our Children from Nature-Deficit Disorder*.[25] Louv calls it the greatest health catastrophe facing today's children. *Avatar* filmmaker James Cameron said, in an address he gave to the Natural Resources Defense Council, that it's not just children who are affected, but that we all suffer from nature-deficit disorder.[26] This is no small disorder. The World Future Society listed children's nature-deficit disorder as the fifth most important global development facing us in 2007 and beyond.[27]

But I don't think the increasing prevalence of poor physical health, behavioral problems, and distractibility are symptoms of a childhood disorder, any more than dwarfism, emotional immaturity, knowledge deficits, and legume anorexia are symptoms of a childhood disorder.[28] They are just standard features of a lot of children. They develop because of the unnatural environments we put children into, and their prevalence is almost completely in our hands. Have you ever heard of an overweight juvenile chimpanzee with attention deficit disorder and high blood pressure? You never will because his parents know better than to sequester him indoors in front of the television set with a bag of Cheetos.

At the same time, a growing number of studies demonstrate that children who spend time outdoors are physically and mentally healthier than their indoor peers. Children's attention can be restored by nature, and the outdoors can kick ADHD symptoms.[29] Free play outside lets children develop social skills they can't pick up from video games or the Internet—or even from playing sports under adult supervision. The outdoors can boost creativity too.[30] There's also evidence that learning through nature-based programs helps kids score higher on standardized tests.[31] One recent study found that students in outdoor science programs improved their science testing scores by 27 percent.[32] That's right. Want your child to get into Harvard? Have her study outdoors.

In my view, a health problem more pressing than children's nature-deficit disorder is an affliction that hits many of today's parents: Minivan-Induced Brain Strain (MIBS). It's a serious disorder with symptoms more debilitating than other common parental afflictions, such as Infectious Laughter and the Hippy Hippy Shakes. Consequently, it seems wise to focus our prevention efforts on MIBS.

How do you know if you have MIBS? The most frequent complaints of sufferers include pulled necks, achy backs, and strained brains. These symptoms are caused mainly by two features of today's minivans: shoddy ergonomics and the constant stress and noise pollution of needy, rowdy children sardined in their car seats.

To address the growing incidence of MIBS, the Occupational Safety and Health Administration (OSHA) has put together a team of experts to develop a plan to reduce the hazards of ferrying children around in minivans. OSHA got involved in this effort because the minivan has been officially designated a "workplace," given the growing number of job-related dealings that happen in their front seats. There are conference calls made on cell phones, presentations written on laptops, e-mails answered on iPads, notes taken on personal recorders, and inventions designed on glove box napkins—all while waiting for children at soccer practice, violin lessons, Cub Scouts, and math tutors.

The brain trauma induced by minivan driving is the most serious symptom of MIBS. It happens slowly as the brain deals with the constant and wearying demands of trafficking children to their various classes, lessons, practices, tutoring sessions, and sporting events. When the brain is flooded with too many demands and too much stimulation from the backseat—"He hit me." "I'm hungry." "I spilled my grape juice." "My gazillion-piece Lego spaceship exploded." "I lost my Super Ball behind the seat and I just can't go on."—it involuntarily shuts down.

The brain area most vulnerable to damage is the parental lobe. This region controls parents' ability to settle backseat arguments, divvy out healthy snacks, pay attention to road signage, maintain seat belt compliance, and navigate to the nearest public restroom—all at the same time. When this brain region goes, the lower-level reflexive parts of the brain take over. This is what causes sufferers to involuntarily blurt, "Don't you make me pull this van over." Sometimes the parental lobe can be reactivated by banging one's head on the steering wheel. But if the head banging doesn't work, then parents should immediately drive home, clear their children's schedules, and release the kids out in the backyard. If they're still in car seats, supervise them lightly, of course. But if they're older, see what they can do on their own.

GREEN SPACE AND GRAY MATTER

The good news for families dealing with MIBS is that even slight lifestyle changes can help. Consider the effects of the outdoors on, say, children's cognitive processes, like attention and memory. Just being in an artificial environment can impair these basic mental skills. The brain is better able to pay attention, hold things in memory, and show self-control after it has been outdoors—and the greener the location, the better.

University of Michigan cognitive neuroscientist Marc Berman and his colleagues have shown that something as simple as a walk in the park can have immediate beneficial effects on attention and memory.[33] Other work has shown that increasing green environmental features, such as more trees in the inner city or a greater variety of plants in urban parks, can boost cognitive performance.[34] Hospital patients recover more quickly if they can see trees outside their windows, and women living in public housing can focus better when their apartments overlook a grassy courtyard.[35] There's also evidence that nature can be calming. Both prisoners and Alzheimer's patients who garden display lower levels of aggressive assaults and hostility.[36] Even viewing pictures of the outdoors can improve brain performance.[37] Why? It seems the outdoors provides a mental break from artificial environments. The mind needs nature, and even a little bit can be a big help.

Let's back up a bit. Artificial environments like city streets, living rooms, and classrooms exploit crucial weak spots of the brain. They're so overstuffed with stimuli that we need to constantly work to redirect our attention so that we aren't distracted by irrelevant things, like the girl who is poking your arm, the boy who is singing his ABCs, the grinding of the pencil sharpener, the classroom guinea pigs squeaking for attention, the box of crayons that fell onto the floor, and the gossiping out in the hallway. To do anything in this kind of environment, we need to use "controlled perception." We need to constantly tell our brains what to pay attention to and what to ignore. But ignoring so many constant sights and sounds takes a lot of energy and effort, and consequently, it requires a lot of brainpower.[38] This is an even more difficult task for children because their attentional abilities are not yet as mature and smoothly tuned as adults' are.

Natural settings, in contrast, don't require the same amount of cognitive effort. University of Michigan psychologist Stephen Kaplan has developed this idea and calls it attention restoration theory, or ART.[39] It's common knowledge in cognitive psychology that attention is a limited resource—it's why you can't pay attention to two different conversations at the same time, or listen simultaneously to both *SportsCenter* and your wife.

It's also well known that our ability to pay attention depletes during the day: it's more difficult to pay attention at the end of the day than at the beginning. Kaplan thinks that the outdoors—because it's made up of natural stimulation rather than artificial distractions—can have a restorative effect on attention. The brain machinery we use to ignore police sirens, backfiring cars, barking dogs, and junk e-mails can relax deeply and replenish itself.

There's also the idea that artificial environments don't just deplete attention but also interfere with self-control.[40] When your seven-year-old is sitting on the couch trying to concentrate on his *Harry Potter* book, his brain is assaulted with temptations—the *SpongeBob* marathon on the television set, the ice-cream truck with rocket pops driving by, the doorbell that his best friend just rang, and the new Mario game peeking out of the Wii. To resist these temptations, he needs to involve his prefrontal cortex—the very same region that's already been taxed all day at school as he tried to focus on his desk work. Because his brain has been barraged all day with such demands, it is less able to garner the neural resources to exert self-control, and consequently, his brain is likely to give in to *SpongeBob*.

This is pretty much the double whammy of modern childhood. Children's overstuffed childhoods subvert their ability to resist the temptations of these same overstuffed childhoods. The result is that children's brains can too easily short-circuit. All it takes is a busy classroom, an unruly lunchroom, or a boisterous Cub Scout meeting. I don't think that we parents and teachers take the fragility of children's attention seriously enough. It's something we should protect. The work of Marc Berman and others shows that nature experience can replenish attention—within minutes—and should be taken seriously. These data suggest that a green brain, restored by time in the outdoors, can concentrate better, can control itself more easily, can remember more, and can keep its temper more reliably. If you're looking for a way to improve your child's cognitive performance, a daily walk in the park might be more effective than another round of flash cards, an extra page of homework, or additional time in the classroom.

NATURAL ENVIRONMENTS

Botanist Luther Burbank wrote, "Every child should have mud pies, grasshoppers, tadpoles, frogs, mud turtles, elderberries, wild strawberries, acorns, chestnuts, trees to climb. Brooks to wade, woodchucks, bats, bees, butterflies, various animals to pet, hayfields, pine cones, rocks to roll, snakes, huckleberries and hornets. And any child who has been deprived of these has been deprived of the best part of education."[41]

That doesn't seem right to our education-obsessed culture. Our No Child Left Behind children certainly are deprived of this "best" part of education. Nonetheless, Burbank's sentiments, I think, strike a nerve in my generation of parents. I tell my children stories of the days when every child knew what happened when you licked a yellow banana slug and not a single one used her thumbs to dial phones. They don't believe me, but I tell them that things have changed in these and countless other ways because children today just aren't getting the rich experiences they're supposed to in the outdoors.

In 1979, psychologist James J. Gibson coined the term "affordance" to refer to action possibilities in the environment.[42] For example, computer keys are for pushing, drawer handles are for pulling, zippers are for zipping, and shirt buttons are for buttoning. From Gibson's vantage, outdoor environments are varied and more open ended, filled with objects that afford more diverse action possibilities than most indoor environments. Both couches and trees afford sitting, but trees also afford climbing, hiding, swinging, and shelter. Rocks afford throwing, grasping, piling, rolling, and sorting. Streams afford endless experiments, and a dirt pile affords an entire imaginative world. In addition, outdoor environments with looseness encourage creativity as children invent new uses for natural elements, like pretending a tree is a spaceship, loose twigs are transmitters, and the fallen leaves are alien currency. These sorts of interactions are not going to happen indoors in video games or with scripted toys.

Diverse *natural* elements are especially important in stimulating creativity and problem solving. On a manufactured jungle gym, children can *only* climb, hang, or fall off. But a varied natural landscape affords endless possibilities. Natural places are also always changing, prone to weather, and to some degree unpredictable. The field and the forest never look the same twice. Yet the jungle gym is always set up in the same way and consequently is totally predictable. All the manufactured playground equipment produced by the best builders in the world could not substitute for the diversity nature offers.

Consistent with these ideas, research shows the pervasive benefits of unstructured outdoor play.[43] Natural outdoor environments invite the kinds of play crucial for healthy development. Younger children are more likely to engage in free play than other types of play outdoors, and outdoor play boosts attention, observational skills, problem-solving abilities, and self-regulation. Playing outside also can serve to reduce children's stress and episodes of bullying. Children whose schools have diverse natural play environments are more physically active, more civil to one another, more likely to cooperate, and more likely to engage in more creative forms of play. Collectively, these ideas and this evidence make the outdoors a critical environment for childhood.

NO JUNGLE IN THE GYM

The camera gun was really a bad idea. It's tough to get your family to smile for a holiday snapshot when you're pointing a .38 revolver at them. Airbag underwear wasn't much better. Those briefs could detect a fall in progress and inflate before you hit the ground, but they just made tripping even more embarrassing. But sticking a forty-thousand-dollar plastic structure into a square of wood chips and calling it a playground—now *that* takes the cake. It is well intentioned, relatively safe, and resilient against lawsuits, but completely boring.

When we were kids, playgrounds were different. They were a place to see how far you could push your physical limits, get a few scrapes and bruises along the way, and learn your place in the social pecking order. There were solid wood swings installed right on the asphalt, so when one hit you, you'd end up with a knot on your head and skinned knees from the fall. The sliding boards were made out of steel, so in the summer time, you'd have to burn the top layer of skin off your legs to make it down. And the teeter-totters were made of splintered wood, so when your friend unexpectedly jumped off the other end, you'd end up with a couple of slivers of lead paint–covered wood in your rear. Summers were all about the smell of Bactine, the pinch of tweezers, and those orange disinfectant stains that took weeks to fade. Plaster casts covered with friends' names written in colorful markers were the trophies of the day. But I never see kids with disinfectant-stained knees anymore. That's a good thing, right?

Today, playgrounds are safe. Swing sets, merry-go-rounds, tube slides, monkey bars, and teeter-totters have all but disappeared. They've been replaced by smooth plastic structures with rounded edges and soft surfaces. Most are low to the ground, enclosed in plastic fences, and situated on rubber mats or wood chips. Even the National Program for Playground Safety has removed the dangerous swing from its logo and replaced it with a low-to-the-ground slide with side rails.

Children are still allowed to play on playgrounds, but at many elementary schools, games like tag, dodgeball, and even Duck Duck Goose, where knees and feelings might get bruised, are being banned. Some school playgrounds, those particularly worried about lawsuits, don't even allow running.[44] What's next? Signs that prohibit walking (to prevent toe-stub litigation), playing (just to keep children as safe as possible), and other children (to avoid children colliding with other children)?

What's the big deal if children no longer have outdoor spaces to climb, hang, swing, and figure out social hierarchies? Children can do all this on the Wii or Xbox, right?

When children spend time outside getting scraped knees and muddy sneakers, itching with poison ivy and stung by wasps, they're learning important lessons—what hurts, when they might trip, when they might fall, how strong their arms are, how high they can jump, and how fast they can run.

Let's face it: life is risky business. There are financial risks, emotional risks, physical risks, and social risks. And so the playground, given its inherent riskiness, might be a good and safe-ish place for the brain to begin to figure out how to deal with risk, conquer challenges, and overcome obstacles. We never would have survived as a species on the savanna if we never took any risks. I think that when we become overly concerned with eliminating every potential bump, bruise, and scrape on the playground, we also squash an important context for the development of essential human skills. In fact, Peter Cornall, head of leisure safety for the United Kingdom's Royal Society for the Prevention of Accidents, has suggested that the lack of outdoor play might in itself boost the accident rate because natural environments provide children opportunities to learn important safety lessons by trial and error: what is unstable, what is steep, what is slippery, and what is unsound.[45] There's also the possibility that standard playground equipment is more dangerous than loosely built natural areas because the standard stuff is predictable and unchanging.[46] See, if children are playing on equipment that has evenly spaced rungs on the monkey bars and a patterned weave on the climbing net, they don't really have to concentrate on where they're putting their hands and feet once they get started. Not only might this lead to accidents if, say, one rung is missing, but the physical lessons learned on such perfectly spaced play structures cannot be translated to the uneven and unpredictable world.

Here's what I think: if the prevailing view is that if the children don't play, they won't get hurt, and if they don't get hurt, we won't get sued, then we've got it all wrong. It's an extreme stance, and it's detrimental to the children, much more so than a scratched knee or bruised elbow.

Safety advocates counter by pointing to the numbers, saying that playground accidents cause two hundred thousand injuries per year.[47] But is there anything worse than a child getting hurt on the playground? How about an entire generation being released into the world without learning the hard way what's dangerous and what isn't, or an entire generation of children who have been protected so much that they haven't developed their own instincts and survival skills?

Remember that time you strayed too far on your bike and faced a dark and scary ride home? You knew it was your own fault, and you had to make it home alone. But you did it, felt infinitely stronger for it, and you knew not to do it again. How will our kids learn those lessons? They're not something you can teach at Sylvan. I'll bet ten bucks that someone will read this and come up with an interactive computer program that'll purport to teach children survival skills from their safe and supervised homes. After a few rounds of virtual outdoor play, the computer will ask, "If Abby jumps from that tree branch, will she break her leg or just sprain an ankle?" And: "Who's hiding behind that bush? Is it a registered sex offender or just a squirrel?"

TONIC OF WILDERNESS

Henry David Thoreau wrote of the "tonic of wildness."[48] A century ago, John Muir observed that "thousands of tired, nerve-shaken, over-civilized people are beginning to find out that going to the mountains is going home; that wilderness is a necessity; and that mountain parks and reservations are useful not only as fountains of timber and irrigating rivers, but as fountains of life."[49]

But in today's high-technology world, can the virtual outdoors be enough? Can television substitute for the real thing? Can we get the benefits of outdoors through nature DVDs, or do we actually need to feel the sun on our faces, hear the crunch of dried leaves under our shoes, and smell the blueberry bushes?

To test these ideas, University of Washington psychologist Peter Kahn exposed adults to a mild stressor and then had them either see a natural setting through a window, look at a plasma version, or stare at a blank wall.[50] It turned out that only the real view of the outdoors calmed the participants. The plasma window was no more restorative than the blank wall. Even high-definition quality can't fool the brain.

TAKE TWO WALKS AND YOU'LL FEEL BETTER IN THE MORNING

What if there were a cure for the ailments caused by the modern world? Well, maybe there is.

Mainstream medicine treats illness with pills or surgery or psychotherapy, but what about a walk in the park? For centuries, philosophers, mystics, and tree huggers have talked up the benefits of nature. And you've already read about a study that shows that a mere walk outside can benefit cognitive processing. Can it cure depression, hostility, and attention deficits?

I asked my family doctor this very question. She told me that a walk in the park won't hurt, but if I want to treat my body or mind, I'll need surgery, medication, or psychotherapy. What she doesn't know is that there have been empirical demonstrations that nature can feed our mental and physical bottom lines. There's the study I alluded to above, in which hospital patients who viewed trees through their room windows left the hospital a day earlier and used fewer pain medications than patients who had a view of a brick wall.[51] Likewise, a walk in the park attenuated children's symptoms of ADHD.[52] When surrounded by trees and animals, children are less likely to have behavioral problems and are better able to focus on a particular task.[53] The greener a girl's view from home, the better she concentrates, the less she acts impulsively, and the longer she can delay gratification.[54] Even a view of nature—green plants and natural landscapes—helps reduce stress among highly stressed children.[55] Residents of housing with trees and green space immediately outside the door experience a host of further benefits: a greater sense of community, a reduced risk of street crime, lower levels of violence and aggression between domestic partners, and a better capacity to cope with life's demands, especially the stresses of living in poverty.[56] Nearby nature can protect the brain and the body from stress and promote psychological well-being.

How exactly does nature do the brain and the body so much good? Other than Kaplan's ideas about attention above, I don't know. No matter; doctors prescribed aspirin for a long time without knowing its exact mechanism, and it still took headaches away. And even though drugs, surgery, and psychotherapy can cure people's problems, they often carry side effects. So treating modern life with nature may be the healthiest way to go—and likely the most cost-effective in a broad sense, since it comes with other benefits as well. Perhaps health plans will allow parents to use their flex dollars for improving green space. There is a cumulative message in all of this: as a society, we need to recognize that trees and green space are not luxuries, but necessary components of a healthy human habitat.

THINKING OUTSIDE THE HOUSE

I don't think that today's children have nature-deficit disorder. The last thing modern children need is another label to deal with. We already call them overweight, unpopular, learning disabled, and attention deficient. And thanks to my psychologist colleagues, we've already got enough labels for every odd behavior imaginable. There's Paris syndrome (a temporary psychosis triggered by visiting the city, almost exclusive to Japanese tourists), the Capgras delusion (a belief that a friend or family member has been replaced by an identical-looking impostor), and reduplicative paramnesia (a belief that a certain location has been copied and exists simultaneously somewhere else). So we really don't need another disorder to add to the already overflowing pile.

The real gem in Louv's work is not his coining of a "disorder," but rather his attaching a framework to a phenomenon everyone knew existed but no one had quite articulated. Louv's book jump-started an international movement that gave birth to the Children and Nature Network and a No Child Left Inside coalition, which lobbies for statewide environmental literacy.

I clicked onto the Children and Nature Network's website, and it invited me to plan an outdoor learning activity and invite a congressperson to attend.[57] I'm not sure how inviting the Honorable Jim Gerlach to the neighborhood children's regular weekend round of sardines and Eastern American toad hunt will help with their nature disorder, but I listened to the website and wrote him an invitation. I'm still waiting to hear back.

CLIF® Bar and Company invites children to submit an idea for an original game in the Backyard Game of the Year contest.[58] The winner receives a ten-thousand-dollar scholarship, a new Trek™ bike, and a trip to New York City. Great contest and super prizes. But if we take seriously the research reviewed in chapter 3 that found that external rewards can squash internally motivated behaviors, then this sort of contest might actually dampen children's tendencies to engage in the very outdoor free play it is trying to promote.

Part of the problem, I think, is that parents have seduced children indoors with toys, video games, computers, and air conditioning. These things aren't damaging in and of themselves, but they definitely pull children inside from the outdoors. We shouldn't convince children that the indoors offers as much as the outdoors. Riding the Fisher-Price® Smart Cycle® in front of the television set does not, as its marketing says, "take kids on learning adventures like no other." The real outdoors does this. Likewise, with the Xbox game Kinectimals™, children can venture into a virtual forest and build relationships with wild animals right in their own living rooms. It's a super-fun invention, but kids should also be running out the back door to learn about the native animals—the insects, birds, and mammals—in their own backyards.

I'm not convinced that we need a national coalition and federal legislation to get children outside. Parents and teachers simply need to take matters into their own hands. If you agree with me that childhood itself is an endangered species, take the surprisingly simple but very radical first step to saving this species. End the Great Indoor Retreat, unplug your kids, and kick them outside—to play, to learn, to relax, and maybe even to smell the blueberries.

Chapter 10

Old School

Don't you get a kick out of urban myths? Like the one about your hair growing back thicker after shaving. Or your eyes popping out of your head if you keep them open when you sneeze. Or swallowed chewing gum staying in your stomach for seven years. And then there's the one about recess being a waste of time. That it elbows out time needed for academics. That it distracts from the schools' primary mission of instruction.

The biggest reason for scrapping recess is the federal No Child Left Behind law. The law mandates that schools get all students testing at a proficient level by 2014. If they don't, teachers can lose their jobs, and administrators can get their schools taken over. Since no state has even gotten close to 100 percent proficiency, there's lots of work to do.

How much work? According to the latest national results, only 38 percent of fourth graders and 33 percent of eighth graders scored at or above the proficient level in math.[1] The results are worse for reading achievement, and there are huge state-by-state differences. In Massachusetts, where educators have carefully reworked standards and instruction, 52 percent of eighth graders scored at or above proficient on the latest math test. Compare that with Mississippi, where only 15 percent of students scored at proficient. This isn't a reason to push the panic button yet, but it's clear our children have no time for recess—especially in Mississippi.

There is all sorts of evidence to suggest that more classroom time should boost children's test scores.[2] The more time children spend in school, the higher their IQs. For each year of schooling children complete, there is an IQ gain of about 3.4 points. In fact, one year of schooling has a greater impact on IQ than does one year of age. We also know that the more children miss school, the more IQ drops. In one study, children who frequently missed school had an IQ of only 60! Then there's the summer slide. With each passing month away from school, children lose ground from their end-of-the-year test scores. So doing away with non-instructional things like recess will afford more opportunities for instruction, which can only positively affect academic achievement.

But here we're still in the realm of urban myths. Often the only truth in urban myths is that they're not true. Not even in the suburbs. Shaving doesn't make hair grow back thicker, or else we wouldn't have so many balding Gen-Xers walking around. Your eyes wouldn't fly out of your head if you propped them open during a sneeze because your eye sockets and your nasal passages don't cross paths. And gum passes on the same schedule as everything else you put in your mouth. The only difference is that gum comes out at the other end relatively unchanged by the trip.

What about recess being a waste of time? But early in the 2000s, educators started hacking away at it to make room for more academics. Today, nearly 40 percent of school districts have reduced or eliminated recess, and at the schools that do still offer it, some teachers take away recess privileges for bad behavior or forgotten homework.[3] Only three states require recess, and only ten recommend it.[4] Schools stubborn enough to have kept it around are placing increasing restrictions on what can go on during this "free time." At my children's school, the board has banned the holy trinity of chase, tag, and dodgeball. Now teachers hand out balls like controlled substances.

But a few decades ago, a strange fate befell education administrators. They started reading the education journals, and their collective breath was taken away. American children were performing better in school before they started losing their recess. The latest results of the National Assessment of Educational Progress show that students' math scores grew faster during the seven years before No Child Left Behind than after.[5] Before the federal law, fourth grade math scores grew by eleven points from 1996 to 2003, and eighth grade scores grew by eight points during the same time. But in the six years since the federal law took effect, both fourth and eighth grade scores gained only five points.

Same goes at the secondary level. Today, only 38 percent of high school seniors are proficient in reading, and only 26 percent in math.[6] The 2010 ACT College Readiness Report says that only 52 percent of graduating seniors are ready for college reading, 43 percent are ready for college math, and 29 percent are ready for college science.[7] Bottom line: our children were doing better before the No Child Left Behind effort to increase classroom time.

To make matters worse, our children are also sliding behind those of other countries. On one global test called Program for International Student Assessment, the United States fell to twenty-fifth in math and twenty-first in science skills out of thirty countries.[8] Other international assessments, we've dropped out of. In 2007, the United States quietly withdrew from the Trends in Mathematics and Science Study.[9] In the past, our high school students have performed shockingly badly. In the last survey, done in 1995, students from only two countries—Cyprus and South Africa—scored lower than Americans.

How can this be? In the past forty years, we've more than doubled the amount of money we spend per student on education. We have the smallest elementary class sizes we've had in forty-five years.[10] So how can our children—even the more affluent, suburban ones—earn worse science and math scores than children in other nations?

Educators are reacting to this news in a variety of ways. Some school officials have decided to lower the difficulty of their standards tests to skirt the No Child Left Behind penalties on failing schools—a process Education Secretary Arne Duncan has called a "race to the bottom."[11] Other schools, not willing to lower their standards, have simply fudged their results or flat-out cheated.[12] For instance, at Normandy Crossing Elementary School outside Houston, the principal, assistant principal, and three teachers resigned over allegations that they made a study guide by "tubing" the state science test. Tubing is the practice of squeezing a test booklet into an open tube so the test questions can be seen without breaking its paper seal. At a charter school in Massachusetts, a principal allegedly instructed teachers to point out students' wrong answers during the state tests. In Virginia, a principal allegedly pressured teachers to use an overhead projector to show special-education students the right answers for the state reading assessments. And in Georgia, 191 schools are under investigation after computer analyses of eraser markings on 2009 tests suggested that teachers changed the students' test answers. Are these one-time mistakes, or do they represent a trend? *Freakonomics* author and *New York Times* blogger Steven D. Levitt and a colleague examined Chicago public school answer sheets and concluded that about

5 percent of teachers cheat.[13] The monetary incentive is certainly there; math and science teachers at Normandy Crossing get a cash prize of $2,850 if their fifth graders test proficiently.[14] But if the incentive is to raise students' achievement, perhaps this money could be better spent on making sure that children have adequate space and play equipment for recess.

THE FOURTH R

The first hint that recess might not be so bad came when developmental psychologists Harold Stevenson and Shin-Ying Lee compared the structure of the school day in first and fifth grades in Minneapolis, Minnesota; Taipei, Taiwan; and Sendai, Japan. They found that although the East Asian children spent more total days in school than children in Minneapolis, the Asian children were given more recess breaks (four versus two in first grade and four or five versus two or fewer in fifth grade) and consequently spent fewer total hours in the classroom than the American children did.[15] In most East Asian elementary schools, children are given a ten-minute break every forty minutes or so. So it seems, perhaps ironically, that East Asian schools, which are characterized by highly rigorous curricula, also seem keenly aware of their children's need for recess breaks.

Does this mean that American parents should box up their children and ship them to the Far East if their children are to stand any chance of becoming academically successful? Can American children benefit from more recess breaks at school, or are Japanese and Taiwanese children the lucky ones? If you're thinking that Stevenson and Lee's study doesn't prove that more recess time in the United States would boost achievement because there might be something else completely unrelated to recess that is responsible for the East Asian children's success, you're right. This is where the next study comes in.

To explore whether recess can have positive effects in US schools, University of Minnesota educational psychologist Anthony Pellegrini and his colleagues experimentally manipulated the timing of school recess for children in kindergarten, second grade, and fourth grade.[16] Two days a week, children's recess was delayed by thirty minutes. Pellegrini found that not only was attention to schoolwork higher after than before recess, but the effects of the recess delay were greatest on the youngest children. Following recess, children were able to sustain attention on tasks and were less likely to fidget in their seats. Not only does recess have immediate benefits to children's attention to classroom tasks, but it also has long-term academic advantages. Other work by Pellegrini and his colleagues has shown that the increased attention facilitated by regular recess breaks can boost children's academic performance.[17] These findings fly in the face of educators who complain that recess leads to disruptive behavior. The data show exactly the opposite—that recess deprivation increases the likelihood of behavioral problems.

How could recess boost classroom performance? It might not be what you're thinking. It has nothing to do with children blowing off steam. Instead, imagine life without coffee breaks. Got it? If you think it has to do with attention, you're right. For anything to get into your brain, you first need to be paying attention to it. If you're not paying attention, it's not getting in. Also, attention is maximized when incoming information is spaced out, rather than massed into one big session. So frequent breaks help because they force you to space things out. And high-demand cognitive tasks—of the sort children often face in school—require sustained and focused attention.

Children benefit especially from breaks away from cognitively demanding tasks because the unstructured nature of play serves to reduce the mental interference that builds up during continued structured work, and consequently, it increases children's ability to pay attention.[18] Physical education classes, however, don't provide the same boost to classroom attention as does recess. This finding suggests that the nature of children's breaks is important. Physical education classes likely don't facilitate children's attention because they are merely another form of instruction and thus don't offer the sort of interruption needed to maximize academic work. But the unstructured nature of recess is cognitive candy to children. This is true especially for younger children because their immature nervous systems make classroom tasks cognitively taxing. Consequently, younger children are very vulnerable to cognitive fatigue during sustained instruction, and the release that unstructured breaks provide is highly beneficial.

What are we to make of these data on school achievement and recess? I think that we've been going about trying to boost students' academic performance the wrong way. Children don't need more schooling.

They don't need more structured intellectual work, which brings diminishing returns, since children's ability to concentrate bottoms out as the length of time between breaks increases. Children need more recess. We have complicated something that is simple and innocent and said that it's dangerous, it encourages flight, it causes disruptive behavior, and it's totally outmoded in the modern school. But children just need playful breaks here and there so they can pay attention in the classroom and so teachers can help develop them into outstanding thinkers, builders, creators, and explorers. Teachers often punish children by taking away recess privileges, but this seems all turned around to me. A teacher wouldn't punish a child by taking away math or science. Recess should be a vital part of the curriculum.

Stevenson and Lee's data on East Asian schools suggest also that American children's school days and school years should be lengthened. More and more districts are moving in this direction, and it would, of course, bring the total number of hours American children attend school in a year closer to that of other countries in the world. The increase should have the corresponding benefit of increased achievement—but the catch is that we'd need to work in frequent breaks, more than most children get now.

VOWEL MOVEMENTS

Educability is our species' claim to fame. We have a unique suite of cognitive, social, and communicative skills that gives us the capacity to build classrooms, develop curricula, knowingly transmit knowledge, and teach new skills. As a result, we achieve the most impressive accomplishments of any species on this planet. We engineer particle accelerators, film motion pictures, fly jet airliners, write comic books, compose symphonies, transplant organs, and choreograph Broadway shows. No other animal even comes close.

The assured way we build institutions designed to pass on our knowledge to our children would make you think we have this education thing in the bag. But we don't. The demands of formal education are one of the clearest examples of how modern children are hindered by the ancient brains that reside in their heads.[19]

For 90 percent of human existence, children were educated in an informal, hands-on manner during natural interactions with more expert peers or adults. New skills were picked up on the job and were relevant to solving a real problem in the context they were acquired. When children learned a new task, the reasons were immediately apparent. Children weren't taught how to, say, grind a stone tool merely so they could demonstrate they had that knowledge on Wednesday's quiz. They were taught this skill so they could open the fruit sitting in front of them. Such was learning for most of human existence.

Then about ten thousand years ago, when we traded in our nomadic lifestyle for stationary, agrarian communities, education started to change. The changes in our way of living increased the amount and complexity of technological knowledge that needed to be passed down to our children. Nonetheless, at first, most education was still done on the job. But as new technological skills developed rapidly, the amount and complexity of knowledge to be transmitted to the next generation amassed exponentially, and instruction "out of context" was soon required.

It has only been within the last several hundred years (at most, and not yet universally) that formal education has been a requirement for our children's success in the world. But formal education is not a task for which children's brains were designed. Today's children come into the world with the very same brains as their hunter-gatherer peers, yet we sit them down in classrooms, give them textbooks, and ask them to take standardized exams. We ask them to learn things that their brains never expected and in contexts that are completely foreign. We expect all children to learn the same set of skills at exactly the same rate. There's little room for individual differences in learning speed or for following one's penchants beyond the state's curriculum. The classroom clearly presents a formidable challenge to the brain's educability. It is an evolutionary novelty that seems to catch a lot of today's children off guard.

As opposed to the real-world learning the human brain was designed to do, most formal education today takes place "out of context," inside a school building. We pull children out of the real world for eight hours a day and sit them down in a classroom. Unfamiliar adults ask them to learn skills "for their own sake" and not to solve some problem immediately relevant for survival. Children count by twos, fives, and tens; sort vocabulary words by vowel sounds; memorize facts about the Civil War; identify the earth's layers; and distinguish between potential and kinetic energy—all for reasons likely not clear to any of them and totally unre-lated to their lives outside the classroom. I've lost count of the number of times my daughter has asked me: "Mom, *why* do I need to memorize all the US presidents when I can just google them? Can you even name them all?" But I doubt this same conversation went on in families ten thousand years ago: "Mom, why do I need to learn how to build a hut?"

Given that schooling is an unnatural experience, we should not be surprised that many children have difficulties with its demands. Nor should we be surprised that many children lack the motivation for the "out of context" learning that goes on in the classroom, especially those children who don't consistently experience the real-world benefits of their new skills. For instance, it's likely tough for a first grader to under-stand why she's being asked to sort similar-sounding words, write sen-tences about new vocabulary words, and then put them in alphabetical order, if no one outside of the classroom ever reads with her. But if her parents regularly read picture books, street signs, cookie recipes, and restaurant menus with her, she's likely to understand not only why she's learning to read in school, but also that reading can be good fun. Like-wise, it's probably difficult for a third grader to understand why he's being asked to estimate the length of various objects, measure the perimeter of polygons, and find the volume of prisms, unless his parents show him why these skills are important outside the classroom.

This evolutionary perspective on schooling suggests that we should consider ways to put children's learning back in context—to make it meaningful and to consequently motivate learning. The motivation to read, for instance, is not motivated by the process itself. It's motivated by the meaning of the words. It's not driven by the thrill of sounding out isolated words, spelling them correctly, or coming up with synonyms. You already know this if you've ever seen a second grader toil over her terribly boring word study homework or had to bribe your fifth grader to write out definitions once again for that week's vocabulary. The moti-vation for reading is driven by being able to do meaningful things like reading stories, writing messages, leaving notes, understanding signs, making out recipes, sending texts, and posting the day's events on Face-book. Likewise, the motivation for learning math is not the excitement of rote counting, estimating whether 7 + 8 will be more than 10, identi-fying symmetrical shapes, or solving long-division equations. It's driven by real-world benefits like being able to figure out whether you have enough money to buy both the action figure and the water gun, to divvy up your jellybeans equally among friends, to know how many pairs of pajamas to pack for your week at the beach, and to estimate how much sand you'll need to fill the new sandbox.

There certainly are a growing number of formal curricula aimed at applying learning to real-world situations, but they're often still centered in a workbook that goes on a desk that stands in a classroom. Parents and teachers need to move some of the learning out of the classroom and into the real world. Otherwise, teaching children is really no different from sitting a bluebird down in a classroom with a bunch of other birds, showing a PowerPoint® presentation on where to find nest construction materials, and then having the birds open their workbooks and fill out the nest-building module. That would be completely silly.

DRILL, BABY, DRILL

Being a mom of two elementary schoolers, I run into a lot of children. But I haven't met a single one who really loves school. Most tolerate it, do the work that's asked of them (some with more whining than others), and really look forward to summer vacation. What do you think happens between the one-year-old who can't get enough of learning about the world to the six-year-old who simply tolerates school? School seems to take a toll on the natural curiosity and enthusiasm for learning with which children begin life.

Sure, the world is not as new and exciting by the time you've been on this planet for six years, but I think that the loss of motivation for learning falls squarely in our laps. In chapter 4, I already talked about how grades and rewards in general can extinguish the natural high that comes from learning new things that serves to motivate further learning. Grades simply tell children to learn to get the grade; they have nothing to do with the joy of gaining new knowledge. As the No Child Left Behind standards movement becomes entrenched, this will certainly continue.

Increasingly, the standards movement has been motivating teachers to "teach to the test" and to focus more on a drill-and-practice educational strategy. This style can teach new facts and lead to gains on academic tests, but in education circles it's often referred to as "drill and kill"—"drill" because you drill children with facts, and "kill" because the practice eventually kills children's motivation to learn. Not only that, is memorizing a bunch of facts really learning? I have an app on my iPhone that offers to drill me until I learn how to make every cocktail ever mixed on *Mad Men*. I think I could learn it all in about a half an hour. It would make me a great bartender at parties, but do we really want our children learning in this manner in school? Why should they when there's an app for that? And it really doesn't take any true thinking to merely memorize.

TEACHING THINKING

Even though I don't know you, I bet you take thinking for granted. That it's something we all do automatically and equally well, like breathing, chewing, and talking. The truth is that without special training, we humans are not naturally good thinkers. We're incredibly gullible and believe almost anything anyone tells us. It takes work to get us to realize that multiple opinions exist and that not everything we hear is true. I didn't learn this until college.

In my sophomore year, I signed up for a cognitive psychology class that required three different textbooks. I thought it superfluous to have three books all describing the same cognitive system, but I went along with it. I read the first, put it down, and felt as if I had gained a basic knowledge of how things like attention, memory, and language worked. I moved on to the second. It completely disagreed with the first, and I didn't know what to do. I must have read it wrong. So I tried the third. That one disagreed with both the first and the second book. It made my head reel. I had been motoring through school, taking notes, regurgitating them on exams, and getting As. I had assumed that whatever I read in books or whatever a teacher told me in class was fact, and that people who were allowed to write books and teach classes always told the gospel truth. Now I had read three books—all written by esteemed professors of psychology—and none of them agreed. I was sure I read at least two of the books wrong; if the authorities disagreed, then how would I, a young college sophomore, know which one was right? There was always only one right answer, after all, and I had always depended on older, smarter people to tell me what it was. I was thrown into my first collegiate metaphysical crisis.

When exam time came, my cognitive professor asked us to explain which text we thought was closest to the truth and why. Holy smokes! I couldn't deal, so I fell back into my old test-taking mode of simply regurgitating material. I failed the exam. And got a note to meet with the professor after class. She sat me down, handed me a tissue, and told me that I hadn't learned how to learn. She explained that she assigned three conflicting texts not because she got a rise out of marking Fs on exams, but to give students a platform to think critically, to evaluate conflicting evidence, to synthesize research findings, and to reason scientifically. I didn't know students were supposed to do that, and her words switched a light on in my head. I ended up acing the rest of my exams for her course, and I spent my junior and senior years as a research assistant in her laboratory. I actually chose developmental psychology as a career path in part because of this experience and because my professor's job seemed like so much fun.

I think that every student needs this sort of "aha" experience about critical thinking—though much sooner than I did, since in today's Google age, conflicting information is ubiquitous.

BOXED LEARNING

So humans are not naturally good thinkers. What do we do with this? It is exactly why we need schools and not just Wikipedia® and an Internet connection. If we were all naturally good thinkers, naturally skeptical and balanced, schools would be superfluous.

The problem is, we don't teach much thinking in our schools. We teach the three Rs—reading, writing, and arithmetic—but not critical thinking. One reason we don't is that today's "standards movement" in education makes us focus mostly on getting children within each grade to learn a certain bunch of facts each school year. But this isn't learning how to think. It's learning how to memorize facts and take tests. It's boxed learning. This approach reminds me of the opening lines in Charles Dickens's novel *Hard Times*. Mr. Thomas Gradgrind, a schoolmaster who sees his students as pitchers to be filled with facts, says, "Now, what I want is, Facts. Teach these boys and girls nothing but Facts. Facts alone are wanted in life. Plant nothing else, and root out everything else. You can only form the minds of reasoning animals upon Facts: nothing else will ever be of any service to them."

But in the Google age, when facts are at our fingertips, children don't need to fill their heads with facts. They don't need to be fed information. They need to learn how to think for themselves. Children need to learn how to think *about* facts, toss them around in their heads, and let them marinate. They need to learn how to weigh some new fact against other facts, consider them critically, think about them skeptically, gather them to solve problems, and put them together in new ways to do something different. It's these critical thinking skills that today's children are lacking. In a clever study, the University of Connecticut's Donald Leu and his colleagues dreamed up an Internet hoax and created a series of bogus websites about the "Pacific Northwest Tree Octopus."[20] Turns out when seventh graders were let loose on the Internet and found the bogus websites, most of the children thought it was a real creature—even after Leu and colleagues explained that the students were looking at fake websites created by the researchers.

Asking children to memorize facts—like presidents, state capitals, and historical dates—has long outlived its usefulness. This isn't to say that children shouldn't be taught about history or the usual school subjects, but asking students to do something like memorizing the Constitution sheds no real light on US history and leaves children with no genuine skills for understanding the significance of the Constitution or, say, the role of the Supreme Court in interpreting the document.

How do we get children to think for themselves? Recreate for them the experimental way of learning that was prominent before formal schooling started. Children need to explore new areas as scientists who learn by trial and error, rather than merely being passive recipients of knowledge discovered by someone else.

When children learn things for themselves, they can take what they're learned and apply it widely. When they learn how to, say, ride a bicycle through trial and error, they can ride any bike, anywhere, anytime. When they learn how to add two small numbers together, they can add anything, anywhere, anytime. But much of the memorization and fact learning that our children do doesn't transfer to different situations. Rather, learning is superficial and limited to only the context in which information is learned. When my daughter was in the third grade, she was asked to memorize her times tables to "demonstrate automaticity with multiplication facts," and she did. She taped her chart next to her bed and studied it every night. Soon, she could rattle off anything between 0×0 and 12×12. But her rote learning didn't really lead to her understanding the concept of multiplication. When we were filling prize bags for her upcoming birthday party with three stickers per bag, I asked her how many we'd need. There were twelve girls coming and we wanted to give each one three stickers, so we'd need a total of? Radio silence. She had no idea that $12 \times 3 = 36$ meant that we'd need 36 stickers if we wanted to give twelve girls three stickers apiece. Her multiplication skills were limited to the box in which she had learned them. We, of course, worked on the problem until she understood. But this example shows that it's important for children to be able to use their knowledge outside of the classroom in which it is picked up. True learning has taken place only when children can transfer the learned skills to new contexts. Otherwise, it's like a circus clown who can juggle tennis balls, but throw him a set of pins or rubber chickens, and he has no idea what to do with them.

ALL BRAINS ARE NOT THE SAME

Last week, my daughter, Izzy, came home with her fifth grade school picture, and, funny thing, not every girl in the class looks exactly like my daughter. Some of them look something like her, but others are at least a foot smaller with rounded, babyish cheeks; shorter arms; and pink T-shirts with unicorns. Others look almost old enough to drive. These girls have thinner faces, longer legs, eye shadow, lip gloss, hips, and brassieres.

Just as these fifth grade bodies are very different, so are the brains inside their heads. Yet their school requires that they all learn the exact same things by the end of each school year. It seems silly to expect that their brains all grow at the same rate, since it's so clear that their arms, legs, heads, and bellies don't.

We learned in chapter 2 that brain growth is largely driven by children's experiences in the world. Because each child has different experiences, their brains are massively different from one another. Such individual differences in brain wiring mean that schools' expectation that every brain learn the same curriculum at the same rate is baseless. This individual variability also suggests that we should bring back the customized learning that was common to children for most of human history.

Individualized learning is by no means a new idea in the modern world. Tutoring companies like Sylvan and Kumon do so well because they offer specialized lessons tailored to children's individual needs. The public education system should take the lead of these companies and apply their approach. This would require knocking the current system down and envisioning something completely different. And it would certainly be a challenge for educators to keep track of their students' inner educational lives—the aptitudes, motivations, understandings, and confusions. The beginnings of figuring out how to tailor teaching to individual students already exist. For instance, Carol McDonald Connor at Florida State University and her colleagues are exploring the benefits of individualized language arts instruction among first graders.[21] Teachers are trained to use software that automatically translates students' assessment results into weekly recommendations of specific instructional activities for each student. The software enables teachers to match students' individual abilities with the amount and type of instruction they'll receive. Importantly, test scores indicate that individualized instruction boosts the growth of children's word reading and reading comprehension skills. This is certainly a step in the right direction. And it provides compelling evidence that today's mass education experiment and the accompanying insistence that all children learn the very same things at the very same rate doesn't make sense, given that their brains develop with profound variability.

This expectation of instructional sameness is like taking Charles Barkley, the former 76ers power forward, and expecting him to have a "proficient" golf swing by the end of a given marking period—even if Barkley had one of the greatest teachers in the world. This actually happened, and I'll tell you the ending if you don't know. Sir Charles is an eleven-time all-star, a Basketball Hall of Famer, 1993 NBA MVP, Olympic gold medalist, and one of only four players ever to compile twenty thousand points, ten thousand rebounds, and four thousand assists.[22] He also has what Golf.com calls the "World's Ugliest Golf Swing."[23] If you've never seen Barkley swing a golf club, google a video right now.

Is his swing really that terrible? John Elway thinks so. When asked to describe the "Round Mound of Rebound's" swing, he said, "I cringe when I see Charles' swing." Joe Theisman added, "It could have a psychological effect on someone who watches his golf swing. It's that bad."

And Jerry Rice admitted, "I had to face the other direction when he got ready to swing."[24]

In 2009, Tiger Woods's former swing coach, Hank Haney, tried to rehabilitate Barkley's swing on a Golf Channel reality show. How'd he do? Haney was so unsuccessful that Barkley went on *Saturday Night Live* to parody his own inability to learn a fluid swing.[25]

How could one of the greatest athletes in history have such a terribly hitched golf swing that it couldn't be fixed by one of the greatest swing coaches in the world? If you've been a dominant professional basketball player, shouldn't golf be a piece of cake, especially if you have Tiger Woods's coach helping you out? After all, both sports simply involve taking a round ball and getting it into the hole, with golf clearly being the easier of the two because ninety-year-olds and overweight players can still be competitive.

It has to do with how Sir Charles's brain is wired. And not even one of the smartest golf coaches could teach him to have a proficient swing. If Barkley couldn't get proficient under these conditions, I'm not sure how we expect all students to get proficient by 2014—especially when we're the ones choosing the areas of proficiency and the rate of learning. That seems like asking Barkley to shoot a golf score of 80.

PACKING THE NEURAL SUITCASE

No Child Left Behind expects 100 percent of students at each grade level to be proficient by 2014. What about 2015? Absent from the standards movement in education is how durable the learning remains after children complete their grade. Fifth graders are required to learn how to calculate the mean, median, and mode for a data set, but not to remember this for even one day past assessment day. Unfortunately, the school year for many students is like speed-packing a cheap suitcase—everything is put in hastily, the new contents are held briefly, and then most everything falls out.

If we really want children to retain what they've learned, they need to pack their neural suitcase carefully and gradually. And if it starts to fall apart, they'll need to give it some support. That way, it'll hold its contents for far longer.

There's both old and new literature in cognitive psychology that demonstrates how to best pack children's brains. First, it's well known that the brain likes to learn in more than one location. Some teachers often tell students to find one comfortable place to study—say, a desk in their bedrooms or a quiet corner in their houses. But research tells the opposite story. In a classic 1978 experiment, University of California, Los Angeles, psychologist Robert Bjork and his colleagues found that students who studied vocabulary words in two different rooms—one windowless, cluttered room and one modern room with an outdoor view—later outperformed those who studied twice in the same room.[26]

Why does location matter to the brain? When the brain is studying, it's constantly making subtle associations between the materials it's learning and everything else around it at the time—sights, sounds, textures, tastes—even though the brain's possessor is completely unaware of it. As your second grader is sorting his vocabulary words into long and short O sounds, his brain is coloring them with the blue paint on his bedroom walls. When he moves into the family room to put the same words in alphabetical order, his brain tags them with the sound of the chickadees chirping at the bird feeder in his backyard. Studying in multiple locations forces the brain to make multiple associations and consequently enriches the material in the brain. This enrichment, then, is thought to slow down the rate of forgetting.

Second, varying the type of material studied during any one session, rather than concentrating on just one skill at a time, also boosts retention. It's good for your sixth grader to do a bit of social studies homework, move on to studying her vocabulary words, switch to some science, and then review her long division for next week's exam. It's why musicians mix up their practice sessions—some scales, then musical selections, and then drills.

The superiority of this "interleaved" practice over "blocked" practice has been demonstrated by psychologists Kelli Taylor and Doug Rohrer. They taught fourth graders to calculate the dimensions of prisms either by studying repeated examples of one type, then another type, and so forth (e.g., *aaabbbccc*), or by mixing example types (e.g., *abcabcabc*).[27] Each group of children had the same total amount of study time. When children were tested a day later on new problems of the type they'd practiced, those who had mixed study did twice as well as the others, outscoring them 77 to 38 percent. These findings have profound implications for boosting student retention, especially because in many school texts, students practice problems of a particular type before moving onto the next type. If you've ever spent any time doing math homework of this blocked sort with your children, you know the problems later on in the set get answered almost automatically. When students see a set of problems all of the same kind, after the first few, they know the strategy to use before they even read the directions. But with mixed practice, each new problem is different from the last, which requires more active problem solving. This is also usually similar to the way their tests are designed, such that each new problem requires starting from the get-go.

The brain also does not like cramming. It would much rather your fifth grader study fifteen minutes on Saturday morning, fifteen on Monday before bed, and then fifteen more on Thursday after dinner, rather than packing all forty-five minutes into Thursday night. Both can get her the same A grade on Friday morning's exam, but the brain is more likely to retain the information past Friday morning if she spaces out her studying.

One last bit of help we can get from the cognitive psychology literature is to reconceptualize the way we view testing. Testing is the goal in today's high-stakes approach to education. Ironically, however, educators rarely think of tests as an educational opportunity—merely an evaluative one. But when students take tests, they're retrieving learned information from memory, manipulating it in their minds, and then communicating it on their test papers. If you think of testing in this manner, doesn't it look like it also might be a place that learning occurs? It does if you know how memory works. When you retrieve information from memory, it's not like walking into a library and pulling the right book from the stacks. Rather, simply retrieving information changes the way it's stored in memory and usually makes it more accessible in the future.

Cognitive psychologists Henry Roediger and Jeffrey Karpicke demonstrated this idea by having students study a prose passage in two back-to-back sessions.[28] When tested on the material immediately, students did well but quickly forgot the material. However, when students studied the passage in just one session and then did a practice test in the second session, they retained the information much longer than the first group did. The moral here is that testing has gotten a bad rap. If testing is such a powerful learning tool, perhaps we should stop complaining that educators are "teaching to the test" and instead advocate testing as a means to learning rather than an end.

So there's your study plan straight from cognitive psychology: change study contexts, mix content, space study sessions, and take tests. One last thing I have to mention, only because I'm a teacher and it drives me crazy. Students who do poorly on exams in my larger lecture classes sometimes drop by my office hours and tell me that they did so poorly because they are tactile-learners or left-brained or can pick up new ideas only through dance. Others who do well sometimes thank me for the PowerPoints I use because they're visual learners, or for the organized lectures because they're good listeners. Everyone seems to know their style of learning, and they like to share how they would prefer information to be presented to them. I can't blame them because teachers talk about learning styles all the time: there are scores of learning-style tests and guidebooks for teachers, and many professional education organizations offer learning-style workshops. However, in a 2008 review of the learning style literature, a team of highly regarded psychologists found virtually no support for the idea of learning styles. They said, "The contrast between the enormous popularity of the learning-styles approach within education and the lack of credible evidence for its utility is, in our opinion, striking and disturbing."[29]

The lack of an evidence base for learning styles doesn't mean that there are no individual differences in learning. It just means that it's not a good use of school resources to devote them to children's learning styles. Instead, those resources would be better used to figure out how to individualize learning in the Carol McDonald Connor style I described earlier.

HEMORRHOIDS AND HOMEWORK

Another consequence of the standardized testing movement is Big Homework. I do mean BIG. Tonight, my fifth grade daughter has to do one word study sheet and one math review sheet, read social studies and complete a questionnaire, review science for a possible quiz, and read a book of her choice for thirty minutes. This constitutes about two hours of homework, give or take. It's a good thing we didn't plan on her joining the rest of her family for an after-school bicycle ride and dinnertime hot dog cookout, or else she'd be behind the rest of her class tomorrow. And she'll only get busier as she moves on toward middle school.

Homework is a good thing, right? It reinforces skills learned in school and teaches children a good work ethic. Or maybe it doesn't. Most of my daughter's homework seems like busywork, and getting it done can cause our family a whole bunch of stress.

Homework is one of the best examples of how the ancient brain inside children's heads is hindered by the demands of formal schooling. It reminds me of hemorrhoids. If you consider our evolutionary history as animals, we've always been active: active predators in the ancient seas, freshwater streams, and boggy marshes; active tree-living primates; active hunter-gatherers as early humans; and active agriculturalists as we settled down. Today, we sit on our butts.

The evolutionary novelty of butt sitting is why so many of us suffer from hemorrhoids. Evolution in no way prepared us for our sedentary lifestyle. Hemorrhoids are one side effect of our modern ways. How so? Quick physiology lesson: Our hearts pump blood to our body parts with our arteries and back to our hearts with our veins. It's quite a job for veins to pump back blood from places down low like our feet because the blood has to travel uphill. We have two design features that help. One is the nifty little valves that let blood move up but stop it from moving back down. The second one is our leg muscles. They contract when we walk, and this contraction serves to pump blood up the veins in our legs. This setup works smoothly in animals that move around a lot. But in a more sedentary species like us, who don't use our legs much, sometimes there are not enough contractions to pump all of the blood up the veins. When this happens, blood pools in the veins, valves fail, and we end up with increasingly swollen veins that can become a literal pain in the butt. Hemorrhoids happen when blood pools in the veins around the rectum—an uncomfortable reminder that we were not built to sit around.

Just as sitting for long periods of time is a foreign element in the natural ecology of the hemorrhoid-ridden truck driver, homework is a foreign element in the natural ecology of the five-year-old. This might explain why, then, most children hate it, and why, at least for elementary schoolers, it does absolutely nothing to improve learning. In fact, when children are asked to do too much homework, it has the opposite effect. Homework has only minimal benefits for achievement in middle school.

It's not until high school that there are clear academic benefits to homework, but again, they start to decline if children are too overloaded.[30]

Many countries with the highest-scoring students on achievement tests, like Japan, the Czech Republic, and Denmark, assign little homework, whereas countries with students who score poorly internationally, such as Greenland, Iran, and Thailand, assign a lot of homework.

Based on data like these, some experts, such as education professor Etta Kralovec at the University of Arizona South, recommend no homework, at least not until middle or high school.[31] The National Education Association and National Parent Teacher Association recommend no more than ten to twenty minutes of homework per night for kindergarten through second grade and thirty to sixty minutes per night in grades three through six.[32]

My take? I won't go as far as the American Child Health Association did in the 1930s, when it blamed homework and child labor as leading killers of children who developed tuberculosis and heart disease.[33] And I realize that recommended levels of elementary school homework are probably less time than many children spend watching *SpongeBob* every day. Nonetheless, I find it striking that we have no evidence that there is any academic benefit to elementary school homework, yet educators feel compelled to assign it, and parents continue to think it helps students. Homework is going to be a hard habit to break, but since it's not related to academic achievement at least until middle school, and then only marginally, why assign it? Can't teachers squeeze all the learning children need into the eight hours a day they already have them at school? It seems to me that all the other pastimes outside of school that are good for children are a much wiser and more fun way for them to spend their after-school time. For high school students, there's no academic benefit from more than two hours of homework, so why pile it on?

But what if you're one of those parents who just want your children to do something "academic" after school? How do you resist your tendency to give them something to do that'll boost their grades? Make the family dinner. A large study by the University of Michigan's Sandra Hofferth found that the single strongest predictor of better achievement scores and fewer behavioral problems for children ages three to twelve was more family mealtime together.[34] Family time spent at meals was a stronger predictor of higher achievement and fewer behavioral problems than time spent at school, doing homework, attending church, playing organized sports, or engaging in art activities.

Also, keep in mind that no homework doesn't necessarily mean no learning after school. We as a society are strangely enamored of homework, even though it's a practice that seems to have few to no positive effects for younger children. Perhaps it is because we worry about what other things children would be getting into if they didn't have homework to fill their time. See chapters 6 through 9 if you worry. If educators and developmental scientists talk with one another, they might be able to come up with a way to eliminate homework and make everyone happy. One simple solution might be to, say, extend the school day by thirty minutes so that elementary schoolers can do their thirty minutes of "homework" at school. This suggestion goes back to Stevenson and Lee's findings regarding East Asian schools above. Longer school days (with frequent recess breaks) equal better achievement. And the suggestions from cognitive psychology in the section above might just eradicate the need for homework. At best, homework just reinforces what's learned in school. But if we can get all the necessary learning accomplished at school using some of the strategies of cognitive psychology, then in the schoolrooms of the future, homework may be unnecessary.

ORANGUTANS ON RITALIN

Ever met an orangutan with attention deficit/hyperactivity disorder (ADHD)? I haven't. But what do you think would happen if you dressed one up in jeans and a T-shirt, put him on a school bus, sent him to kindergarten, handed him a pencil, and told him to sit quietly in his seat and do a geometry worksheet? I bet he'd seem easily distracted, make careless mistakes, seem not to listen when spoken to directly, have trouble sustaining his attention, fidget, and try to leave his seat before he finished his work. During recess, I bet he would have trouble playing quietly or waiting his turn and would intrude into others' games. These are common symptoms of ADHD, and if you sent him to the doctor, I bet he'd come home with a prescription for Ritalin.

In chapter 9, we learned that increasing numbers of children are being diagnosed with ADHD and medicated for it. People have blamed this rise on everything from television sets to pesticides, from head injuries to food allergies, from bad genes to terrible parenting. But you know what's really not good for children who still have a limited ability to sustain attention and a healthy appetite for rambunctious play? Stuffing them into a classroom for eight hours a day.

If you've ever spent any serious time with young children, you know that they simply have trouble paying close and sustained attention. You also know that their play can be vigorous, if not raucous, at times. Such tendencies, especially among boys, don't fit well with hours of sitting quietly in seats, minding their own business, and concentrating on desk work. Yet schools generally discourage children's natural active tendencies, which makes me wonder whether much of the disruptive behavior might simply be due to children's naturally limited attention spans and their drive to play actively and explore.

Early childhood education specialists Anthony Pellegrini and Michael Horvat have wondered whether many children have been misdiagnosed with ADHD simply because they are naturally active and have a natural desire to explore.[35] Of course, highly active, attention-shifting children, even when not the most extreme, can be disruptive to a classroom. But perhaps the classroom setting shares some of the blame. You wouldn't take a recovering alcoholic—someone with a drive to drink—to a bar and then ask him not to have a gin and tonic. So why put children—youngsters who can't help but shift their attention and be rowdy—in a classroom and ask them to sustain attention and be sedentary for long periods of time? Wouldn't that make you an enabler?

I'm not trying to argue that ADHD isn't a real condition or that it's merely an artifact of the classroom, but that a lot of restless, rambunctious children have been misdiagnosed. In any given kindergarten class, those children born just before the cutoff date (that is, those who are young for their grade) are more likely to be diagnosed with ADHD (and prescribed stimulant medication) than those born just after the cutoff (those who are old for their grade).[36] Because there's no reason to suspect that incidence rates in any given year would be greater than in any other, these findings provide compelling support for the idea that a mismatch between the demands of the classroom and the typical behaviors of children has led to some degree of overdiagnosis. The findings suggest that the younger children's more immature behavior made them more likely to be tagged as having ADHD.

This overdiagnosis might not seem like a big deal until I tell you that more than half of all children diagnosed with ADHD use stimulants. They're even prescribed liberally for preschoolers. Stimulants, of course, often work well to reduce hyperactivity, but the question is open as to whether or not they also reduce the desire and opportunity to play—which, as we learned in chapter 6, is one of the main means through which children learn important cognitive and social skills.

There's also some evidence that recess might be part of a solution to this growing misdiagnosis problem—or at least a better solution than Ritalin. Jaak Panksepp, a behavioral neuroscientist at Washington State University, created a rat model of ADHD (by destroying the right frontal cortex—the region of the brain responsible for paying attention, planning ahead, and being sensitive to social cues).[37] This model should translate to humans because children diagnosed with ADHD often have delayed frontal lobe development. When Panksepp observed these rats playing, he discovered that they had more overall activity and engaged in more rough-and-tumble play than rats with intact brains. So the rats with damaged frontal cortices not only had brains like children with ADHD, but also behaved hyperactively like them. Then Panksepp gave his ADHD rats extra opportunities to play—which generally took the form of play fighting—and their behavior later showed reduced hyperactivity. Do these findings mean that extra play can reduce ADHD symptoms in children? That research still needs to be done. But if we consider Anthony Pellegrini's studies, reviewed above, showing that recess breaks reduce fidgeting and increase attention (two dimensions of ADHD), there's likely no harm in treating children's inattention and hyperactivity with a recess break before asking for a prescription of Ritalin.

JUGGLING CHICKENS

Have you ever seen a circus clown who could juggle only one thing—who could juggle three tennis balls, but had no idea how to juggle pins, hoops, or rubber chickens? Of course you haven't. Any clown worth his weight in red foam noses can transfer his knowledge of tennis-ball juggling to new contexts, like rubber chickens, and can even add other skills to do something more complex, like juggling rubber chickens while balancing on one foot.

This is what we need today's children to do. They need to be able to take the new skills they're learning in school, transfer them to new contexts, and use them to do new and more complex things. If we teach them how to juggle with tennis balls, and they can't figure out how to juggle with pins, then they haven't truly learned how to juggle.

We also need to keep in mind that the classroom is a species-atypical environment, so we should not be surprised that formal schooling is often difficult for children and that not all of them thrive in it. Children may not have evolved for school learning, but they're capable of it, and the perpetuation of our culture is dependent upon their continued mastery of the basic technological skills of writing and mathematics. Given that schooling is an unnatural experience, it's best to keep in mind that education can be best achieved when we take children's natural dispositions and abilities into consideration.

Chapter 11

Evolutionary Baggage

Think about how weird this is. If moms and dads kept up with the developmental science journals and applied the findings to their parenting, every child in the world would be out in the backyard playing pickup games with their friends until it got dark. But moms and dads don't do this. Instead, moms and dads strap their babies in bouncy seats and flip on Baby Einstein, even though it's through social interaction and not television sets that real intelligence is made. They teach their toddlers basic addition with flash cards, even though math is better learned by divvying up their Goldfish snacks among two and not three friends. They enroll their preschoolers in academic programs, even though these curricula can squash children's drive to learn. They sit their kindergartners in front of large-screen televisions and hand out video game controllers, even though too much gaming time can lead to attention problems. They jump at the chance to enroll their elementary schoolers in soccer leagues, even though their children would learn more about cooperation and self-regulation if they were left to their own devices with a ball and some friends. And, somehow, moms and dads feel good about this. If I were a Vulcan researching parenting behavior on Earth, this would seem like an irrational mess. But I am a psychologist, and based on what my field has discovered about the human brain, this makes perfect, ironic sense. We are born to make bad decisions.

HOW THE MODERN WORLD CAN MAKE YOU HAND OVER YOUR BRAIN

So how is it that you've been suckered into thinking that piping sounds into your pregnant belly could boost your fetus's IQ, or that Your Baby

Can Read could actually teach your baby to read, or that listening to Mozart would make your child a genius? Because information sources like *MommyBlog*, *The View*, Disney, and Olympic gold medalist Shannon Miller told you so. And you're more likely to listen to them than a bunch of egghead scientists you don't even know.

Part of the reason parents do things for their children that go against what science recommends is that many of us believe we're all equally qualified at everything—especially at giving child-rearing advice. Technology has played a central part in generating this belief because it allows mom bloggers and reality television personalities to weigh in about the pros and cons of educational toys, infant learning programs, and preschool curricula alongside tenured faculty who specialize in child development. On the Internet, TED (Technology, Entertainment, Design) webinars given by elite brain scientists go up against Hollywood celebrities who promote baseless agendas on YouTube and marketers who give groundless advice. We believe Jenny McCarthy when she tells us that the measles, mumps, rubella (MMR) vaccine caused her son's autism, even though there is no epidemiological evidence linking any vaccine to autism.[1] We've arrived at a place where we think that giving advice on child rearing is the same as giving advice on what color to paint the family room or what dress to wear to a high school reunion. But it's not. People who give advice on how to raise children should know what they're doing.

You wouldn't take advice on how to drywall your basement or remove a computer worm from your laptop from just anyone who knows how to write a blog or lucked into their own reality show. So why take advice from people who are not experts when it comes to raising your children? We're not all equally qualified in that area, just like we're not all equally qualified to do open heart surgery, pilot a helicopter, walk a tightrope, or rescue avalanche victims in the Andes. If I had a brain tumor, I'd want advice on treatment options from a well-qualified medical specialist who kept up with the latest in therapies and knew their risks and success rates—not from a Disney Channel infomercial, my neighbor, a blog on GroundlessMedicalAdvice.com, or some celebrity.

Likewise, if you have children, you want advice on child rearing from a well-qualified developmental specialist who has kept up with the latest research and who knows the pros and cons of common parenting decisions. You want this because you're not going to read a developmental science journal for yourself. Only developmental scientists read them. They contain sentences like, "The pattern of fcMVPA feature weights indicated that functional maturation is driven both by the segregation of nearby functional areas, through the weakening of short-range functional connections, and the integration of distant regions into functional networks, by strengthening of long-range functional connections."[2] Try to use that to tell your spouse why you shouldn't let your infant watch too much Baby Einstein.

Besides the equal-qualification fallacy, the other part of the reason that parents disregard science is that many of us confuse facts with opinions and think that we can have opinions about facts. You can have an opinion about the dancing Elvis doll your mother-in-law brought you from Graceland, the sweater your boss wears at Christmas that beeps out "Jingle Bell Rock," or whether *American Idol* is better with or without Paula Abdul. But you can't have an opinion about the number of bones in a giraffe's neck, how high a flea can jump, how long it takes to digest an Oreo®, or whether rushing children to grow up is a bad idea. These are facts, and your opinion about them has no effect on them. Just like we learned in chapter 2, BabyPlus does absolutely nothing for your child's brain, and thinking that it does won't suddenly make it any less of a sham.

We're prone to this sort of thinking because it's pervasive in the media. Consider a study carried out by Nanette Gartrell of the University of California, San Francisco, and Henry Bos of the University of California, Los Angeles. After following children throughout childhood and early adolescence, Gartrell and Boss found that children raised by lesbian parents performed better academically, had greater self-esteem and confidence, and demonstrated fewer behavioral problems than children raised by heterosexual parents.[3] This study was published in the journal *Pediatrics* and underwent the typical rigorous peer review process. No matter. Wendy Wright, president of Concerned Women for America, a group that supports biblical values, opined that she is "a little suspicious of any study that says children being raised by same-sex couples do better or have superior outcomes to children raised with a mother and father. It just defies common sense and reality."[4] The thing is, Ms. Wright, if we relied only on common sense and not science, we'd still think that the earth is the center of the universe, that microbes are not evolving, that things that taste good are always good for us, and that E does not equal MC². You can have an opinion about whether or not homosexuality is moral, and you can question the technical rigor of any study's methods, the appropriateness of its statistical analyses, or whether the authors' conclusions are substantiated by the data, but you can't have an opinion about peer-reviewed scientific findings.[5]

WITH A SIDE OF IRRATIONALITY

A frequent myth in cognitive science is that human brains go about acting logically. If this were true, a guinea pig would be a pig from Guinea and not a rodent indigenous to South America, a koala bear would be a bear and not a marsupial, and a titmouse would both be a mouse and have mammilla. There would be ham in hamburgers, egg in eggplant, and at least either pine or apples in pineapple.

So you see, it's not your fault that you're more persuaded by commercials, celebrities, and your Mothers of Preschoolers group than scientists. We're illogical beings.

The real problem is that evolution didn't give us a way of systematically making decisions. We can't thoroughly search our entire bank of memories or objectively judge if the woman on *The Dating Game* should choose bachelor number one, two, or three, though this is what we'd need to do to make objective decisions. Just as political polls are most accurate if they're drawn from a group that is representative of the entire population, our decisions would be most accurate if they could be taken from a balanced set of evidence. The problem is that evolution never discovered the statistician's rule of a representative sample, so we never get from our brains a representative set of data. Instead, our brains mess with information before they hand it over to us.

This happens because we essentially have two decision-making systems—one old and one new—and both of them jockey for influence.[6] The evolutionarily older system is quick and automatic, but shortsighted. We're largely unaware of its goings-on. Our newer system is slower but deliberate and judicious; it chews over the incoming data and does its best to take the long view. The older system relies on older brain parts like the cerebellum and basal ganglia (implicated in motor control) and the amygdala (associated with emotion). The newer system involves the frontal cortex, and it can be one of the last neural areas to know when a decision is made.

The deliberate system is indeed deliberate, but it's not necessarily rational, though it tries to be. Likewise, the automatic system is not always irrational—it's just not been updated to work well in the modern world. Its decisions would have served well back in the day to help us flee, fight, eat, and reproduce—in other words, make all those automatic survival decisions. But now that the newer, conscious system has been installed, this antique system can make us behave irrationally in the modern world.

Our newer, deliberate system has never fully taken over because it relies on secondhand information that older systems feed it. In other words, even when we try to reason completely objectively, there's no guarantee that the older system has handed over a balanced set of data. Worse, if our emotions are deeply stirred (or if we're tired, stressed, or distracted), our newer, more logical chunks of brain can go completely quiet and leave us entirely at the mercy of the older, reflexive regions. So we have the equipment to reason deliberately, but evolution hasn't built in a way for us to do so without any interference or a way to ensure that our newer systems stay in the game. As a result, we often feel as if our decisions are based on cold, hard facts, but they're shaped by our ancestral system in subtle ways that we are not even aware of.

In fact, the effects of this ancestral system can be so strong that its automatic reactions can trump our efforts at logic and reason. For instance, these influences make anecdotes much more compelling to us than statistics. Our brains are belief engines that employ associative learning to seek and find patterns. This has helped us survive for millions of years: "I ate that purple plant yesterday and then got sick. That plant must have made me sick, so I won't eat it again." This tendency makes us ignore the Statistics 101 mantra, "Correlation does not imply causation," and automatically associate phenomena that occur at roughly the same time. If two things coexist, the brain often tells us, they must be related. Historically, this was an effective strategy because false positives (believing there is a connection between a purple plant and the plague, when there is not) generally are not harmful, whereas false negatives (believing there is no connection between a purple plant and the plague, when there is) may take you out of the gene pool. So this tendency to connect closely occurring happenings is millions of years old, and science, with its ways of controlling for intervening variables to circumvent false positives, is brand-new by comparison. Which is why we're much more persuaded by our neighbor telling us her Baby Einstein Discovery Cards turned her little girl into a genius ("I used the cards, and now she's so smart") than by a cold, dry academic journal paper telling us that there is no positive statistical association between children's IQ scores and the number of hours their parents flip flash cards in front of their faces. Likewise, even though there's no scientific basis for BabyPlus, if you used one and your baby turns out to be advanced, you're likely to be bamboozled by your brain into thinking the prenatal device caused your baby's smartness—even though her smartness is likely to have something to do with all the other supportive things you did for her development. You can almost feel the invitation to irrationality the moment you hold your child in your arms for the first time and realize that you'd do anything for her if anyone told you it worked.

A frustrating example of how our ancestral ways can contaminate our rationality is in the controversy over whether vaccinations cause autism. In 1998, Andrew Wakefield was the lead author on a study published in the *Lancet* that suggested there may be a link between autism and the MMR vaccine.[7] Soon, parents began to notice that shortly after their children were vaccinated, autistic symptoms appeared. Their conclusion: the vaccine must have caused the autism. Since then, the MMR/autism interpretation of the 1998 article has been retracted by ten of Wakefield's coauthors. And in a historic move in February 2010, the *Lancet* retracted the entire study. Later that year, Wakefield was banned from practicing medicine and found by the General Medical Council to have acted "dishonestly and irresponsibly."[8]

Scientists other than Wakefield have been unable to find any causal link between autism and the MMR vaccine. Let me make this clear: there is no scientific reason to think that the vaccine could cause autism. Twelve studies have found no connection between the MMR vaccine and autism, six studies have found no association between thimerosal (a preservative containing ethylmercury that has largely been removed from vaccines since 2001) and autism, and three other studies have found no evidence that thimerosal causes even minor neurological damage.[9]

But, according to a 2008 survey, that hasn't stopped as many as one in four people from believing in the vaccine connection.[10] How could they do otherwise when US senators like John Kerry of Massachusetts and Chris Dodd of Connecticut both have trumpeted the idea that vaccines cause autism?[11] Or when Robert F. Kennedy Jr. writes a 2005 piece for *Rolling Stone* and *Salon* titled "Deadly Immunity" that accuses the government of protecting drug companies from litigation by concealing evidence that mercury in vaccines may have caused autism in thousands of children?[12] And then there's celebrity Jenny McCarthy, who continues to blame the MMR vaccine for giving her son autism. This message has won McCarthy a wide audience and three best-selling books on autism.[13] Plus, there are antivaccine websites, Facebook groups, e-mail alerts, and lobbying organizations.

These stories hold power despite contrary facts and even in the face of long-dormant diseases like measles, meningitis, and pertussis (whooping cough) that are returning due to dropping immunization rates.[14] Is this a problem? Only if it worries you that the risk of an infected infant dying of pertussis is about 1 percent, but the risk of an infant dying from the pertussis vaccine is practically nonexistent. This fact makes Jenny McCarthy more of a threat to public health than any vaccine.

The autism/vaccine story is an unsettling example of why it's important for parents to be good consumers of science. The modern world is stuffed with groundless claims, baseless opinions, affecting anecdotes, bad science, and elegant research about children and their development. Making good decisions about how to rear and educate your children can be tough enough without your brain suckering you into inventing problems that don't exist.

DECIDEDLY SEEKING NONSCIENCE

With our brains marinating in our heads in all sorts of frothy, ancient influences, trying to increase our scientific literacy can be an uphill battle. A study by Imperial College London's Katrina Brown and her colleagues demonstrates that wall we're up against. Brown reviewed thirty-one studies of parents' beliefs about the MMR vaccine and came up with a few things relevant to our discussion.[15] First, parents generally felt that they didn't have enough information, especially regarding the dangers of not vaccinating. Second, parents did not trust health professionals or officially endorsed research, but they did trust friends and the media. Third, parents said they were heavily influenced by information about risks.

These findings are in line with our discussion so far and suggest where we need to go to boost our scientific literacy. Brown's first finding, about parents feeling as if they don't have enough information to make informed decisions, is an easy one to fix. That was the purpose of the first ten chapters of this book. But Brown's two other findings make it clear that more information is not enough. You can't just pile it on and expect it to take hold. You have to do more.

What do we do with Brown's second finding: that parents trust their peers and the media more than experts? What's so bad about experts? Experts are evolutionary novelties, and so we're not sure what to do with them. It makes sense, then, that parents would be more inclined to believe a familiar person or a shiny ad that shows a familiar-looking family. Historically, it probably was vastly more risky to ignore advice from a peer than to take it.

So, from the perspective of our ancestors, a bias in favor of the familiar likely made sense; what Great-Great-Great-Grandma knew didn't kill her was a safer bet than what she didn't know—which might do her in. But our preference for the familiar can be problematic in the modern world, especially when we don't realize that it can lead to irrational decisions. For example, we know that people prefer social policies that are already in place to those that are not. This is the case even if there are no solid data demonstrating that the current policies are effective. Rather than analyze the costs and benefits, we apply a simple rule: "If we're using it, it must be working." One recent study showed that people prefer current policies over proposed ones even when they have no idea what the current policies are. People's bias to favor the familiar is so strong that the study's participants had no trouble formulating reasons to support current-but-unknown policies. In fact, people prefer the familiar over the unfamiliar even when the familiar is known to be the worse option.[16] This reasoning explains, for instance, why the school policy recommendations made in chapter 10 haven't yet made their way into the school system.

Then there's Brown's third finding: that people's decisions are more compelled by fear than by assurance. Objectively speaking, decisions should be made by an evenhanded appraisal of risks versus benefits, but emotionally, we are swayed more by the potential for danger than for gain. Here, again, we're more affected by a moving story even if there is only a remote chance that it'll ever happen again. This is why everyone is out of the water the moment they hear of a shark attack. But not only are shark-bite fatalities rare (only about eight people per year worldwide die from shark attacks), up to a hundred million sharks die every year at the hands of humans.[17] We're a bigger threat to them than they are to us. Humans are more likely to be bitten by another human than a shark, but that doesn't stop us from inviting people over for dinner parties.

There's a second study, by the University of Maryland's Heather Ridolfo and her colleagues, that I'd like to bring into this discussion.[18] This one hits at the meat of our mistrust in science. Ridolfo persuaded participants that either 25 or 90 percent of the general public believed in the reality of ESP and that scientists either did or did not accept ESP. When participants thought that ESP was widely believed in by the public, they, too, were likely to believe. This makes sense. People are compelled by the beliefs of their peers. But when participants thought that ESP was accepted by the scientific community, they claimed disbelief. So, all things being equal, people took the opposing view to the scientists. This seems absurd. Shouldn't people believe experts who spend their lives toiling in their laboratories with their bubbling beakers and fancy microscopes? Does this mean that people automatically believe the opposite of anything that comes out of a scientist's mouth? Do people really think that cigarettes are good for your lungs and that moderate exercise at least three times a week will make you obese? Instead of publishing their findings in peer-reviewed journals, perhaps scientists need to embed themselves in PTAs and moms' groups and tell stories of one representative participant: "This one mom I know, she let her baby watch those Baby Einstein videos all the time. You know, the ones that are supposed to turn your kid into a genius. Well, now her daughter has a smaller vocabulary than the other one-year-olds in her Gymboree® class. Isn't that terrible?" There's also a well-known effect in psychology that as soon as people feel they're being manipulated toward one choice, they do the opposite—so this might have something to do with people's tendency to reject science. But regardless of the explanation, we scientists need to tread carefully when our data have a story to tell.

RATIONAL PARENTING

So what do we do about our illogical, science-flinging brains? Ever try to tickle yourself? You can't do it. You can't because your brain knows it is coming and can predict the sensation. The same perhaps might go for decision making.[19] If you know what's coming (say, that you're going to get all worked up over Jenny McCarthy's story), perhaps you can predict your response (that you're going to feel compelled to withhold vaccinations from your children) and stop yourself from being tickled.

Here's why I think so. You've already learned that much of the brain's decision making goes on behind the scenes at an unconscious level (not in the Freudian Oedipal complex sense, but in the sense that you aren't aware of it), even though it all feels totally conscious. Whatever decisions we make, it feels like we meant to make them. "I meant to come home from Bullseye with the hundred-dollar Blinky McNeutron Bounce 'n' Figure electronic math tutor/bouncy seat because I read on the box that it'll teach my three-month-old the 'advanced computational skills' she'll need to get into a good preschool." But this "I meant to do it" feeling is really an illusion that the brain creates. What's really going on is that those older parts of the brain grab the incoming information first, quickly weigh various pieces using some completely unconscious algorithm, and then present that choice to the conscious mind. This system is so slick that it fools us into thinking the whole thing was conscious. And our consciousness is very good at retrofitting a logical explanation for whatever we've decided to do—see the Blinky McNeutron example above. We know that this goes on because Yale University's John Bargh and his colleagues have shown that if our unconscious algorithms are changed by priming them with something, for example, the decision-making process is changed, too.[20]

In a series of experiments, Bargh has shown that he can alter people's judgments just by handing them a cup of coffee (a.k.a. the prime).[21] When study participants were asked to momentarily hold a cup of iced coffee, they later rated a hypothetical person as much colder, less social, and more selfish than did participants who held hot coffee. You read that right. The temperature of a cup of coffee was all it took to unknowingly change people's descriptions of a person. As unbelievable as this seems, similar findings involving priming have been pouring in over the last decade. For instance, people tidy up more thoroughly when there is a faint scent of cleaning products in the air, and they are more competitive if there is a briefcase in view—all without being aware of the change or what prompted it.[22]

This line of investigation demonstrates just how influential our old, unconscious systems are and how everyday sights, sounds, and smells can trigger them. Just like tickling, priming doesn't work if you're aware of it. That's why I'm about to tell you what most likely primes your bad child-rearing decisions.

THE SWING SET IS OUT TO GET YOU

It's a funny thing: our decision making is riddled with errors and biases that make rational humans seem irrational, but researchers studying nonhuman animals in their natural environments have been increasingly impressed by how they often make sound choices that approximate decision making that's consistent with elaborate mathematical models of optimality.[23] We appear to have a paradox on our hands: How can humans be so foolish and animals so intelligent?

The problem, according to evolutionary psychologists Leda Cosmides and John Tooby, is that humans only seem irrational because we're not looking at our behavior in our natural environment.[24] Rather, we're looking at these behaviors in a newfangled modern environment for which our brains haven't had the time to adjust. In other words, the brain has evolved to make decisions of the adaptive sort: those dealing with food, shelter, mates, allies, and enemies. But because modern human life is so cushy, most of our decisions have little, if any, impact on our ability to survive and reproduce.

The result? Our brains are lousy at assessing modern risks. To see this, just think about your child visiting a playground on her own. You're likely to wonder: Is that man with the long beard who plays his guitar under the tree a child molester? Does that recycled tire climber contain carcinogens or other dangerous chemicals? Does that swing set have dangerously high levels of lead-based paint, or is it teaming with drug-resistant bacteria? This place is too dangerous for my child—but wait! Not getting enough outdoor free play is bad for children. So why does it feel like even the playground is out to get them? As I pointed out, it's because the human brain was not designed to evaluate risks like these.

The brain is biased to make certain decisions when faced with risks. Our biases reflect the choices that kept our ancestors alive. Our ancient ancestors mainly based their decisions on their own observations, which were accumulating counts of natural frequencies, such as, "We were attacked by another tribe the last three out of four times we hunted across the river to the west." But we have yet to evolve similarly effective responses to statistics, pushy advertisements, and fearmongering news reports. Twenty-four-hour news channels and infomercials are evolutionary novelties that we haven't yet developed strategies to deal with. Nonetheless, a line of research carried out in the last thirty or so years, principally by two psychologists, the late Amos Tversky of Stanford University and Daniel Kahneman of Princeton University, explains how we've come to deal with a range of modern risks and provides insight into how we could use this information to make more logical decisions.[25]

One of the most irrational classes of decisions we make as parents are those that have to do with fear—fear that a vaccine will cause autism, that the outdoors is dangerous, and that our children will fall behind if we don't keep up with the Joneses. Fear comes from a super-fast risk assessment that is driven by various primate parts of our brain. The amygdala flags certain perceptions, sends an alarm signal, and—before you're even aware of it—floods your brain with adrenaline. This is the way our ancestors assessed risk before we had statistics. So we're built to gauge fear reflexively, before the entirety of the situation is consciously perceived—not to first read *Consumer Reports*, google the risks, confer with friends, think it through, and only then determine if we should be afraid. If our species carried on like this on the savanna, humans would have gone extinct long ago.

WE FEAR STRANGERS AND NOT MINIVANS

Here's a decision for you: are there more words in the English language that start with the letter *k* or that have *k* in the third position? If you're like the participants in a study by Tversky and Kahneman, then you probably judged that *k* is found more often at the beginning of words. In fact, *k* appears about twice as often in the third position.[26]

What happened? It's much easier to think of words that begin with *k* than those in which *k* comes third. So your judgment was biased by the availability of information from memory. This availability rule of thumb makes sense usually because much of the time, what is available from memory will lead to accurate judgments.

So if you judge dodgeball to be a less dangerous pastime for your kids than heli-skiing, availability is serving you well. But if you think your child is more likely to be kidnapped than be involved in a fatal accident in your minivan, you're wrong. The likelihood of your child being killed in an auto accident is about twelve times higher than the likelihood of your child being abducted by a stranger.[27] There are about twelve hundred child vehicular fatalities per year, or more than three a day; the evening news doesn't cover those three deaths per day because it wouldn't be newsworthy or attract ratings to report the same thing every night. The media does cover child abductions, so abductions are more memorable. The more we see something, the more common we think it is, even if we are watching the same footage over and over.

So we routinely take whatever memories are the most recent or the most easily remembered to be much more important than any other data. Much of our everyday interpersonal friction comes from this same failure to consider how well our samples represent reality. When we squabble with our spouse about whose turn it is to wash the dinner dishes, we (without realizing it) remember better the previous times we ourselves did them (as compared to the times our spouse did), and we rarely compensate for that imbalance—so we come to believe we've done more work than we have and end up in a self-righteous huff. Studies show that in virtually any collaborative venture, from household duties to writing academic papers, the sum of each individual's perceived contributions exceeds the total amount of work done.[28]

Also, because fear strengthens memory, memories of fearful events, like child abductions, salmonella poisonings, and acts of terrorism, are more easily brought to mind than memories of everyday, ordinary events. Consequently, the ease with which we remember fearful events makes them seem more frequent than they actually are. As a result, we overestimate the odds of dreadful but infrequent events and underestimate how risky ordinary events are. The dramatic quality and spectacular features of improbable events make them appear to be more common. This likely was an adaptive strategy for our ancestors—to pay attention to whatever seemed the most dramatic. In our modern mode of safer, more relaxed living, we often have the luxury of reflecting on every contingency and counter-alternative—we just don't realize the benefits of doing so.

Our tendency to be swayed by the dramatic is exacerbated by the fact that this is often exactly what the media covers. An example of how memory availability can hurt: Nearly a million and a half people changed their travel plans to avoid flying in the three months following September 11, 2001. Most chose to drive instead, but driving is more dangerous than flying. You're statistically more likely to die in a car than in an airplane, but we fear airplanes, and this was especially true following 9/11. Much of this fear was due to media coverage. Demonstrating the danger of relying on such availability, a study by the University of Michigan's Transportation Research Institute found that the decision to drive rather than fly caused an additional 1,018 fatalities from car crashes.[29] In other words, 1,018 people who chose to drive following 9/11 wouldn't have died had they flown instead.

None of this is to say that children's risk from strangers is nonexistent. Some neighborhoods are truly dangerous, particularly in inner cities, and that reality must be addressed before all of our children can play freely outdoors. But when the number of child abductions per year is about one hundred in a country of seventy-five million children (approximately .000133 percent), it's important to understand that it is a rare event. Children are more likely to die in the bathtub than they are in the backyard, yet we don't keep children from taking baths. My point is that we shouldn't limit children's lives because of a fear based on a very remote danger. My neighbor lets her eleven-year-old daughter walk one hundred yards by herself over to our house to play. But she has to call her parents the second she arrives safely at our door, as if she's been dodging sniper fire.

WE FEAR STRANGERS AND NOT OBESITY

So we have our brains set up to deal with traditional dangers to our children like hungry predators and angry neighbors, not modern childhood dangers like video games, the television set, and a sedentary lifestyle. As opposed to traditional dangers, many modern dangers don't produce an immediate negative effect, so the snap judgments our ancestral systems cause us to make are unhelpful for negotiating childhood experiences that somewhere down the line might be unhealthy. We tend, then, not to fear things that aren't immediate threats. As a result, we're less frightened of obesity, stress, or the inability to focus than we should be.

Attention deficiencies, for example, are the end result of actions that one at a time (one *SpongeBob* rerun) aren't especially dangerous, but, repeated over months and even years, can have harmful consequences. Because our brains are built to react in the moment, we tend to overvalue what's happened in the last few seconds, relative to everything else that has happened or will happen. We don't fear that the television set might cause attention problems in our children because we don't see it happening. It's not as though after an afternoon of vegging on the couch to a *Clone Wars* marathon, our children will exhibit new attention problems in school the very next day. This shortsighted tendency is pretty much like considering only yesterday's stock market returns while ignoring everything else that's happened in the past ten years.

Generally, things that build up very slowly are difficult for us to see. We focus on the short term, even if we know the long-term risk. Consider, for instance, that many children today spend hours indoors playing video games and watching television. Indeed, this move indoors was spurred by our desire to protect our children. But the unfortunate consequence of this modern trend is that children's lives have become more sedentary; they are more overweight than ever and at a greater risk of developing hypertension, diabetes, and heart disease at younger ages. Likewise, there's evidence that this lifestyle has led to behavioral problems and difficulties in learning. A ten-year-old who's developed diabetes is very upsetting, but because we don't see a lack of physical activity causing health problems, we don't worry about diabetes. So even though staying inside might be more dangerous for children in the long run than going outside, we tend to ignore risks that creep up on us.

WE FEEL SAFER IF WE (THINK WE) ARE IN CONTROL

If we feel we can control what happens, or if we choose to take a risk voluntarily, it often feels less dangerous. This is why when you move to the passenger's seat from the driver's seat during a road trip, the car in front of you suddenly starts to look closer, and you mash your foot on an imaginary brake. You're less scared behind the steering wheel because you're in control and that's reassuring. It's also why your spouse can't help but criticize your driving.

The false sense of safety we feel when we're in control and the fear we feel about dangers we can't control both explain why, for example, we get nervous about our children walking home from school alone, even though we felt perfectly fine when we did it at their age. It's why we huddle children indoors under our care—because we feel they're safer under our watchful eye. Surprising as this may sound, elementary school– and middle school–aged children are more likely to die under our care while we're driving the minivan than by unintentional injuries that occur outside the home.[30] In the same vein, a lot of parents feel safer driving children to school themselves than putting them on a school bus or letting them walk to school. But being driven to school in a passenger vehicle is by far the most dangerous way to get to school. Riding on a school bus is the safest. Seventy-five percent of fatalities and 84 percent of injuries take place while children are in passenger vehicles, whereas only 2 percent of student deaths and 4 percent of injuries result from travel by school bus.[31]

THE MOTHER OF ALL BIASES

What's known as the confirmation bias is the mother of all human reasoning problems. The confirmation bias refers to our tendency to seek or interpret evidence in line with our beliefs and to ignore or reinterpret evidence contrary to our beliefs.

To demonstrate the first half of this bias, in 1983, Princeton University psychologists John Darley and Paget Gross showed participants a video of a child taking a test. Half of the participants were told that the child was from a high socioeconomic class, and half were told the child was from a low socioeconomic class. When later asked to evaluate the academic abilities of the child on the basis of the test results, those who believed the child was from a high socioeconomic class tended to rate the child's performance at an above-grade level, whereas those who believed they were looking at the results from a low-socioeconomic-class child tended to give a below-grade rating.[32] In other words, the very same objective data were rated differently based on the expectations of the evaluators. Following Darley and Gross's investigation, hundreds of studies have demonstrated that people's expectations can be extremely persuasive. Hypochondriacs interpret minor pains as indications of major illness, whereas normal people interpret them as no big deal.[33] People who hold prejudiced views of racial or religious groups tend to interpret the behaviors of all members of those groups in line with their expectations.[34] Depressed people interpret everyday events and information in a glass-half-empty fashion and ignore any evidence to the contrary that suggests that things may be looking up.[35]

Part of the reason this bias happens has to do with the way we search our memory.[36] When you use Google, your computer systematically searches all relevant data. Our memories, however, find things that match, and so we can't help but be better at noticing occurrences that confirm the things we already believe. People led to believe that either tooth brushing or caffeine consumption was bad for their health remembered themselves as brushing their teeth or drinking coffee less often than those who were told that tooth brushing or caffeine consumption was good for them.[37]

The other side of the confirmation bias is what's known as motivated reasoning, or the tendency to ignore or reinterpret evidence contrary to our beliefs.[38] When both men and women were asked to read a study claiming that caffeine was risky for women, women who were heavy caffeine drinkers tended to doubt the study. Women who were light caffeine drinkers and men showed no motivated-reasoning effect. Only those participants whose behavior was termed risky by the study doubted its truth.

This same effect happens outside the laboratory, too. For instance, when the surgeon general's 1964 report on smoking was released, claiming that smoking caused lung cancer, smokers were less persuaded by the report than nonsmokers. Smokers used all sorts of anecdotal evidence to counter the statistics, like, "I know a lot of smokers who haven't been sick a day in their life." Or simply reasoned away the dangers: "Drinking is worse than smoking," or, "Smoking is better than being fat."[39]

I tell you this because it means that if your child is already (or planning on) going to an academic preschool, is spending a lot of time playing video games, is enrolled in organized sports, or is watching a lot of early learning videos, you're likely to find holes in my arguments, argue that you could be doing much worse, or think that I'm a quack. However, now that you know your brain's tendencies, you can try to be rational. This sounds ridiculous, I know; of course you always attempt to be rational. But this is an "illusion of objectivity." The research reviewed here suggests that the evaluation of scientific evidence is biased in accordance with whether people want to believe its conclusions. But people are not at liberty to believe anything they'd like; they are constrained by their prior beliefs.

However, there is evidence that telling people to consider their answers before responding, to be analytic and rational, and to resist answering with their gut reactions reduces motivated reasoning.[40] With practice, you could prime yourself to do things I've mentioned, like considering long-term risks (rather than focusing merely on the short-term ones) and examining whether you're doing something because certain memories are readily available. If you know the weakness of your mental system, I see no reason why you can't smooth out the rough spots evolution has left.

BUT I'M SMART

Don't think that because you're intelligent, you're off the hook. It turns out that high intelligence simply makes you more skilled at defending the beliefs arrived at for nonsmart reasons. Psychologist David Perkins found a positive relationship between intelligence and the ability to justify beliefs, and a negative relationship between intelligence and the ability to consider other beliefs as viable.[41] So smart people are better at rationalizing their beliefs with reasoned arguments, but as a consequence, they are less open to considering other positions. Although intelligence does not affect what you believe, it does influence how those beliefs are justified, rationalized, and defended.

SPECIAL BRAIN EDUCATION

Do you know how your liver works? How about your spleen or your thymus? Knowledge of our bodies doesn't come naturally. We don't enter the world knowing about the brain's functions. Even scientists didn't figure out until the seventeenth century what the brain did. Aristotle, for one, thought that the brain cooled the blood.[42] This made sense at the time. He inferred backward from the observation that large-brained humans were less "hot blooded" than other, smaller-brained animals.

But now that you know some of the brain's irrational tendencies—and why it's been built that way—you have more power to resist the pressures to rush childhood, the seductions of consumerism, and the tendency to say "yes" because it's easier than saying "no" and it'll make your children like you better. You now have the knowledge to restore some of the freedoms and fun our generation took for granted when we were children. As we wipe clean the family calendar, turn off the technology, and let the children out to play, we need to face up to some of our fears. It'll begin to chip away at the free-floating anxiety that can make us do odd things to young brains.

Chapter 12

Thinking outside
the Sandbox

Volunteers wanted: Must be patient and willing to sit through birthday parties, T-ball games, band concerts, Cub Scout pack nights, and field trips to the dairy farm. Must know how to cook mac 'n' cheese, cupcakes, and hot dogs. Must know how to sew a cherry tomato costume for the school play about the food pyramid. Must hold hands, give hugs, and kiss boo-boos. Must have the dexterity to crawl into a minivan backseat to comfort an ornery toddler without stepping on the driver's crotch or waking up a sleeping baby. Must be willing to listen to the play-by-play of the daily lunchroom happenings and Tiffany who thinks she's *so* great. The cost will be more than two hundred thousand dollars, before student loans. No sick days or vacation time. On call twenty-four hours a day, seven days a week. The successful candidate will turn into a lifetime worrywart, but will lead a very fulfilled life.

We usually go to school to major in an academic field closely related to whatever job we'll eventually have. If you want to be a business executive, you major in business; if you want to be a journalist, you major in journalism; and if you want to be a nurse, you go to nursing school. So why don't parents have to go to parenting school before they get the job? We have childbirth classes to prepare us for childbirth, but after that, we're on our own. There are no instruction manuals or study guides. Not even a 1-800 help line.

Without a formal education in parenting, it's terribly difficult to know if you're doing the right things as a parent. If you're a nurse and you mess up enough times, someone is going to point it out to you. If you give out the wrong medication, ignore an intravenous line, or mistake a meat thermometer for an ear thermometer, you'll know pretty quickly. But as a parent, there's no one there to catch your mistakes. You're on your own.

You can try to keep up with the research literature, but the scientific journals are incredibly boring. And, of course, the rules for parenting keep changing midgame. Now babies should sleep on their backs, not fronts; Mozart doesn't turn toddlers into geniuses; too many classroom drills can hurt school performance; and children's cold medicine isn't recommended for children with colds. And the layers of research findings are difficult to untangle. Should I or shouldn't I let my children wander around in the stream behind our house if its banks are covered in a bubbly, yellow, toxic-looking foam? Will making mud pies in the backyard protect my children from the pesticides in the grass, the smog in the air, and the mercury in the dolphin-safe tuna sandwich they had for lunch? There's simply no way to do everything perfectly in our imperfect world. This shouldn't stop you from trying; just don't beat yourself up if your kids occasionally spend an afternoon indoors with a *SpongeBob* marathon. They'll be all right.

SCIENCE-Y PARENTING

The big point of this book is not to say that the evolutionary developmental perspective is a cure-all for the side effects of modern childhood. Parents shouldn't overapply this framework and revert to a nomadic lifestyle. I hope this book will raise awareness of evolutionary developmental ideas and persuade parents and teachers to consider the long-range causes of today's children's behavior as well as work through the consequences of their novel, modern lifestyle. For a species that evolved to grow up in small primate tribes on the African savanna, today's childhood is strikingly different, and our brains simply haven't had time to adapt. Instead of raising children in wide-open outdoor spaces, we stuff them into classrooms, ballparks, family rooms, and minivans. Their brains never expected this. It's important, then, that we consider the implications of these shifts in the decisions we make for our children. In recent years, a burgeoning research literature has demonstrated that much of the modern world is producing unexpected side effects. And this is what this book has been all about.

The problem is, much of this scientific knowledge about development has been collecting dust in journals. It's not getting to parents and teachers. It's not affecting what they do. Instead, we have the media, marketers, and mom blogs peddling child-rearing advice that is largely made up and not evidence based. Much of the knowledge that parents and teachers have about the brain and its development is wrong, or at least far off in some significant way.

Given that science has produced a rich developmental research literature, a particular goal of mine is to advocate for science-based parenting and science-based teaching. I want to build a more effective connection between science and child-rearing practice and between science and education. It's my goal to bridge the gap between developmental science and the toys we buy for our children, the ways we teach them in our schools, and the kinds of activities with which we fill their time. To truly prepare children for life in the modern world, we can no longer afford to be data blind and ignore a healthy literature that I think can greatly improve children's lives. The research presented in this book gives some idea of how to do this. Some ideas are small, some are provocative, some might be surprising, and some require tearing everything down and starting over.

MORE LEARNING, LESS SCHOOLING

The contrast between what scientists know about children's learning and what goes on in most classrooms is staggering. Scientists know that the human brain has been designed by millions of years of evolution to learn through close observation of real phenomena, active experimental investigation, self-correcting problem solving, and a process of guided apprenticeship in meaningful contexts.

But almost none of this happens in the average classroom. In many of our schools (not all, of course), there's a focus on drills, memorization, and teaching to the test. Even in college, the typical professor lectures while the students write down what the professor says. How can we expect children to go out into the real world and solve its problems if we sequester them in a classroom for the majority of their education? Imagine if your doctor never saw a patient until after he had listened to eight years of lectures about patients.

One solution for which some of the loudest arguments are offered, driven by the No Child Left Behind philosophy and our children's slower than expected progress toward 100 percent proficiency, is to give kids more schooling: more drills, more memorization, more standardized tests, more assessments, more grades, and more homework. More schooling translates into less play, less exploration, less experimentation, and less fun. That means less self-discovery, less critical thinking, less socialization and self-regulation, and less internal motivation for learning. The state of today's schools is completely contrary to authoritative research showing that children learn best by playing freely and through exploration, experimentation, and guided discovery in meaningful real-world contexts. Some schools give lip service to these ideas but then go ahead and create curricula that preclude play and exploration.

Think about the most valuable lessons you learned in school. They probably didn't come from preparing for standardized tests. Most likely, they happened during those times when you were given the freedom to fully and deeply play and when your mentors helped you discover for yourself and follow your own interests. That's how children acquire the social-cognitive skills, the emotional and moral values, the new ideas and ways of thinking, and the deep information that stay with them throughout their lives. Perhaps most important, that's also how they discover what they truly enjoy doing—which is the first step in building a fulfilling adult life.

So every time we require another hour of homework, add another standardized assessment, ask children to memorize another word study list, or coax them into another adult-directed after-school extracurricular activity, we're taking away another opportunity to play, explore, experiment, and reflect and to experience the joys, frustrations, and lessons of the world. The more we do this, the deeper we drive a wedge into our school system, pushing away more and more children who weren't designed for formal education in the first place.

The research we have reviewed offers several prescriptions for schools—that is, for designing learning environments that gel with how the human brain has been designed to develop. This literature tells us that children should have more recess and less homework. Grades and other rewards for learning should be scrapped. Lessons should be individualized. New information should be self-discovered (not passively picked up). And education should be carried out in mainly meaningful contexts. Teachers and parents need to stop telling children they're smart and worrying about bursting their self-esteem. Instead, we should praise children's specific accomplishments, foster their self-respect, and support the maintenance of their natural internal motivation. If we're going to keep children in the classroom, we need to remind ourselves that it is a demanding, unexpected, and evolutionarily novel context for children's brains. We can help ease the brain's transition to this new educational context by letting it outside to play and replenish its ability to pay attention.

These changes would require tearing down much of our school system and starting over. I realize that's a lot to ask. But the skill sets essential for No Child Left Behind proficiency—memorizing times tables, vocabulary words, the water cycle, and the roles of the three branches of government—are not those that develop creative and wise minds. In our twenty-first-century world, where information is doubling every two and a half years and Google makes any fact readily available, we don't need children who excel at computing facts and knowing bits of information. We need wise and creative thinkers—children who can interpret existing information, make new discoveries, and solve pressing problems.

There are extant programs that already use some of these practices. Montessori education, for example, follows the lead of children's interests and doesn't use tests or grades.[1] But this is the exception rather than the norm, especially in public schools. There are also curricula that focus on developing thinking rather than amassing facts. The Philosophy for Children program, as its name suggests, centers on engaging children in philosophical issues and thinking about thinking.[2]

The Philosophy for Children movement got its start in the early 1970s with Matthew Lipman's *Harry Stottlemeier's Discovery*. In the book, Harry writes an essay called, "The Most Interesting Thing in the World." He writes about thinking: "To me, the most interesting thing in the whole world is thinking. I know that lots of other things are also very important and wonderful, like electricity, and magnetism, and gravitation. But although we understand them, they can't understand us. So thinking must be something very special."[3] I love this kid. And this is exactly the type of program that trains children to deeply understand their world. It might even help them to better understand their own brains and perhaps outwit the evolutionary baggage I talked about in chapter 11. The Philosophy for Children program likely wouldn't boost scores on state-standardized exams, but it fosters more independent, creative, and critical thinking. Which schooling option makes more sense to you?

MASTERS OF THEIR OWN PLAY

Play is something else we need to fix. Play is the main business of childhood—it's what children do—but it's never seemed more like work than it does in today's world. With toy stores overstuffed with battery-powered, scripted, and "educational" toys, play has become serious, stressful, and pretty expensive. It's clearly broken.

What's the fix? Parents and teachers need to put the fun and freedom back into play. Someone siphoned it out when we weren't looking, and it's time we filled it back up. If the story line is already there, be it in a plastic talking dollhouse or a space war video game, there's no room left for children's imaginations. We need toys that are loose and flexible and require a heavy dose of social-cognitive, communication, and fantasy skills to pull off. We also need to put parts of play back in children's hands. When children rely on themselves to play—improvising props, making up story lines, negotiating ground rules with friends—they are developing the social-cognitive skills that most boxed toys can't foster.

Remember the chapter 6 mantra: buy toys that are 90 percent children and 10 percent toy. Toys that aren't enough child foster not deep and active play, but shallow and passive observation. Just because a toy claims to be "interactive" or "educational" doesn't mean it is. True interaction and true education go on only in the real world and in meaningful contexts with fleshy people.

Toy companies' dirty little secret is that the very best toys are those that require little or no monetary investment, battery power, or directions to assemble. Newborns have their fingers and toes stuck right on their hands and feet. Newborns can move, feel, and touch with them for free. They don't cost a cent. Why even buy your baby a pacifier when she has two thumbs already attached to her? Her thumb won't get lost, fall onto the floor, or get swallowed by the dog. Take the advice of chapter 5 and ramp up your floor, face, and lap time with children. Retire the stationary entertainers, the bungee seats, and the play yards.

For older babies, crumpled paper, pillow mountains, and empty boxes make for fantastic toys. Pots and pans and plastic containers with spatulas are excellent instruments. For toddlers, nothing beats turning appliance boxes into row homes, slipping on some of Mom and Dad's old clothes, and drawing chalk roads on the sidewalk.

Remember that play is an activity. It's not about the toys. We need to foster this activity and focus less on the toys. This is going to take resisting the hype of toy marketers (though I realize that asking your child to bring crumpled paper as a birthday gift to his best friend's party would be totally inappropriate). The key is to buy simple toys that allow for active exploration and experimentation and resist those that require passive memorization or mesmerization. What we really need is for toy companies to invent more toys that have much looseness and can serve as open-ended props for children's creativity and imaginations. We need more toys that keep the fun rolling in everyday interactions with friends and family members and that expand the boundaries of children's ordinary experiences in their everyday lives.

Bringing back play also means making more time for it. It means opening up children's schedules and reducing children's leagues, lessons, and other activities that are regulated by adults. The brain expects a heavy dose of childhood opportunities so it can practice regulating itself and building executive functions. It expects a generous side order of free play, make-believe, and freeze tag to learn how to control its impulses. That's how the brain learns to regulate itself in school and with friends and how to stop itself when it gets angry and wants to punch or yell.

Bringing back play also means unplugging your children. Real play doesn't happen on a two-dimensional screen with artificially intelligent friends, virtual pets, or animated cities and towns. If your children are doing most of their playing with others online or on the television set, you might want to power them down for a bit and let them out in the backyard to play.

If your play-deprived children have any trouble getting started, you can give them a jump start by bringing play back into your life. Humans are born to learn from models. So there's a strong incentive for making our lives more playful, too. It'll be fun—give it a try. How do you do it? Think of the fishmongers at Seattle's Pike Place Market and the playful people at Google. It'll give you the vision, the moxie, the chutzpah to give play back to children and to take back the fun of parenting.

TAKE IT OUTSIDE

For 99 percent of our history, children grew up mainly outdoors. Compelling evidence suggests that we need to reverse the recent migration indoors and give children ample opportunities to spend time in nature. The out-of-doors can replenish children's easily depleted attention and help soften the blow of their overstuffed and overstimulating world. Importantly, time on the ball field doesn't have the reparative effects of time in more natural areas. It's because adults usually run the show when children are on the field, but also because manicured, flat, open spaces seem to be the least beneficial outdoor settings for the brain. Outdoor spaces with diverse plants and trees confer the best psychological benefits.

This is why natural spaces are great places for children's brains. They're diverse, unpredictable, and even sometimes risky.[4] That makes them great places for children to observe, explore, experiment, and learn how to deal with and manage risks.

Unfortunately, a lot of today's children's outdoor time is spent on artificial playgrounds. Don't get me wrong; playgrounds are well meaning, for sure. But most are padded, plastic, lawsuit-proof, and completely predictable. Good play is rarely predictable, and no one piece of playground equipment designed by an adult is going to match the product of a child's imagination or the randomness of nature. Evolutionarily speaking, it is humankind's adaptability—our ability to adjust to the changing demands of the environment—that propelled us to dominate the planet. So, it seems unnatural to invite human children to play in unchanging and completely predictable settings. Danish "natural playground designer" Helle Nebelong echoes this sentiment and in fact argues that while the usual modern predictable play structure might seem safer, in the long run it might be more dangerous: "I am convinced that standardized playgrounds are dangerous, just in another way: When the distance between all the rungs in a climbing net or a ladder is exactly the same, the child has no need to concentrate on where he puts his feet. Standardization is dangerous because play becomes simplified and the child does not have to worry about his movements."[5]

Another problem with playgrounds is that not even the best and most expensive manufactured play structure can substitute for the deep organic experience afforded by nature. Artificial play pieces are too sterile to compete with the rich sights, sounds, smells, and tactile experiences in nature: the motion of the waves in the surf, the endless experiments in the stream, the cold *whap* of a snowball strike, the crush of dried leaves in your hands, the squish of wrestling with friends in the mud, and the imaginary world in a pile of pebbles. You don't get any of this at even the swankiest neighborhood parks.

It seems to me that outdoor play is one childhood experience that we should return to its primal roots. To bug hunting, tree climbing, river wading, den building, sand digging, and mud pie making. The twentieth-century adventure playgrounds in Europe most closely resemble this sort of experience. In these playgrounds, children use a mixed collection of natural elements, loose parts, everyday tools, and found building materials to design and build their own play equipment.[6] Instead of the usual mammoth, multitiered plastic structures we're used to seeing, these playgrounds are anchored by nature. There are hollowed logs, climbing trees, sand pits, rock piles, mud bogs, makeshift bridges, ponds and streams, overgrown fields, and mini-forests.

So which brand of outdoor play do you think has more play value? Which do you think leads to more creative, challenging, and cooperative play? Which do you think improves social-cognitive skills and teaches children to recognize and cope with potentially hazardous conditions? And which do you think would be less expensive to design and build? The mega-level plastic giant at your neighborhood park, or a natural playground made of loose parts, natural materials, and found junk? We need to think very differently about children's playgrounds. Again, to do the right thing, we might need to tear down everything and start over.

Some scientists who do brain and behavioral research are starting to dabble in landscape design. They're looking for ways to make modern life less damaging to the brain. The good news is that even minor changes, such as planting more trees in the inner city or creating parks with a greater variety of plants and trees, can significantly reduce the negative side effects of our cosmopolitan lifestyle. There's also a small movement to design more natural outdoor spaces for children. In some schools, this means butterfly gardens and small vegetable gardens. And a few places, like the Elizabeth Ann Clune Montessori School in Ithaca, New York, and the Blanchie Carter Discovery Park in Southern Pines, North Carolina, have been brave enough to build playgrounds that incorporate natural elements.[7] Landscape architect Robin Moore, who directs North Carolina State University's Natural Learning Initiative and had a hand in the design of both of these outdoor spaces, sees landscape architecture as a public health intervention. Children's (and our) minds need nature, and even a little bit can be a big help.[8]

Want to start reconnecting your children with nature now and don't know where to start? This can be tough if you're an inner-city family. My advice? Start small. Encourage your children to get to know some small patch of nature. Try to resist media fearmongering and remember that children learn to be safe through experience. Encourage other children to join. Criminologists have long known that in streets, parks, and playgrounds, there is safety in numbers. And get outside with your children. Spread the outdoor vibe. Your children will learn from your example, and the attention you'll replenish from your time in nature will save you a bunch on coffee.

TONIC OF CHILDHOOD

So now you know what you need to do to fix childhood and to lessen the side effects of the modern world. But I hope you continue to follow this evolving story. You know that scientists are doing extraordinary things in their labs: developing new technologies to screen for cancer, designing new medications to treat Alzheimer's, inventing new surgical techniques to repair wounded brains, and engineering artificial limbs. And there are also scientists who are continuing to study the seemingly simple problem of how to best raise children. They're doing this because it's not so simple and because there's never going to be one right way to do it. So keep up with their story. The more you and I learn about how the brain develops, the better we can care for and educate our children, and the better we can raise old brains in a new world.

Notes

PREFACE

1. David F. Bjorklund and Anthony D. Pellegrini, *The Origins of Human Nature: Evolutionary Developmental Psychology* (Washington, DC: American Psychological Association, 2002), p. 24.

2. David J. Linden, *The Accidental Mind: How Brain Evolution Has Given Us Love, Memory, Dreams, and God* (Cambridge, MA: Belknap, 2007), pp. 6–21.

3. Foundation for Child Development, "Child and Youth Well-Being Index," http://www.soc.duke.edu/~cwi/section_d.html (accessed December 22, 2010).

4. Kathleen Ries Merikangas et al., "Lifetime Prevalence of Mental Disorders in U.S. Adolescents," *Journal of the American Academy of Child and Adolescent Psychiatry* 49, no. 10 (October 2010): 980–89.

5. Centers for Disease Control and Prevention, "Increasing Prevalence of Parent-Reported Attention Deficit/Hyperactivity Disorder among Children: United States, 2003 and 2007," *Morbidity and Mortality Weekly Report* 59, no. 44 (November 12, 2010): 1439–43.

6. Merikangas, "Lifetime Prevalence of Mental Disorders in U.S. Adolescents," 980–89.

7. Centers for Disease Control and Prevention, "Prevalence of Autism Spectrum Disorders: Autism and Developmental Disabilities Monitoring Network, United States, 2006," *Morbidity and Mortality Weekly Report Surveillance Summaries* 58, no. 9 (December 18, 2009): 1–20.

8. Julie Magno Zito et al., "Psychotropic Practice Patterns for Youth: A 10-Year Perspective," *Archives of Pediatric and Adolescent Medicine* 157, no. 1 (January 2003): 14–16.

9. National Center for Education Statistics, "The Nation's Report Card: Grade 12 Reading and Mathematics 2009 National and Pilot State Results," National Assessment of Educational Progress, http://nces.ed.gov/nationsreportcard/pubs/main2009/2011455.asp#section1 (accessed January 10, 2011).

10. Michael Shayer, Denise Ginsburg, and Robert Coe, "Thirty Years On: A Large Anti-Flynn Effect? The Piagetian Test Volume and Heaviness Norms 1975–2003," *British Journal of Educational Psychology* 77, no. 1 (March 2007): 25–41.

CHAPTER 1: OLD BRAIN, NEW WORLD

1. David J. Linden, *The Accidental Mind: How Brain Evolution Has Given Us Love, Memory, Dreams, and God* (Cambridge, MA: Belknap, 2007), pp. 5–28; Georg F. Striedter, *Principles of Brain Evolution* (Sunderland, MA: Sinauer Associates, 2004), pp. 297–344.

2. Chimpanzee Sequencing and Analysis Consortium, "Initial Sequence of the Chimpanzee Genome and Comparison with Human Genome," *Nature* 437 (September 1, 2005): 69–88. To be fair, humans also share about 40 percent of their genes with bananas, so even small variations in genes can be associated with big differences in what a thing turns out to be. See David F. Bjorklund, *Why Youth Is Not Wasted on the Young: Immaturity in Human Development* (Malden, MA: Blackwell, 2007), p. 24.

3. Jared M. Diamond, *The Third Chimpanzee: The Evolution and Future of the Human Animal* (New York: Perennial, 1992), p. 2.

4. The most recent evidence indicates that humans and chimpanzees developed into distinct species less than 6.3 million years ago and probably more recently than 5.4 million years ago. After that initial split, however, members of the two new species are thought to have interbred. Fertile hybrid offspring then likely mated back into one or both original populations, bringing in genes from the other species and leaving traces in their respective genetic codes. See Nick Patterson et al., "Genetic Evidence for Complex Speciation of Humans and Chimpanzees," *Nature* 441 (June 26, 2006): 1103–1108.

5. Though *Homo erectus*'s tool kit was more impressive than that of its australopithecine ancestors, it would be irresponsible of me if I left you with the impression that early humans made sophisticated tools. Their tool kit consisted largely of rocks that had been made sharper by slamming them into other rocks. And tool making isn't uniquely human. Chimpanzees, for example, crack nuts with stone tools and de-leaf sticks to force termites out of their mounds.

6. Richard Potts and Chris Sloan, *What Does It Mean to Be Human?* (Washington, DC: National Geographic, 2010); Chris Stringer and Peter Andrews, *The Complete World of Human Evolution* (New York: Thames and Hudson, 2005). See Potts and Sloan for more extensive descriptions of human evolution and early behaviors.

7. Potts and Sloan, *What Does It Mean?*

8. Given the historical difficulties humans have had dealing with people of different races, ethnicities, and social classes, imagine the troubles we'd have if there still were more than one species of us!

9. Our relatives who stayed in the tropical jungles developed into chimpanzees and later, bonobos—both of which still live in the tropics and have not had to adapt to too many changes, and thus, evolutionarily speaking, have not changed much since branching from our common ancestor.

10. Nicholas Humphrey, *The Inner Eye: Social Intelligence in Evolution* (New York: Oxford

University Press, 2002), pp. 65–75; Michael Tomasello and Malinda Carpenter, "Shared Intentionality," *Developmental Science* 10, no. 1 (2007): 121–25.

11. Neil Shubin, *Your Inner Fish: A Journey into the 3.5-Billion-Year History of the Human Body* (New York: Vintage Books, 2009), pp. 174–184.

12. Steven R. Quartz and Terrence J. Sejnowski, *Liars, Lovers, and Heroes: What the New Brain Science Reveals about How We Become Who We Are* (New York: William Morrow, 2002), p. 16.

13. For a more detailed description of brain design and function, see Linden, *The Accidental Mind: How Brain Evolution Has Given Us Love, Memory, Dreams, and Love*, pp. 5–27.

14. Beatrice de Gelder et al., "Navigation Skills after Bilateral Loss of Striate Cortex," *Current Biology* 18, no. 24 (December 23, 2008): R1128–29.

15. When awake, the collective efforts of the brain generate about twenty-five watts of electricity, enough to illuminate a night light.

16. Gilbert Gottlieb, "Probablistic Epigenesis," *Developmental Science* 10, no. 1 (January 2007): 1–11; John P. Spencer et al., "Short Arms and Talking Eggs: Why We Should No Longer Abide the Nativist-Empiricist Debate," *Child Development Perspectives* 3, no. 2 (2009): 79–87.

17. Konrad Lorenz, "The Companion in the Bird's World," *Auk* 54, no. 3 (1937): 245–273.

18. Gilbert Gottlieb, *Synthesizing Nature-Nurture: Prenatal Roots of Instinctive Behavior.* (Mahwah, NJ: Erlbaum, 2007).

19. Olivier Pascalis, Michelle de Haan, and Charles A. Nelson, "Is Face Processing Species-Specific during the First Year of Life?" *Science* 296, no. 5571 (May 17, 2002): 1321–23.

20. Robert Lickliter, "The Role of Sensory Stimulation in Perinatal Development: Insights from Comparative Research for Care of the High-Risk Infant," *Developmental and Behavioral Pediatrics* 21, no. 6 (December 2000): 437–47.

21. Martha Constantine-Paton, "Pioneers of Cortical Plasticity: Six Classic Papers by Wiesel and Hubel," *Journal of Neurophysiology* 99, no. 6 (June 2008): 2741–44.

22. Daphne Maurer and Tarri L. Lewis, "Visual Acuity: The Role of Visual Input in Inducing Postnatal Change," *Clinical Neuroscience Research* 1, no. 4 (July 2001): 239–47.

23. Nora Schultz, "Generation Specs: Stopping the Short-Sight Epidemic," *New Scientist* 2733 (November 6, 2009), http://www.newscientist.com/article/mg20427331.100 -generation-specs-stopping-the-shortsight-epidemic.html (accessed December 15, 2010).

24. Charles H. Hillman, Kirk I. Erickson, and Arthur F. Kramer, "Be Smart, Exercise Your Heart: Exercise Effects on Brain and Cognition," *Science and Society* 9 (January 2008): 58–65.

25. Robert Lickliter, "Premature Visual Stimulation Accelerates Intersensory Functioning in Bobwhite Quail Neonates," *Developmental Psychobiology* 23, no. 1 (January 1990): 15–27.

26. R. Witt Hall and K. J. S. Anand, "Short- and Long-Term Impact of Neonatal Pain and Stress: More Than an Ouchie," *Neoreview* 6, no. 2 (2005): 69–75.

27. Heidelise Als et al., "Early Experience Alters Brain Function and Structure," *Pediatrics* 113, no. 4 (April 2004): 846–57.

28. Not unlike the advanced visual abilities of quails that are prematurely shown patterned light, premature babies who spend time in neonatal units often exhibit areas of accelerated development, such as mathematics, along with motor and cognitive delays. As the result of findings by Als and others demonstrating developmental impairments in premature infants who found themselves in superstimulating hospital rooms, increasing numbers of neonatal intensive care units are dimmed and hushed to resemble the dark and quiet environment premature infants expect: the womb.

CHAPTER 2: SUPERSIZED CHILDHOOD

1. Sharon E. Fox, Pat Levitt, and Charles A. Nelson, "How the Timing and Quality of Early Experiences Influence the Development of Brain Architecture," *Child Development* 81, no. 1 (January/February 2010): 28–40; Joan Stiles, *The Fundamentals of Brain Development: Integrating Nature and Nurture* (Cambridge, MA: Harvard University Press, 2008). The information on brain development discussed in this chapter comes largely from these two sources.

2. David J. Linden, *The Accidental Mind: How Brain Evolution Has Given Us Love, Memory, Dreams, and God* (Cambridge, MA: Belknap, 2007), pp. 50–52.

3. Neurons in the hippocampus, the olfactory bulb, and possibly regions of the neurocortex continue to be generated in adulthood.

4. Mikhail Lazarev, "The Science of BabyPlus," BabyPlus, http://www.baby plus.com/clinicaltrial.php (accessed December 1, 2010). The following quote represents the "theory" behind BabyPlus, taken from the product's website: "The theory proposes that because the imprinting window concludes shortly after normative gestation is complete, and the at-rest maternal cardiation rhythm is the only detectable pattern to so register, progressions from this indigenous baseline will sonically lead the fetal brainwave rate to higher levels, thereby enhancing memoric and synaptic functions where neuronal apoptosis will be mitigated, resulting in a more mature cognitive structure at birth." The theory refers to the closing of an "imprinting window" and a notion that higher levels of "fetal brainwaves" reduce "neuronal apoptosis" (or cell death) which, in turn, produces a "more mature cognitive structure at birth." This so-called theory is groundless. There is no such thing as a neural "imprinting window," nor is there any compelling reason to want a more mature "cognitive structure" (whatever that is) at birth. Most important, brain cell death during the prenatal period does not need mitigating because it is a normal consquence of healthy development.

5. Pamela Weintraub, "Report on Baby+ Research," *OMNI* 11, no. 11 (August 1989), at BabyPlus, http://www.babyplus-education.co.uk/acatalog/babyplus_in_the_news.html (accessed December 1, 2010).

6. Missing from the BabyPlus literature is an interesting claim that I found on Daddytypes.com. A blog entry says that Susedik claims to have come up with his best new inventions after aliens dressed in "foil-type uniforms" took him aboard their spaceship. Is this for real? Decide for yourself: Greg Allen, "BabyPlus Prenatal Audio System Makes Normal Babies Look Like Geniuses Compared to Their Stupid Parents," Daddytypes .com, August 30, 2007, http://daddytypes.com/2007/08/30/babyplus_prenatal_audio _system_makes_normal_babies_look_like_geniuses_compared_to_their _stupid_parents .php (accessed December 1, 2010).

7. To demonstrate for yourself that fetuses can hear sounds outside the womb, next time you are pregnant, wait until the beginning of your final trimester and then make a smoothie in your blender. If your fetus is not snoozing, chances are you'll feel someone startle in your belly. Research by Anthony DeCasper at the University of North Carolina at Greensboro and his colleagues has demonstrated that newborns can recognize recurrent maternal sounds heard while in utero. In a now classic study, mothers were asked to recite a poem aloud twice a day during their last six weeks of pregnancy. Once the babies were born, they preferred to listen to the Dr. Seuss book that contained the poem over other children's literature. Anthony J. DeCasper and Melanie J. Spence, "Prenatal Maternal Speech Influences Newborns' Perception of Speech Sounds," *Infant Behavior and Development* 9, no. 2 (April–June 1986): 133–50.

8. Pamela Paul, "Extract One: Parenting, Inc.," *Telegraph*, May 28, 2008, http:// www.telegraph.co.uk/education/3356199/Extract-one-Parenting-Inc.-by-Pamela -Paul.html (accessed December 1, 2010).

9. Edward M. Hubbard, "Neurophysiology of Synesthesia," *Current Psychiatry Reports* 9, no. 3 (2007): 193–99.

10. Luyuan Pan et al., "The Drosophila Fragile X Gene Negatively Regulates Neuronal Elaboration and Synaptic Differentiation," *Current Biology* 14, no. 20 (October 26, 2004): 1863–70.

11. Cynthia M. Schumann et al., "Longitudinal Magnetic Resonance Imaging Study of Cortical Development through Early Childhood in Autism," *Journal of Neuroscience* 30, no. 12 (March 24, 2010): 4419–27.

12. William T. Greenough, James E. Black, and Christopher S. Wallace, "Experience and Brain Development," *Child Development* 58 (1987): 539–59.

13. Michael J. Renner and Mark R. Rosenzweig, *Enriched and Impoverished Environments: Effects on Brain and Behavior* (New York: Springer-Verlag, 1987).

14. Charles Darwin, *The Descent of Man, and Selection in Relation to Sex* (New York: D. Appleton, 1871), pp. 141–42.

15. Yes, rats again. The rat is the animal of choice for many scientists because rats

are easy to breed, a piece of cake to keep in captivity, and good at cleaning up after themselves. They're also easily tamed and smart.

16. Norman E. Spear and Laura Hyatt, "How the Timing of Experience Can Affect the Ontogeny of Learning," in *Developmental Time and Timing*, ed. Gerald Turkewitz and Darlynne Devenny (Hillsdale, NJ: Erlbaum, 1993), pp. 167–209.

17. Harry F. Harlow, "The Development of Learning in the Rhesus Monkey," *American Scientist* 47 (December 1959): 459–79.

18. In 2009, Baby Einstein put the lid on their explicit claims of brain growing because, in 2006, the Campaign for a Commercial-Free Childhood (CCFC) filed a Federal Trade Commission complaint against Baby Einstein, arguing that the toy marketers were misleading parents by stating that their products are beneficial for babies' brain growth. As a result of the CCFC's complaint, Baby Einstein has completely redesigned its website and products and is no longer making such claims about its DVDs and videos. The Walt Disney Company, which acquired Baby Einstein in 2001, has offered refunds to parents who bought these videos. For more information, see Tamar Lewin, "No Einstein in Your Crib? Get a Refund," *New York Times*, October 23, 2009, http://www.nytimes.com/2009/10/24/education/24baby.html (accessed December 12, 2010).

19. Frederick J. Zimmerman, Dimitri A. Christakis, and Andrew N. Meltzoff, "Associations between Media Viewing and Language Development in Children under Age Two Years," *Journal of Pediatrics* 151 (October 2007): 364–68.

20. American Academy of Pediatrics, Committee on Public Education, "Children, Adolescents, and Television," *Pediatrics* 107, no. 2 (February 2001): 423–26.

21. "Awards," Baby Einstein, http://www.babyeinstein.com/en/our_story/awards/ (accessed December 12, 2010).

22. NICHD Early Child Care Research Network, "The NICHD Study of Early Child Care: Contexts of Development and Developmental Outcomes over the First Seven Years of Life," in *Early Child Development in the 21st Century*, ed. Jeanne Brooks-Gun, Allison Sidle Fuligni, and Lisa J. Berlin (New York: Teachers College Press, 2003), pp. 181–201.

23. Philip Shaw et al., "Intellectual Ability and Cortical Development in Children and Adolescents," *Nature* 440 (March 30, 2006): 676–79.

24. Linden, *The Accidental Mind*, p. 78.

25. "Start Your Baby Reading Today," Your Baby Can Read, http://www.yourbabycanread.com/?uid=PT1_GS1_YBCR_TM_TAQR&gclid=CKz1oPj2l6gCFQbe4AodjUhTCw (accessed December 12, 2010).

26. Maryanne Wolf, *Proust and the Squid: The Story and Science of the Reading Brain* (New York: HarperCollins, 2007), p. 96.

27. "Nobel Prize Laureates (Per Capita) (Most Recent) by Country," NationMaster.com, http://www.nationmaster.com/graph/peo_nob_pri_lau_percap-nobel-prize-laureates-per-capita (accessed December 1, 2010); "Why Junior Kumon?" Kumon, http://www.kumon.com/WhyJrKumon.aspx (accessed December 1, 2010).

28. Anthony J. Perri and Sylvia Hsu, "A Review of Thalidomide's History and Current Dermatological Applications," *Dermatology Online Journal* 9, no. 3 (2003): 5, http://dermatology.cdlib.org/93/reviews/thalidomide/hsu.html (accessed December 1, 2010).

29. Terri L. Lewis and Daphne Maurer, "Multiple Sensitive Periods in Human Visual Development: Evidence from Visually Deprived Children," *Developmental Psychobiology* 46, no. 3 (April 2005): 163–83.

30. Susan Curtiss, *Genie: A Psycholinguistic Study of a Modern-Day "Wild Child"* (New York: Academic, 1977).

31. Celia Beckett et al., "Do the Effects of Early Severe Deprivation on Cognition Persist into Early Adolescence? Findings from the English and Romanian Adoptees Study," *Child Development* 77, no. 3 (May/June 2006): 696–711.

32. The discussion of the adaptive nature of humankind's extended immaturity comes from the work of David Bjorklund and his colleagues. See David F. Bjorklund and Anthony D. Pellegrini, "Child Development and Evolutionary Psychology," *Child Development* 71, no. 6 (November/December 2000): 1687–708; Bjorklund and Pellegrini, *The Origins of Human Nature: Evolutionary Developmental Psychology* (Washington, DC: American Psychological Association, 2002).

33. Child mortality rates in hunter-gatherer societies are about 50 percent, compared to 67 percent to nearly 90 percent in other primates. See Jane B. Lancaster and Chet S. Lancaster, "Parental Investment: The Hominid Adaptation," in *How Humans Adapt: A Biocultural Odyssey*, ed. Donald J. Ortner (Washington, DC: Smithsonian Institution Scholarly, 1984), pp. 33–65.

34. Humans' delayed maturation was a major gamble. Paleoanthropologists suggest that humans were close to extinction one hundred thousand to two hundred thousand years ago, with as few as ten thousand adults living worldwide. The gamble paid big—there are now seven billion of us, and we're threatened by no predator (except for viruses and our own kind).

35. This defense of childhood is supported by analyses of humans' primate kin. Those nonhuman primates that are most neurologically well endowed also have the longest childhoods and the most complex lifestyles.

36. Patricia K. Kulh et al., "Early Speech Perception and Later Language Development: Implications for the Critical Period," *Language Learning and Development* 1, no. 3/4 (2005): 237–64.

37. David F. Bjorklund, *Why Youth Is Not Wasted on the Young: Immaturity in Human Development* (Malden, MA: Blackwell, 2007), pp. 2–14.

CHAPTER 3: THE TWENTY-YEAR SCIENCE PROJECT

1. Alison Gopnik, Andrew N. Meltzoff, and Patricia K. Kuhl, *The Scientist in the Crib: Minds, Brains, and How Children Learn* (New York: HarperCollins, 1999); Alison Gopnik, *The Philosophical Baby: What Children's Minds Tell Us about Truth, Love, and the Meaning of Life* (New York: Farrar, Straus, and Giroux, 2010). These wonderful, lucid books by Gopnik and her colleagues lay out the case for characterizing babies and young children as scientists who are driven by an insatiable need to know and who dabble heavily in fantastic worlds.

2. Robert W. White, "Motivation Reconsidered: The Concept of Competence," *Psychological Review* 66 (September 1959): 297–333.

3. Gopnik, Meltzoff, and Kuhl, *Scientist in the Crib*, p. 9.

4. Robert Dawley, "A CIE Introduction to the Galileo Texts," Ursinus College, 2003, http://www.scribd.com/doc/22939584/An-Introduction-to-Galileo, (accessed December 13, 2010).

5. The rotational speed of the Earth at the latitude of Athens (38° north) is [1000 mph] x [cos 38] = 788 mph. Paul Butterworth and David Palmer, "Ask an Astrophysicist," NASA Goddard Space Flight Center, http://imagine.gsfc.nasa.gov/docs/ask_astro/answers/970401c.html (accessed December 10, 2010).

6. Nearly one out of every five Americans still thinks that Galileo's ideas are fantasy. In a 1999 Gallup poll that asked, "As far as you know, does the Earth revolve around the sun, or does the sun revolve around the Earth?" 18 percent replied that the sun revolves around Earth. Steve Crabtree, "New Poll Gauges Americans' General Knowledge Levels: Four-Fifths Know Earth Revolves around the Sun," *Gallup News Service*, July 6, 1999, http://www.gallup.com/poll/3742/new-poll-gauges-americans-general-knowledge-levels.aspx (accessed December 10, 2010).

7. Esther Herrmann et al., "The Structure of Individual Differences in the Cognitive Abilities of Children and Chimpanzees," *Psychological Science* 21, no. 1 (January 2010): 102–10.

8. Andrew Whiten et al., "Cultures in Chimpanzees," *Nature* 399, no. 6737 (June 17, 1999): 682–85.

9. Esther Herrmann et al., "Humans Have Evolved Specialized Skills of Social Cognition: The Cultural Intelligence Hypothesis," *Science* 317, no. 5843 (September 7, 2007): 1360–66.

10. Michael Tomasello and Malinda Carpenter, "Shared Intentionality," *Developmental Science* 10, no. 1 (2007): 121–25; Michael Tomasello, *Why We Cooperate* (Cambridge, MA: MIT Press, 2009), pp. 68–76.

11. David F. Bjorklund and Jesse M. Bering, "The Evolved Child: Applying Evolutionary Developmental Psychology to Modern Schooling," *Learning and Individual Differ-*

ences 12, no. 4 (2002): 1–27; Michael Tomasello, Ann Cale Kruger, and Hilary Horn Ratner, "Cultural Learning," *Behavioral and Brain Sciences* 16 (1993): 495–552.

12. Cormac McCarthy, *The Road* (New York: Vintage Books, 2006), p. 3.

13. Amanda Ripley, "Should Kids Be Bribed to Do Well in School?" *Time*, April 8, 2010, http://www.time.com/time/printout/0,8816,1978589,00.html (accessed December 12, 2010).

14. Kelly D. Davis, Adam Winsler, and Michael Middleton, "Students' Perceptions of Rewards for Academic Performance by Parents and Teachers: Relations with Achievement and Motivation in College," *Journal of Genetic Psychology* 167, no. 2 (June 2006): 211–20.

15. I mention M&Ms because at SAS, a business analytics software company in North Carolina, free M&Ms are served in bowls to its employees every Wednesday. The company goes through an estimated twenty-two tons of M&Ms every year. I find it no coincidence that SAS was named *Fortune* magazine's number-one best place to work in 2010. David A. Kaplan, "SAS: A New No. 1 Best Employer," *Fortune*, January 22, 2010, http://money.cnn.com/2010/01/21/technology/sas_best_companies.fortune/ (accessed April 28, 2011). Hear that, Ursinus College (my place of employment)?

16. Helen M. Hendy, Keith E. Williams, and Thomas S. Camise, "'Kids Choice' School Lunch Program Increases Children's Fruit and Vegetable Acceptance," *Appetite* 45, no. 3 (December 2005): 250–63.

17. Alan E. Kazdin, "The Token Economy: A Decade Later," *Journal of Applied Behavior Analysis* 15, no. 3 (Fall 1982): 431–45; K. Daniel O'Leary and Ronald Drabman, "Token Reinforcement Programs in the Classroom: A Review," *Psychological Bulletin* 75, no. 6 (June 1971): 379–98.

18. White, "Motivation Reconsidered."

19. I am not being facetious. Really. Here's some video proof: B. F. Skinner Foundation, "Pigeon Ping Pong Clip," YouTube video, 0:39, posted April 1, 2009, http://www.youtube.com/watch?v=vGazyH6fQQ4 (accesssd April 28, 2011).

20. Mark R. Lepper, David Greene, and Richard E. Nisbett, "Undermining Children's Intrinsic Interest with Extrinsic Reward: A Test of the 'Overjustification' Hypothesis," *Journal of Personality and Social Psychology* 28, no. 1 (October 1973): 129–37.

21. Mark R. Lepper and David Greene, "Turning Play into Work: Effects of Adult Surveillance and Extrinsic Rewards on Children's Intrinsic Motivation," *Journal of Personality and Social Psychology* 31, no. 3 (March 1975): 479–86.

22. Edward L. Deci, Richard Koestner, and Richard M. Ryan, "A Meta-Analytic Review of Experiments Examining the Effects of Extrinsic Rewards on Intrinsic Motivation," *Psychological Bulletin* 125, no. 6 (November 1999): 627–68.

23. Kenneth O. McGraw and John C. McCullers, "Evidence of a Detrimental Effect of Extrinsic Incentives on Breaking a Mental Set," *Journal of Experimental Social Psychology* 15, no. 3 (May 1978): 285–94.

24. Jennifer Henderlong and Mark R. Lepper, "The Effects of Praise on Children's Intrinsic Motivation: A Review and Synthesis," *Psychological Bulletin* 128, no. 5 (September 2002): 774–95.

25. Alfie Kohn, *Punished by Rewards: The Trouble with Gold Stars, Incentive Plans, As, Praise, and Other Bribes* (Boston: Houghton Mifflin, 1999), pp. 142–59.

26. John Dewey, *The School and Society* (Chicago: University of Chicago Press, 1915); John Holt, *How Children Fail* (New York: Pitman, 1964); Alfred North Whitehead, *The Aims of Education and Other Essays* (New York: Free Press, 1929).

27. Neil Swidey, "Rush, Little Baby," *Boston Globe*, October 28, 2007, http://www .boston.com/news/globe/magazine/articles/2007/10/28/rush_little_baby/ (accessed December 15, 2010).

28. In 1928, Stanford University psychologist Louis Terman began a still-going longitudinal study of young geniuses (defined by Terman as children who scored 140 or higher on his new IQ test, the Stanford-Binet). More than one hundred scientific articles and a dozen books have been written on Terman's geniuses, who took to calling themselves "Termites." Gregory Park, David Lubinski, and Camilla P. Benbow, "Recognizing Spatial Intelligence: Our Schools, and Our Society, Must Do More to Recognize Spatial Reasoning, A Key Kind of Intelligence," *Scientific American*, November 2, 2010, http://www.scientificamerican.com/article.cfm?id=recognizing-spatial-intel (accessed December 15, 2010).

29. Rebecca Coffey, "20 Things You Didn't Know About Genius," *Discover*, October 2008, http://discovermagazine.com/2008/oct/01-20-things-you-didnt-know-about -genius (accessed December 15, 2010).

30. Nancy Faber, "An Irrelevant Best-Seller by Nobel Laureate Richard Feynman Gives Nerds a Good Name," *People*, July 22, 1985, http://www.people.com/people/ archive/article/0,,20091337,00.html (accessed May 25, 2011).

31. Carol S. Dweck, *Mindset: The New Psychology of Success* (New York: Random House, 2006).

32. Po Bronson, "How Not to Talk to Your Kids: The Inverse Power of Praise," *New York*, February 11, 2007, http://nymag.com/news/features/27840/ (accessed December 13, 2010).

33. Claudia M. Mueller and Carol S. Dweck, "Praise for Intelligence Can Undermine Children's Motivation and Performance," *Journal of Personality and Social Psychology* 75, no. 1 (July 1998): 33–52.

34. Nathaniel Branden, *The Psychology of Self-Esteem: A Revolutionary Approach to Self-Understanding That Launched a New Era of Modern Psychology* (Kalamazoo, MI: Nash Publishing, 1969).

35. "Now, the California Task Force to Promote Self-Esteem," *New York Times*, October 11, 1986, http://www.nytimes.com/1986/10/11/us/now-the-california-task-force -to-promote-self-esteem.html (accessed December 13, 2010).

36. Po Bronson and Ashley Merryman, *NurtureShock: New Thinking about Children* (New York: Twelve, 2009), p. 18.

37. Steven F. Maier, Christopher Peterson, and Barry Schwartz, "From Helplessness to Hope: The Seminal Career of Martin Seligman," in *The Science of Hope and Optimism*, ed. Jane E. Gillham (Radnor, PA: Templeton Foundation, 2000), pp. 11–37.

38. Carol S. Dweck, "Messages That Motivate: How Praise Molds Students' Beliefs, Motivation, and Performance (in Surprising Ways)," in *Improving Academic Achievement: Impact of Psychological Factors on Education*, ed. Joshua Aronson (San Diego, CA: Academic, 2002), pp. 37–60.

39. Ibid., p. 46.

40. Dweck, *Mindset*, p. 72.

41. Lisa S. Blackwell, Kali H. Trzesniewski, and Carol S. Dweck, "Implicit Theories of Intelligence Predict Achievement across an Adolescent Transition: A Longitudinal Study and an Intervention," *Child Development* 78, no. 1 (January/February 2007): 246–63.

42. Dweck, *Mindset*, p. 36.

43. Roy F. Baumeister et al., "Does High Self-Esteem Cause Better Performance, Interpersonal Success, Happiness, or Healthier Lifestyles?" *Psychological Science in the Public Interest* 4, no. 1 (May 2003): 1–44.

44. Anjana Ahuja, "Forget Self-Esteem and Learn Some Humility," *Times*, May 17, 2005, http://www.timesonline.co.uk/tol/life_and_style/article523219.ece (accessed April 28, 2011).

45. K. Anders Ericsson, William G. Chase, and Steve Faloon, "Acquisition of a Memory Skill," *Science* 208, no. 4448 (June 6, 1980): 1181–82.

46. Ibid., 1181.

47. Debra A. Gusnard et al., "Persistence and Brain Circuitry," *Proceedings of the National Academy of Science of the United States of America* 100, no. 6 (March 18, 2003): 3479–84.

48. David Shenk, *The Genius in All of Us: Why Everything You've Been Told about Genetics, Talent, and IQ Is Wrong* (New York: Doubleday, 2010), pp. 25–34.

49. Thomas J. Bouchard Jr. et al., "Sources of Human Psychological Differences: The Minnesota Study of Twins Reared Apart," *Science* 250, no. 4978 (October 12, 1990): 223–28.

50. Gilbert Gottlieb, "Probablistic Epigenesis," *Developmental Science* 10, no. 1 (January 2007): 1–11; John P. Spencer et al., "Short Arms and Talking Eggs: Why We Should No Longer Abide the Nativist-Empiricist Debate," *Child Development Perspectives* 3, no. 2 (2009): 79–87.

51. Avshalom Caspi et al., "Influence of Life Stress on Depression: Moderation by a Polymorphism in the 5-HTT Gene," *Science* 301, no. 5631 (July 18, 2003): 386–89.

52. Jeffrey H. Dyer, Hal B. Gregersen, and Clayton M. Christensen, "The Innovator's DNA," *Harvard Business Review*, December 2009, http://hbr.org/2009/12/the-innovators-dna/ar/1 (accessed December 14, 2010).

53. Jeffrey H. Dyer and Hal B. Gregersen, interview by Bronwen Fryer, "How Do Innovators Think?" *Harvard Business Review* (blog), September 28, 2009, http://blogs .hbr.org/hbr/hbreditors/2009/09/how_do_innovators_think.html (accessed December 14, 2010).

CHAPTER 4: NOT ENOUGH TORTOISE, TOO MUCH HARE

1. Robert J. Samuelson, "A Path to Downward Mobility: Today's Youngest Generation of Americans Are Likely to Be Worse Off Than Their Parents," *Newsweek*, October 13, 2009, http://www.newsweek.com/2009/10/13/a-path-to-downward-mobility.html (accessed December 15, 2010).

2. George H. W. Bush, "Presidential Proclamation 6158," Project on the Decade of the Brain, July 17, 1990, http://www.loc.gov/loc/brain/proclaim.html (accessed December 15, 2010).

3. Ross A. Thompson and Charles A. Nelson, "Developmental Science and the Media: Early Brain Development," *American Psychologist* 56, no. 1 (January 2001): 5–15.

4. Rob Reiner, "Parents' Action for Children," *Huffington Post*, May 26, 2005, http://www.huffingtonpost.com/rob-reiner/parents-action-for-childr_b_1430.html (accessed December 15, 2010).

5. Kathy Hirsh-Pasek, Roberta M. Golinkoff, and Diane Ever, *Einstein Never Used Flash Cards: How Our Children Really Learn and Why They Need to Play More and Memorize Less* (Emmaus, PA: Rodale, 2003), p. 3.

6. National Institutes of Health, National Institute of Child Health and Human Development, "Back to Sleep Public Education Campaign," http://www.nichd .nih.gov/sids/ (accessed December 15, 2010).

7. These descriptions of sleep positioners were copied from each manufacturer's website on December 15, 2010. Since then, each product has been removed from the manufacturer's webiste and is no longer for available for purchase. The quoted manufacturer's product descriptions, however, are still posted on several shopping websites. See, for example: http://www.amazon.com/First-Years-Airflow-Infant-Positioner/dp/B002 NH3TME, http://www.happynursery.com/dex_sleeping_products.htm, and http://www .amazon.com/Dexbaby-Safe-Universal-Wedge-White/dp/B00067AUP2 (accessed April 28, 2011). "Supreme Sleep Positioner/ Ultimate Sleep Positioner by Basic Comfort, Inc.," iParenting Media Awards, http://iparentingmediaawards.com/winners/14/1387 -15-167.php (accessed December 15, 2010).

8. US Food and Drug Administration, "Infant Sleep Positioners Pose Suffocation Risk," September 29, 2010, http://www.fda.gov/ForConsumers/ConsumerUpdates/ ucm227575.htm (accessed December 15, 2010); US Consumer Product Safety Commis-

sion, "Deaths Prompt CPSC, FDA Warning on Infant Sleep Positioners," September 29, 2010, http://www.cpsc.gov/cpscpub/prerel/prhtml10/10358.html (accessed December 15, 2010).

9. BabyPlus, "Celebrity Moms Use BabyPlus, You Should Too," *BabyPlus* (blog), May 23, 2010, http://blog.babyplus.com/blog/babyplus-distributors/celebrity-moms-use-babyplus-you-should-too (accessed December 15, 2010).

10. BabyPlus, http://babyplus.com/ (accessed April 28, 2011).

11. BabyPlus, "What Is It?" http://babyplus.com/ (accessed December 15, 2010).

12. Timothy D. Wilson, Daniel Gilbert, and Thalia Wheatley, "Protecting Our Minds: The Role of Lay Beliefs," in *Metacognition: Cognitive and Social Dimensions*, ed. Vincent Y. A. Yzerbyt, Guy Lories, and Benoit Dardenne (New York: Sage, 1998), 171–201.

13. "What Is It?" BabyPlus, http://www.babyplus.com/WhatIsIt.php (accessed July 28, 2010).

14. Maria C. Caselli et al., "A Cross-Linguistic Study of Early Lexical Development," *Cognitive Development* 10, no. 2 (April–June 1995): 159–99.

15. "What Is It?" BabyPlus.

16. Uffe Schjoedt et al., "The Power of Charisma: Perceived Charisma Inhibits the Frontal Executive Network of Believers in Intercessory Prayer," *Social Cognitive and Affective Neuroscience* 6, no. 1 (January 6, 2011): 119–27.

17. B(l)aby, http://www.blabybaby.com/blaby%20about%20page.html (accessed April 28, 2011).

18. Cindy Wallander, "You're Never Too Young to Learn," *BabyPlus* (blog), http://blog.babyplus.com/blog/babyplus-customer-service/youre-never-too-young-to-learn-v2 (accessed April 28, 2011).

19. Christine M. Moon and William P. Fifer, "Evidence of Transnatal Auditory Learning," *Journal of Perinatology* 20, no. 8s (December 2000): S37–S44.

20. Mark Prigg, "The Baby Bump iPod," *London Evening Standard*, April 17, 2009, http://www.thisislondon.co.uk/standard/article-23677164-the-baby-bump-ipod.do. (accessed December 15, 2010).

21. Frances H. Rauscher, Gordon L. Shaw, and Katherine N. Ky, "Music and Spatial Task Performance," *Nature* 365 (October 14, 1993): 611.

22. Nikhil Swaminathan, "Fact or Fiction? Babies Exposed to Classical Music End up Smarter: Is the So-Called 'Mozart Effect' a Scientifically Supported, Developmental Leg up or a Media-Fueled 'Scientific Legend'?" *Scientific American*, September 13, 2007, http://www.scientificamerican.com/article.cfm?id=fact-or-fiction-babies-ex (accessed December 15, 2010).

23. Don Campbell, The Mozart Effect Resource Center, www.mozarteffect.com (accessed December 15, 2010).

24. Baroque-A-Bye Baby, http://www.workingmusic.co.uk/ (accessed December 15, 2010).

25. Kevin Sack, "Georgia's Governor Seeks Musical Start for Babies," *New York Times*, January 15, 1998, http://www.nytimes.com/1998/01/15/us/georgia-s-governor-seeks -musical-start-for-babies.html (accessed December 15, 2010).

26. Thompson and Nelson, "Developmental Science and the Media."

27. Christopher F. Chabris, "Prelude or Requiem for the 'Mozart Effect'?" *Nature* 400 (August 26, 1999): 826–27; Kristin M. Nantais and E. Glenn Schellenberg, "The Mozart Effect: An Artifact of Preference," *Psychological Science* 10, no. 4 (July 1999): 370–73.

28. Jakob Pietschnig, Martin Voracek, and Anton K. Formann, "Mozart Effect–Shmozart Effect: A Meta-Analysis," *Intelligence* 38, no. 3 (May/June 2010): 314–23.

29. Swaminathan, "Fact or Fiction?"

30. Nantais and Schellenberg, "The Mozart Effect."

31. "At Five Months, Babies Have the Raw Ability to Add," *Life*, July 1993, http://pantheon.yale.edu/~kw77/LIFE_article.html (accessed May 24, 2011).

32. H. Keith Rodewald, "Application of Bower's One-Element Model to Paired-Associate Learning by Pigeons," *Journal of Experimental Animal Behavior* 19, no. 2 (March 1973): 219–23.

33. Oskar Pfungst, *Clever Hans (The Horse of Mr. Von Osten): A Contribution to Experimental Animal and Human Psychology* (Ithaca, NY: Cornell University Library, 1911).

34. Kristian Smock, "Creative Child Magazine Has Honored 'Your Baby Can Read!' with Six Awards for Educational Excellence!" *Business Wire*, July 14, 2010, http:// www.pr-inside.com/creative-child-magazine-has-honored-your-r2003145.htm (accessed December 15, 2010).

35. "Start Your Baby Reading Today," Your Baby Can Read, http://yourbabycan read.com/(accessed December 15, 2010).

36. According to PsycINFO, which is the database for searching psychological literature, Titzer has coauthored two studies. His *Psychological Review* paper (on which he is the third author) deals with a common hide-and-seek error that infants make: Linda B. Smith et al., "Knowing in the Context of Acting: The Task Dynamics of the A-Not-B Error," *Psychological Review* 106, no. 2 (April 1999): 235–60. Titzer's second publication explores motor performance in adults: John B. Shea and Robert C. Titzer, "The Influence of Reminder Trials on Contextual Interference Effects," *Journal of Motor Behavior* 25, no. 4 (December 1993): 264–74.

37. Campaign for a Commercial-Free Childhood, "Complaint and Request for Investigation and Relief, in the Matter of Your Baby Can, LLC, and Dr. Robert Titzer," http:// www.commercialfreechildhood.org/pdf/ybcrftccomplaint.pdf (accessed April 28, 2011).

38. Fred M. Hechinger, "About Education," *New York Times*, November 22, 1989, http://www.nytimes.com/1989/11/22/us/education-about-education.html (accessed December 15, 2010).

39. Mabel Vogel Morphett and Carleton Washburne, "When Should Children Begin to Read?" *Elementary School Journal* 31 (1931): 496–503.

40. Philip H. K. Seymour, Mikko Aro, and Jane M. Erskine, "Foundation Literacy Acquisition in European Orthographies," *Journal of British Psychology* 94, no. 2 (May 2003): 143–74.

41. Maryanne Wolf, *Proust and the Squid: The Story and Science of the Reading Brain* (New York: HarperCollins, 2007), pp. 81–133.

42. Tomoko Ishibashi et al., "Astrocytes Promote Myelination in Response to Electrical Impulses," *Neuron* 49, no. 6 (March 16, 2006): 823–32.

43. Elizabeth McFarlane, "World Book Day: Just Leave It to Captain Underpants," *Times*, March 6, 2008, http://women.timesonline.co.uk/tol/life_and_style/women/the_way_we_live/article3490039.ece (accessed December 16, 2010).

44. "Child Development," Your Baby Can, http://www.yourbabycan.com/Child Development (accessed April 28, 2011).

45. Roberta M. Golinkoff and Kathy Hirsh-Pasek, *How Babies Talk: The Magic and Mystery of Language Acquisition* (New York: Penguin, 1999), pp. 25–34.

46. Roberta M. Golinkoff, "I Beg Your Pardon? The Preverbal Negotiation of Failed Messages," *Journal of Child Language* 13, no. 3 (October 1986): 455–76.

47. Susan Goldin-Meadow and Carolyn Mylander, "Gestural Communication in Deaf Children: The Effects and Non-Effects of Parental Input on Early Language Development," *Monographs of the Society for Research in Child Development* 49, no. 3/4 (1984): 1–151.

48. Patricia K. Kuhl, Feng-Ming Tsao, and Huei-Mei Liu, "Foreign-Language Experience in Infancy: Effects of Short-Term Exposure and Social Interaction on Phonetic Learning," *Proceedings of the National Academy of Sciences* 100, no. 15 (July 22, 2003): 9096–101.

49. Kathleen Vail, "Ready to Learn: What the Head Start Debate about Early Academics Means for Your Schools," *American School Board Journal* 190, November 2003, http://www.asbj.com/MainMenuCategory/Archive/2003/November/Ready-to-Learn.html?DID=275878 (accessed December 15, 2010).

50. Carollee Howes and Alison Guerra Wishard, "Revisiting Shared Meaning: Looking through the Lens of Culture and Linking Shared Pretend Play through Proto-Narrative Development to Emergent Literacy," in *Children's Play: The Roots of Reading*, ed. Edward Zigler, Dorothy G. Singer, and Sandra J. Bishop-Josef (Washington, DC: Zero to Three, 2004), pp. 143–58.

51. Susan B. Neuman and Kathy Roskos, "Literacy Objects as Cultural Tools: Effects on Children's Literacy Behaviors during Play," *Reading Research Quarterly* 27, no. 3 (Summer 1992): 203–23.

52. Sue Bredekamp, "Play and School Readiness," in *Children's Play: The Roots of Reading*, ed. Edward Zigler, Dorothy G. Singer, and Sandra J. Bishop-Josef (Washington, DC: Zero to Three, 2004), pp. 159–74; Dorothy G. Singer, Roberta M. Golinkoff, and Kathy Hirsh-Pasek, *Play=Learning: How Play Motivates and Enhances Children's Cognitive and Social-Emotional Growth* (New York: Oxford University Press, 2006).

53. Deborah J. Stipek et al., "Good Beginnings: What Differences Does the Program Make in Preparing Young Children for School?" *Journal of Applied Developmental Psychology* 19, no. 1 (January–March 1998): 41–66; Deborah J. Stipek et al., "Effects of Different Instructional Approaches on Young Children's Achievement and Motivation," *Child Development* 66, no. 1 (February 1995): 209–33.

54. Singer, Golinkoff, and Hirsh-Pasek, *Play=Learning*.

55. David P. Weikart and Lawrence J. Schweinhart, "Disadvantaged Children and Curriculum Effects," *New Directions for Child and Adolescent Development* 53 (Fall 1991): 57–64.

56. Margot Adler, "Growth Spurt: The Rise of Tutoring in America," *National Public Radio*, June 5, 2005, http://www.npr.org/templates/story/story.php?storyId=4676496 (accessed December 16, 2010).

57. "Sylvan's Personalized Pre-K Programs Will Encourage Your Child to Love Reading," Sylvan Learning Centers, http://tutoring.sylvanlearning.com/pre_k_tutoring.cfm (accessed April 28, 2011).

58. "Why Junior Kumon?" Kumon, http://www.kumon.com/madison-west/whyjrkumon/instilladesire (accessed April 28, 2011).

59. "StartingPoints: Adventure Begins When You Learn to Read!" KnowledgePoints, http://www.knowledgepoints.com/StartingPoints.html (accessed April 28, 2011).

60. Greg J. Duncan et al., "School Readiness and Later Achievement," *Developmental Psychology* 43, no. 6 (November 2007): 1428–46.

61. Pamela Paul, "Tutors for Toddlers," *Time*, November 21, 2007, http://www.time.com/time/magazine/article/0,9171,1686826,00.html (accessed December 16, 2010).

62. Lloyd de Mause, "The Evolution of Childhood," in *The History of Childhood*, ed. Lloyd de Mause (New York: Psychohistory, 1974), pp. 1–73.

63. Jean-Jacques Rousseau, *Emile* (New York: Dutton, 1762), p. 100. Quite ironically, Rousseau placed all five of his children in orphanages so that they wouldn't interfere with his work.

64. Henry David Thoreau, *The Writings of Henry David Thoreau*, Vol. 7 (Boston: Houghton Mifflin, 1892), p. 222.

65. Friedrich Froebel, *The Education of Man* (Mineola, NY: Dover, 2005), p. 30.

66. Stanford University psychologist Lewis Terman famously dispelled this myth by following a group of high-IQ children—dubbed "Termites"—for thirty-five years. Terman found that at midlife, his gifted group were taller, healthier, physically better developed, and more socially adept than average-IQ children—and had attained an impressive list of accomplishments. Of just the 857 gifted males in Terman's study, 70 were listed in *American Men of Science*, 3 were elected to the National Academy of Sciences, 10 had entries in the *Directory of American Scholars*, and 31 appeared in *Who's Who in America*. Together, the Termites had published more than 2,000 scientific and technical papers, written more than 60 books and monographs, and had been granted at least 230 patents.

Sure, that's an impressive list, but some have argued that the Termites' accomplishments could have been predicted on the basis of their socioeconomic status alone—mostly white and raised in middle-class to upper-middle-class families.

67. David Elkind, *The Hurried Child* (Cambridge, MA: Da Capo, 1981), p. 7.

68. Kathy Hirsh-Pasek et al., *A Mandate for Playful Learning in Preschool: Presenting the Evidence* (New York: Oxford University Press, 2009), p. xi.

69. Edward F. Zigler and Sandra J. Bishop-Josef, "The Cognitive Child vs. the Whole Child: Lessons from 40 Years of Head Start," in *Play=Learning: How Play Motivates and Enhances Children's Cognitive and Social-Emotional Growth*, ed. Dorothy G. Singer, Roberta M. Golinkoff, and Kathy Hirsh-Pasek (New York: Oxford University Press, 2006), pp. 15–35.

70. David Elkind, "Our President: Acceleration," *Young Children* 43, no. 4 (May 1988): 2.

71. Joseph Stone, Henrietta Smith, and Lois Murphy, *The Competent Infant: Research and Commentary* (New York: Basic Books, 1973).

72. Institutes for the Achievement of Human Potential, "Glenn Doman, Founder," http://www.iahp.org/ (accessed April 28, 2011).

73. Karen Wynn, "Psychological Foundations in Number: Numerical Competence in Human Infants," *Trends in Cognitive Sciences* 2 (1998): 296–303.

74. Jonathan I. Flombaum, Justin A. Junge, and Marc D. Hauser, "Rhesus Monkeys (*Macaca mulatta*) Spontaneously Compute Addition Operations over Large Numbers," *Cognition* 97, no. 3 (October 2005): 315–25.

75. Rosa Rugani et al., "Arithmetic in Newborn Chicks," *Proceedings of the Royal Society of London* 276, no. 1666 (2009) 2451–60.

76. Kelly S. Mix, Janellen Huttenlocher, and Susan Cohen Levine, *Quantitative Development in Infancy and Early Childhood* (New York: Oxford University Press, 2001), pp. 23–49.

77. Melissa W. Clearfield and Kelly S. Mix, "Infants Use Continuous Quantity—Not Number—to Discriminate Small Visual Sets," *Journal of Cognition and Development* 2 (2001): 243–60.

78. "Awards, Badges, Bridging, and Other Insignia," Girl Scouts, http://www.girlscouts.org/program/gs_central/insignia/ (accessed April 28, 2011).

79. Alvin Rosenfeld, "Over-Scheduling Children and Hyper-Parenting: The Need for a National Family Night," Hyper-Parenting.com, http://www.hyper-parenting.com/nationalfamilynight/mission.htm (accessed April 28, 2011).

80. Stacy, "21 Things to Do Before Summer Ends," Putting Family First, http://www.puttingfamilyfirst.org/ (accessed April 28, 2011).

81. "Putting Family First Challenge," Putting Family First, http://www.puttingfamilyfirst.org/challenge/(accessed April 28, 2011).

82. Alvin Rosenfeld, "The Over-Scheduled Child," Hyper-Parenting.com, http://www.hyper-parenting.com/start.htm (accessed April 28, 2011).

83. Shaw et al., "Intellectual Ability and Cortical Development."

84. Schumann et al., "Longitudinal Magnetic Resonance Imaging Study."

85. University of Victoria psychologist Stephen Lindsay and his colleagues have demonstrated that showing people doctored photographs of themselves taking a hot-air balloon ride (that never happened) and then asking them to work on remembering the event can lead large numbers of people to wrongly report memories of the event. Kimberly A. Wade et al., "A Picture Is Worth a Thousand Lies: Using False Photographs to Create False Childhood Memories," *Psychonomic Bulletin and Review* 9, no. 3 (September 2002): 597–603.

86. John Mordechai Gottman, Lynn Fainsilber Katz, and Carole Hooven, *Meta-Emotion: How Families Communicate Emotionally* (Mahwah, NJ: Erlbaum, 1997), pp. 86–105.

87. David F. Bjorklund, *Why Youth Is Not Wasted on the Young: Immaturity in Human Development* (Malden, MA: Blackwell, 2007), p. 1.

88. David F. Bjorklund and Brandi L. Green, "The Adaptive Nature of Cognitive Immaturity," *American Psychologist* 47, no. 1 (January 1992): 46–54.

89. Leo Lionni, *Fish Is Fish* (New York: Dragonfly Books, 1974).

90. David F. Bjorklund, "The Role of Immaturity in Human Development," *Psychological Bulletin* 122, no. 2 (September 1997): 153–69.

91. David F. Bjorklund, "A Note on Neonatal Imitation," *Developmental Review* 7, no. 1 (March 1987): 86–92.

92. Gerald Turkewitz and Patricia A. Kenny, "Limitations on Input as a Basis for Neural Organization and Perceptual Development: A Preliminary Theoretical Statement," *Developmental Psychobiology* 15, no. 4 (July 1982): 357–68.

93. Rats are born blind and deaf—their early survival depends on smell. Bjorklund, "Role of Immaturity."

94. Elissa L Newport, "Constraining Concepts of the Critical Period for Language," in *The Epigenesis of Mind: Essays on Biology and Cognition*, ed. Susan Carey and Rochel Gelman (Hillsdale, NJ: Erlbaum, 1991), pp. 111–30.

95. Hilary Horn Ratner, Mary Ann Foley, and Nicole Gimpert, "The Role of Collaborative Planning in Children's Source-Monitoring Errors and Learning," *Journal of Experimental Child Psychology* 81, no. 1 (January 2002): 44–73.

96. David F. Bjorklund, Jane F. Gaultney, and Brandi L. Green, "I Watch, Therefore I Can Do: The Development of Meta-Imitation over the Preschool Years and the Advantage of Optimism in One's Imitative Skills," in *Emerging Themes in Cognitive Development*, ed. Robert Pasnak and Mark L. Howe (New York: Springer-Verlag, 1993), pp. 79–102.

97. Laura E. Berk, "Children's Private Speech: An Overview of Theory and the Status of Research," in *Private Speech: From Social Interaction to Self-Regulation*, ed. Rafael M. Diaz and Laura E. Berk (Hillsdale, NJ: Erlbaum, 1992), pp. 17–53.

CHAPTER 5: THE WORST SEAT
IN THE HOUSE

1. Jean-Jacques Rousseau, *Emile* (New York: Dutton, 1762), p. 35; William James, *The Principles of Psychology* (New York: Henry Holt, 1890), p. 488.

2. J. Gavin Bremner and Theodore D. Wachs, *The Wiley-Blackwell Handbook of Infant Development*, Vol. 1, *Basic Research*, 2nd ed. (Malden, MA: Wiley-Blackwell, 2010), pp. 33–314.

3. University of California, Berkeley, developmental psychologist Alison Gopnik is well known for her characterization of humans as bags of skin. Alison Gopnik, Andrew N. Meltzoff, and Patricia K. Kuhl, *The Scientist in the Crib: Minds, Brains, and How Children Learn* (New York: HarperCollins, 1999), pp. 4–9.

4. Chris Frith, *Making Up the Mind: How the Brain Creates Our Mental World* (Malden, MA: Blackwell, 2007), pp. 83–160.

5. Gopnik, Meltzoff, and Kuhl, *Scientist in the Crib*, p. 6.

6. Monty Newborn, *Kasparov versus Deep Blue: Computer Chess Comes of Age* (New York: Springer, 1997).

7. John Markoff, "Computer Wins on 'Jeopardy!': Trivial, It's Not," *New York Times*, February 16, 2011, http://www.nytimes.com/2011/02/17/science/17jeopardy -watson.html?pagewanted=1&_r=1 (accessed April 28, 2011).

8. Psychologist Umberto Castiello at the University of Padua in Italy has demonstrated that our brain automatically prepares action programs for objects around us, even when we have no conscious intention to act. He found that the hand preshapes itself on its way to the object, adjusting the distance between the thumb and the fingers to match the size of the object. If you're reaching for a tennis ball, you'll open your hand wider than if you're going for a marble. But if you reach for a marble when a tennis ball is sitting next to it, you'll open your hand wider than if you just saw the marble alone. This happens because the action for grasping a tennis ball interferes with your action for gripping a marble. Umberto Castiello, "The Neuroscience of Grasping," *Nature Reviews Neuroscience* 6 (September 1, 2005): 726–36.

9. Janette Atkinson, "Human Visual Development over the First Six Months of Life: A Review and a Hypothesis," *Human Neurobiology* 3, no. 2 (1984): 61–74.

10. M. Suzanne Zeedyk, "What's Life in a Baby Buggy Like? The Impact of Buggy Orientation on Parent-Infant Interaction and Infant Stress," National Literacy Trust, November 21, 2008, http://www.literacytrust.org.uk/assets/0000/2531/Buggy_research .pdf (accessed December 20, 2010).

11. Another word of caution: Zeedyk's stroller research has not yet been published in a peer-reviewed journal. To date, these data exist only on the websites of Dundee University and the National Literacy Trust.

12. Jennifer Bleyer, "The Latest in Strollers? Mom and Dad," *New York Times*, March 10, 2010, http://www.nytimes.com/2010/03/11/fashion/11BABY.html (accessed December 20, 2010).

13. US Consumer Product Safety Commission, "Infant Deaths Prompt CPSC Warning About Sling Carriers for Babies," March 12, 2010, http://www.cpsc.gov/CPSCPUB/PREREL/prhtml10/10165.html (accessed December 20, 2010).

14. Jim Sears, "Babywearing," AskDrSears.com, http://www.askdrsears.com/html/5/t051100.asp (accessed December 20, 2010).

15. Urs A. Hunziker and Ronald G. Barr, "Increased Carrying Reduces Crying: A Randomized Controlled Trial," *Pediatrics* 77, no. 5 (May 1986): 641–48.

16. Ronald G. Barr et al., "Carrying as Colic 'Therapy': A Randomized Controlled Trial," *Pediatrics* 87, no. 5 (May 1991): 623–30.

17. Jerome Kagan, *The Temperamental Thread: How Genes, Culture, Time, and Luck Make Us Who We Are* (New York: Dana, 2010).

18. Ronald G. Barr, Ian St. James-Roberts, and Maureen R. Keefe, "New Evidence on Unexplained Early Infant Crying: Its Origins, Nature, and Management," Johnson and Johnson Pediatric Institute, 2001, http://www.baby.com/jjpi/for-professionals/New-Evidence-on-Unexplained-Early-Infant-Crying-Its-Origins-Nature-and-Management.pdf (accessed December 20, 2010).

19. Ibid.

20. Sarah B. Hrdy, *Mother Nature: A History of Mothers, Infants, and Natural Selection* (New York: Pantheon Books, 1999), p. 452.

21. Jane Mildred et al., "Play Position Is Influenced by Knowledge of SIDS Sleep Position Recommendations," *Journal of Pediatrics and Child Health* 31, no. 6 (December 1995): 499–502.

22. Tamis Pin, Beverly Eldridge, and Mary P. Galea, "A Review of the Effects of Sleep Position, Play Position, and Equipment Use on Motor Development in Infants," *Developmental Medicine and Child Neurology* 49, no. 11 (November 2007): 858–67.

23. Shenandoah Robinson and Mark Proctor, "Diagnosis and Management of Deformational Plagiocephaly: A Review," *Journal of Neurosurgery: Pediatrics* 3, no. 4 (2009): 284–95.

24. John Persing et al., "Clinical Report: Prevention and Management of Positional Skull Deformities in Infants," *Pediatrics* 112, no. 1 (July 2003): 199–202.

25. Karen E. Adolph, "Learning to Move," *Current Directions in Psychological Science* 17, no. 3 (June 28, 2008): 213–18.

26. Michael Tomasello, "For Human Eyes Only," *New York Times*, January 13, 2007, http://www.nytimes.com/2007/01/13/opinion/13tomasello.html (accessed December 20, 2010).

27. Michael Tomasello, *Why We Cooperate* (Cambridge, MA: MIT Press, 2009), pp. 14–17.

28. Michael Tomasello, *Origins of Human Communication* (Cambridge, MA: MIT Press, 2008), pp. 5–12.

29. Amy Vaughan Van Hecke et al., "Infant Joint Attention, Temperament, and Social Competence in Preschool Children," *Child Development* 78, no. 1 (January/February 2007): 53–69.

30. Costanza Colombi et al., "Examining Correlates of Cooperation in Autism: Imitation, Joint Attention, and Understanding Intentions," *Autism* 13, no. 2 (March 2009): 143–63; Peter Mundy and Lisa Newell, "Attention, Joint Attention, and Social Cognition," *Current Directions in Psychological Science* 16, no. 5 (October 1, 2007): 269–74.

31. Tamar Lewin, "No Einstein in Your Crib? Get a Refund," *New York Times*, October 23, 2009, http://www.nytimes.com/2009/10/24/education/24baby.html (accessed December 12, 2010).

32. Dimitri A. Christakis et al., "Audible Television and Decreased Adult Words, Infant Vocaliations, and Conversational Turns: A Population-Based Study," *Archives of Pediatrics and Adolescent Medicine* 163, no. 6 (June 2009): 554–58; Dimitri A. Christakis et al., "Early Television Exposure and Subsequent Attention Problems in Children," *Pediatrics* 113, no. 4 (April 1, 2004) 708–13.

33. Campaign for a Commercial-Free Childhood, "FTC Complaint against Baby Einstein, Brainy Baby, & BabyFirstTV," http://www.commercialfreechildhood.org/babyvideos/ftccomplaint.htm (accessed December 20, 2010).

34. Campaign for a Commercial-Free Childhood, "CCFC Victory: Disney Offers Refunds on Baby Einstein Videos," http://www.commercialfreechildhood.org/babyeinstein refund.html (accessed December 20, 2010).

35. "New Discovery Kits," Baby Einstein, http://www.babyeinstein.com/en/discovery _kits/?src=home (accessed April 29, 2011).

36. Baby Einstein, "Baby's Favorite Places: First Words around Town DVD," Disney Store, http://www.disneystore.com/baby-einstein-babys-favorite-places-first-words -around-town-dvd/mp/1195978/1000316/#productDetailsAnchor (accessed January 13, 2011).

37. Patricia K. Kuhl, Feng-Ming Tsao, and Huei-Mei Liu, "Foreign-Language Experience in Infancy: Effects of Short-Term Exposure and Social Interaction on Phonetic Learning," *Proceedings of the National Academy of Sciences* 100, no. 15 (July 22, 2003): 9096–101.

38. Judy S. DeLoache et al., "Do Babies Learn from Baby Media?" *Psychological Science* 21, no. 11 (November 1, 2010): 1570–74.

39. Laura Chaddock et al., "A Neuroimaging Investigation of the Association between Aerobic Fitness, Hippocampal Volume, and Memory Performance in Preadolescent Children," *Brain Research* 1358 (October 28, 2010): 172–83.

40. Laura Chaddock et al., "Basal Ganglia Volume Is Associated with Aerobic Fitness in Preadolescent Children," *Developmental Neuroscience* 32, no. 3 (August 2010): 249–56.

41. Sabine Schaefer et al., "Cognitive Performance Is Improved while Walking: Differences in Cognitive-Sensorimotor Couplings between Children and Young Adults," *European Journal of Developmental Psychology* 7, no. 3 (2010): 371–89.

CHAPTER 6: TOYING WITH CHILDREN

1. Alix Spiegel, "Old-Fashioned Play Builds Serious Skills," *National Public Radio*, February 21, 2008, http://www.npr.org/templates/transcript/transcript.php?storyId=19212514 (accessed January 8, 2011).

2. Howard Chudacoff, *Children at Play: An American History* (New York: New York University Press, 2007). See also Yumi Gosso et al., "Play in Hunter-Gatherer Society," in *Play in Humans and Great Apes*, ed. Anthony D. Pellegrini and Peter K. Smith (Mahwah, NJ: Erlbaum, 2005), pp. 213–53.

3. Jay Belsky and Robert K. Most, "From Exploration to Play: A Cross-Sectional Study of Infant Free Play Behavior," *Developmental Psychology* 17, no. 5 (September 1981): 630–39; Vonnie C. McLoyd, "The Effects of the Structure of Play Objects on the Pretend Play of Low-Income Preschool Children," *Child Development* 54, no. 3 (June 1983): 64–66.

4. I did not make this up. Playmobil's Jewel Thieves is a real toy; see Playmobil, http://store.playmobilusa.com/on/demandware.store/Sites-US-Site/en_US/Product-Show?pid=4265 (accessed April 29, 2011). Back in the 1970s, in the German market, Playmobil sold a construction worker set that came with three cases of beer. The packaging showed two of the figures talking: "That's my fifth bottle today," says one worker. "Don't worry, we've got enough beer," says the other. Kate Muir, "The Dark Ages: Reinventing Playmobil for Modern Times," *Times*, May 3, 2008, http://women.timesonline.co.uk/tol/life_and_style/women/the_way_we_live/article3831553.ece (accessed April 29, 2011). Playmobil still sells the jewel heist, but you'll have to go to eBay for the Playmobeer.

5. Pamela Paul, *Parenting, Inc.* (New York: Times Books, 2008), p. 138.

6. "Young Explorer," Little Tikes, http://www.littletikes.com/toys/young-explorer.aspx (accessed April 29, 2011).

7. David Elkind, *The Power of Play: How Spontaneous, Imaginative Abilities Lead to Happier, Healthier Children* (Cambridge, MA: DaCapo, 2007); Dorothy G. Singer, Roberta M. Golinkoff, and Kathy Hirsh-Pasek, *Play=Learning: How Play Motivates and Enhances Children's Cognitive and Social-Emotional Growth* (New York: Oxford University Press, 2006).

8. Kenneth R. Ginsburg, the Committee on Communication, and the Committee on the Psychosocial Aspects of Child and Family Health, "The Importance of Play in Promoting Healthy Child Development and Maintaining Strong Parent-Child Bonds," *Pediatrics* 119, no. 1 (January 2007): 182–91.

9. Kathy Hirsh-Pasek and Roberta M. Golinkoff, "Brains in a Box: Do New Age Toys Deliver the Promise?" in *Child Development in a Changing Society*, ed. Robin Harwood, Scott A. Miller, and Ross Vasta (Hoboken, NJ: Wiley, 2008), http://udel.edu/~roberta/pdfs/Harwood%20piece%20-toys11-16-05%20Brains%20in%20Box.pdf (accessed January 13, 2011).

10. George Eisen, *Children and Play in the Holocaust: Games among the Shadows* (Amherst: University of Massachusetts Press, 1990).

11. Robin Marantz Henig, "Taking Play Seriously," *New York Times*, February 17, 2008, http://www.nytimes.com/2008/02/17/magazine/17play.html (accessed April 29, 2011).

12. Deborah K. Tinsworth and Joyce E. McDonald, "Injuries and Deaths Associated with Children's Playground Equipment," US Consumer Product Safety Commission, http://www.cpsc.gov/library/playgrnd.pdf (accessed January 9, 2011).

13. Robert Harcourt, "The Development of Play in the South American Fur Seal," *Ethology* 88, no. 3 (July 2010): 191–202.

14. Heather C. Bell, Sergio M. Pellis, and Bryan Kolb, "Juvenile Peer Play Experience and the Development of the Orbitofrontal and Medial Prefrontal Cortices," *Behavioural Brain Research* 207, no. 1 (February 11, 2010): 7–13.

15. Heather C. Bell et al., "The Role of the Medial Prefrontal Cortex in the Play Fighting of Rats," *Behavioral Neuroscience* 123, no. 6 (December 2009): 1158–68.

16. Marc Bekoff, "Animal Play and Behavioral Diversity," *American Naturalist* 109, no. 969 (September/October 1975): 601–03.

17. Anthony D. Pellegrini, *The Role of Play in Human Development* (New York: Oxford University Press, 2009).

18. Dimitri A. Christakis, Frederick J. Zimmerman, and Michelle M. Garrison, "Effects of Block Play on Language Acquisition and Attention in Toddlers," *Archives of Pediatric and Adolescent Medicine* 161(2007): 967–71; Kathy Hirsh-Pasek et al., *A Mandate for Playful Learning in Preschool: Presenting the Evidence* (New York: Oxford University Press, 2009), pp. 29–51; Anthony D. Pellegrini et al., "A Short-Term Longitudinal Study of Children's Playground Games across the First Year of School: Implications for Social Competence and Adjustment to School," *American Educational Research Journal* 39, no. 4 (Winter 2002): 991–1015; Jerome L. Singer, "Cognitive and Affective Implications of Imaginative Play in Childhood," in *Child and Adolescent Psychiatry: A Comprehensive Textbook*, ed. Andres Martin and Fred R. Volkmar (Philadelphia, PA: Lippincott Williams and Wilkins, 2002), pp. 252–63.

19. Adele Diamond et al., "Preschool Program Improves Cognitive Control," *Science* 318, no. 5855 (November 30, 2007): 1387–88.

20. Laura E. Berk, "Why Children Talk to Themselves," *Scientific American*, November 1994, 78–83; Kimberlee Bonura, "Academic Learning and Play," in *Encyclopedia of Play in Today's Society*, ed. Rodney P. Carlisle (Thousand Oaks, CA: Sage, 2009), pp.

1–5; Helena Kopecky et al., "Performance and Private Speech of Children with Attention-Deficit/Hyperactivity Disorder while Taking the Tower of Hanoi Test: Effects of Depth of Search, Diagnostic Subtype, and Methylphenidate," *Journal of Abnormal Child Psychology* 33, no. 5 (October 2005): 625–38.

21. Greg J. Duncan et al., "School Readiness and Later Achievement," *Developmental Psychology* 43, no. 6 (November 2007): 1428–46.

22. Spiegel, "Old-Fashioned Play."

23. Gordon M. Burghardt, *The Genesis of Animal Play: Testing the Limits* (Cambridge, MA: MIT Press, 2005), p. 81.

24. Masao Kawai, "Newly Acquired Pre-Cultural Behavior of the Natural Troop of Japanese Monkeys on Koshima Islet," *Primates* 6, no. 1 (1965): 1–30.

CHAPTER 7: Wii LITTLE CHILDREN

1. Victoria J. Rideout, Ulla G. Foehr, and Donald F. Roberts, "Generation M2: Media Use in the Lives of 8- to 18-Year-Olds," Henry J. Kaiser Family Foundation, January 2010, http://www.kff.org/entmedia/upload/8010.pdf. (accessed December 14, 2010).

2. Amanda Lenhart, "Teens, Cell Phones and Texting: Text Messaging Becomes Centerpiece Communication," Pew Research Center, April 20, 2010, http://pewresearch.org/pubs/1572/teens-cell-phones-text-messages. (accessed December 14, 2010).

3. Gary Small and Gigi Vorgan, *iBrain: Surviving the Technological Alteration of the Modern World* (New York: Harper, 2008), pp. 14–17.

4. Ibid., pp. 20–22.

5. Alvaro Pascual-Leone et al., "The Plastic Human Brain Cortex," *Annual Review of Neuroscience* 28 (2005): 377–401.

6. Kaveri Subrahmanyam and Patricia Greenfield, "Online Communication and Adolescent Relationships," *Future of Children* 18, no. 1 (Spring 2008): 119–46, http://www.futureofchildren.org/futureofchildren/publications/journals/article/index.xml?journalid=32.&articleid=59 (accessed January 14, 2011).

7. Marc A. Brackett, Susan E. Rivers, and Peter Salovey, "Emotional Intelligence: Implications for Personal, Social, Academic, and Workplace Success," *Social and Personality Psychology Compass* 5, no. 1 (2011): 88–103; Howard E. Gardner, *Frames of Mind: The Theory of Multiple Intelligences* (New York: Basic Books, 1983), pp. 237–76.

8. Ray Bradbury, *Golden Apples of the Sun* (New York: Perennial, 1997), p. 55.

9. American Academy of Pediatrics, Committee on Public Education, "Children, Adolescents, and Television," *Pediatrics* 107, no. 2 (February 2001): 423–26.

10. Victoria J. Rideout and Elizabeth Hamel, "The Media Family: Electronic Media in the Lives of Infants, Toddlers, Preschoolers, and Their Parents," Henry J.

Kaiser Family Foundation, May 2006, http://www.kff.org/entmedia/upload/7500.pdf. (accessed December 14, 2010).

11. Elizabeth A. Vandewater, David S. Bickham, and June H. Lee, "Time Well Spent? Relating Television Use to Children's Free Time Activities," *Pediatrics* 117, no. 2 (February 2006): 181–91.

12. Jeffrey G. Johnson et al., "Television Viewing and Aggressive Behavior during Adolescence and Adulthood," *Science* 295, no. 5564 (March 29, 2002): 2468–71.

13. Frederick J. Zimmerman et al., "Early Cognitive Stimulation, Emotional Support, and Television Watching as Predictors of Subsequent Bullying among Grade-School Children." *Archives of Pediatrics and Adolescent Medicine* 159, no. 4 (April 2005): 384–88.

14. Dimitri A. Christakis et al., "Early Television Exposure and Subsequent Attention Problems in Children," *Pediatrics* 113, no. 4 (April 1, 2004) 708–13.

15. Jeffrey G. Johnson et al., "Extensive Television Viewing and the Development of Attention and Learning Difficulties during Adolescence," *Archives of Pediatrics and Adolescent Medicine* 161, no. 5 (May 2007): 480–86.

16. Centers for Disease Control and Prevention, "Prevalence of Autism Spectrum Disorders: Autism and Developmental Disabilities Monitoring Network, United States, 2006," *Morbidity and Mortality Weekly Report Surveillance Summaries* 58, no. 9 (December 18, 2009): 1–20.

17. Michael Waldman et al., "Does Television Cause Autism?" Working Paper No. 12632, National Bureau of Economic Research, October 2006, http://papers.ssrn.com/sol3/papers.cfm?abstract_id=938958 (accessed December 22, 2010).

18. Craig J. Newchaffer et al., "The Epidemiology of Autism Spectrum Disorders," *Annual Review of Public Health* 28 (2007): 235–58.

19. Andrew N. Meltzoff, "Imitation of Televised Models By Infants," *Child Development* 59, no. 5 (October 1988): 1221–29.

20. Patricia J. Bauer, "Long-Term Recall Memory: Behavioral and Neuro-Developmental Changes in the First Two Years of Life," *Current Directions in Psychological Science* 11, no. 4 (2002): 137–41.

21. Richard M. Ryan, C. Scott Rigby, and Andrew Przybylski, "The Motivational Pull of Video Games: A Self-Determination Theory Approach," *Motivation and Emotion* 30, no. 4 (2006): 347–64.

22. B. F. Skinner, *Science and Human Behavior* (New York: Macmillan, 1953), p. 70.

23. Jaak Panksepp and Joseph R. Moskal, "Dopamine and SEEKING: Subcortical 'Reward' Systems and Appetitive Urges," in *Handbook of Approach and Avoidance Motivation*, ed. Andrew J. Elliot (New York: Taylor and Francis Group), pp. 67–87.

24. EA Video Games, http://www.ea.com/platform/pc-games (accessed June 1, 2011).

25. "How the Nintendo Wii Will Get You Emotionally Invested in Video Games:

A Console to Make You Wiip," *Seed*, November 16, 2006, http://seedmagazine.com/content/article/a_console_to_make_you_wiip/ (accessed January 7, 2011).

26. Steven Johnson, *Everything Bad Is Good for You: How Today's Popular Culture Is Actually Making Us Smarter* (New York: Penguin, 2005).

27. Steven J. Kirsh, *Media and Youth: A Developmental Perspective* (Malden, MA: Wiley-Blackwell, 2009); Victor C. Strassburger, Barbara J. Wilson, and Amy B. Jordan, *Children, Adolescents, and the Media* (Thousand Oaks, CA: Sage, 2009).

28. American Academic of Pediatrics, "Joint Statement on the Impact of Entertainment Violence on Children," Congressional Public Health Summit, July 26, 2000, http://www.aap.org/advocacy/releases/jstmtevc.htm (accessed January 3, 2011).

29. Karen Springen, "This Is Your Brain on Violence," *Newsweek*, November 28, 2006, http://www.newsweek.com/2006/11/27/this-is-your-brain-on-violence.html (accessed January 7, 2011).

30. Craig A. Anderson and Brad J. Bushman, "Effects of Violent Video Games on Aggressive Behavior, Aggressive Cognition, Aggressive Affect, Physiological Arousal, and Prosocial Behavior: A Meta-Analytic Review of the Scientific Literature," *Psychological Science* 12, no. 5 (September 2001): 353–59.

31. Plato, *Phaedrus* (370 BC; Project Gutenberg, 1998), http://www.gutenberg.org/ebooks/1636 (accessed June 2, 2011).

32. Steven Yantis, interview by Nora Young, *Spark Plus*, CBC Radio, February 10, 2010, http://castroller.com/podcasts/Spark/1458902-Full%20Interview%20Steven%20Yantis%20on%20Multitasking (accessed January 7, 2011).

33. Heather L. Kirkorian, Ellen A. Wartella, and Daniel R. Anderson, "Media and Young Children's Learning," *Future of Children* 18, no. 1 (Spring 2008): 39–62, http://www.princeton.edu/futureofchildren/publications/docs/18_01_03.pdf (accessed January 3, 2011).

34. Elizabeth Zack et al., "Infant Imitation from Television Using Novel Touch-Screen Technology," *British Journal of Developmental Psychology* 13, no. 1 (March 2009): 13–26.

35. Marie Evans Schmidt and Elizabeth A. Vandewater, "Media and Attention, Cognition, and School Achievement," *Future of Children* 18, no. 1 (Spring 2008): 63–86, http://futureofchildren.org/futureofchildren/publications/docs/18_01_04.pdf (accessed January 3, 2011).

36. Rideout, Foehr, and Roberts, "Generation M2."

37. Ofer Malamud and Christian Pop-Eleches, "Home Computer Use and the Development of Human Capital," Working Paper No. 15814, National Bureau of Economic Research, March 2010, http://www.nber.org/papers/w15814 (accessed January 4, 2011).

38. Johnson, *Everything Bad Is Good*, pp. 25–62.

39. Council on Science and Public Health, "Emotional and Behavioral Effects, Including Addictive Potential, of Video Games," American Medical Association, June

2007, http://www.ama-assn.org/ama/no-index/about-ama/17694.page?# (accessed April 23, 2011).

CHAPTER 8: ORGANIZED CRIME

1. Sandra L. Hofferth and John F. Sandberg, "Changes in American Children's Time, 1981–1997," in *Children at the Millennium: Where Have We Come From, Where Are We Going?*, ed. Sandra L Hofferth and T. J. Owens (New York: JAI, 2001), pp. 193–229; Sandra L. Hofferth, "Changes in Children's Time, 1997–2003," *Electronic International Journal of Time Use Research* 6, no. 1 (September 2009): 26–47, http://www.ncbi.nlm.nih.gov/pmc/articles/PMC2939468/ (accessed December 15, 2010).

2. Curt Hinson, *6 Steps to a Trouble-Free Playground* (Hockessin, DE: PlayFit Education, 2001).

3. Ibid.

4. Mark Powell, "The Hidden Curriculum of Recess," *Children, Youth, and Environments* 17, no. 4 (2007): 86–106.

5. Dennis Cauchon, "Children's Pastimes Are Increasingly Moving Indoors," *USA Today*, December 12, 2005, http://www.usatoday.com/news/nation/2005-07-11-pastimes-childhood_x.htm (accessed December 15, 2010).

6. Steven F. Asher and John D. Coie, *Peer Rejection in Childhood* (Cambridge: Cambridge University Press, 1990), pp. 253–308.

7. Anthony D. Pellegrini, *The Role of Play in Human Development* (New York: Oxford University Press, 2009); Dorothy G. Singer, Roberta M. Golinkoff, and Kathy Hirsh-Pasek, *Play=Learning: How Play Motivates and Enhances Children's Cognitive and Social-Emotional Growth* (New York: Oxford University Press, 2006).

8. Nakia S. Gordon et al., "Socially Induced Brain Fertilization: Play Promotes Brain-Derived Neurotrophic Factor Expression," *Neuroscience Letters* 341 (2003): 17–20.

9. Nathaniel Branden, *The Psychology of Self-Esteem: A Revolutionary Approach to Self-Understanding That Launched a New Era of Modern Psychology* (Kalamazoo, MI: Nash Publishing, 1969).

10. Ellen J. Langer, *Counterclockwise: Mindful Health and the Power of Personality* (New York: Ballantine Books, 2009); Ellen J. Langer, *Mindfulness* (Cambridge, MA: Perseus Books, 1989).

11. Langer, *Mindfulness*, pp. 43–204.

12. Michael Tomasello, *Why We Cooperate* (Cambridge, MA: MIT Press, 2009).

13. Hillary L. Burdette and Robert C. Whitaker, "Resurrecting Free Play in Young Children: Looking beyond Fitness and Fatness to Attention, Affiliation, and Affect," *Archives of Pediatric and Adolescent Medicine* 159, no. 1 (January 2005): 46–50.

14. Imagination Playground, http://www.imaginationplayground.org/ (accessed December 21, 2010).

15. Barbara H. Fiese, "Playful Relationships: A Contextual Analysis of Mother-Toddler Interaction and Symbolic Play," *Child Development* 61, no. 5 (October 1990): 1648–56.

16. Mark R. Lepper and David Greene, "Turning Play into Work: Effects of Adult Surveillance and Extrinsic Rewards on Children's Intrinsic Motivation," *Journal of Personality and Social Psychology* 31, no. 3 (March 1975): 479–86.

17. Anthony Pellegrini, "The Effect of Dramatic Play on Children's Generation of Cohesive Text," *Discourse Processes* 7, no. 1 (1984): 57–67; Jane C. Perlmutter and Anthony D. Pellegrini, "Children's Verbal Fantasy Play with Parents and Peers," *Educational Psychology* 7, no. 4 (1987): 269–81.

18. Pellegrini, *Role of Play,* pp. 16–23, 184–97; Singer, Golinkoff, and Hirsh-Pasek, *Play=Learning,* pp. 7–88.

19. Roger Mackett et al., "Children's Independent Movement in the Local Environment," *Built Environment* 33, no. 4 (December 2007): 454–68.

CHAPTER 9: AN INSIDE JOB

1. Sandra L. Hofferth and John F. Sandberg, "Changes in American Children's Time, 1981–1997," in *Children at the Millennium: Where Have We Come From, Where Are We Going?,* ed. Sandra L Hofferth and T. J. Owens (New York: JAI, 2001), pp. 193–229; Lia Karsten, "It All Used to Be Better? Different Generations on Continuity and Change in Urban Children's Daily Use of Space," *Children's Geographies* 3, no. 3 (December 2005): 275–90; Rhonda Clements, "An Investigation of the State of Outdoor Play," *Contemporary Issues in Early Childhood* 5, no. 1 (2004): 68–80; Pamela Wridt, "An Historical Analysis of Young People's Use of Public Space, Parks, and Playgrounds in New York City," *Children, Youth and Environments* 14, no. 1 (2004): 86–106.

2. Gersh Kuntzman, "New Face of Vandalism?" *Brooklyn Paper,* October 13, 2007, http://www.brooklynpaper.com/stories/30/40/30_40graffitigirl.html (accessed June 3, 2011).

3. Victoria J. Rideout, Ulla G. Foehr, and Donald F. Roberts, "Generation M2: Media Use in the Lives of 8- to 18-Year-Olds," Henry J. Kaiser Family Foundation, January 2010, http://www.kff.org/entmedia/upload/8010.pdf. (accessed December 14, 2010).

4. Andrew Balmford et al.,"Why Conservationists Should Heed Pokémon," *Science* 295, no. 5564 (March 29, 2002): 2367.

5. National Center for Chronic Disease Prevention and Health Promotion, "Healthy Youth," http://www.cdc.gov/HealthyYouth/obesity/index.htm (accessed December 29, 2010).

6. Foundation for Child Development, "Child and Youth Well-Being Index," http://www.soc.duke.edu/~cwi/section_d.html (accessed December 22, 2010).

7. World Health Organization, *Population-Based Prevention Strategies for Childhood Obesity, Report of a WHO Forum and Technical Meeting, Geneva, 15–17 December 2009* (Geneva, Switzerland: WHO Press, 2010), http://www.who.int/dietphysicalactivity/childhood/child-obesity-eng.pdf (accessed Demember, 29, 2010).

8. S. Jay Olshansky et al., "A Potential Decline in Life Expectancy in the United States in the 21st Century," *New England Journal of Medicine* 352, no. 11 (March 17, 2005): 1135–37.

9. Roger L. Mackett and James Paskins, "Children's Physical Activity: The Contribution of Playing and Walking," *Children and Society* 22, no. 5 (September 2008): 345–57; Trina Hinkley et al., "Preschool Children and Physical Activity: A Review of Correlates," *American Journal of Preventive Medicine* 34, no. 5 (May 2008): 435–41.

10. Janice F. Bell, Jeffrey S. Wilson, and Gilbert C. Liu, "Neighborhood Greenness and 2-Year Changes in Body Mass Index of Children and Youth," *American Journal of Preventive Medicine* 35, no. 6 (December 2008): 547–53.

11. Juhi Kumar et al., "Prevalence and Associations of 25-Hydroxyvitamin D Deficiency in US Children: NHANES 2001–2004," *Pediatrics* 124, no. 3 (September 2009): 362–70.

12. Heidi J. Kalkwarf et al., "The Bone Mineral Density in Childhood Study: Bone Mineral Content and Density According to Age, Sex, and Race," *Journal of Clinical Endocrinology and Metabolism* 92, no. 6 (June 2007): 2087–99.

13. Kathryn A. Rose et al., "Outdoor Activity Reduces the Prevalence of Myopia in Children," *Ophthalmology* 115, no. 8 (August 2008): 1279–85.

14. Patricia N. Pastor and Cynthia A. Reuben, "Diagnosed Attention Deficit Hyperactivity Disorder and Learning Disability: United States, 2004–2006," *Vital and Health Statistics* 10, no. 237 (July 2008): 1–14.

15. Centers for Disease Control and Prevention, "Increasing Prevalence of Parent-Reported Attention Deficit/Hyperactivity Disorder among Children: United States, 2003 and 2007," *Morbidity and Mortality Weekly Report* 59, no. 44 (November 12, 2010): 1439–43.

16. Nancy M. Wells, "At Home with Nature: Effects of Greenness on Children's Cognitive Functioning," *Environment and Behavior* 32, no. 6 (2000): 775–95.

17. Andrea Faber Taylor, Frances E. Kuo, and William C. Sullivan, "Coping with ADD: The Surprising Connection to Green Play Settings," *Environment and Behavior* 33, no. 1 (2001): 54–77.

18. Andrea Faber Taylor and Frances E. Kuo, "Children with Attention Deficits Concentrate Better after a Walk in the Park," *Journal of Attention Disorders* 12, no. 3 (May 2009): 402–09.

19. David Derbyshire, "How Children Lost the Right to Roam in Four Generations," *Daily Mail*, June 15, 2007, http://www.dailymail.co.uk/news/article-462091/How-children-lost-right-roam-generations.html. (accessed December 23, 2010).

20. Lenore Skenazy, "More from America's Worst Mom: 9-Year-Old on the Subway, Continued," *Huffington Post*, April 10, 2008, http://www.huffingtonpost.com/lenore-skenazy/more-from-americas-worst_b_96175.html (accessed April 29, 2010).

21. Foundation for Child Development, "Child and Youth Well-Being Index," http://www.soc.duke.edu/~cwi/section_d.html (accessed December 22, 2010).

22. National Center for Health Statistics, "10 Leading Causes of Injury Deaths by Age Group Highlighting Unintentional Injury Deaths, United States—2007," http://www.cdc.gov/injury/wisqars/pdf/Unintentional_2007-a.pdf (accessed December 27, 2010).

23. "Missing Children: Christopher Michael Barrios," *America's Most Wanted*, http://www.amw.com/missing_children/brief.cfm?id=43915. (accessed December 27, 2010).

24. Jeanne Van Cleave, Steven L. Gortmaker, and James M. Perrin, "Dynamics of Obesity and Chronic Health Conditions among Children and Youth," *Journal of the American Medical Association* 303, no. 7 (2010): 623–30.

25. Richard Louv, *Last Child in the Woods: Saving Our Children from Nature-Deficit Disorder* (Chapel Hill, NC: Algonquin Books, 2005).

26. Deborah Schoeneman, "James Cameron Goes Green," *Huffington Post*, February 24, 2010, http://www.huffingtonpost.com/deborah-schoeneman/james-cameron-goes-green_b_473855.html (retrieved December 23, 2010).

27. World Future Society, "Futurists Release Top Forecasts for 2007 and Beyond," http://www.wfs.org/pr2nd06.htm (accessed December 23, 2010).

28. These "symptoms" of childhood come from University of Pennsylvania's Jordan W. Smoller's satirical piece called "The Etiology and Treatment of Childhood." Check it out—it's a hoot: http://harvardmedicine.hms.harvard.edu/fascinoma/funnybone/etiology.php (accessed January 4, 2011).

29. Stephen Kaplan, "The Restorative Benefits of Nature: Toward an Integrative Framework," *Journal of Environmental Psychology* 15, no. 3 (1995): 169–82; Taylor, Kuo, and Sullivan, "Coping with ADD"; Taylor and Kuo, "Children with Attention Deficits."

30. Janetta Mitchell McCoy and Gary W. Evans, "The Potential Role of the Physical Environment in Fostering Creativity," *Creativity Research Journal* 14, no. 3/4 (2002): 409–26; Mark A. Runco, *Creativity: Theories and Themes: Research, Development, and Practice* (Burlington, MA: Elsevier, 2007), pp. 328–29.

31. California Department of Education, State Education and Environment Roundtable, "California Student Assessment Project, Phase Two: The Effects of Environment-Based Education on Student Achievement," January 2005, http://www.seer.org/pages/research/CSAPII2005.pdf (accessed December 27, 2010).

32. American Institutes for Research, "Effects of Outdoor Education Programs for Children in California," January 31, 2005, http://www.childrenandnature.org/downloads/outdoorschool_finalreport.pdf (accessed December 27, 2010).

33. Marc G. Berman, John Jonides, and Stephen Kaplan, "The Cognitive Benefits of Interacting with Nature," *Psychological Science* 19, no. 12 (December 2008): 1207–12.

34. Andrea Faber Taylor, Frances E. Kuo, and William C. Sullivan, "Views of Nature and Self-Discipline: Evidence from Inner-City Children," *Journal of Environmental Psychology* 22, no. 1/2 (March 2002): 49–63; Wells, "At Home with Nature."

35. Frances E. Kuo and William C. Sullivan, "Aggression and Violence in the Inner City: Effects of Environment via Mental Fatigue," *Environment and Behavior* 33, no. 4 (July 2001): 543–71; Roger S. Ulrich, "View through a Window May Influence Recovery from Surgery," *Science* 27, no. 4647 (April 27, 1984): 420–21.

36. Patrick Mooney and P. Lenore Nicell, "The Importance of Exterior Environment for Alzheimer Residents: Effective Care and Risk Management," *Healthcare Management Forum* 5, no. 2 (Summer 1992): 23–29; Jay Stone Rice and Linda L. Remy, "Impacts of Horticultural Therapy on Psychosocial Functioning among Urban Jail Inmates," *Journal of Offender Rehabilitation* 26 (1998): 169–91.

37. Michael D. Hunter et al., "The State of Tranquility: Subjective Perception Is Shaped by Contextual Modulation of Auditory Connectivity," *NeuroImage* 53, no. 2 (November 1, 2010): 611–18; Rita Berto, "Exposure to Restorative Environments Helps Restore Attentional Capacity," *Journal of Environmental Psychology* 25 (2005): 249–59.

38. Berman, Jonides, and Kaplan, "Cognitive Benefits of Interacting with Nature."

39. Stephen Kaplan, "The Restorative Benefits of Nature: Toward an Integrative Framework," *Journal of Environmental Psychology* 15, no. 3 (September 1995): 169–82; Stephen Kaplan, "Meditation, Restoration, and the Management of Mental Fatigue," *Environment and Behavior* 33, no. 4 (July 2001): 480–506.

40. Taylor, Kuo, and Sullivan, "Nature and Self-Discipline."

41. Luther Burbank, *The Training of the Human Plant* (New York: DeVinne Press, 1907), p. 91.

42. James J. Gibson, *The Ecological Approach to Visual Perception* (Boston: Houghton Mifflin, 1979), pp. 33–46.

43. Anne C. Bell and Janet E. Dyment, "Grounds for Health: The Intersection of Green School Grounds and Health-Promoting Schools," *Environmental Education Research* 14, no. 1 (2008): 77–90; Hillary L. Burdette and Robert C. Whitaker, "Resurrecting Free Play in Young Children: Looking beyond Fitness and Fatness to Attention, Affiliation, and Affect," *Archives of Pediatric and Adolescent Medicine* 159, no. 1 (January 2005): 46–50; Ingunn Fjørtoft, "The Natural Environment as a Playground for Children: The Impact of Outdoor Play Activities in Pre-Primary School Children," *Early Childhood Education Journal* 29, no. 2 (Winter 2001): 111–17; F. Mårtensson et al., "Outdoor Environmental Assessment of Attention Promoting Settings for Preschool Children," *Health and Place* 15, no. 4 (December 2009): 1149–57; Stuart Lester and Martin Maudsley, "Play, Naturally: A Review of Children's Natural Play," Children's Play Council, http://www.playday .org.uk/PDF/play-naturally-a-review-of-childrens-natural%20play.pdf (accessed December 27, 2010); Nancy M. Wells and Gary W. Evans, "Nearby Nature: A Buffer of Life Stress among Rural Children," *Environment and Behavior* 35, no. 3 (May 2003): 311–30.

44. Drake Bennett, "Back to the Playground," *Boston Globe*, April 15, 2007, http://www.boston.com/news/globe/ideas/articles/2007/04/15/back_to_the_playground/ (accessed May 3, 2011); Jane E. Brody, "A Classroom of Monkey Bars and Slides," *New York Times*, April 3, 2007, http://www.nytimes.com/2007/04/03/health/03brody.html (accessed May 3, 2011).

45. Richard Louv, "Nurture with Nature," *Sunday Times*, July 15, 2007, http://women.timesonline.co.uk/tol/life_and_style/women/families/article2075239.ece (accessed January 10, 2011).

46. Tim Gill, "How to Let Your Children Run Free," *Independent*, October 3, 2005, http://www.independent.co.uk/environment/how-to-let-your-children-run-free-509400.html (retrieved December 27, 2010).

47. Craig W. O'Brien, "Injuries and Investigated Deaths Associated with Playground Equipment, 2001–2008," US Consumer Product Safety Commission, October 2009, http://www.cpsc.gov/library/foia/foia10/os/playground.pdf (retrieved December 27, 2010).

48. Henry David Thoreau, *Walden; Or Life in the Woods* (Boston: Shambhala, 2004), at Princeton University, http://www.princeton.edu/~batke/thoreau/ (accessed June 3, 2011).

49. John Muir, *Our National Parks* (Boston: Houghton Mifflin, 1901), at Sierra Club, http://www.sierraclub.org/john_muir_exhibit/writings/our_national_parks/ (accessed June 3, 2011).

50. Peter H. Kahn, Rachel L. Severson, and Jolina H. Ruckert, "The Human Relation with Nature and Technological Nature," *Current Directions in Psychological Science* 18, no. 1 (February 2009): 37–42.

51. Ulrich, "View through a Window."

52. Taylor and Kuo, "Children with Attention Deficits."

53. Burdette and Whitaker, "Resurrecting Free Play"; Fjørtoft, "Natural Environment as a Playground"; Mårtensson et al., "Outdoor Environmental Assessment."

54. Taylor, Kuo, and Sullivan, "Nature and Self-Discipline."

55. Wells and Evans, "Nearby Nature."

56. Kuo and Sullivan, "Aggression and Violence."

57. Children and Nature Network, http://www.childrenandnature.org/ (accessed December 27, 2010).

58. "CLIF Kid Backyard Game of the Year," CLIF Bar and Company, http://www.clifkidbackyardgame.com/ (accessed May 3, 2011).

CHAPTER 10: OLD SCHOOL

1. US Department of Education, "National Snapshot," ED Data Express, http://www.eddataexpress.ed.gov/state-report.cfm?state=US. (accessed December 23, 2010).

2. Jeffrey Bisanz, Frederick J. Morrison, and Maria Dunn, "Effects of Age and

Schooling on the Acquisition of Elementary Quantitative Skills," *Developmental Psychology* 31, no. 2 (March 1995): 221–36; Steven J. Ceci, "How Much Does Schooling Influence General Intelligence and Its Cognitive Components? A Reassessment of the Evidence," *Developmental Psychology* 27, no. 5 (September 1991): 703–22.

3. Robert Wood Johnson Foundation, *The State of Play: Gallup Survey of Principals on School Recess*, http://www.rwjf.org/files/research/stateofplayrecessreportgallup.pdf (accessed June 3, 2011), p. 4.

4. Debra Nussbaum, "Before Children Ask, 'What's Recess?'" *New York Times*, December 10, 2006, http://www.nytimes.com/2006/12/10/nyregion/nyregionspecial2/10Rrecess.html (accessed January 2, 2011).

5. Amanda Ripley, "*Waiting for 'Superman'*: A Call to Action for Our Schools," *Time*, September 23, 2010, http://www.time.com/time/specials/packages/article/0,28804,2019663_2020590_2020592,00.html (accessed January 10, 2011).

6. National Center for Education Statistics, "The Nation's Report Card: Grade 12 Reading and Mathematics 2009 National and Pilot State Results," National Assessment of Educational Progress, http://nces.ed.gov/nationsreportcard/pubs/main2009/2011455.asp#section1 (accessed January 10, 2011).

7. ACT News, "College and Career Readiness Growing among ACT-Tested US High School Graduates," August 10, 2010, http://www.act.org/news/2010/08/18/college-career-readiness/ (accessed January 2, 2011).

8. Organization for European Economic Cooperation, Program for International Student Assessment, "PISA 2006: Science Competencies for Tomorrow's World: OECD Briefing Note for the United States," http://www.oecd.org/dataoecd/16/28/39722597.pdf (accessed January 2, 2011).

9. "Dropouts: The United States Has Quietly Withdrawn from an International Study Comparing Math and Science Students," *Newsweek*, August 9, 2007, http://www.newsweek.com/2007/08/08/dropouts.html (accessed January 2, 2011).

10. Ripley, "*Waiting for 'Superman.'*"

11. Sam Dillon, "Sluggish Results Seen in Math Scores," *New York Times*, October 14, 2009, http://www.nytimes.com/2009/10/15/education/15math.html?_r=1&ref=no_child_left_behind_act (accessed January 3, 2011).

12. Trip Gabriel, "Cheat Sheet: Under Pressure, Teachers Tamper with Tests," *New York Times*, June 10, 2010, http://www.nytimes.com/2010/06/11/education/11cheat.html (accessed January 2, 2011).

13. Steven D. Levitt and Stephen J. Dubner, *Freakonomics: A Rogue Economist Explores the Hidden Side of Everything* (New York: William Morrow, 2005), p. 34.

14. Gabriel, "Cheat Sheet."

15. Harold W. Stevenson and Shin-Ying Lee, "Contexts of Achievement: A Study of American, Chinese, and Japanese Children," *Monographs of the Society for Research in Child Development* 55, no. 1/2 (1990): 1–123.

16. Anthony Pellegrini, "Give Children a Break: An Obsession with Schools' Results Is Missing the Wider Point about Schools' Socializing Role," *Taipei Times*, March 27, 2005, http://www.taipeitimes.com/News/editorials/archives/2005/03/27/20032479 72/1 (accessed January 2, 2011); Anthony D. Pellegrini and Catherine M. Bohn, "The Role of Recess in Children's Cognitive Performance and School Adjustment," *Educational Researcher* 34, no. 1 (January/February 2005): 13–19.

17. Ibid.

18. Olga S. Jarrett et al., "The Impact of Recess on Classroom Behavior: Group Effects and Individual Differences," *Journal of Educational Research* 92, no. 2 (1998): 121–26; Pellegrini and Bohn, "Role of Recess"; Rachel Seabrook, Gordon D. A. Brown, and Jonathan E. Solity, "Distributed and Massed Practice: From Laboratory to Classroom," *Applied Cognitive Psychology* 19, no. 1 (January 2005): 107–22.

19. David F. Bjorklund and Jesse M. Bering, "The Evolved Child: Applying Evolutionary Developmental Psychology to Modern Schooling," *Learning and Individual Differences* 12, no. 4 (2002): 1–27; Barbara Rogoff, *Apprenticeship in Thinking: Cognitive Development in Social Context* (New York: Oxford University Press, 1990), pp. 25–41.

20. Donald J. Leu et al., "What Is New about the New Literacies of Online Reading Comprehension?" in *Secondary School Literacy: What Research Reveals for Classroom Practices*, ed. Leslie S. Rush, A. Jonathan Eakle, and Allen Berger (Urbana, IL: National Council of Teachers of English, 2007), pp. 37–68. Check out the endangered Pacific Northwest Tree Octopus for yourself: http://zapatopi.net/treeoctopus/. Remember, it is a bogus website created by researchers to study how gullible we are to Internet content.

21. Carol McDonald Connor et al., "Individualizing Student Instruction Precisely: Effects of Child by Instruction Interactions on First Graders' Literacy Development," *Child Development* 80, no. 1 (2009): 77–100.

22. NBA Encyclopedia: Playoff Edition, "Charles Barkley Bio," http://www.nba .com/history/players/barkley_bio.html (accessed January 4, 2011).

23. "Charles Barkley: World's Ugliest Swing," Golf.com video, 1:06, http:// www.golf.com/golf/video/article/0,28224,1655177,00.html (accessed January 4, 2011).

24. Ibid.

25. "Barkley Golf," NBC.com video, 2:47, originally aired during *Saturday Night Live*, January 9, 2010, http://www.nbc.com/saturday-night-live/video/barkley-golf/1191666/ (accessed January 4, 2011).

26. Steven M. Smith, Arthur Glenberg, and Robert A. Bjork, "Environmental Context and Human Memory," *Memory and Cognition* 6, no. 4 (1978): 342–53.

27. Kelli Taylor and Doug Rohrer, "The Effects of Interleaved Practice," *Applied Cognitive Psychology* 24, no. 6 (September 2010): 837–48.

28. Henry L. Roediger III and Jeffrey D. Karpicke, "Test-Enhanced Learning: Taking Memory Tests Improves Long-Term Retention," *Psychological Science* 17, no. 3 (March 2006): 249–55.

29. Harold Pashler et al., "Learning Styles: Concepts and Evidence," *Psychological Science in the Public Interest* 9, no. 3 (December 2008): 105–19.

30. David P. Baker and Gerald K. LeTendre, *National Differences, Global Similarities: World Culture and the Future of Schooling* (Palo Alto, CA: Stanford University Press, 2005), pp. 117–133; Harris M. Cooper, *The Battle over Homework: Common Ground for Administrators, Teachers, and Parents* (Thousand Oaks, CA: Corwin Press, 2005), pp. 17–40.

31. Etta Kralovec and John Buell, *The End of Homework: How Homework Disrupts Families, Overburdens Children, and Limits Learning* (Boston: Beacon Press, 2000).

32. National Education Association, "Research Spotlight on Homework," http://www.nea.org/tools/16938.htm (accessed May 3, 2011); National Parent Teacher Association, "Homework Help," http://www.pta.org/2039.htm (accessed May 3, 2011).

33. Valerie Strauss, "As Homework Grows, So Do Arguments against It," *Washington Post*, September 12, 2006, http://www.washingtonpost.com/wp-dyn/content/article/2006/09/11/AR2006091100908.html (accessed January 3, 2011).

34. Sandra L. Hofferth, "How American Children Spend Their Time," *Journal of Marriage and the Family* 63, no. 2 (May 2001): 295–308.

35. Anthony D. Pellegrini and Michael Horvat, "A Developmental Contextualist Critique of Attention Deficit Hyperactivity Disorder," *Educational Researcher* 24, no. 1 (January/February 1995): 13–19.

36. William N. Evans, Melinda S. Morrill, and Stephen T. Parente, "Measuring Inappropriate Medical Diagnosis and Treatment in Survey Data: The Case of ADHD among School-Age Children," *Journal of Health Economics* 29, no. 5 (September 2010): 657–73.

37. Jaak Panksepp et al., "Modeling ADHD-Type Arousal with Unilateral Frontal Cortex Damage in Rats and Beneficial Effects of Play Therapy," *Brain and Cognition* 52, no. 1 (June 2003): 97–105.

CHAPTER 11: EVOLUTIONARY BAGGAGE

1. "Time to Look beyond MMR in Autism Research," *Lancet* 359, no. 9307 (February 23, 2002): 637.

2. Nico U. F. Dosenbach et al., "Prediction of Individual Brain Maturity Using fMRI," *Science* 10, no. 5997 (September 10, 2010):1358–61.

3. Nanette Gartrell and Henry Bos, "US National Longitudinal Lesbian Family Study: Psychological Adjustment of 17-Year-Old Adolescents," *Pediatrics* 128, no. 1 (July 2010): 1–9.

4. Madison Park, "Kids of Lesbians Have Fewer Behavioral Problems, Study Suggests," *CNN*, June 7, 2010, http://www.cnn.com/2010/HEALTH/06/07/lesbian.children.adjustment/index.html (accessed December 30, 2010).

5. I also think you can't pick and choose the science you want to believe and the

science you don't. How could someone choose to disbelieve in evolution (which is as close to a fact as you're going to get in science) but choose to believe in penicillin (when they're sick with a sinus infection)? You can't only believe in some science—shouldn't it be all or nothing? Perhaps if we withheld all science from rainy-day believers (no penicillin until you also believe in evolution), they'd see my point.

6. Gary Marcus, *Kluge: The Haphazard Construction of the Human Mind* (Boston: Houghton Mifflin, 2008), pp. 69–94.

7. Andrew J. Wakefield et al., "Ileal-Lymphoid-Nodular Hyperplasia, Non-Specific Colitis, and Pervasive Developmental Disorder in Children," *Lancet* 351, no. 9103 (February 28, 1998): 637–41, http://www.thelancet.com/journals/lancet/article/PIIS0140-6736%2897%2911096-0/abstract (accessed May 3, 2011).

8. Scott Hensley, "Lancet Renounces Study Linking Autism and Vaccines," *National Public Radio*, February 12, 2010, http://www.npr.org/blogs/health/2010/02/lancet_wakefield_autism_mmr_au.html (accessed May 3, 2011).

9. Amy Wallace, "An Epidemic of Fear: How Panicked Parents Skipping Shots Endangers Us All," *Wired*, October 19, 2009, http://www.wired.com/magazine/2009/10/ff_waronscience/3/ (accessed December 30, 2010).

10. Ibid.

11. Ibid.

12. Robert F. Kennedy Jr., "Deadly Immunity," originally published in *Rolling Stone* and *Salon*, June 16, 2005, http://www.robertfkennedyjr.com/articles/2005_june_16.html (accessed May 3, 2011). Since the article was published, *Rolling Stone* has issued a series of corrections and clarifications discrediting the article for, among other things, overestimating the amount of mercury in childhood vaccines by more than a hundred times. See also, Kerry Lauerman, "Correcting Our Record: We've Removed an Explosive 2005 Report by Robert F. Kennedy Jr. about Autism and Vaccines: Here's Why," *Salon*, January 16, 2011, http://www.salon.com/about/inside_salon/2011/01/16/dangerous_immunity/index.html (accessed May 3, 2011).

13. Karl Taro Greenfeld, "The Autism Debate: Who's Afraid of Jenny McCarthy?" *Time*, February 25, 2010, http://www.time.com/time/nation/article/0,8599,1967796,00.html (accessed May 3, 2011).

14. Jason M. Glanz et al., "Parental Refusal of Pertussis Vaccination is Associated with an Increased Risk of Pertussis Infection in Children," *Pediatrics* 123, no. 6 (June 2009): 1446–51.

15. Katrina F. Brown et al., "Factors Underlying Parental Decisions about Combination Childhood Vaccinations Including MMR: A Systematic Review," *Vaccine* 28, no. 26 (June 11, 2010): 4235–48.

16. Wray Herbert, *On Second Thought: Outsmarting Your Mind's Hard-Wired Habits* (New York: Crown, 2010), pp. 53–64; Ab Litt et al., "Pressure and Perverse Flights to Familiarity," *Psychological Science* 22, no. 4 (2011): 523–31.

17. Lisa Ling, "Shark Fin Soup Alters an Ecosystem," *CNN*, December 10, 2008, http://articles.cnn.com/2008-12-10/world/pip.shark.finning_1_shark-fin-shark-populations-top-predator?_s=PM:WORLD (accessed May 3, 2011).

18. Heather Ridolfo, Amy Baxter, and Jeffrey W. Lucas, "Social Influences on Paranormal Belief: Popular versus Scientific Support," *Current Research in Social Psychology* 15 (February 7, 2010): 33–40.

19. Sarah-Jayne Blakemore, Daniel Wolpert, and Chris Frith, "Why You Can't Tickle Yourself," *Neuroreport* 11(2000): R11–R16.

20. John A. Bargh and Ezequiel Morsella, "The Unconscious Mind," *Perspectives on Psychological Science* 3, no. 1 (January 2008): 73–79.

21. Lawrence E. Williams and John A. Bargh, "Experiencing Physical Warmth Promotes Interpersonal Warmth," *Science* 322, no. 5901 (October 24, 2008): 606–07.

22. Rob W. Holland, Merel Hendriks, and Henk Aarts, "Smells Like Clean Spirit: Nonconscious Effects of Scent on Cognition and Behavior," *Psychological Science* 16, no. 9 (September 2005): 689–93; Aaron C. Kay et al., "Material Priming: The Influence of Mundane Physical Objects on Situational Construal and Competitive Behavioral Choice," *Organizational Behavior and Human Decision Processes* 95, no. 1 (September 2004): 83–96.

23. Leslie A. Real, "Paradox, Performance, and the Architecture of Decision-Making in Animals," *American Zoologist* 36, no. 4 (1996): 518–29.

24. Leda Cosmides and John Tooby, "Better than Rational: Evolutionary Psychology and the Invisible Hand," *American Economic Review* 84, no. 2 (May 1994): 327–32; Leda Cosmides and John Tooby, "Are Humans Good Intuitive Statisticians After All? Rethinking Some Conclusions of the Literature on Judgment under Uncertainty," *Cognition* 58 (1996): 1–73.

25. Amos Tversky and Daniel Kahneman, "Judgment under Uncertainty: Heuristics and Biases," *Science* 185, no. 4157 (September 27, 1974): 1124–31.

26. Ibid.

27. Andrea J. Sedlak et al., "National Estimates of Missing Children: An Overview," Office of Juvenile Justice and Deliquency Prevention, October 2002, http://www.ncjrs.gov/html/ojjdp/nismart/01/index.html (accessed December 29, 2010); US Department of Transportation, "Fatality Analysis Reporting System/General Estimates System 2008 Data Summary," 2010, http://www-nrd.nhtsa.dot.gov/Pubs/811171.pdf (accessed December 29, 2010).

28. Eugene Caruso, Nicholas Epley, and Max H. Bazerman, "The Costs and Benefits of Undoing Egocentric Responsibility Assessments in Groups," *Journal of Personality and Social Psychology* 91, no. 5 (November 2006): 857–71.

29. University of Michigan Transportation Research Institute, "Roadway Deaths Up after 9/11," *UMTRI Research Review* 35, no. 4 (October–December 2004): 6–7, http://www.umtri.umich.edu/content/rr35_4.pdf (accessed December 29, 2010).

30. US Centers for Disease Control and Prevention, "Ten Leading Causes of Death and Injury," http://www.cdc.gov/injury/wisqars/LeadingCauses.html (accessed January 2, 2011).

31. American Academy of Pediatrics, Committee on Injury, Violence, and Poison Prevention and Council on School Health, "School Transportation Safety," *Pediatrics* 120, no. 5 (May 2007): 213–20.

32. John M. Darley and Paget H. Gross, "A Hypothesis-Confirming Bias in Labeling Effects," *Journal of Personality and Social Psychology* 44, no. 1 (January 1983): 20–33.

33. James W. Pennebaker and J. A. Skelton, "Psychological Parameters of Physical Symptoms," *Personality and Social Psychology Bulletin* 4, no. 4 (October 1978): 524–30.

34. David L. Hamilton, Patricia M. Dugan, and Tina K. Trolier, "The Formation of Stereotypic Beliefs: Further Evidence of Distinctiveness-Based Illusory Correlations," *Journal of Personality and Social Psychology* 48 (1985): 5–17.

35. Aaron T. Beck, *Cognitive Therapy and the Emotional Disorders* (New York: International Universities Press, 1976), pp. 24–131.

36. Ellen Berscheid et al., "Outcome Dependency: Attention, Attribution, and Attraction," *Journal of Personality and Social Psychology* 34 (1976): 978–89.

37. Ziva Kunda, "The Case for Motivated Reasoning," *Psychological Bulletin* 108, no. 3 (November 1990): 480–98.

38. Ibid.

39. Harold H. Kassarjian and Joel B. Cohen, "Cognitive Dissonance and Consumer Behavior," *California Management Review* 8 (Fall 1965): 55–64.

40. Seymour Epstein et al., "Irrational Reactions to Negative Outcomes: Evidence for Two Conceptual Systems," *Journal of Personality and Social Psychology* 62, no. 2 (February 1992): 328–39; Mario B. Ferreira et al., "Automatic and Controlled Components of Judgment and Decision Making," *Journal of Personality and Social Psychology* 91, no. 5 (November 2006): 797–813.

41. D. N. Perkins, *The Mind's Best Work* (Cambridge, MA: Harvard University Press, 1981), p. 303.

42. John E. Mendoza and Anne L. Foundas, *Clinical Neuroanatomy: A Neurobehavioral Approach* (New York: Springer, 2008), p. 273.

CHAPTER 12: THINKING OUTSIDE THE SANDBOX

1. Angeline Lillard and Nicole Else-Quest, "Evaluating Montessori Education," *Science* 313, no. 5795 (September 29, 2006):1893–94.

2. "What is 'Philosophy for Children?'" Institute for the Advancement of Philosophy for Children, http://cehs.montclair.edu/academic/iapc/whatis.shtml (accessed May 3, 2011).

3. Matthew Lipman, *Harry Stottlemeier's Discovery* (Upper Montclair, NJ: First Mountain Foundation, 1985); Michael Pritchard, "Philosophy for Children," Stanford Encyclopedia of Philosophy, http://plato.stanford.edu/entries/children/ (accessed May 3, 2011).

4. Richard A. Fuller et al.,"Psychological Benefits of Greenspace Increase with Biodiversity," *Biology Letters* 3, no. 4 (August 22, 2007): 390–94.

5. Helle Nebelong, "Designs on Play," Free Play Network, http://www.freeplaynetwork.org.uk/design/nebelong.htm (accessed May 3, 2011).

6. Joe L. Frost, *A History of Children's Play and Play Environments: Toward a Contemporary Child-Saving Movement* (New York: Routledge, 2009), pp. 173–97.

7. "Elizabeth Ann Clune Montessori School of Ithaca," Natural Learning Initiative, North Carolina State University, http://www.naturalearning.org/content/elizabeth-ann-clune-montessori-school-ithaca (accessed May 3, 2011); Anne Raver, "Human Nature: Tutored by the Great Outdoors," *New York Times*, October 7, 1999, http://www.nytimes.com/1999/10/07/garden/human-nature-tutored-by-the-great-outdoors.html (accessed May 3, 2011).

8. Robin C. Moore, "A New Role for Landscape Architecture," Natural Learning Initiative, North Carolina State University, http://www.naturalearning.org/content/new-role-landscape-architecture (accessed May 3, 2011).